GREGORY T.K. WONG, Ph.D. (2005) in Hebrew and Old Testament Studies, New College, University of Edinburgh, has lectured at the University of Edinburgh and has published numerous articles on the book of Judges.

Compositional Strategy of the Book of Judges

Supplements
to
Vetus Testamentum

VOLUME 111

Compositional Strategy of the Book of Judges

An Inductive, Rhetorical Study

by

Gregory T.K. Wong

BRILL

LEIDEN • BOSTON
2006

This book is printed on acid-free paper.

Library of Congress Cataloging-in-Publication Data

Wong, Gregory T. K.
Compositional strategy of the book of Judges : an inductive, rhetorical study / by Gregory T.K. Wong.
p. cm. — (Supplements to Vetus Testamentum, ISSN 0083-5889 ; v. 111)
Includes bibliographical references and indexes.
ISBN-13: 978-90-04-15086-7 (hardback : alk. paper)
ISBN-10: 90-04-15086-2 (hardback : alk. paper)
1. Bible. O.T. Judges—Language, style. 2. Rhetoric in the Bible. I. Title.

BS1305.6.R5W66 2006
222'.32066—dc22

2006049078

ISSN 0083-5889
ISBN-13: 978 90 04 15086 7
ISBN-10: 90 04 15086 2

PRINTED IN THE NETHERLANDS

To
Robert B. Chisholm, Jr.
and
A. Graeme Auld

With gratitude and appreciation

CONTENTS

ABBREVIATIONS

ActO	Acta Orientalia (Copenhagen)
BBB	Bonner biblische Beitrage
BDB	Brown-Driver-Briggs-Gesenius Hebrew Lexicon
BETL	Bibliotheca Ephemeridum Theologicarum Lovaniensium
Bib	Biblica (Rome)
BibInt	Biblical Interpretations: A Journal of Contemporary Approaches (Leiden)
BJS	Brown Judaic Studies
BN	Biblische Notizen (Bamberg)
BSac	Bibliotheca Sacra (Dallas)
BT	The Bible Translator (Aberdeen)
BTB	Biblical Theology Bulletin (Jamaica, NY)
BZ	Biblische Zeitschrift (Paderborn)
CBQ	Catholic Biblical Quarterly (Washington D.C.)
Communio	Communio: Internationale katholische Zeitschrift (Paderborn)
EI	Eretz-Israel: Archaeological, Historical, and Geographical Studies (Jerusalem)
ExpTim	Expository Times (Edinburgh)
HALOT	Hebrew and Aramaic Lexicon of the Old Testament
HAR	Hebrew Annual Review (Columbus)
HUCA	Hebrew Union College Annual (Cincinnati)
IJT	Indian Journal of Theology (Serampore)
Int	Interpretation (Richmond)
JANES	The Journal of Ancient Near Eastern Society (New York)
JAOS	Journal of the American Oriental Society (New Haven)
JBL	Journal of Biblical Literature (Atlanta)
JETS	Journal of the Evangelical Theological Society (Wheaton)
JHS	Journal of Hebrew Scripture (Edmonton)
JNES	Journal of Near Eastern Studies (Chicago)
JNSL	Journal of Northwest Semitic Languages (Leiden)
JRR	A Journal from the Radical Reformation
JSOT	Journal for the Study of the Old Testament (Sheffield)
JSOTSup	Journal for the Study of the Old Testament, Supplement Series

JSPSup	Journal for the Study of the Pseudepigrapha, Supplement Series
JTS	Journal of Theological Studies (Oxford)
NIV	New International Version
NJB	New Jerusalem Bible
OTS	Oudtestamentische Studiën
PEQ	Palestine Exploration Quarterly (London)
Proc	Proceedings: Eastern Great Lakes and Midwest Biblical Society
Proof	Prooftexts: A Journal of Jewish Literary History (Bloomington)
PRS	Perspectives in Religious Studies (Murfreesboro)
RB	Revue Biblique (Jerusalem and Paris)
RTR	Reformed Theological Review (Melbourne)
SBLDS	SBL Dissertation Series
SBLSS	SBL Semeia Studies
Semeia	Semeia (New York)
SJOT	Scandinavian Journal of the Old Testament (Copenhagen)
TDOT	Theological Dictionary of the Old Testament
TLZ	Theologische Literaturzeitung (Leipzig)
Trans	Transactions of the Glasgow University Oriental Society (Glasgow)
TWOT	Theological Wordbook of the Old Testament
TynBul	Tyndale Bulletin (Cambridge)
USQR	Union Seminary Quarterly Review (New York)
VE	Vox Evangelica (London)
VT	Vetus Testamentum (Leiden)
VTSup	Supplements to Vetus Testamentum
WTJ	Westminster Theological Journal (Philadelphia)
ZAW	Zeitschrift für die alttestamentliche Wissenschaft (Berlin)

CHAPTER ONE

SETTING THE STAGE: PREVIOUS SCHOLARSHIP AND CURRENT ISSUES

Critical Survey of Previous Scholarship on Judges

Within the last century, scholarship on the book of Judges has taken some significant turns.

1. *Historical-Critical Scholarship and Noth's Deuteronomistic History Hypothesis*

At the dawn of the 20th Century, scholarship on Judges was largely dominated by historical criticism. Interest was mainly on discovering the sources that underlie the book, and Wellhausen's approach to the Pentateuch so widely accepted at the time was applied also to the study of Judges.

Under this approach, diversity of language and style and perceived repetitions and duplications in the various narratives in Judges are seen as indicative of distinct, underlying sources.[1] In particular, words and phrases that are thought to characterise two of the underlying sources for the book seem to correspond respectively to the language of J and E that supposedly underlie the Hexateuch. This suggests that J and E did not end their histories with the conquest of Canaan, but must have extended their respective histories to the period of the judges and beyond. Thus, the redactor who united J and E into one composite history for the Hexateuch is seen as likely also having brought J and E together into a pre-Deuteronomic book of Judges.[2] This non-ideological pre-Deuteronomic Judges, redacted mainly for harmonistic purpose, is then thought to have been revised by a Deuteronomic redactor,[3] who gave the work a definite theological

---

[1] Moore, xx, xxiv; Burney, xxxvii.

[2] Moore, xxv–xxvii, xxxiii–xxxiv; Cooke, xx–xxi; Burney, xxxviii, xli, xlix.

[3] Burney (xli–l) thinks that the portion usually attributed to a Deuteronomic redactor was in fact the work of a redactor who was influenced by the later Ephraimitic school of prophetic teachers and who did his work prior to the promulgation of

perspective by adding framework passages to individual hero stories, arranging the stories according to a cyclical framework, and giving the book a programmatic introduction.[4] This Deuteronomic redaction then went through further revision by a post-exilic redactor, who not only restored older material from pre-Deuteronomic Judges that the Deuteronomic redactor had left out, but also added minor glosses and material of his own.[5] As this post-exilic redactor is said to demonstrate traits associated with the Priestly school,[6] this essentially results in the presence in Judges of all four major redactional sources, J, E, D, and P, that supposedly underlie the Hexateuch.

But a significant drawback of this type of source analysis is that it leaves the text highly fragmented. Nowhere is this more obvious than in Simpson's meticulous attempt to separate the entire book into its various strands of sources.[7] However, this would soon change with the introduction of Noth's Deuteronomistic History hypothesis in 1943.[8]

In this work, Noth argues that the division of Deuteronomy to Kings into separate books in their current form actually represents a secondary development. At their inception, these books originally constituted one continuous narrative composed by an exilic historian Noth calls the Deuteronomist (Dtr). Although Dtr also made extensive use of older traditional materials and incorporated them into his composition, Noth maintains that Dtr was not just another redactor in the source-critical sense. Instead, he should be considered the author of a history as he was the one who brought together materials from highly varied traditions and, along with summaries he himself composed to anticipate and recapitulate events at different points of the narrative, organised them into a coherent and connected

---

Deuteronomy. His work is marked as E^2. To Burney, the resemblance of this work to Deuteronomy is largely a result of this redactor's thoughts influencing the shaping of Deuteronomy rather than vice versa.

[4] Moore, xxxiv–xxxv; Cooke, xxi–xxiii; Burney, xxxv–xxxvii, xli.

[5] Moore, xxxv; Cooke, xxiii–xxiv; Burney, xxxvii. The material restored by the exilic redactor is generally believed to include 1:1–2:5, 9:1–57, 16:1–31, and 17:1–21:25. Notices of the minor judges in 10:1–5 and 12:8–15, as well as other glosses, are seen to be this redactor's own contribution.

[6] Cooke, xxiii; Burney, l.

[7] Simpson, 9–147.

[8] The English translation published by JSOT in 1991 is a translation of pp. 1–110 of the third German edition of Noth's *Überlieferungsgeschichtliche Studien* published in 1967.

account of the history of Israel from the conquest to the exile.[9] To Noth, Dtr's main concern was to teach the true meaning of Israel's history. This means the recognition that YHWH was continuously at work in Israel's past, meeting the accelerated moral decline with warnings and punishments, and finally, when these proved fruitless, with total annihilation.[10] This monumental piece of history writing Noth calls Deuteronomistic History (DH).

Within this DH, Noth considers Dtr's contribution to the history of the period between the conquest and the monarchy especially significant. In fact, to Noth, Dtr practically created the 'period of the judges' as he combined diverse traditional materials and shaped them into an integrated yet distinctive period within the larger history of Israel. According to Noth, the record of this period extends from Judg. 2:6 to 1 Samuel 12, bracketed by two major speeches found in Joshua 23 and 1 Samuel 12.[11] The material Dtr utilised to construct the Judges portion of this period came from two basic traditions: a series of stories about various tribal heroes and their victories over foreign enemies, and a list of 'judges' with short accounts of their birthplaces, periods of office, places of burial, and some odd detail about their lives. The presence of Jephthah in both the hero stories and the judges list was what facilitated the merging of the two traditions, thus allowing the term 'judge' to be applied also to the tribal heroes.[12]

Concerning the stories about the tribal heroes, although these may have been collected prior to the time of Dtr, it was Dtr who gave them thematic unity as he added to each hero story framing material that echoes the programmatic introduction he composed for the period in 2:6–11, 14–16, 18–19. The Othniel story (3:7–11) and the two divine rebukes found in 6:7–10 and 10:6–16 are also considered to have been composed by Dtr,[13] although the prologue (1:1–2:5), epilogue (17:1–21:25), and 2:20–3:6 are considered post-Deuteronomistic additions.[14] The Samson narratives in 13:2–16:31 may also have been

[9] Noth, 1991:24–26,120.
[10] Ibid., 134.
[11] Ibid., 69.
[12] Ibid., 69–72.
[13] Ibid., 73–76.
[14] Ibid., 20–24, 77 n. 2. Here, Noth implies that the prologue and epilogue may have been added when DH was separated into the present canonical books, whereas 2:20–3:6 probably represent secondary expansions to 2:6–19 rather than an attempt at systematic revision.

later additions for two main reasons: they show no sign of having been worked on by Dtr, and Samson's name is not included in 1 Sam. 12:9–11, which Noth thinks aims at being comprehensive.[15]

From the above survey, it seems clear that compared to the source analysis that preceded Noth, Noth's DH hypothesis offers a much simpler and more holistic view of the compositional history behind the text of Judges. This in turn allows for the exploration of a substantial portion of the text without the kind of fragmentation that characterises previous attempts. For even though Noth concedes the presence of later additions to Dtr's work, the majority of these additions are thought to consist of larger units of texts being inserted or appended to Dtr's work rather than systematic attempts at reworking the text at the micro-level.

2. *Subsequent Modifications to Noth's Hypothesis*

Although Noth's hypothesis was readily accepted by the scholarly community and its influence remains to this day, it did not take long before modifications to Noth's original hypothesis were brought forth. One such modification relating to Judges came from Richter.

In Noth's hypothesis, it was Dtr who composed the framing passages around the hero stories that give thematic unity to these stories. But Richter contends that even before Dtr, these stories had already gone through significant development as a collection and had been given an interpretive framework. This is based on the fact that typical Deuteronomistic language and thought, especially the term 'judge (שׁפט)' found repeatedly in 2:6–11, 14–16, 18–19, occur neither in the framing material around the hero stories nor in the Othniel story in 3:7–11.[16] Richter therefore concludes that the framing material as well as the Othniel story must not have been the work of Dtr himself, but rather, must have come from his sources.[17] He thus postulates three pre-Deuteronomistic redactions as follows.

Around the time of King Jehu, a northern redactor first compiled a 'Retterbuch' from diverse traditions.[18] This book began with Ehud

[15] Ibid., 84–85.
[16] Richter (1964:25,61) considers 3:10, where the term שׁפט occurs, a later addition.
[17] Ibid., 61–62.
[18] Richter, 1963:339–40.

and ended with the story of Abimelech, and was compiled as an anti-monarchical polemic against the northern kingdom.[19] A later redactor (Rdt_1) then added framing material around the hero stories involving Ehud, Deborah/Barak, and Gideon, thus making divine retribution a theological motivation for the periods of oppression.[20] After that, another redactor (Rdt_2), possibly associated with Josiah's reforms, added the paradigmatic Othniel account as an introduction to this 'Retterbuch', thus providing some southern content and expanding on the theology of Rdt_1 by identifying the evil Israel did as the worship of foreign gods.[21]

It is only after these redactions were completed that DtrG, which is Richter's designation for Noth's Dtr, came into the picture. He was the one who combined the hero stories with the minor judges, adopted the term 'judge' for the leaders of the period, added the Jephthah and Samson narratives, and composed the programmatic introduction in Judg. 2:6–11, 14–16, 18–19.[22]

But if Richter's theory focuses primarily on the redaction history of Dtr's source material, two schools represented respectively by Cross and Smend offer further modifications to Noth's hypothesis by identifying later attempts at systematic revision of the work of Dtr.

Although Cross basically agrees with Noth's separation of DH from the Tetrateuch and endorses Noth's view of Dtr as a creative author,[23] he disagrees with Noth in that he sees two different layers of redaction in the material Noth attributes solely to Dtr.

Exploring thematically the portion of DH found in Kings, Cross sees the main redaction as following the twin themes of judgment on the northern kingdom on account of apostasy, and YHWH's eternal and unconditional promises to the house of David and to Jerusalem.[24] But Cross also notices that beginning with the Manasseh pericope in 2 Kings 21, the hope that is based on YHWH's promises to David seems to have been presented as futile as the promises on which that hope is based are recast as conditional promises that can be forfeited if Judah breaks the covenant.[25] From this, Cross concludes

---

[19] Ibid., 320, 336–39.
[20] Richter, 1964:113–14.
[21] Ibid., 114–15.
[22] Ibid., 44–49, 115–18, 127–31.
[23] Cross, 274.
[24] Ibid., 279–85.
[25] Ibid., 285–86.

that two different redactions must have been merged together, and argues that the primary Deuteronomistic redaction (Dtr^1) may have been Josianic rather than exilic as Noth maintains. This Josianic redaction was then updated by an exilic redactor (Dtr^2), who overwrote the work of Dtr^1 to make it relevant to an audience whose hope in the Josianic era had already passed.[26]

To Cross, this second layer of exilic redaction is limited in scope and is found primarily in Kings and Deuteronomy, and in six verses in Joshua 23 and 1 Samuel 12.[27] No evidence of this exilic revision is found in Judges. Subsequent to Cross, however, some of his followers have seen traces of Dtr^2 even in Judges.

Nelson, for example, sees Judg. 2:1–5 and 6:7–10 as the work of Dtr^2 based primarily on the secondary nature of these passages, the presence of non-Dtr^1 expressions, and a more pessimistic view of Israel.[28] He also thinks that Judges 1 may have been inserted, though not composed, by Dtr^2 to provide the context for the angel's rebuke in 2:1–5.[29] And because of their association with 1:1–2:5, Nelson sees 2:17, 20–23 as possibly also the work of Dtr^2.[30]

Boling, also influenced by Cross, offers a somewhat different understanding of Judges. Like Richter, Boling also sees the cyclical framework that organises the hero stories as having been established prior to the primary Deuteronomistic redaction.[31] However, he differs from Richter with regard to the extent of what he calls a 'pragmatic' collection, which seems to include the programmatic introduction, the minor judges, as well as the Jephthah and much of the Samson stories.[32] This collection was incorporated into the larger history of DH by a Josianic historian whom he calls a 'Deuteronomic' redactor.[33] Understanding 2:1–5 and 17:1–18:31 as a polemic against the northern rivals to the Jerusalem cult, Boling sees these also as the work of this redactor.[34] Likewise 6:7–10 and 10:11–14, as they seem to

[26] Ibid., 287–88.
[27] Ibid., 287.
[28] R. Nelson, 1981:43–53.
[29] Ibid., 47.
[30] Ibid., 20, 25, 49.
[31] Ibid., 35–36.
[32] This is inferred from Boling's chart (1975:30).
[33] Ibid., 34–35. This 'Deuteronomic' redactor is presumably the equivalent of Cross's Dtr^1.
[34] Ibid., 36, 66–67, 184–85, 258.

demonstrate similarities with 2:1–5.[35] This Josianic redaction then went through subsequent updating by an exilic 'Deuteronomistic' redactor,[36] who added Judges 1 from previously neglected traditions to anticipate the angel's rebuke in 2:1–5, and incorporated Judges 19–21 as a balance to Judges 1 so that the book which begins with the disintegration of Israel would end with the nation being united at last.[37]

On a somewhat parallel development with Cross, Smend also sees the work of Noth's Dtr as having been overlaid and reworked by a later redactor. As he examines Josh. 1:7–9, which Noth considers a secondary addition to the work of Dtr,[38] Smend discovers that some of its thought and language can also be found in other passages in Joshua and Judges that Noth considers secondary. To Smend, these passages signal the existence of a layer of redaction that focuses specifically on Israel's relationship with the nations and the issue of obedience to the law.[39] He therefore calls its redactor the nomistic redactor (DtrN). In Judges, 2:17, 20–21, 23 would be the work of DtrN,[40] while 1:1–2:5 was inserted also by DtrN from a pre-existing unit he did not himself compose.[41]

Subsequently, Dietrich extended Smend's analysis to Kings, and concludes that a further redactor known as DtrP had been responsible for inserting prophetic speeches, fulfilment notices, and other prophetic material to the work of DtrG.[42] But while Dietrich does not see any evidence of DtrP having updated the Judges portion of DH, Roth subsequently argues that Judg. 2:13–15, 18–19 and 8:22–23 also belong to the work of DtrP.[43] Thus, counting the work of DtrG, which Dietrich thinks was composed just after the fall of Judah, and that of DtrN, which followed DtrG, Dietrich sees three layers of exilic redactions where Noth sees only one.

But the scope of the DtrN's influence on Judges is to be further expanded by Veijola, who sees the two divine rebukes in 6:7–10 and

---

35 Ibid., 36.
36 Boling's 'Deuteronomistic' redactor is presumably the equivalent of Cross's Dtr^2.
37 Boling, 1975:36–38.
38 Noth, 1991:62.
39 Smend, 1971:494–509.
40 Ibid., 504–06.
41 Ibid., 507–09.
42 Dietrich, 1977:133–34.
43 Roth, 545–46, 547–48.

10:6–16, Jotham's fable in 9:8–15 with its surrounding context, and the evaluative statements about Abimelech in 9:24, 57 as also the work of DtrN.[44] Furthermore, in contrast to Noth, who sees the narratives in Judges' epilogue (17–21) as a later addition that intrudes into the original work of Dtr when DH was separated into individual books, Veijola sees Judges 17–21 as the work of DtrG. For Veijola considered the refrain in the epilogue to be clearly Deuteronomistic, and discerned other Deuteronomistic words and phrases within these chapters.[45] To Veijola, the narratives in the epilogue fit well into the cyclical framework of the period because they essentially depict the evil Israel did in the apostasy part of the final cycle.[46] And because the refrain that links these narratives together seems clearly promonarchical, Veijola disputes Noth's characterisation of Dtr as basically anti-monarchical. Instead, he attributes the anti-monarchical strands in DH to subsequent revisions by DtrN and DtrP in general, and to DtrN in particular for the Judges portion.[47]

In recent years, there seems to be some movement towards the merging of certain features of the Cross and Smend schools. Mayes and O'Brien, for example, accept both Cross's view that DtrG was basically a Josianic redactor whose work was further subjected to an exilic revision, and Smend's view that this exilic revision was redacted out of an emphasis on Israel's disobedience to the law.[48] Concerning Judges, however, Mayes and O'Brien continue to differ with regard to the extent of the two redactions. Thus, while Mayes takes 6:7–10 and the Samson narrative in 13:2–16:31 as the work of DtrG, for example, O'Brien considers 6:7–10 the work of DtrN[49] and the Samson narrative a later post-Deuteronomistic addition which nonetheless preceded the insertion of Judges' epilogue.[50]

In a more recent monograph-length study of Judges that explores the book's layers of Deuteronomistic redactions, Becker advocates a

[44] Veijola, 43–48, 100–14.

[45] Ibid., 15–27. Such phrases include איש הישר בעיניו יעשה in 17:6 and 21:25 (cf. Deut. 12:8); והוא גר־שם in 17:7 (cf. Deut. 18:6); למיום עלות בני־ישראל מארץ מצרים עד היום הזה in 19:30 (cf. Deut. 9:7; 1 Sam. 8:8; 2 Sam. 7:6; 1 Kgs. 8:16; 2 Kgs. 21:15), and other minor phrases.

[46] Ibid., 28–29.

[47] Ibid., 115–22. Veijola, like Dietrich, does not see evidence of DtrP having worked on Judges.

[48] Mayes, 1983:58–80, 134–35, 137; 1985:12–13; O'Brien, 82–98.

[49] O'Brien, 88 n. 21, 24.

[50] Ibid., 94–96.

return to Noth by rejecting Richter's view of pre-Deuteronomistic redactions and crediting Dtr as the one who was primarily responsible for the shaping of the Judges portion of DH from diverse traditional source materials.[51] But he does recognise DtrN as among the various exilic updatings of Dtr's work, even though he holds significantly different views from Veijola, Mayes, and O'Brien regarding the extent of each redaction. Thus, for example, while Veijola attributes Judges 17–21 to DtrG, and Mayes and O'Brien see these chapters as post-Deuteronomistic additions, Becker attributes 17–18 to DtrN and 19–21 to a priestly redactor from the same circle as the priestly redactor of the Pentateuch.[52] And while Mayes and O'Brien agree with Richter in seeing Judges 9 as a part of the pre-Deuteronomistic source material, and Veijola sees Jotham's fable and the evaluative statements of Abimelech as the work of DtrN, Becker takes only the evaluative statements as the work of DtrN but sees Jotham's fable as the work of DtrG.[53] Furthermore, Becker also disagrees with Veijola regarding the nature of DtrG's redaction. Thus, while Veijola sees DtrG as essentially pro-monarchical, Becker sees DtrG as fundamentally anti-monarchical. The pro-monarchical sentiment, to Becker, came from the final priestly redactor.[54]

Thus, from the above survey of developments subsequent to Noth, three things become apparent. First, not only is there little consensus regarding the nature, setting, and extent of the basic Deuteronomistic composition, there is also little consensus regarding the nature, number, and extent of subsequent redactions to that basic composition.[55] Second, with the various modifications to Noth's original hypothesis, the contribution of Dtr to the shaping of the Judges portion of DH is significantly reduced. For not only is Dtr generally seen as no longer responsible for introducing the cyclical framework that organises the history of the period, he is also seen by some as no longer the author of the Othniel story in 3:7–11 and the two divine rebukes in 6:7–10 and 10:6–16. And these, ironically, are some of

[51] Becker, 300–01.
[52] Ibid., 302–03.
[53] Ibid., 300, 302.
[54] Ibid., 303–06.
[55] This lack of consensus regarding the basic thematic thrust of the supposedly Deuteronomistic editing and the number of editions involved is especially highlighted by Polzin (15).

the very passages that first enabled Noth to detect the creative presence of Dtr in the Judges portion of DH.

But finally and most importantly, with the introduction of the various modifications, the simplicity of Noth's hypothesis that is its greatest strength has now been significantly weakened. For with three layers of pre-Deuteronomistic redactions and another two to three layers of Deuteronomistic redactions detected for the Judges portion of DH, the fragmentation that characterises pre-DH scholarship has once again returned with a vengeance.

3. *The Rise of Synchronic Studies*

It is perhaps in reaction to this kind of fragmentation that a number of scholars in the late 1960's and early 1970's began calling for a new and more holistic approach to the study of Hebrew Scripture in general and the historical narratives in particular. Where Judges is concerned, one can probably consider as a turning point Lilley's 1967 article, in which he expressly call for "a fresh appraisal of Judges as a literary work, starting from the assumption of authorship rather than of redaction".[56]

To be sure, Lilley recognises that the assumption of authorship does not necessarily rule out the possibility of additions and later redactions, or the identification of sources. But what he objects to is an interpretive assumption that inherently supports a bias towards fragmentation. For recognising that purpose of composition is inevitably bound up with authorship, prior attempts at literary analysis seem to have implicitly assumed that each author is restricted to only a single purpose in a composition, such that when different purposes expressed through different themes are discerned, these are automatically assigned to separate hypothetical authors. But Lilley argues that an author may conceivably be motivated by more than one purpose in a composition, and not all such purposes are equally in view in any one paragraph or section. Because the evaluation of a work on the basis of purpose can often prove subjective and inconclusive, Lilley thus advocates a focus on language, style, and the arrangement of material as a more objective alternative for literary analysis.[57]

[56] Lilley, 95.
[57] Ibid., 95–96.

To demonstrate the viability of this new approach, Lilley then proceeds with a brief analysis of Judges in its current form, and argues that such an analysis reveals a unity of design that points towards the book being substantially a single piece of historical writing. In particular, Lilley disputes the popular belief that the central section of the book was organised around a repetitive cyclical pattern, but argues that the book was arranged according to a progressively deteriorating structure.[58] Since this deterioration seems to be elaborating a theme already introduced in the prologue of the book, Lilley sees the two sections as intricately related at the compositional level.[59] As for the epilogue, the two stories are also seen as contributing to the author's purpose as they provide a fitting conclusion to the period by dramatically displaying the religious and moral failures of Israel that underlay their political misfortune.[60] Thus, what Lilley tries to demonstrate is that the meaning of the book in its current form is actually discoverable synchronically through a careful consideration of its structure, content, and overall thematic development. In fact, to Lilley, this approach provides a more satisfying explanation of the way the final redactor handled the source material than any consideration of separate redactors' schemes.[61]

In the years that follow, the number of studies following the approach advocated by Lilley multiplied significantly. These studies can roughly be divided into three types.

The first type consists of relatively short literary studies the aim of which is to show how Judges in its current form displays a unity of design that makes sense without first needing to separate the book into various layers of redaction. Gros Louis, for example, explores the selection and arrangement of the material in the prologue and central section by showing how the narratives are woven together by recurring motifs that are continually developed as the book progresses.[62] Meanwhile, Gooding tries to argue for an overall unity in

[58] Ibid., 97–99.

[59] Ibid., 101.

[60] Ibid., 99–100. Note, however, that Lilley did not provide any formal ties that actually link the epilogue to the rest of the book.

[61] Ibid., 99, 101–02.

[62] Gros Louis, 141–62. These include unexpected choices of deliverers; the use of treachery by Ehud, Jael, and in the conquest of Bethel; the lack of faith of Barak and Gideon; the refusal of Israelite cities and tribes to help their judges; and the killing of heroes such as Sisera, Abimelech, and Samson by women.

the book's design by showing how the book is symmetrically arranged into a series of concentric pairs where the second member of each pair represents deterioration from the first.[63]

In a somewhat lengthier study, Polzin also tries to focus on the overall literary aspects of the text using analytical techniques rooted in Russian structuralism. Although Polzin basically accepts DH as a unified piece of work,[64] his view of DH differs significantly from Noth. Rather than seeing a continuous narrative whose division into separate books represents a secondary development, he seems to see DH as having been conceived originally as a series of distinct literary units corresponding to the current canonical books.[65] Yet to Polzin, the entire DH corpus is united by the presence of a subtle, on-going dialogue between two different ideological perspectives,[66] which Polzin calls authoritarian dogmatism[67] and critical traditionalism.[68] The former, which focuses on retributive justice, is expressed through the voice of Moses in Deuteronomy and various prophetic speeches elsewhere in DH.[69] The latter, which reflects the tradition of a God who is both merciful and just, is expressed through the narration of God's gracious dealing with Israel throughout her history, repeatedly delivering her instead of destroying her on account of her sin.[70]

---

[63] Gooding, 73–77.

[64] Polzin, 18.

[65] Although Polzin does not state this explicitly, such a view is strongly implied in the way he speaks of structural parallels and distinct perspectives discernible along the lines of the current canonical set-up. For example, instead of seeing Judges as continuing on where Joshua left off, Polzin (147) sees Judges as consciously recapitulating a central position described in Joshua and applying it to the period after Joshua's death in much the same way that Joshua recapitulates the central position of Deuteronomy and applies it to the period after Moses' death. Moreover, Polzin (160–61) also speaks of Dtr's focus on divine justice in the book of Deuteronomy measurably softening in the book of Joshua and taking a major turn in the book Judges to reveal the weaknesses and limitations of all ideologies. These comments thus seem to suggest that Polzin sees DH as comprising distinct literary units rather than one continuous narrative.

[66] Ibid., 22–23.

[67] Ibid., 59, 65.

[68] Ibid., 67.

[69] Ibid., 19–20.

[70] The dialogue between these two voices is most cogently argued for by Polzin (36–69) in his discussion of Moses' first two addresses in Deuteronomy. However, Polzin (43) also makes it clear that "the interplay of the two voices involved in this dialogue is an essential constituent of . . . the ultimate semantic authority that unifies not only Deuteronomy, but . . . the entire Deuteronomistic History."

For Judges, the many ambiguities and surprises embedded within its narratives are further seen as part of a conscious strategy by Dtr not only to reflect the growing chaos Israel faced during the period,[71] but also to undermine any certainty a reader may place on authoritarian dogma or critical traditionalism. This weakness or limitation of ideology is seen as a unifying factor discernible in every major segment of the book.[72]

What is particularly noteworthy about Polzin's approach is that even though he acknowledges the existence of discordant perspectives in close proximity within the text, instead of assigning them to different redactional layers, he opens up the possibility that their juxtaposition may well be a conscious literary strategy that serves to bring out the author's message.[73] This suggests, therefore, that synchronic solutions may well exist for problems that were previously thought to be answerable only through diachronic considerations.[74]

In a parallel development with these literary studies of the whole book, the mid 1970's and beyond also saw the emergence of a second type of literary analysis of Judges. These are characterised by in-depth explorations of specific narrative units within the book, focusing particularly on the narrative structure and thematic development that allow the author to effectively accomplish his rhetorical goals. Notable examples include Younger's studies on the conquest narrative in Judges 1,[75] Murray's study on the Deborah-Barak narrative,[76] the studies of Globe and Vincent on Deborah's song,[77] Boogaart's study on the Abimelech narrative,[78] Webb's study on the Jephthah narrative,[79] Beem's study on the minor judges,[80] Exum's studies on

[71] Ibid., 165–66.

[72] Ibid., 146–204.

[73] More recently, Marais argues a similar point using Judges as a test case. Although Marais (1–5) approaches the issue primarily from an epistemological standpoint rather than a literary one, he nonetheless sees the juxtaposition of different and even paradoxical perspectives as explainable apart from diachronic considerations. To Marais (6, 59–167), this juxtaposition in fact constitutes a typical mode of representation for Old Testament narratives in general, and for Judges in particular.

[74] In this regard, while Polzin (23) affirms the value of the historical critical approach, he nonetheless calls for operational priority to be given to the kind of synchronic, literary approach he advocates.

[75] Younger, 1994:207–27; 1995:75–92.

[76] Murray, 158–89.

[77] Globe, 1974:493–521; 1975:169–84; Vincent, 61–82.

[78] Boogaart, 45–56.

[79] Webb, 1986:34–43.

[80] Beem, 147–72.

the Samson narratives,[81] Wilson's study on Judges 17–18,[82] and the studies of Revell and Satterthwaite on the narrative of the Benjaminite war in Judges 20.[83]

With the proliferation of the above two types of studies arguing for the literary unity of the book as a whole and of its constituent parts, it is perhaps a matter of time before the third and most ambitious type of literary study of Judges emerges. From the mid-1980's to the late 1990's, four major monograph-length studies have come out, all of which represent attempts to apply to the whole book the kind of in-depth literary analysis that has been used to study specific narrative units. What distinguishes these studies from previous ones is that, rather than focusing on the demonstration of literary unity, these simply assume the existence of unity for the book in its final form, and proceed from there in an attempt to discover the book's thematic centre.

In general, most of these studies share the assumption that the final form of the book is redacted on the basis of specific purposes, and that these purposes, which hold the key to understanding the selection and arrangement of material within the book,[84] are discoverable from a synchronic examination of the book as attention is paid to literary and rhetorical features such as plot, characterisation, points of view, narrative structures, wordplays, allusions, and recurring themes and motifs.[85] Interestingly, however, in spite of a great deal of commonality with regard to approach and emphasis, the four major studies all yield very different conclusions.

Although Webb's main concern is not specifically to discover the rhetorical purpose that unites the book as he focuses on the structure of the text and what it means as a complex whole, he nonetheless concludes that the fundamental issue the book addresses is the non-

---

[81] Exum, 1980:43–59; 1981:3–29.

[82] Wilson, 73–85.

[83] Revell, 417–33; Satterthwaite, 1992:80–89.

[84] Amit (1998:27), for example, states that the examination of the book "from a viewpoint which takes into consideration the editorial line, contributes to explaining the selection and combination of all those details that compose it."

[85] That the redactional purpose is discoverable through attention to literary and rhetorical features is explicitly affirmed by O'Connell (10), who states that the aim of his work is to "discern the primary rhetorical purpose of Judges from its formal structure and poetics." Likewise, Amit (1998:25) also speaks of the reconstruction of editorial guidelines as attention is paid to elements of poetics such as structural models, analogies, points of view, repetition of motifs, and so on.

fulfilment of YHWH's oath to give the whole land to Israel. This in turn is related to Israel's persistent apostasy and the freedom of YHWH's action over against Israel's presumption that she can use Him.[86] In face of Israel's persistent apostasy, Webb sees YHWH being portrayed in the book not so much as dispensing rewards and punishments as oscillating between punishment and mercy. This contrast between "the 'knowable' aspect of divine providence" and "the contrariness-to-expectation, freedom, and 'unknowability' of YHWH's actions" thus directs the reader away from "a simplistic moralism or a mechanical theory of history".[87] In this respect, Webb's understanding of the central issue of book is not dissimilar to that of Polzin's, a fact Webb himself also recognises.

With her monograph published a year after Webb's, Klein sees irony as the dominant literary device that gives the book unity. This irony is expressed both through content and narrative structure, and is developed progressively throughout the book, "touching on every level from non-ironic to multi-layered irony".[88] Thus, from the non-ironic base with which the book opens, the sequence of narratives increases in instances and intensity of irony, until irony permeates the resolution, which according to Klein, does not really resolve but simply "devolves in disorder".[89] The book therefore moves progressively towards highlighting human limitations for ethical judgment, making it increasing clear that apart from YHWH, who is the only judge in the book, the nation will inevitably descend into chaos.

Of the four works, O'Connell's probably represents the most thorough literary/rhetorical analysis of Judges. To O'Connell, two distinct yet related rhetorical concerns can be discerned throughout the book. The first, which O'Connell calls the tribal-political schema, aims at portraying Judah as the pre-eminent tribe consistently favoured by YHWH to lead the other tribes.[90] The second, which O'Connell calls the deuteronomic schema, highlights Israel's repeated failure to fulfil its covenant responsibilities with regard to occupation of the land, inter-tribal covenant loyalty, cultic order, and social justice.[91]

[86] Webb, 1987:208.
[87] Ibid., 209.
[88] Klein, 1988:20. See also Klein's subsequent article (1990:83–90), where she further develops her ironic structure around male-female relationships.
[89] Klein, 1988:190.
[90] O'Connell, 12–19.
[91] Ibid., 10,19–57.

From these two concerns, O'Connell infers that the rhetorical purpose of Judges is to enjoin its readers to endorse a divinely appointed Judahite king, who, in contrast to the judges, would uphold such deuteronomic ideals as expelling foreigners from the land and maintaining inter-tribal loyalty to YHWH's cult and to regulations concerning social justice.[92]

As for Amit's monograph, although it seems to be the most recent of the four, in actuality, it is the earliest because the current English version is simply an updated translation of her 1984 dissertation published in Hebrew. Basically, Amit sees the book as being redacted out of two complementary editorial guidelines: signs and leadership. To Amit, the first editorial guideline having to do with signs aims at emphasising YHWH's intervention in history in order to heighten the awareness that YHWH alone is the God and deliverer who is not to be abandoned in favour of other gods.[93] As for the second editorial guideline focusing on leadership, Amit thinks that the events of the book are arranged to instil a sense of disappointment with the judges. This leads to a gradual recognition that a change of government is inevitable, thus paving the way for the acceptance of monarchy as a necessary though not altogether desirable compromise solution.[94] Thus, according to Amit, the integration of the two guidelines shows the reader that, despite the large number of signs that confirm YHWH's role in shaping history, the people still need continuous human leadership.[95]

4. *Some Critique of Synchronic Scholarship on Judges to Date*

From the above survey of the four major synchronic studies, it is clear that despite the claims of all four authors to use basically the same synchronic, literary/rhetorical approach to uncover the rhetorical purpose of Judges, they have each arrived at a very different conclusion. For even though all four studies in some way acknowledge the failure of the nation and the inadequacies of her judges, yet they diverge markedly in the way they view the solution to this failure that lies at the centre of the book. Thus, for Webb, the answer

---

[92] Ibid., 1, 10, 343.
[93] Amit, 1998:27–59.
[94] Ibid., 59–118.
[95] Ibid., 118–19.

to Israel's repeated apostasy is YHWH's surprising mercy to preserve an undeserving people out of His freedom. For Klein, however, the rapid disintegration of the nation exacerbated by the leadership of flawed judges represents an implicit call to return to YHWH and to YHWHistic values and judgments. For O'Connell, the solution is more political in nature as the author prepares his readers to endorse a divinely appointed Judahite king who would uphold deuteronomic ideals. For Amit, however, while the book's author may see the advantage of continuous leadership, monarchy is at best a less-than-desirable compromise solution.

But not only do the four studies disagree when it comes to the central message of Judges, they also differ significantly when it comes to the interpretation of certain narratives within the book. Take the narrative of Ehud, for example. While Amit sees the narration of the chain of events contributing to Ehud's success as a 'sign' pointing to YHWH's decisive intervention behind the scene,[96] Webb thinks that the author has deliberately constructed the narrative to direct the readers towards identifying with Ehud and enjoying the sheer virtuosity of his performance.[97] Klein, however, took an almost exact opposite view from Webb, and sees Ehud as an ironic figure who is used by YHWH in spite of his dishonourable actions that betray an unwillingness to rely on Him.[98] As for O'Connell, his position is somewhere between those of Webb and Klein. While he acknowledges that the narrative seems to glorify Israel's hero Ehud along with her God YHWH, he also observes that in light of the larger context of the book, where a growing concern surfaces with regard to the leadership qualities of Israel's judges, one may discern a subtle attempt to characterise Ehud as a self-promoting opportunist.[99]

That such a significant divergence in interpretation can arise in spite of the fact that all four studies basically share the same approach to the text is precisely what prompted Andersson in his recent monograph to question the very validity of this type of synchronic study. To Andersson, this type of synchronic study is flawed because it seeks to interpret individual narratives in the context of the book as

[96] Ibid., 171–98.
[97] Webb, 1987:128–32.
[98] Klein, 1988:37–39, 46.
[99] O'Connell, 84–100.

a whole as if these narratives have already been absorbed into the larger text and reduced into a single consistent voice. But Andersson argues that individual narratives at the micro level are autonomous, and thus, are resistant to being absorbed at the macro level. And since individual narratives at the micro level do not necessarily provide points of view consistent with the overall message of the book at the macro level, this results in there being many different voices within the book that cannot be harmonised and reduced to one.[100] What Andersson proposes instead, is to read Judges as a collection of narratives so that each narrative is understood on its own without the need to harmonise it with other narratives or to look for significance within the larger text.[101]

Unfortunately, although Andersson's approach is novel, careful scrutiny reveals that his main thesis regarding narrative autonomy and the resistance of narratives to reworking is fundamentally flawed and unsustainable.[102] Furthermore, in light of how Andersson repeatedly highlights divergences of interpretation in the synchronic studies in question to cast doubt on the validity of this approach,[103] it is somewhat ironic that in the one narrative where there seems to be broad agreement among the synchronic scholars, it is Andersson who proposes a dissenting interpretation of the Samson narrative that is controversial for its rejection of the implicitly assumed moral context.[104]

But perhaps Andersson is making too much of this lack of consensus among the synchronic studies in question. After all, the narratives in Judges are surprisingly devoid of direct evaluative statements.[105] Con-

---

[100] Andersson, 115–16, 124–25, 220–23.

[101] Ibid., 124–25, 142, 221.

[102] For a critical response to Andersson, see Wong, 2006b: forthcoming.

[103] See, for example, Andersson, 43–49.

[104] Contrary to the view of most synchronic scholars, Andersson (171–80) actually sees Samson being portrayed essentially as a hero.

[105] Other than the negative evaluation of the Israelites by the narrator for their idolatry (2:11–13,19; 3:7,12; 4:1; 6:1; 8:33–34; 10:6; 13:1) and failure to show covenant loyalty to Gideon and his family (8:35), there is hardly any editorial evaluation of individual characters in the book. The only exception is the negative evaluation of Abimelech and the citizens of Shechem in 9:23–24, 56–57. Considering the plethora of protagonists that appear one after another throughout the book, this surprising lack of direct editorial evaluation is certainly a feature that adds challenge to the task of interpretation.

sequently, divergent interpretations are to be expected as interpreters have to sift through each narrative looking for subtle contextual clues to help them evaluate the events and characters involved. In fact, this is not unlike what one finds in the study of literature in general, where the lack of direct editorial evaluation in a novel or short story often gives rise to rival interpretations. Thus, contrary to what Andersson implies, the lack of consensus among existing synchronic studies may not necessarily be indicative of any fundamental weakness of the approach itself as it is of the inherent difficulty in interpreting the kind of subtle narrative found in Judges.

But even so, Andersson's work does raise one issue that perhaps deserves further attention. Although his suggestion that one reads Judges as a loose collection of independent narratives is based primarily on flawed arguments regarding narrative autonomy and the resistance of narratives to reworking, the suggestion itself is in fact not dependent upon those flawed arguments. For in the end, whether a narrative is to be interpreted in the context of the larger whole or on its own really depends on whether significant relationships can be demonstrated between that narrative and other narratives within the larger whole. If such relationships can be demonstrated, such that each narrative, in association with other narratives within the larger whole, is seen to be contributing towards an overall structure, a continuous plot, and the progressive development of recurrent themes, then a case can be made for each narrative to be interpreted in the context of the larger whole. For these relationships would constitute a strong argument that each individual narrative is intended to be read as a component part of an integrated work. But absent such relationships, and each narrative should perhaps be interpreted on its own without its meaning being affected by narratives in the surrounding context. In such a case, one would then be looking at the kind of loose collection or anthology that Andersson suggests.

The question for Judges, then, is whether the narratives in the book in fact demonstrate the kind of significant relationships with each other that justify their being read as an integrated whole in the first place. Unfortunately, this is a question that none of the four major synchronic works have directly addressed.

For as much as all four major synchronic works analyse Judges with the assumption that the book can and should be read as an integrated whole, no direct attempt has been made to first justify this assumption of unity on the basis of significant relationships between narratives.[106] Thus, Klein's decision to regard the work as a single entity with a single author is based simply on her belief that one hand must have given the book its present form.[107] This belief, however, was never thoroughly justified. Likewise, although O'Connell states explicitly that the aim of his work is to present a coherent reading of the present form of the book,[108] he offers no prior justification to show that the book deserves to be read as a coherent whole.[109]

As for Amit, while she concedes that the biblical text in general is formed out of a series of redaction over time,[110] she nonetheless argues for the legitimacy of a unified, synchronic reading based on her theory that the successive redactors who worked on the text essentially followed the same central editorial line as their predecessors. This, therefore, gives the majority of the components of a biblical book the sense of combining towards the same goal.[111] But the problem with Amit's position is that her assumption that successive editors were guided by the same implicit editorial line as their predecessors is an assumption that simply cannot be proven. In fact, once this essentially philosophical assumption of editorial unity is adopted, one may be predisposed to a biased reading of the text that glosses over differences in perspective in favour of a unified reading. Thus, rather than justifying her integrated approach to Judges, Amit's assumption actually does the opposite by highlighting her inherent bias.

---

[106] Although the distinction seems subtle, yet it cannot be emphasised enough that procedurally, there is a world of difference between finding significant relationships between narratives in order to establish unity, and assuming unity and then trying to show how the narratives are related within that unity. The former represents an inductive process whereby the acceptance or rejection of literary unity basically results from an objective consideration of the available evidence. The latter, however, allows for a certain degree of circularity in that, once unity is assumed, one would be predisposed to look for relationships between component parts to maintain that assumption of unity. This can result in the establishment of tenuous literary relationships that may not be fully justified.

[107] Klein, 1988:11.

[108] Ibid., 1.

[109] O'Connell (365–66, 368) seems to also tie his assumption of literary unity to the existence of a final redactor, but this is only inferred from comments he made in an excurses.

[110] Amit, 1998:5.

[111] Ibid., 9, 14–18.

Of the four works, Webb's comes closest to offering a thorough defence of an integrated, synchronic approach to Judges as a self-contained literary unit. Webb essentially justifies his integrated reading on the basis of three lines of argument: the historical view of the book as a distinct, meaningful literary unit,[112] the apparent success of the final redaction to redefine the period of the judges according to the boundaries set by the book,[113] and evidence of literary design.[114] Of the three lines of argument, however, the first two are essentially based on extrinsic considerations not directly derived from the text. While these arguments do add weight to the case, how the book has historically been understood does not in itself prove the correctness of that understanding.

To the present author, Webb's third line of argument offers the greatest potential because this line of argument deals more directly with the discovery of significant relationships between narratives within the larger text. Unfortunately, here Webb merely refers to works of other scholars rather than presents new arguments of his own. This weakens his argument in two ways. First, even as Webb himself concedes, the various studies he refers to are all "modest in scope and are not characterised by the kind of systematic attention to detail normally expected in major studies."[115] Second, as insightful as these analyses are, they have by no means provided definitive 'proof' for the literary unity of the book.

Take Gros Louis' article, for example, to which Webb refers. While Gros Louis indeed points out a number of related themes that are progressively developed throughout the first sixteen chapters of the book, his article makes no mention at all of the final five chapters of Judges. But since these final chapters are generally regarded by historical critical scholars to be a later addition unrelated to the main body of Judges, by not including them in his analysis, Gros Louis comes across as having implicitly conceded the point to the historical critical scholars. Therefore, at best, the article succeeds in defending of the literary unity of the first sixteen chapters of Judges, but falls short of defending the literary unity of the book as a whole.

---

[112] Webb, 1987:13–19, 38.
[113] Ibid., 28.
[114] Ibid., 28–36.
[115] Ibid., 35.

As for the symmetrical structure Gooding posits for the whole book, to which Webb also refers, valid questions can also be raised about the strength of Gooding's case. Chief among them is the fact that some of the symmetries Gooding proposes strike one as being somewhat forced. An example would be how Gooding manages to boil down the lengthy narratives of Samson into a mere couple of points to serve as counterbalance to the very brief Othniel narrative in 3:7–11. Not only so, but the points to which Gooding refers under the Othniel narrative are not even derived from 3:7–11, but from related texts in 3:6 and 1:11–15![116] As for the balance Gooding sees between the Ehud and Jephthah narratives, while the emphasis on messages to kings and battles at the fords of Jordan seems to make sense, this leaves the significant episode concerning the sacrifice of Jephthah's daughter entirely unaccounted for under the proposed schema. In light of these weaknesses, one is perhaps justified in wondering whether Gooding has in fact succeeded in definitively demonstrating the literary unity of the book as a whole.

And yet, on the basis of these somewhat flawed studies, Webb concludes that there is strong enough evidence of overall literary design in Judges to justify a detailed analysis of the book in its final form.[117] To the present author, however, the case for an integrated, synchronic approach to Judges has by no means been sufficiently established.

Goal and Method of the Present Study

Methodologically, like the works of other synchronic scholars, the present study seeks to examine Judges through careful attention to literary and rhetorical features such as narrative structure, recurring themes and motifs, allusions, wordplays, points of view, plot, and characterisation. For it is believed that these are the most common literary tools used by an author to establish continuity and link various constituent parts together in a unified literary composition.

Yet, the present study is not intended to be another integrative study of Judges in the same way that the four major synchronic studies are. For while the four major synchronic studies all proceed

[116] Gooding, 77–78.
[117] Webb, 1987:35–36.

from the assumption that Judges is an integrated text, the present study makes no such assumption. Rather, the primary goal of the present study is to answer the more fundamental question of whether the approach taken by Amit, Webb, Klein, and O'Connell to explore Judges as an integrated whole and to interpret individual narratives in light of the larger context can indeed be justified.

To accomplish this goal, the present study will focus on exploring whether significant rhetorical links exist between narratives from different sections of Judges on the basis of language and plot parallels. The underlying assumption is that if such links indeed exist through which narratives from different sections of the book interact to reinforce the same basic points of view and contribute towards the unfolding of the same continuous plot and the progressive development of the same themes and motifs, then such a display of unity of design will constitute a strong argument that a single creative mind stood behind the present form of the book, and that each constituent narrative is to be read as an integral part of the larger whole.

But still, given the large number of individual narratives that make up the book, how does one go about exploring possible rhetorical links among them? In this matter, the task is actually made easier by some of the conclusions of historical critical scholars.

As is clear from the earlier survey of historical critical scholarship in Judges, there seems to be a general consensus that the book in its current form is divisible into three major sections. For the central section of the book (2:6–16:31), which is seen as a part of the larger Deuteronomistic History, the existence of a certain degree of compositional/redactional unity is by and large beyond dispute. This unity is primarily seen in the recurrence of certain formulaic phrases that frame each of the hero stories, thus transforming individual hero stories into integral parts of a larger cyclical pattern that dominates the entire section. As for the epilogue of the book (17:1–21:25), the repetition of the same basic refrain that seems to act as a transitional link between the various narratives within that section also seems to point towards some kind of compositional/redactional unity for the section as a whole. The prologue of Judges (1:1–2:5) is admittedly brief, but the fact that much of the material making up this section seems to show a significant dependence on Joshua also gives it a certain redactional unity.

But as much as critical scholars seem to recognise that each of the three major sections demonstrates a degree of compositional/redactional unity within itself, the three sections are nonetheless viewed essentially as independent compositions unrelated to each other. In fact, the general consensus is that both the prologue and the epilogue are later additions appended separately and artificially to the central section.[118] In light of this general consensus, it seems all the more necessary for some sort of justification to be made for treating all three major sections of Judges as integral parts of a unified work before synchronic scholars can present their integrated readings of the book in its current form.

Therefore, in the following three chapters of the present study, attempts will be made to discover if significant rhetorical links in fact exist that connect the narratives in the three major sections of Judges to one another. Possible links between narratives in the prologue and the epilogue will first be examined in chapter 2, followed by a similar examination of possible links between the epilogue and the central section in chapter 3, and finally, between the prologue and the central section in chapter 4. The approach taken for each of these explorations will be inductive in nature, which means that instead of assuming a certain conclusion at the outset and trying to prove its validity, the available evidence will first be examined before a conclusion is allowed to emerge from that evidence. And should the evidence point towards the existence of significant rhetorical links that connect the narratives in one section to another, the implications of such links will also be explored from the compositional standpoint, to see if they are further indicative of common authorship behind the sections in question.

Furthermore, recognising that any claim of compositional unity for Judges would inevitably have to answer questions regarding apparent discrepancies in points of view within the book, a further chapter is devoted to exploring one of the main issues concerning which critical scholars have discerned divergent voices. As has already been

[118] Although, as has been noted, Veijola has attempted to argue for the epilogue being an integral part of DH, his argument has generally not been accepted by the scholarly community. As for the prologue, even though scholars in both the Cross and Smend schools have credited it to later deuteronomistic redactors, they also seem to have taken pains to point out that whoever inserted Judges 1 did not compose it himself, but that the material was taken from older traditional sources. In fact, O'Doherty (1–2) and Mullen (1984:34–35) continue to note that there appears to be no contextual connection between the prologue and the central section of the book.

noted in the earlier survey of critical scholarship, critical scholars seem divided about whether Judges is essentially pro-monarchical or anti-monarchical. While Noth sees Dtr as anti-monarchical, and Richter basically agrees although he attributes this anti-monarchical ideology to Dtr's source rather than Dtr himself, Veijola sees DtrG as basically pro-monarchical and attributes the anti-monarchical sentiments to later deuteronomistic redactors such as DtrN and DtrP. Becker, on the other hand, supports Noth, and instead attributes the pro-monarchical sentiments to a later priestly redactor. What this seems to show is that regardless of which position one takes, one still has to contend with the fact that both pro- and anti-monarchical sentiments appear to exist within Judges. Regarding this, the solution critical scholars generally take is to attribute opposing sentiments to different redactors. In this respect, Buber's view that the current book of Judges really consists of two books, one anti-monarchical, the other pro-monarchical, each complete within itself and each being redacted from an opposing biased viewpoint,[119] is essentially predicated on the assumption that the central section and the epilogue of Judges are separate and distinct compositions. But if it can indeed be shown that significant rhetorical links exist between the central section and the epilogue of Judges, such that common authorship becomes a distinct possibility, then how is one to reconcile this apparent divergence of viewpoints regarding the monarchy?

In an attempt to answer this question, an examination of the allegedly pro-monarchical refrain in the epilogue will be conducted in chapter 5 to determine if the 'king (מלך)' referred to is indeed a reference to the monarchy as both critical and synchronic scholars seem to think. Noting the existence of significant rhetorical links that seem to join together several narratives relating to kingship from all three sections of Judges, an attempt will be made to explore the possibility of an alternative interpretation of the refrain that has the potential of eliminating the problem of divergent viewpoints within the book with regard to monarchy.

In the final chapter of the present study, the various observations and conclusions drawn in previous chapters will be brought together to be synthesised into a more comprehensive theory regarding the

[119] Buber, 68.

overall compositional strategy of Judges. If a strong case can indeed be made for compositional unity of the book in its current form, then a further attempt will be made to discover the overall rhetorical purpose of Judges based on what is implied by the rhetorical links that join the three major sections into a unified whole.

CHAPTER TWO

THROUGH THE LENS OF JOSHUA: LINKS BETWEEN THE PROLOGUE AND EPILOGUE OF JUDGES

In historical critical scholarship, the prologue and epilogue of Judges are generally taken to be later additions that do not belong to the original core of the book. Under the Deuteronomistic History hypothesis, these sections are especially seen as "intrusions into a continuous account which relates Joshua to Judges and Judges to Samuel".[1]

And in a way, such a view is not unjustified. For while the central section of Judges is seen as fitting naturally into the continuous narrative of Deuteronomistic History,[2] when it comes to the two peripheral sections, significant linguistic, stylistic, and thematic differences seem to set them apart from the central section.[3] These observations thus lead to the conclusion that the prologue and epilogue must have been derived from a different hand than the one responsible for the central section, and that in all likelihood, they were independent compositions that were only later appended to the central section under different circumstances. Perhaps for this reason, historical critical scholarship has generally shown little interest in exploring any formal relationship between the prologue and epilogue of Judges.[4]

[1] Mayes, 1985:13.

[2] See Noth, 1991:17–26. Note, however, that in recent years, Auld has begun questioning not only the extent to which Judges should be considered 'Deuteronomistic' (1998:120–26), but also whether the term is in fact an appropriate description of the Former Prophets (1999:116–26; 2000:353–67). See also Greenspahn, 1986:285–96.

[3] See Mayes (1985:13–16) for a detailed presentation of these differences.

[4] One notable exception is Boling (1975:29–38), who argues for definite redactional relationships between the prologue and the epilogue. But rather than taking the prologue and epilogue each as a distinct unit, Boling sees two concentric frameworks being supplied by different redactors at different points in time. In his view, the inner framework was composed by a seventh century deuteronomic redactor and includes 2:1–5 of the prologue, 17:1–18:31 of the epilogue, as well as 6:7–10; 10:6–16; 16:1–31 of the central section. This inner framework is then bracketed by an outer framework which was composed by a sixth century deuteronomistic redactor and comprises 1:1–36 of the prologue and 19:1–21:25 of the epilogue.

With the rise of literary/rhetorical studies, however, the search for links between the major sections of the book to justify an integrated reading has resulted in an awareness that certain themes introduced in the prologue actually emerge again in the epilogue. An obvious example is the selection of Judah in 1:2 and 20:18 to take the lead in two very different military campaigns. Unfortunately, discussions of such links are inevitably brief, and seem to comprise little more than observations about thematic associations at the most superficial level.[5] Thus, while some view such links as evidence that one unifying mind must have been responsible for the compilation of the book in its present form,[6] little attempt has been made to further validate this through careful consideration of the language and rhetorical significance of the links to see if they are in fact indicative of common authorship at the compositional level.

In view of such deficiencies, in the following discussion, episodes in the prologue and epilogue that seem to be thematically related will be closely examined to determine if there is more to these links than superficial thematic association. If there is, an attempt will then be made to determine whether such links point to conscious design, since that would imply a closer relationship between the two sections than is generally recognised. After all, conscious design is often indicative of common authorship.

In addition, another distinctive feature that seems to be shared by the prologue and epilogue of Judges will also be explored. This concerns the pervasive use of references in both sections to the book of Joshua. While the more direct references to Joshua have long been noted and discussed by historical critical scholars interested in the source and ideology of Judges' prologue,[7] it is the more subtle and frequently overlooked allusions to Joshua in both the prologue and epilogue of Judges that seem most intriguing. These cases of subtle allusions will thus be closely examined to determine if collectively, they provide further indication as to whether the prologue and epilogue of Judges are related at a compositional level.

---

[5] See, for example, Gooding, 75–77; Webb, 1987:197–98; Gunn and Fewell, 120.

[6] See, for example, Gooding, 72.

[7] See, for example, O'Doherty, 1–7; Weinfeld, 1967:93–113; 1993a:387–99; Auld, 1975:261–85; Mullen, 1984:33–54; 1993:121–30.

Thematic Links Between the Prologue and Epilogue

When it comes to thematic unity, five episodes can be identified in the epilogue for which thematic links with episodes in the prologue seem to exist. In fact, as the following discussion shows, these links to the prologue seem to bring an extra interpretive dimension to the related episodes in the epilogue, such that in each case, the episode in the epilogue receives clarity or added significance when viewed in light of the corresponding episode in the prologue. These five episodes are as follows.

1. *Jebusite threat implied in the prologue actualised by Israelites in the epilogue*

In 1:21 in the prologue, the inability of Benjamin to dislodge the Jebusites living in Jerusalem is mentioned. This resulted in the Jebusites continuing to live among Benjaminites there.

Placed near the beginning of a section that gives a series of quick reports of the various tribes' attempts to dispossess the peoples of the land (1:19–34), this failure of Benjamin sets an ominous tone for the whole section. In fact, as the rest of the narrative shows, this failure was not restricted to Benjamin either, but also characterises other tribes such as Manasseh (1:27), Ephraim (1:29), Zebulun (1:30), Asher (1:31–32), Naphtali (1:33), and Dan (1:34). The resulting presence of the nations among the tribes thus serves to highlight the danger of enemies living in the midst of Israel.

But this mention of Jebusites continuing to live among Benjaminites in Jerusalem may be significant in another way. For while neither the Jebusites nor Jerusalem comes up again through the central section of the book, both reappear in Judges 19 as a foil to the Benjaminites living in Gibeah in the story of the Levite and his concubine.

In that narrative, a Levite, his concubine, and his servant were travelling from Bethlehem to hill country of Ephraim. Towards the evening, they came near Jebus (that is, Jerusalem). The servant of the Levite suggested spending the night there, but this was rejected by the Levite because the Jebusites living there were non-Israelites. The implication is obviously that it would be dangerous to spend the night among people who were not part of the covenant community. So, they journeyed on until they reached Gibeah, an Israelite town within Benjaminite territory. As it turns out, not only were the citizens of Gibeah slow to extend hospitality as they should, the overnight stay of the Levite and his company also went horribly wrong as it ended in the death of the concubine at the hands of the wicked townsfolk.

Here, the irony is unmistakable. The Levite's attempt to bypass the potential danger of the Jebusites only led him and his company into a far more lethal danger, one that is all the more unexpected because it came from his fellow countrymen.

But what is noteworthy here is that in order for this irony to be properly appreciated, there must be prior knowledge of the relationship between the Jebusites and the Israelites. Otherwise one can conceivably draw wrong conclusions about the story, such as misunderstanding the horrific death of the concubine as a harsh but necessary lesson aimed at correcting the Levite's xenophobic paranoia and racial bias.[8] Thus, it is only with the realisation that the Jebusites were in fact Israel's enemies whom Israel had previously attempted unsuccessfully to dispossess that the Levite's reluctance to spend the night in Jebusite territory becomes understandable. And it is only then that the later atrocity committed in supposedly 'friendly' Israelite territory becomes all the more horrifying and unthinkable.

But what is most curious here is that within the narrative of Judges 19, this background information so vital for the full appreciation of this irony is not provided. The Levite's reluctance to spend the night in Jebus is simply explained in terms of its people not being Israelite. This apparent omission of what appears to be crucial background information can only be explained in one of three ways.

To be sure, this omission could be due to a significant oversight on the part of the author. But this seems unlikely, seeing how careful he was to note the new name of Jebus as Jerusalem. Alternatively, the omission could be due to the author's assumption that his readers were already well-informed regarding interracial relationships between Israelites and Jebusites. But this too seems unlikely, for had the author considered his readers up-to-date with regard to Israelite-Jebusite relationship, he would not have needed to explain that Jebus was in fact Jerusalem. The final option then, is that the author

[8] Fokkelman (1992:44–45; 1999:111) in fact takes just such a view, and faults the Levite for his prejudice! A similar stance is also taken by Jüngling (292–93), who faults the Levi for avoiding Jerusalem.

simply saw no need to repeat information that has already been previously given, namely, in 1:21 of the prologue.[9]

If this last option indeed seems the most plausible of the three, then the implication is that certain compositional unity must exist between the epilogue and the prologue. For if information deemed necessary for the proper understanding of a specific episode in the epilogue is spared repetition because it has already been given in the prologue, then what this suggests is that the epilogue could not have been composed independently of the prologue, but rather, as a complement to the prologue even from its inception. And to the extent that information conveyed about the Jebusites in 1:21 turns out to be exactly what is needed to fill the rhetorical gap in Judges 19 in order for the irony there to be fully appreciated, one can argue that one of the rhetorical functions of 1:21 may in fact be to anticipate Judges 19. If so, this may also offer additional possibilities towards resolving the textual issue of 1:21.

For it has long been recognised by scholars that Judg. 1:21 and Josh. 15:63 are in some kind of dependent relationship. But while Josh. 15:63 attributes the failure to dispossess the Jebusites in Jerusalem to Judah, in Judg. 1:21 the same failure is blamed on Benjamin. In light of the almost identical wording of the two verses and the general dependence of Judg. 1:9–36 on Joshua 14–19, there seems little doubt that Judg. 1:21 represents a revision of Josh. 15:63. Until now, however, most arguments in support of this direction of dependence are primarily theological or historical-critical.[10] But to these, it may now be possible to add another argument of a different nature, namely, that this attribution to Benjamin of the failure to dispossess the Jebusites in Jerusalem may have arisen partly as a rhetorical device to link Judg. 1:21 to the narrative of the Levite and his concubine in Judges 19. After all, in Judges 19, Benjaminites are portrayed as living in a town right next to the Jebusites in Jerusalem. The attribution to Benjamin of the failure to dispossess the Jebusites in 1:21 would therefore provide the crucial setting needed to understand the subsequent narrative in Judges 19.

---

[9] Notice that the information given in 19:10 about Jebus being equivalent to Jerusalem is actually a piece of new information not previously given in 1:21.

[10] See, for example, O'Doherty, 2; J. Gray, 250; Auld 1975:274–75; Van Seters, 335–42; Fishbane, 203 n. 88; Mullen, 1984:46, 1993:126; Lindars, 1995:47.

2. *Similar oracular consultations in the prologue and epilogue end with different results*

One of the most obvious links between the prologue and the epilogue is probably the selection of Judah as the first among the tribes to engage in battle in 1:2 and 20:18.[11] A closer examination of the two texts, however, reveals that there is more to link the two episodes together than simply the selection of Judah.

First, both incidents begin with an Israelite consultation of YHWH that employs the language of oracular inquiry. For שׁאל ב- followed by a noun associated with a deity or his representative[12] frequently signals an oracular inquiry. In fact, it is believed that such inquiries made to YHWH often involve the more archaic practice of using the Urim and Thummim.[13]

Moreover, while this kind of oracular inquiry has been referred to on numerous occasions in Samuel and 1 Chronicles,[14] the five occurrences in Judges are restricted only to the prologue and epilogue of the book.[15] Of these, the three occurrences in Judges 20 are found in essentially the same episode. Like 1:1, they also represent pre-war inquiries for specific guidance in battle.

But not only do Judg. 1:1 and 20:18 both involve pre-war oracular inquiries, when it comes to how the actual inquiries were phrased, there are also remarkable similarities. In both episodes, the main question posed by Israel begins with the identical מי יעלה־לנו. And in both cases, the issue of priority is also raised by the use of בתחלה.

Furthermore, not only are two questions similar, the report of YHWH's answer in both cases is also almost identical. In response to the inquiry in the prologue, YHWH's answer is reported in 1:2 as ויאמר יהוה יהודה יעלה. In the epilogue, it is reported in 20:18 as ויאמר יהוה יהודה בתחלה.

---

[11] In fact, Boling (1975:53), Webb (1987:198), O'Connell (16–17), and Block (1999:559) all understand this as a framing device such as an inclusio.

[12] Within Hebrew Scripture, שׁאל ב- is almost always followed by יהוה or אלהים when the following noun is associated with the deity. Notable exceptions are in 1 Chron. 10:13, where Saul inquired of a medium, and in Hos. 4:12 and Ezek. 21:26, where inquiries are made respectively of a piece of wood presumably representing an idol made of that material, and of the teraphim.

[13] See Lindars (1995:11) and Block (1999:86).

[14] 1 Sam. 10:22; 14:23; 22:10,13,15; 23:2,4; 28:6; 30:8; 2 Sam. 2:1; 5:19,23; 1 Chron. 14:10,14.

[15] 1:1; 18:5; 20:18,23,27.

The suspicion that such similarities are not accidental but represent a conscious attempt to link the two episodes together is further confirmed by the fact that Judah's selection to lead the tribes in the war against Benjamin seems wholly unmotivated by plot necessity in its immediate context. For while the mention of Judah's selection to lead the campaign against the Canaanites in the prologue seems contextually necessary in light of the immediately following report of the tribe's initial successes in 1:3–19a, the mention of a similar selection of Judah to lead the campaign against Benjamin seems puzzling. For in the immediately ensuing account of the war against Benjamin, Judah actually plays no distinguishable role from any of the other tribes within the Israelite coalition. In fact, Judah was not even mentioned again either in the battle account that follows or in the rest of the book. Consequently, one can argue that this lack of contextual relevance suggests that the report of Judah's selection at the beginning of the Benjaminite war may have been present primarily as a link to the similar selection of the tribe at the beginning of the book.

But granted that similarly phrased reports of Judah's selection in the two pre-war inquiries seem to suggest a conscious attempt at establishing a thematic link, the question 'To what end?' remains.

From a rhetorical standpoint, that two similar questions were asked and two similar responses were given in the two pre-war inquiries raises the expectation that the ensuing outcomes would also be similar. But surprisingly, this is not the case. For while the selection of Judah at the beginning of the book is followed immediately by reports of successes, the selection of Judah in the epilogue is followed immediately by reports of failures. And as one is forced to go back to the text to look for clues that might explain the different outcomes, one notices that a promise of victory accompanying YHWH's selection of Judah in the prologue has gone missing in the similar selection of Judah in the epilogue. With no promise of victory accompanying Judah's selection in 20:18, the Israelite coalition thus went on to suffer two crushing defeats in the hands of Benjamin. Not until the Israelites came back for a third oracular inquiry was the promise of victory, also involving the phrase נתן . . . ביד as in 1:2, finally given (20:28).

But why was there a delay in YHWH's promise of victory? And what accounts for this stark difference in immediate outcome if the oracular inquiries in 1:1 and 20:18 seem so similar in so many ways?

As it turns out, the key may be found in the one difference that sets the two episodes apart. While the inquiry in the prologue concerns battle with the Canaanites, a people whom Israel had already received instructions to dispossess,[16] the consultation in the epilogue concerns battle with Benjamin, who, as Israel concedes in 20:23,28, is actually a brother. Thus, the possibility exists that not only is the question מי יעלה־לנו in 20:18 inappropriate because the Israelites had yet to receive instructions from YHWH to fight against Benjamin,[17] the very act of making such an inquiry may also be deemed problematic because this kind of pre-battle oracular inquiry is typically reserved for war against external enemies rather than brothers.[18]

In any case, what is important is that even though the oracular inquiries in the prologue and epilogue each has its plot-driven function in the immediate context, it is only when they are examined together that their full rhetorical significance becomes apparent. For it is only when the remarkable similarities between the two episodes are noticed that attention is drawn to the stark difference in outcome, thereby forcing an alert reader to look for plausible explanations to account for that difference. What this seems to indicate

[16] See, for example, Deut. 20:17–18.

[17] Notice that in similar oracular inquiries such as in 1 Sam. 14:37; 23:2; 30:8; 2 Sam. 2:1; 5:19; 1 Kgs. 22:6,15; 1 Chron. 14:10, when no clear prior instructions have been received from YHWH, the first question is often one seeking direction as to whether one should go or not. But such a question is conspicuous by its absence in Judges 20. This is probably what prompted Lasine (50) to assert that Israel had asked the wrong question when she came to YHWH for advice.

[18] Although an oracular inquiry could be made about a variety of issues, such as the direction and prospects of a journey (Judg. 18:5; 2 Sam. 2:1) or the whereabouts of a person (1 Sam. 10:22), when it comes to pre-war inquiries, they were mostly reserved for fighting against external enemies. This may have to do with the fact that external enemies were generally regarded also as YHWH's enemies by virtue of the fact that they opposed YHWH's people. Therefore, implicit to the act of inquiry is the conviction that YHWH would guide His people as they fight against His and their enemies. Thus, for example, the consultation in Judg. 1:1 concerns going up against the Canaanites, the consultations in 1 Sam. 14:37; 23:2, 4; 28:6; 2 Sam. 5:19, 23 (also recorded in 1 Chron. 14:10,14) all concern fighting against the Philistines, and the consultation in 1 Sam. 30:8 concerns going after the Amalekites. As it turns out, Judg. 20:18,23,27 actually represent the only instances in Hebrew Scripture where such an inquiry was made concerning a battle against fellow Israelites. Considering that the above-mentioned battles against external enemies generally went well whenever YHWH responded to His people's inquiries, the fact that the battle against Benjamin did not go well even after YHWH had responded seems to suggest that something was fundamentally wrong with this inquiry to begin with.

is that the series of oracular inquiries in the epilogue may have been designed to be read in light of the similar inquiry in the prologue. If so, this again points to the likelihood that the prologue and epilogue of Judges may not have been composed independently of each other, since they seem to be linked to each other by conscious design.

3. *Specific military action appropriately applied in the prologue but inappropriately applied in the epilogue*

As has already been pointed out, by seeking an oracular inquiry in their war against Benjamin, the Israelites were essentially applying a procedure normally reserved for war against external enemies to a war against their brothers. This blurring of distinction by the Israelites between external and internal war is further highlighted by the use of specialised war terms depicting actions usually reserved for external enemies in war. These include חרם and the related הכה . . . לפי־חרב, both of which, incidentally, occur only in the prologue and the epilogue but not in the central section.[19]

Concerning חרם, there is admittedly little consensus with regard to the nature and origin of the concept.[20] But a good case can be made that the term has sacral connotations and may have at its core

[19] The absence of these relatively common war terms in the central section is somewhat surprising, especially considering how many wars were fought under the leadership of various judges that resulted in the complete destruction of Israel's foreign enemies (e.g. 4:16; 7:25; 8:10–12; 11:32–33).

[20] For example, while Stern (217–26) sees the concept as rooted in the mythic battle against chaos and thus represents an attempt to bring moral and physical order to an ethnic group, R. Nelson (1997:39–54) sees the concept as a historical reflection of Israel's system of cultural classification. Here, Nelson's view is not dissimilar to Malul's (824–27), who thinks the concept was rooted in the idea of separation and transferral to an outside sphere. Weinfeld (1993b:154–60), however, sees the חרם laws in Deuteronomy as utopian laws originating during the time of Saul. As such, he thinks they were never actually carried out against the Canaanites in history. In contrast, Brekelmans (476) seems to see חרם as having been actually applied in its earliest historical phase, and that Saul's failure to fully execute it against Amelek represents a transition to a phase where the war ban was no longer applied from the royal period on. Like Weinfeld, Hoffman (196–210) also considers the חרם passages in Deuteronomy and Joshua late insertions. But unlike Weinfeld, he sees their insertion as primarily Deuteronomistic and arising out of an ideologically motivated attempt to combat separatist-nationalistic politics during the post-exilic era. For other views, see also Lohfink, 1986:180–99; 1989:104–12; Niditch, 1993:28–77; Schäfer-Lichtenberger, 270–75.

the idea of devotion to YHWH.[21] This idea of devotion is manifested in two distinct but related nuances. On the one hand, Lev. 27:28 speaks of a positive kind of devotion where an object of value is irrevocably devoted to YHWH for His use. On the other hand, חרם can also be associated with a different kind of devotion where objects deemed offensive to YHWH and injurious to His cause are devoted for destruction. Both acts are, however, equally regarded as proof of devotion.

For objects devoted to destruction, these specifically include idolatrous cultic objects (Deut. 7:26), as well as persons embracing such idolatry, be they Israelites (Exod. 22:19; Deut. 13:13–19) or the surrounding nations that Israel was to fight against in their attempt to take possession of the land (Deut. 7:1–4; 20:16–18).

In particular, it is likely on account of the explicit commands of Deut. 7:1–4 and 20:16–18 that the utter destruction of Israel's foreign enemies under the חרם came to be presented almost as standard military practice as Israel began taking possession of the land.[22] That such a practice is essentially religiously motivated is seen in that the justification given in Deut. 7:1–4 and 20:16–18 has to do explicitly with the prevention of idolatry-related apostasy. That its execution is looked upon as an expression of devotion to YHWH is seen in that the utter destruction of the nations is offered up as a vow in Num. 21:2.[23]

But what is noteworthy is that even though utter destruction under the חרם can be applied to Israelites in cases of idolatry[24] or illegal appropriation of objects devoted to YHWH,[25] in the context of war, חרם seems to have been reserved mainly for Israel's non-YHWHist foreign enemies.[26] And it is in precisely this context that חרם appears

---

[21] For arguments for sacral connotations, see Kaminsky, 329–36.

[22] Lohfink (1986:183) notes the regular appearance of חרם in wars of conquest against enemy cities. These include Deut. 2:34; 3:6; Josh. 6:17,21; 8:26; 10:28–40; 11:11–12,21; Judg. 1:17.

[23] Incidentally, the use of חרם in the extra-biblical Mesha Inscription to describe the total destruction of Nebo as an act of devotion to the God Ashtar-Kemosh seems to show that this religiously motivated practice was not unique to Israel.

[24] See Exod. 22:19; Deut. 13:13–19. In later prophetic writings such as Isa. 43:28; Jer. 25:9; Mal. 3:24, YHWH also warned about Himself applying the חרם to Israel for her idolatry and waywardness.

[25] Deut. 7:26; Josh. 6:18; 7:11–12.

[26] Of course, one can argue that since civil wars are never a normal, anticipated development, naturally, no rules exists to govern military conduct under such circumstances. However, if the application of the חרם is indeed religiously motivated,

in Judg. 1:17, where the word is used in connection with Israel's destruction of Zephath and the subsequent renaming of the city as Hormah.

Interestingly, however, חרם shows up again in Judg. 21:11 in the epilogue, where it is applied by the Israelites to every male and non-virgin female in Jabesh Gilead for the town's non-participation in the war against Benjamin.[27] And reminiscent of Num. 21:2, this application of the חרם was also connected to a vow (21:5).[28] But as Jabesh Gilead is clearly presented as an Israelite settlement in 21:5,8, and its offence is clearly unrelated to idolatry or the illegal possession of devoted objects, it raises the question of whether such an application of חרם is really justified.

As for הכה . . . לפי־חרב, evidence seems to suggest that the phrase is used practically synonymously with חרם.[29] In seventeen of its twenty-six occurrences in Hebrew Scripture, the phrase is used in the context of Israel's war against the nations.[30] Of these, the phrase is used interchangeably with or in close proximity to חרם thirteen times.[31] In the remaining nine occurrences where the phrase is not specifically used in the context of war with the nations,[32] most of them nonetheless hint at actions associated with the חרם.[33]

---

then it goes to reason that unless it is to deal with systemic apostasy of the kind mentioned in Deut. 13:13–19, there is little basis for it to be applied to fellow-worshippers of YHWH. This may be why nearly all the war-related applications of the חרם by Israel recorded in Hebrew Scripture are against foreign, non-YHWHist enemies.

[27] This is actually the only instance in Hebrew Scripture where חרם is explicitly said to be directed against fellow Israelites.

[28] As Lohfink (1986:184) points out, the solemn oath (השׁבועה הגדולה) in 21:5 is tantamount to a vow. After all, שׁבועה is used synonymously and in parallel with נדר in Num. 30:3.

[29] Greenfield (5) in his discussion of the Aramaic idiom *nkh tkwh bhrb* in the Sefire Treaty Inscriptions compares it to the Hebrew equivalent of הכה . . . לפי־חרב and recognises that the latter is used for the total annihilation of a city. This perhaps represent some kind of intuitive recognition that חרם and הכה . . . לפי־חרב may be semantically closer than most realise. Likewise, Niditch (1993:63) also speaks of the phrase as formulaic banning language, but offers no formal attempt to link the two.

[30] Num. 21:24; Deut. 13:16; 20:13; Josh. 8:24; 10:28,30,32,35,37,39; 11:11,12,14; 19:47; Judg. 1:8,25; 18:27.

[31] The clearest examples are in Deut. 13:16 and the nine occurrences in Josh. 10:28–39 and 11:11–14. In these instances, חרם and הכה . . . לפי־חרב are often used together in the same verse almost as synonyms.

[32] Judg. 20:37,48; 21:10; 1 Sam. 22:19; 2 Sam. 15:14; 2 Kgs. 10:25; Job 1:15,17; Jer. 21:7.

[33] For example, Jehu's slaying of the priests of Baal in 2 Kgs. 10:25 certainly seems to fall within the mandate of the חרם in relation to idolatrous influences.

But if לפי־חרב ... הכה is indeed synonymous with חרם, then one can argue that while לפי־חרב ... הכה is reasonable and indeed expected in the context of Israel's war against her foreign enemies in Jerusalem and Luz in Judg. 1:8 and 1:25, the same action taken against the Benjaminites in 20:37,48 and the citizens of Jabesh Gilead in 21:10 raises the question of propriety. After all, the Benjaminites and the citizens of Jabesh Gilead were both clearly Israelite, and the conditions under which the חרם can be applied to Israelites, namely, idolatry and the illegal appropriation of devoted objects, are simply not present.

Besides, the only other incidents in Hebrew Scripture where לפי־חרב ... הכה is described as being applied by Israelites to their fellow countrymen are in 1 Sam. 22:19 and 2 Sam. 15:14, where Saul's חרם-style slaughter at Nob and the possibility of Absalom applying the same kind of destruction to Jerusalem serve respectively to highlight the extent of Saul's spiritual/moral decline and Absalom's ruthlessness. Thus in both instances, the one who would לפי־חרב ... הכה fellow Israelites is presented in extremely negative light.

In view of this, one can argue that even though in the epilogue of Judges, the author has not overtly portrayed Israel's actions against the Benjaminites and the citizens of Jabesh Gilead as inappropriate, yet his subtle disapproval may have been conveyed through references to military action that appears to have been misapplied.

Incidentally, a similar disapproval related to the use of לפי־חרב ... הכה may also be found in a different episode within the epilogue of Judges. In this case, however, the problem has to do not so much with the recipients of destruction being Israelite as with the legitimacy of applying such destruction to a non-Israelite population.

In 18:27, the Danites are reported as having struck with the sword (לפי־חרב ... הכה) the people of Laish as they took possession of the town.[34] While Laish was clearly a non-Israelite settlement, and no

---

Likewise, YHWH's determination to hand Zedekiah and the people of Judah over to Nebuchadnezzar to be struck with the sword in Jer. 21:7 may also represent YHWH's attempt to apply the חרם to His apostate people. In fact, in a similar statement in Jer. 25:8, חרם is explicitly used. In Judg. 21:10–11, לפי־חרב ... הכה and חרם also occur in close proximity, both referring to the same action. As for the destruction of Nob in 1 Sam. 22:19, although חרם is not explicitly used, the description of the destruction in that verse is certain reminiscent of descriptions of other destructions under the חרם such as in Josh. 6:21 and 1 Sam. 15:3.

[34] Boling (1974:43) also thinks that חרם is hinted at in Judg. 18:27–28. Note the typographic error in Boling's text where 8:22–28 should probably read 18:27–28.

overt value judgement has been provided regarding the incident, one can nonetheless detect a subtle disapproval of the Danites' actions. For twice within the narrative in 18:7,27, the people of Laish are described as at rest and unsuspecting (שקט ובטח).[35] This is significant because the four other times שקט is used in Judges are to refer to the 'rest' for the land secured by the judges after Israel's foreign enemies have been defeated.[36] That they were 'unsuspecting (בטח)' is also mentioned a third time in 18:10, coming from no less than the mouths of the Danites spies themselves. Furthermore, that the Laishians seems to be living in contentment with their relative isolation is twice emphasised by their description in 18:7,28 as living at a distance (רחוק) from the Sidonians and having no relationship with anyone else.

But one suspects that these facts about the Laishians were not emphasised simply to arouse sympathy. Rather, they seem to be included specifically with the rule of military conduct given in Deut. 20:10–15 in mind. For Deut. 20:15 specifically dictates that in dealing with cities that are "at a great distance from you (הרחקת ממך מאד)", the Israelites are to first make an offer of peace (20:10). If such an offer is accepted, then there is to be no taking of life (20:11). But even if the offer is rejected and battle ensues which leads to the defeat of that city, it is still only the men who are to be struck with the sword (הכה . . . לפי־חרב); the women, children, livestock, and everything else are to be spared (20:12–14).

Given that the Laishians are described asliving at a distance (רחקים) not just from the main Israelite settlement but also from the Sidonians who themselves lived far from Israel's territories, and given that these Laishians have repeated been described as 'at rest and unsuspecting (שקט ובטח)', one gets the impression that had they been offered peace as Deut. 20:10–15 dictates, they would probably have accepted the offer. What this suggests then, is that the Danites really had no basis upon which to struck with the sword (הכה . . . לפי־חרב) the whole population of Laish had YHWH's explicit instructions in Deut. 20:10–15 been followed.

Therefore, the two specialised war terms, חרם and הכה . . . לפי־חרב, each found only in the prologue and epilogue in Judges, appear to

[35] In fact, according to Ezek. 38:10–11, attacking a people described with exactly the same two roots as 'at rest' and 'unsuspecting' (השקטים ישבי לבטח) is characterised as an evil scheme (מחשבת רעה)!

[36] Judg. 3:11,30; 5:30; 8:28.

have been set up to create an intentional contrast in the way certain military actions have been applied by Israel in the two sections. While actions associated with both terms seem to have been appropriately applied to Israel's enemies in the prologue, in the epilogue, the same actions are consistently presented as having been applied under questionable circumstances. What this implies is that in contrast to the very beginning of the book where the חרם-laws are appropriately applied, Israel seems subsequently to have lost her ability to apply these laws with understanding and discernment. If so, what this again suggests is that the prologue and epilogue of Judges must have been integral parts of the same composition rather than two separate and independent compositions. For the contrast between appropriate applications of a specific military strategy in the prologue and questionable applications of the same strategy in the epilogue seems too neat to be accidental.

4. *Diminishing national fortune twice wept over at Bethel*

A fourth link between the prologue and epilogue of Judges involves the weeping of Israel at Bokim in the prologue and at Bethel in the epilogue.

Although openly weeping is a fairly common occurrence in biblical narrative with the verb בכה having occurred over a hundred times in Hebrew Scripture, on certain occasions, the verb occurs in conjunction with other words or phrases to convey an increased intensity in mourning. One such example involves the use of נשׂא . . . קול immediately before בכה.

Now the combination of נשׂא . . . קול ובכה is not uncommon in Hebrew Scripture.[37] However, in Judges, it occurs only twice: towards the end of the prologue in 2:4, and towards the end of the epilogue in 21:2.[38]

A closer examination of the two instances reveals further similarities. For example, both instances involve the entire Israelite community having gathered together to weep over the prospect of a

[37] The combination is found in Gen. 21:16; 27:38; 29:11; Num. 14:1; Judg. 2:4; 21:2; Ruth 1:9,14; 1 Sam. 11:4; 24:17; 30:4; 2 Sam. 3:32; 13:32; Job 2:12.

[38] Mullen (1993:131–32) speaks of the two 'weeping' in 2:1–5 and 21:2 as forming some kind of inclusio, although he also includes 20:23,26 as a part of this inclusio. But in 20:23,26, only בכה is used. Unlike 2:4 and 21:2, it is not further qualified with נשׂא . . . קול.

bleak future. The immediate cause for weeping at Bokim in 2:4 was the oracle given by the angel of YHWH, rebuking the Israelites for their disobedience in not having dealt with the foreign occupants of the land as they were instructed. The immediate cause for weeping at Bethel in 21:2, on the other hand, was the realisation that the Israelites were on the verge of eliminating one of their own tribes as a result of their own actions and decisions.

While the immediate cause for the two 'weeping' seems at first glance to be very different, as one takes a deeper look, interesting correlations appear. For if one traces the chain of events that finally led to the two 'weeping', they are ultimately traceable to the two oracular inquiries in 1:1 and 20:18.

At the beginning of the prologue in 1:1, the Israelites sought guidance from YHWH as they readied themselves to fight against the nations to take possession of the land. The question they asked and the subsequent actions they took to dispossess the nations were essentially appropriate, although unfortunately, they were unable to complete the task. In the end, it was precisely this failure that resulted in the rebuke by the angel of YHWH, and hence, the subsequent weeping.

In 20:18 in the epilogue, the Israelites also sought guidance from YHWH as they readied themselves to fight against Benjamin, their errant brother. However, as has already been noted, the question they asked was the wrong one, as were the actions they were planning to take.[39] But ironically, they almost succeeded in accomplishing what they had set out to do, and that success was what eventually also resulted in their weeping before YHWH.

In other words, one can argue that the events described in the prologue and in the latter half of the epilogue are practically two sides of the same coin. While one records Israel's failure to do what was right, the other records Israel's success in doing what was wrong, and both resulted in a diminishing of national fortune that justifiably deserved to be loudly wept over and mourned.

---

[39] From the oath they took at Mizpah before the battle, reported retrospectively in 21:1, it seems clear that the Israelites were prepared to excommunicate the entire tribe of Benjamin. The action they took during battle also makes it clear that the Israelites were prepared to utterly destroy their brothers through an application of the חרם.

Moreover, if Bokim is indeed to be identified as Bethel as many seem to think,[40] then what we have at the beginning and the end of Judges are two oracular inquiries which set into motion a chain of events that ultimately resulted in the whole nation weeping loudly over diminished national fortune at Bethel. And that, perhaps more so than simply the oracular inquiries that resulted in the selection of Judah, seems to provide an extended inclusio which neatly ties the whole book together, giving it closure from a rhetorical standpoint.[41] This, of course, would point towards unity of design between the prologue and epilogue at a structural level, thus again suggesting common authorship.

5. *An appropriately arranged marriage in the prologue contrasted with inappropriately arranged marriages in the epilogue*[42]

In Judges, the giving of daughters to others as wives is mentioned six times.[43] Each time, the key words נתן, בת, and אשה occur in close proximity. Apart from 3:6 where intermarriage with Israel's foreign neighbours is in focus, the other five all concern marriages within the Israelite community. Incidentally, these five instances are distributed between two narratives located respectively in the prologue and epilogue of Judges. The two are the narrative about Caleb's giving of his daughter in marriage in 1:11–15, and the attempt of the Israelite elders to find wives for the Benjaminites in 21:1–23.

---

[40] See Cundall, 1968:63; Boling, 1974:37–38; Auld, 1984:140; Talmon, 46–47; Lindars, 1995:76; Block, 1999:112; Amit, 2000:121–31.

[41] The selection of Judah as well as the weeping at Bethel, albeit in 20:18,26 rather than in 21:2, are among the factors that prompt Webb (1987:197–98) to speak of the epilogue as providing "literary bracketing or closure" as elements from the prologue are picked up and repeated. This, according to Webb, signals the completion of the literary unit and invites the readers to compare and contrast the circumstances the characters find themselves in at the close of the unit with the circumstances they were in at the beginning.

[42] Because Judg. 1:11–15 is substantially the same as Josh. 15:15–19, the following discussion can conceivably be placed in the next section of the chapter entitled 'Literary/Rhetorical Dependence on Joshua' as a case of allusion to unrelated events in Joshua. But the fact that the author of the prologue saw fit to repeat Josh. 15:15–19 almost word for word in Judg. 1:11–15 seems to suggest that he had in mind a definite rhetorical function for the episode. This episode is therefore treated here as an integral part of Judges' prologue rather than simply an episode in Joshua that is alluded to in Judges.

[43] Judg. 1:12,13; 3:6; 21:1,7,18.

Other than the presence of the three key words and the fact that both narratives involve marriages within Israelite community, there are also other features that hint at a conscious attempt to link the two narratives.

First, it is worth noting that in both narratives, talk about the giving or not giving of daughters in marriage is immediately brought on by war. While Caleb promised to give his daughter in marriage essentially as a prize incentive to whomever would succeed in taking Kiriath Sepher in battle (1:12), the Israelites, ready to fight against the Benjaminites their brother, swore in advance of the battle not to give their daughters to any Benjaminite in marriage (21:1,7). Thus, in both cases, the pre-war pledge to give or not to give daughters in marriage plays a not-insignificant role in the politics of war.

Second, in both instances, after the respective wars have been fought and won, the narratives also report on follow-up actions specifically related to the pre-war pledges. But while Caleb is reported as fulfilling his pre-war pledge in 1:13 by giving his daughter Achsah to Othniel as wife, the Israelite assembly and its elders are portrayed in 21:10–22 as trying to come up with schemes that would allow them to circumvent their pre-war pledge.

This leads to a third link between the two episodes that may hinge upon a subtle but significant contrast involving the association of the two narratives with the opposing concepts of blessing (ברך) and cursing (ארר).

That blessing and cursing represent a significant pair of binary opposites in Hebrew Scripture can be seen from the frequency with which the two are juxtaposed to provide direct contrast. In this regard, although the contrast is commonly expressed through the juxtaposition of the nouns ברכה and קללה,[44] on certain occasions, this contrast is also expressed through the juxtaposition of the roots ברך and ארר.[45] Interestingly, in the two narratives in question, it just

[44] Gen. 27:12; Deut. 11:26–29; 23:6; 28:2,15; 30:1,19; Josh. 8:34; Ps. 109:17; Zech. 8:13.

[45] See, for example, Gen. 12:3; 27:29; Num. 22:6,12; 24:9; Jer. 20:14; Mal. 2:2. In addition, areas in which Israel is said to be blessed (ברוך) in Deut. 28:3–8 if she obeys YHWH are repeated almost precisely in 28:16–19 as the very areas that will be cursed (ארור) if she disobeys Him. This seems to suggest that even though Deut. 28:3–8 and 28:16–19, both written in verse, are separated by intervening material in prose form, they were composed as complementary parts and are meant to be read as such.

so happens that the root ברך is associated with one while the root ארר is associated with the other.

In the narrative about Caleb and his daughter, the fulfilling of Caleb's pre-war pledge to give Achsah in marriage to Othniel is followed immediately by an account involving the asking and granting of a blessing (ברכה). The fact that Achsah asked for a blessing in the form of springs of water and Caleb immediately granted it to her seems to cast the entire narrative in a very positive light. Caleb's readiness to bless his daughter can thus be seen as characterising his relationship with her throughout the narrative, thus retroactively casting his giving her in marriage to Othniel and the giving of land to her in the Negev also as benevolent acts intended as blessings.[46]

In contrast, the pre-war oath of the Israelites not to give their daughters in marriage to any Benjaminite is an oath that, according to 21:18, came in the form of a curse (ארור). Because of the excessive zeal with which the oath was first uttered, the Israelites came to regret it in the aftermath of war. Therefore, in an attempt to circumvent this curse without violating the letter of the oath, in one of their schemes, the elders decided to allow Benjaminites to abduct daughters of Shiloh and take them away as wives even as they were dancing in celebration at a festival of YHWH.

Here, it is interesting to note that the two verbs used to describe this act of sanctioned abduction, חטף in 21:21 and גזל in 21:23, both carry very negative connotations. חטף, used only three times in Hebrew Scripture, is twice used in Ps. 10:9 to describe the violent seizing of the helpless as a lion would. גזל, on the other hand, is regularly used to speak of robbery and oppression,[47] and even the flaying of people's skin and flesh from their bodies (Mic. 3:2). In fact, גזל is even used twice in Deut. 28:29,31 in the context of covenant curses.

What the use of these two verbs seems to indicate, therefore, is that even though the elders thought they had found a way to cir-

[46] While some might object to Caleb using his daughter as a prize of war, the fact remains that by offering her to the one who succeeds in taking Kiriath Sepher, Caleb was guaranteeing that she would be married to a valiant warrior who is able to fulfil YHWH's command to dispossess the enemy.

[47] Gen. 21:25; Lev. 5:21,23; Deut. 28:29,31; Judg. 9:25; Job 20:19; 24:9; Pss. 35:10; 62:11; Prov. 22:22; Eccl. 5:7; Isa. 10:2; Jer. 21:12; 22:3; Ezek. 18:7,12,16,18; 22:2; Mic. 2:2.

cumvent the curse that came with their oath, in reality, the curse remained. For inasmuch as the oath not to give their daughters in marriage to any Benjaminite eventually forced the elders to adopt a solution that resulted in the violent abduction of the daughters of Israel, one can indeed say that the oath itself had become a curse to the community.

But still, if the association of the two pre-war pledges respectively with ברך and ארר is meant to offer a subtle contrast between the two, what is the point of this contrast? To answer this question, perhaps a final parallel between the two narratives needs to be noted.

In both narratives, the ones who exercised control over the fate of their daughters' marriages happen to be those in leadership positions in Israel. While the elders in 21:16 clearly function as leaders of the assembly in their generation, Caleb, as one of only two adult males of his generation allowed to enter the land,[48] was effectively the only Israelite leader of his generation left after the death of Joshua. In view of the distinction made in Judg. 2:6–10 between Joshua's generation and the generation of those who came after him, it may not be insignificant that Caleb and the elders of Judges 21 happen to represent precisely those two generations.

If so, then while Caleb's pre-war promise to give his daughter in marriage to the one who succeeds in taking Kiriath Sepher seems to represent a wise move that merged concern for the fulfilment of YHWH's promise with concern for his daughter's welfare, the pre-war oath of Israel's leadership not to give their daughters in marriage to any Benjaminite seems to represent a rash and foolish decision made out of muddled thinking and excessive vindictiveness. And to the extent that the former opened up further blessings to Caleb's daughter, while the latter ended up cursing both the community and the daughters of Israel, the contrast between the leadership qualities of the two generations could not have been starker.

And as one shall see in the next section of this chapter, this contrast between the generations is not an isolated incident either, but seems to constitute a rhetorical theme that repeatedly emerges in the prologue and epilogue through allusions to events found in the book of Joshua. But before moving on to this, there is still one final observation worth noting.

---

[48] Num. 14:26–35; 26:63–65; 32:10–13; Deut. 1:34–40.

While the episode in the epilogue concerning the pre-war oath not to give the daughters of Israel in marriage to any Benjaminite seems integral to the overall narrative about the Benjaminite war,[49] the inclusion in the prologue of the story concerning Caleb's daughter is somewhat curious. After all, the focus of the prologue seems to be on the effort and accomplishments of the various tribes in taking possession of the land. The story of Caleb's domestic affairs involving his daughter's marriage therefore seems out of place in the immediate context. This leads to two significant implications.

First, the lack of contextual motivation for the inclusion of this episode about Caleb and his daughter in the prologue makes it more likely that Judg. 1:11–15 was borrowed directly from Josh. 15:15–19 than vice versa. After all, in the context of boundary information for Judah's allotment in Joshua 15, this episode fits in relatively well as it concerns not only Caleb's portion in Hebron and Debir, but also the granting of land in the Negev along with the upper and lower springs to Caleb's daughter.

Second, in light of the many parallels and contrasts this episode has with the episode concerning the elders' decision not to give the daughters of Israel in marriage to the Benjaminites in the epilogue, one can argue that not only was this episode borrowed directly from Joshua, it was also inserted into the prologue specifically to foster a rhetorical link with the related episode in the epilogue.

If so, this again argues strongly for a direct relationship between the prologue and epilogue at the compositional level. For not only has the episode in the epilogue gained additional interpretive significance through links with the corresponding episode in the prologue, the decision regarding what material to include in the prologue also seems to be influenced by the possibility of thematic links with the epilogue. What this suggests is that, if the prologue and epilogue are indeed directly related at a compositional level, that relationship is not simply unidirectional but bi-directional, with the prologue and the epilogue each contributing to the shaping of the other. This, therefore, argues strongly for the prologue and epilogue being the work of a single author, who crafted each section with the other in mind.

[49] It is integral because it provides a much-needed explanation of how Benjamin continued to survive as a tribe in spite of the fact that all its women and children were killed off and only 600 men survived.

Shared Dependence on the Book of Joshua

In addition to thematic links cited above, the use of another significant albeit not immediately obvious literary device in both the prologue and the epilogue also suggests the possibility of compositional unity between the two sections. This involves the pervasive use of references in both sections to the book of Joshua,[50] both directly and more subtly through allusions. In fact, in certain cases, one can even argue that the full rhetorical significance of certain episodes in the prologue and epilogue can simply not be grasped apart from an awareness of their dependence on Joshua.[51]

In trying to delineate these instances of dependence, it seems useful to divide them into three main categories: significant word for word correspondences referring to the same events in Joshua, casual references to related events in Joshua, and allusions to apparently unrelated events in Joshua.

The first and most direct category involves significant word-for-word correspondences as the same events are referred to in Joshua and the prologue or epilogue of Judges. These include the conquest of Hebron and Debir and the giving of Acsah in marriage to Othniel in Josh. 15:13–19 and Judg. 1:20,10–15, the failure to dispossess the Jebusites in Josh. 15:63 and Judg. 1:21 but attributed to a different tribe, the failure of Manasseh to dispossess the Canaanites in Josh. 17:11–13 and Judg. 1:27–28, the failure of Ephraim to dispossess the Canaanites in Josh. 16:10 and Judg. 1:29, and the naming of

[50] Incidentally, references to the book of Joshua are by and large absent from the central section of Judges except at the beginning of the introductory framework in 2:6–9. As the boundary between the prologue and the central section is still controversial, some actually suggest, partly on the basis of this reference to Joshua, that the prologue extends to 2:9.

[51] I am aware that even within scholarly circles, no unanimity as yet exists concerning the direction of dependence between Joshua and Judges 1. The problem seems complex. Lindars (1995:42–43), for example, sees Judg. 1:18–21 as basically dependent on various passages in Joshua. But he also sees both Judg. 1:27–28 and Josh. 17:1–3 as dependent on an older source (1995:56), and Josh. 16:10 and 19:47 as dependent respectively on Judg. 1:29 and Judg. 1:34–35; 18:29 (1995:60,69). Auld (1975:277–78), however, argues for the dependence of Judg. 1:34–35 on Josh. 19:47. Because the critical issues involved would demand the kind of attention not feasible within the scope of the present study, for the remainder of this chapter, it will simply be assumed that overall, Judges is dependent on Joshua. A more concrete literary/rhetorical argument for this direction of dependence will be presented subsequently within this chapter after the relevant passages have been examined.

Dan in Josh. 19:47b and Judg. 18:28b–29. Notice, however, that in spite of the presence of significant word-for-word correspondences, the same events are never described in the two books in exactly the same way.[52]

Second, there are also a number of verses in the prologue of Judges that seem to make casual references to related passages in Joshua. Unlike the previous category, however, the related passages here do not refer to the same events. Nonetheless, it is still possible to argue for some kind of definite link between them because most of these references seem to be of a similar type: where allotment of specific cities to specific tribes is recorded in Joshua, the related passages in Judges follow up on the matter by describing the ability or inability of these tribes to take possession of their allotted cities.[53] A comparison between these sets of passages shows, however, that apart from Judah, the other tribes basically failed to take possession of the cities allotted to them. Thus, on the whole, perhaps except for Judah, these casual references to Joshua seem to paint an unfavourable picture of the generation of the judges.

Apart from this group, however, there appears to be one other reference to a related event in Joshua that operates on a slightly different set of dynamics. Instead of being linked by city names and tribe names, this reference is linked by the phrase 'iron chariots (רכב ברזל)', which appears in Josh. 17:16,18 and again in Judg. 1:19. Here, although the 'iron chariots' appear in relation to the Joseph tribes in Joshua, whereas in Judges they are related to Judah, what is noteworthy is that the only occurrences of this phrase[54] in Hebrew Scripture are in Joshua and Judges.[55] Furthermore, the specific association of iron chariots with the Canaanites living in the plains (העמק) in both Josh. 17:16 and Judg. 1:19 also makes it virtually certain that the same basic group is being referred to in both cases. It is

[52] For more in-depth discussion, see Auld (1975), Lindars (1995), Mullen (1984), and Weinfeld (1967).

[53] These include Josh. 15:20,45–47 and Judg. 1:18; Josh. 18:21,28 and Judg. 1:21; Josh. 19:10,15 and Judg. 1:30; Josh. 19:24,28–30 and Judg. 1:31; Josh. 19:32,38 and Judg. 1:33; and Josh. 19:40,42 and Judg. 1:34–35.

[54] Although the noun רכב on its own is fairly common within Hebrew Scripture, what is at issue here appears to be specifically רכב ברזל since this is the type of chariot that apparently gave Israel trouble. Besides, ברזל has only been used three times in Judges, all of which occur in the phrase רכב ברזל (1:19, 4:3,13). This seems to justify taking the entire phrase as an integrated unit.

[55] The phrase is found only in Josh. 17:16,18; Judg. 1:19; 4:3,13.

therefore likely that the references in the two books are related by design. But still, what is the point to this link?

In Josh. 17:14–18, the Joseph tribes complain to Joshua about the insufficiency of their allotment. In response to Joshua's suggestion that they clear the forests in the hill country, the Joseph tribes reiterated that even then, it would still not be enough as they were unable to move into the plains because the Canaanites there had 'iron chariots'. Joshua, however, disputed their perception of reality. Pointing to their great number and strength, Joshua expressed confidence in them even as he challenged them to take on the Canaanites and dispossess them in spite of their 'iron chariots'.

But if Joshua's last word on the matter in Josh. 17:18 suggests quite clearly that iron chariots should not be an issue for the Joseph tribes in their effort to take possession of the land, in Judg. 1:19, the same 'iron chariots' apparently re-emerge as an issue for Judah. The fact that Judah's inability to dispossess the Canaanites from the plains is attributed primarily to the Canaanites' iron chariots thus creates a direct contrast between Joshua's earlier confidence and Judah's present failure.[56] Thus, rather than it being an indictment of Joshua's excessive optimism, what this link seems to highlight is Judah's failure to live up to its full potential.[57] If so, what this seems to suggest is that its initial successes not withstanding, Judah may not to be doing significantly better than the other tribes after all when it comes to carrying out its full mandate to dispossess the Canaanites and occupy the land.[58]

While the previous two types of dependence are relatively obvious, there is yet a third type of dependence that is much more subtle, and hence has not received the kind of attention it deserves. This type of dependence makes reference to Joshua primarily by means

[56] Granted, Joshua's earlier confidence is directed at the Joseph tribes. Yet given the repeated incidents of unlikely successes recorded in Joshua, there is little reason to think that Joshua's confidence in victory over the enemy's iron chariots would in any way be diminished had a different tribe been involved.

[57] O'Connell (64) notes that the subsequent triumph of Barak over similar 'iron chariots' Sisera possessed (4:3,13) "retroactively nullifies the legitimacy of Judah's excuse for failing to occupy its allotment".

[58] This point is also noted by Niditch (1999:200), and puts a dent in the assertions of Brettler (1989a:401–02, 2002:97–102), Mullen (1984:43–54, 1993:126–29), O'Connell (12–19), Sweeney (527), and Weinfeld (1993a:398) that a strong pro-Judah polemic is found in the prologue. For further evidence against an alleged pro-Judah polemic, see Wong, 2005:84–110.

of allusion, as apparently unrelated events are artificially drawn together for comparison and contrast.

As defined in Abrams' *A Glossary of Literary Terms*, "allusion in a work of literature is a brief reference, explicit or indirect, to a person, place, or event, or to another literary work or passage."[59] As the phrase 'explicit or indirect' implies, an allusion can be made with different levels of directness.

On the most indirect level, an allusion can be made without explicit reference to the subject alluded to or without any repetition of key words and phrases that usually serve to provide a direct link. Instead, the allusion is only broadly hinted at through plot parallels or similar contextual circumstances. In such cases, caution needs to be exercised in determining whether an allusion is indeed intended or whether resemblances are only coincidental. As a rule, however, the more points of correspondence there are between two accounts, the greater the likelihood that an allusion is indeed intended.[60]

On the other hand, there are also allusions that are quite explicit. These either refer directly to the subject alluded to, or use linguistic correspondences such as parallel syntax or repetition of key words and phrases to create direct links between two accounts. In the present situation, it appears that both direct and indirect allusions to Joshua are found in the prologue and epilogue of Judges.

After an allusion is identified, the next step is to discover the point of the allusion. As Abrams also notes, the point of an allusion is usually to enlarge upon or enhance a particular subject, although it can also be used ironically to undercut a subject through discrepancies between the subject and the allusion.[61]

As will be evident from the following discussion, allusions to Joshua in the prologue and epilogue of Judges seem to fall primarily into the category of ironic use. For where allusions are made to Joshua, the events alluded to all seem to have successful outcomes and are generally portrayed in a positive light in their original contexts. These include the spying and taking of Jericho in Joshua 2 and 6, the campaign against Ai in Joshua 8, and the resolution of potential internal conflict at Shiloh in Joshua 22.

---

[59] Abrams, 8.

[60] A similar point is also made by Amit (1988:388–89) concerning the discernment of analogies.

[61] Abrams, 8.

But in contrast, episodes in the prologue and epilogue of Judges where allusions to Joshua are discernible all seem to fall short of having satisfactory results. In fact, even when there seems to be success in these episodes, that success is portrayed as short-term and superficial at best, as they lead invariably to further complications that ultimately result in failure. These episodes include the taking of Luz in Judg. 1:22–26, the sending of Danite spies in Judges 18, the attempt to deal with internal problems in Judg. 20:1–14, and the subsequent war against Benjamin in Judg. 20:15–48. These allusions and their significance will now be examined one by one in greater detail.

1. *Allusion to the successful taking of Jericho in the account of the taking of Luz*

The incident concerning the spying and subsequent taking of Jericho in Joshua 2 and 6 is briefly alluded to in the account of the taking of Luz in Judg. 1:22–26.

In the Judges account, spies sent by the house of Joseph made an offer to a man coming out of Luz in exchange for a way into the city. The offer made to treat the man with kindness (ועשׂינו עמך חסד) is almost a word for word repetition of the promise "we will treat you with kindness and faithfulness (ועשׂינו עמך חסד ואמת)" made to Rahab by the two Israelite spies in Josh. 2:14.[62]

Furthermore, after Israel had struck Luz with the sword (הכה ... לפי־חרב), the sending away of the man and his family (ואת־האישׁ ואת־כל־משׁפחתו שׁלחו) in Judg. 1:25 also echoes the bringing out of Rahab and her family in Josh. 6:23 (ויציאו את־רחב ... ואת כל־משׁפחותיה הוציאו) after the Israelites had similarly struck Jericho with the sword (הכה ... לפי־חרב).

Finally, as both narratives come to a close and one last piece of information is given about each of the two survivors, the building of a new Luz by the man from the old Luz and the integration of Rahab into Israelite community are both qualified by 'until this day

[62] The combination of עשׂה plus עם, with חסד as direct object, is found only four times in Joshua and Judges: in Josh. 2:12(x2),14 and Judg. 1:24. Since all three occurrences in Joshua are in the context of Rahab's dialogue with the spies, this seems to support the contention that the unique occurrence of the clause in Judg. 1:24 represents a conscious attempt to allude to the Rahab episode in Joshua 2.

(עד היום הזה)', a phrase often used to stress the enduring significance of specific acts or states.[63] This seems to suggest that what happened to Rahab and the man from Luz after each was spared is regarded by the authors of Joshua and Judges as at least having long-term significance.

But if the linguistic correspondences cited above indeed suggest an allusion to Jericho in the account of the taking of Luz, what then is the point of the allusion?

First, in the Jericho account, after Rahab and her family were brought out of Jericho and spared, they lived among the Israelites. Rahab presumably lived among them until her death.[64] Thus, the Jericho account not only records a military victory in which enemies who stood in the way of Israel's possession of the land were destroyed, it also records an incident in which a non-Israelite woman who had shown faith in YHWH (Josh. 2:8–13) was eventually allowed a place within the covenant community.

But in contrast, this is not the case regarding the man from Luz. Although like Rahab, he and his family were spared when his city was destroyed, unlike Rahab, he did not attach himself to the covenant community. Instead, he went away and built a new city, which he promptly named after the city just destroyed. The inclusion of this piece of information in the narrative is surely intended to highlight the incompleteness of Israel's triumph. For although the house of Joseph appeared to have won a military victory when Luz was

---

[63] The phrase is frequently used in the Former Prophets in connection with naming or the establishment of customs and monuments (Josh. 4:9; 5:9; 7:26; 8:28–29; Judg. 1:26; 6:24; 10:4; 15:19; 18:12; 1 Sam. 5:5; 6:18; 30:25; 2 Sam. 6:8; 18:8; 1 Kgs. 9:13; 2 Kgs. 2:22; 14:17), and the status of places and peoples over an extended period of time (Josh. 6:25; 9:27; 13:13; 14:14; 15:63; 16:10; Judg. 1:21; 1 Sam. 27:6; 2 Sam. 4:3; 1 Kgs. 8:8; 9:21; 12:19; 2 Kgs. 8:22; 16:6; 17:23).

[64] Although Rahab was not mentioned again in Hebrew Scripture, yet according to Matt. 1:5 in the New Testament, she eventually married an Israelite named Salmon and became the mother of Boaz, who was a direct ancestor of King David. Since Matthew's Gospel is generally regarded as having been written for a Jewish audience, one can only assume that the record of Jesus' genealogy must at least reflect accepted traditions concerning the more prominent individuals. Moreover, in the New Testament books of Hebrews and James, both of which also display strong Hebraist features, Rahab is again mentioned in a positive light and placed alongside men of faith like Abraham, Moses, Samuel, and David (Heb. 11:31, Jas. 2:25). In fact, Talmudic literature has her marrying Joshua and becoming the ancestress of eight priests who were also prophets. Thus, according to Jewish tradition, not only was Rahab's integration into Israelite community relatively successful, she also came to be highly regarded by subsequent generations.

destroyed,[65] yet the spirit of Luz lived on through its survivor and his family. And that spirit immediately manifested itself in a different context, as the re-emergence of a new Luz is recounted in the very next verse. Thus, if Rahab's living in the midst of the Israelites 'until this day' is meant to be an enduring testimony to Israel's total success at Jericho, then the existence of a new Luz 'until this day' seems to serve as an enduring reminder of the failure of the house of Joseph at Luz.

But if this is true, what accounts for the difference? This is probably another significant point the allusion tries to address. For in the Jericho account, the spies promised Rahab to deal with her with kindness (חסד) and faithfulness. In the Luz account, an almost identical promise to show חסד was also made to the man from Luz. In view of the divergent outcome of the two promises, an alert reader is thus forced to consider whether the promise of חסד to the man from Luz was appropriate in the first place. For despite superficial similarities, a closer examination reveals that circumstances surrounding the promises are actually quite different.

First, in the case of Rahab, the promise of חסד was made in response to her request to be shown חסד. And that request in turn was made only after she had made an unambiguous profession of faith in YHWH's invincibility and supremacy (Josh. 2:9–11), backed by concrete action as she sheltered the spies sent by YHWH's people. Thus, the promise of חסד here may simply be an appropriate response to one who has already declared her allegiance to YHWH by word, and shown חסד to His people by deed. Therefore as such, it should not be construed as part of a bargain or deal.[66]

[65] It is actually debatable whether the taking of Luz was indeed a military success. For as Gunn and Fewell (160) point out, Jericho was taken by walking around its walls and blowing trumpets. Thus, no direct human contribution was needed, either from Rahab or from anyone else. The taking of Luz, on the other hand, seems to depend to a large extent on the help of its eventual survivor. Thus, the deal with the man from Luz seems to imply an inability of the house of Joseph to enter the city without his help. This makes it doubtful that the apparent military victory is in fact really a victory at all.

[66] Although the conditions set by the spies in Josh. 2:14,17–20 make it seem as if a deal is being struck, the requirement for Rahab not to tell what they were doing may simply be a test to make sure her profession of faith was genuine and not just a ploy to gain immunity. As for the scarlet chord, since that was solely for the benefit of Rahab and not the spies, it is probably best interpreted as a practical arrangement rather than a condition for showing חסד.

But unlike Rahab, there was no prior profession of faith on the part of the man from Luz. In fact, the offer of חסד was probably made at the spies' first encounter with the man as a one-time business transaction solely on condition that he would show the Israelites the way into town. This explains why, after the man has fulfilled his part of the bargain, he promptly went away and built a new Luz, thus re-creating what he had helped destroy in the first place.

What this seems to show then, is that unlike the case of Rahab, the offer of חסד to the man from Luz was never based on any preexistent relationship between the man and YHWH or YHWH's people. As his subsequent actions make abundantly clear, his receiving of חסד also did nothing to change the fundamental relationship between the two parties involved. If so, the offer and subsequent demonstration of חסד may indeed be inappropriate because the very essence of חסד was actually violated.

For although חסד is generally considered a covenant term when used of YHWH's dealing with His people, when applied to dealings between fellow human beings, the predominant idea seems to be the demonstration of benevolence appropriate to specific underlying relationships.[67]

If so, then the offer of חסד to the man from Luz may have violated of the very essence of חסד because in spite of what appears to be a covenant-like setting when the deal was struck, there was no underlying prior relationship between the man and YHWH or YHWH's people to allow for a meaningful offer of חסד. Without such a relationship, חסד is thus reduced from relational benevolence to a mere bargaining chip in a business transaction.

Moreover, a survey of the use of חסד between individuals also seems to indicate that reciprocity is a significant if not indispensable

[67] *HALOT* actually defines חסד as joint obligation between relatives, friends, host and guest, master and servant. It notes that חסד results from a close relationship between two people, with obligations being largely the same. Granted, as pointed out in *TWOT* (305–6), whether חסד is obligatory or freely given is still debated. But while 'obligation' may seem too strong, חסד is nonetheless regarded as the appropriate, and at times, even expected, response to the demands of specific relationships. These include relationships between a son and his dying father (Gen. 47:29), a wife and her husband (Gen. 20:13), relatives (Ruth 2:20), friends (2 Sam. 9:1), and people who have bestowed and received past favours (Gen. 40:14; 2 Sam. 2:5; 1 Kgs. 2:7). Thus, a specific underlying relationship between two people seems to be the key in the request or demonstration of חסד.

feature. Therefore, just as a request or demonstration of חסד often recalls past acts of benevolence in a relationship,[68] so any demonstration of חסד also makes it almost incumbent upon its recipient to remain faithful to the relationship and to reciprocate חסד in due course. This is why past demonstrations of חסד not reciprocated are inevitably regarded almost as an act of betrayal.[69]

But in the present case, the sparing of the man from Luz, presumably an act of חסד, did not result in a continuation of faithful relationship. Unlike Rahab, whose decision to live among the Israelites may be understood as a reciprocation of חסד received, the man from Luz simply did his part of the bargain, accepted חסד as rightful payment, and moved on to a new life without any desire or attempt to foster further relationship with the Israelites or with their God. This would certainly constitute an aberration of the unspoken rules of חסד.

In other words, the conditions may have never been present to begin with for a real and meaningful offer of חסד to the man from Luz. This probably accounts for the inability of the Israelites to enjoy the same kind of success in Luz that their predecessors enjoyed in Jericho. For by trying superficially to copy a past strategy of success without paying attention to the circumstances that made the application of that strategy successful, the Israelites were destined to fail from the beginning. And that is very likely the point of the allusion to Jericho.

2. *Allusion to Joshua's sending out of spies in the account of Danite migration*

The account of the sending out of spies in Joshua 2 is also alluded to in the account of Danite migration in the epilogue of Judges.[70]

---

[68] Examples include Abimelech's appeal for חסד on the basis of his past חסד to Abraham (Gen. 21:23), Rahab's appeal for חסד on the basis of her חסד to the spies (Josh. 2:12), and Saul's sparing of the Kenites on the basis of their past חסד to the Israelites (1 Sam. 15:6).

[69] Examples include Israel's failure to show חסד to Gideon's family for the good he did for them (Judg. 8:35), and Joash's failure to remember the חסד of Jehoiada by having his son killed (2 Chron. 24:22). Abner's anger at Ish-Bosheth in 2 Sam. 3:8 was also due to Ish-Bosheth's accusation in spite of Abner having shown חסד to the house of Saul his father in the past.

[70] In fact, Bauer (2000:37–40) notes that parallels exist between the story of Danite migration and other spy stories in general, and calls Judges 18 an 'anti-spy story'. For further discussion on parallels between Judges 18 and other conquest traditions, see Malamat, 1970:1–16; Pennant, 262–63.

This is seen especially through parallels in the way the two accounts are introduced.

First, the place of commission is specified in each case: Zorah and Eshtaol[71] in Judges, and Shittim in Joshua.

Second, the number of men sent out is also specified, and in each case, further description of the men is given by means of an apposition. In Judg. 18:2, the five men (חמשה אנשים) are further described as "men of valour (אנשים בני־חיל)", whereas Josh. 2:1 literally reads, "two men, spies (שנים־אנשים מרגלים)".

Third, in both cases, the specific commission is quoted directly, and in both cases, it involves a double imperative with לכו being the first and את־הארץ being the direct object of the second. Thus, in Judg. 18:2, the Danite spies were told, "Go, explore the land (לכו חקרו את־הארץ)" while in Josh. 2:1, the spies were told, "Go, look over the land (לכו ראו את־הארץ)".

Finally, in both cases, the spies' follow-up action is immediately reported after the commission, with the main action being described with ויבאו. Not only so, in each case the spies' journey came to a temporary halt at a house whose owner is named: "the house of Micah (בית מיכה)" in Judg. 18:2, and "the house of a prostitute named Rahab (בית־אשה זונה ושמה רחב)" in Josh. 2:1. And in each case, the spies decided to make a stopover there, thus, "they spent the night there (וילינו שם)" in Judg. 18:2, and "they lay down there (וישכבו־שמה)" in Josh. 2:1.

From the above parallels, it seems clear that some kind of allusion is at work. The point of the allusion seems to be as follows. If the sending of spies to Jericho represents the first step of what turned out to be a successful campaign, then by adopting similar language, the author of the epilogue may be portraying the sending of Danite spies as an attempt to reduplicate that same success. But as the narrative unfolds, the attempt falls flat. For while the spies of Jericho found shelter in the house of an alien woman who decided to put her trust in YHWH, the Danite spies ended up spending the night in the house of an Israelite man who practised idolatry. And so,

[71] While the language of the verse makes it possible to take Zorah and Eshtaol as places of origin for the spies rather than places of their commissioning, a comparison with Judg. 18:8 seems to show that the two cities were in fact where the commissioning took place. For it was to the two cities that the spies returned to report their findings.

even as Rahab the prostitute became the most unlikely heroine, who, by aiding the spies, secured her own deliverance, Micah and Jonathan, the grandson of Moses, became the most unexpected villains whose idolatry ended up ensnaring the entire tribe of Dan.

As for the spies from Dan, unlike their counterparts in Joshua who dealt with their former hostess with חסד, they instead led a group of armed men back to their former host to steal from him, even threatening violence when discovered. Thereafter, they went up and attacked a peaceful and unsuspecting people living a distance from anyone else, effectively annihilating the entire population. In so doing, these 'men of valour (בני־חיל)' showed themselves ironically to be anything but that.

Thus, by alluding to the Jericho account right at the beginning of the account of Danite migration, and by showing the main characters in both narratives as essentially doing the same things at that initial stage, the author of the epilogue may in fact be inviting his audience to continue comparing the actions of the two sets of main characters. And the starker the contrast is between the faithfulness of one set of spies and the lack of principle of the other, the more one sees the validity of the author's evaluation of the period through the oft-repeated refrain. For the Danites, it seems, can certainly be counted among those who 'did what was right in their own eyes'.[72]

3. *Allusion to the successful Ai campaign in the campaign against Benjamin*

That the account of Israel's campaign against Benjamin in Judg. 20:29–48 bears much resemblance to the account of her campaign against Ai in Josh. 8:3–29 is readily apparent even from a cursory reading of the two texts.[73] After all, both describe military campaigns in which ambush is featured prominently. Precisely for this reason, one may initially be tempted to dismiss the resemblance as arising purely out of similarity in subject matter.

However, a survey of the use of ארב and the related מארב reveals that other accounts of military ambush have been recorded in Hebrew

---

[72] As Amit (1990:6), Wilson (74), McMillion (232, 237), and Mayes (2001:242) have noted, although the second part of the refrain is not explicitly repeated in 18:1 and 19:1, the closeness between the full and partial refrain makes it likely that the ellipsis would have been automatically supplied and understood.

[73] This has been variously noted by Cundall (1968:204), Boling (1975:287), Auld (1984:248), Satterthwaite (1993:84), and Block (1999:568).

Scripture. These include Saul's ambush against the Amalekites in 1 Sam. 15:4–6, Jeroboam's ambush against Asa's army in 2 Chron. 13:13–16, YHWH's divine ambush against the invading Ammonite-Moabite-Edomite coalition in 2 Chron. 20:22, and Abimelech's ambush against Gaal and the Shechemites in Judg. 9:30–45.[74] Granted, some of these accounts are exceedingly brief, but nonetheless, it is worth noting that other than the two accounts on which we are currently focusing, these others accounts are variously described and share little resemblance with each other. Thus, one cannot attribute the resemblance between Judges 20 and Joshua 8 to mere similarity of subject matter.

Besides, of all the allusions to Joshua being considered in the prologue and epilogue of Judges, perhaps none is as involved and as comprehensive as this. For parallels between the two accounts can actually be found at three different levels: plot, vocabulary, and rhetorical technique.

First, at the plot level, the accounts of the two military campaigns basically share an identical plot. In both cases, an initial failure (or failures) leads to a further attempt at re-engaging the enemy. In both re-engagements, a false retreat during a frontal attack is used to draw a complacent enemy away from the target city, thus allowing an ambushing battalion to successfully take the largely undefended city. In both cases, the undefended city, once taken, is set on fire so that the rising smoke would serve as a signal for those pretending to flee to turn around and start attacking their pursuers. The ambushing battalion then joins the battle from behind, thus trapping the enemy in the middle. In both cases, once the enemy is totally annihilated, the combined forces then return to the city to execute whoever remains and set the city (and even surrounding towns) on fire.

As one can see, when it comes to the main plot, the two accounts match each other almost point for point. If both indeed represent accurate descriptions of what actually happened, then one has to conclude that the Israelites in the campaign against Benjamin were consciously borrowing a successful military strategy their predecessors had previously used against Ai. And by recording the campaign

---

[74] There are also accounts of ambushes against individuals recorded in Judg. 16:2,9,12; Pss. 10:8–9; 59:4; Prov. 1:11; 24:15; Mic. 7:2; Lam. 4:19. However, as these fall outside our present focus on military ambushes, they will not be further considered in the present discussion.

against Benjamin with minimal plot variation from the account of the campaign against Ai, the author of the epilogue seemed to be intentionally preserving this connection between the two accounts, so that the campaign against Benjamin is viewed as some kind of re-enactment of the campaign against Ai.

But not only do the two accounts share the same basic plot, the language used to describe the campaigns is also remarkably similar. While some similarity in vocabulary is to be expected on account of the similarity in plot,[75] the two accounts also share a number of highly marked words and phrases.

For example, although יצא . . . לקרא is a common expression used frequently in Numbers and Deuteronomy to describe opposing troops marching to engage each other in battle,[76] the phrase is used in this specific sense in Joshua and Judges only in Josh. 8:5,14,22 and Judg. 20:25,31.[77] Considering how many battles are recorded in the two books, the absence of יצא . . . לקרא in other battle accounts seems to indicate that the military use of this phrase is highly marked in these two books. If so, the use of the expression in Judg. 20:25,31 may represent a conscious attempt to draw a connection with the only account in Joshua where this expression is used.

Then there is also נתק, a verb that does not appear elsewhere in the Former Prophets except in Joshua and Judges. Used in the sense of 'drawing away', נתק appears in this portion of Hebrew Scripture only in Josh. 4:18, 8:6,16, and Judg. 20:31,32.[78] Here, the verb appears less marked in Joshua as its use in the same sense in Josh. 4:18 is unrelated to the campaign against Ai. But since נתק is not used in this sense elsewhere in Judges,[79] it may point to another

[75] These would include terms such as 'ambush (ארב)', 'flee (נוס)', 'in the previous time (בראשׁון)', 'smoke (עשׁן)', 'strike (הכה)', and 'strike with the sword (הכה . . . לפי־חרב)'.

[76] Num. 20:18,20; 21:23,30; Deut. 1:44; 2:32; 3:1; 29:6. It is also used in this sense in 1 Sam. 4:1; 2 Sam. 18:1; and 2 Chron. 35:20.

[77] The expression is used in the more general sense of meeting someone in Judg. 4:18,22 and 11:31,34.

[78] It is also used in Judg. 16:9,12, but in the sense of 'break' or 'tear to pieces'.

[79] As a point of interest, it is worth noting that the verb משׁך is used in Judg. 4:7 to describe a very similar drawing away of Sisera's troops to a specific location by YHWH. Another synonym is פתה, used in Judg. 14:15; 16:5; 1 Kgs. 22:20–22 to denote 'entice'. As such, this seems to put פתה in close semantic range with נתק in Judg. 20:31,32. Of course, if the authors of the epilogue and the central section of Judges are distinct individuals, then the presence of these synonyms in the central section would be of little significance. But if the author of the epilogue also

conscious attempt at establishing a direct link between the two accounts.

The climaxes of the two battles are also characterised by a similar combination of words. The moment of truth for Benjamin is described in Judg. 20:40 as "The Benjaminites turned behind them, and behold, the whole city had gone up into the sky (ויפן בנימן אחריו והנה עלה כליל־העיר השמימה)". This is almost a word for word parallel with the description in Josh. 8:20: "The men of Ai turned behind them and looked, and behold, the smoke of the city had gone up into the sky (ויפנו אנשי העי אחריהם ויראו והנה עלה עשן העיר השמימה)"

Somewhat related to this is also the use of הפך, one meaning of which is broadly synonymous with פנה and שוב. While all three verbs are used in Joshua 8 to denote some kind of turning around,[80] the preferred verb in Judges 20 appears to be פנה.[81] Yet within the climactic section of the Judges account, a sudden switch of verb occurs such that the anticipated and actual turning around of the Israelite troops pretending to flee are twice described with הפך in 20:39,41. This is significant in that first, הפך is otherwise hardly used at all in Judges.[82] Second, the use of this verb in Judg. 20:41 also occurs at almost exactly the same point in the narrative as its use in Josh. 8:20: to mark the sudden turning around of the Israelite troops just as the enemies had become aware of their precarious position. Thus, one can argue that the sudden switch of verb in 20:41 from the otherwise preferred פנה to the more highly marked הפך may reflect a desire to preserve the same vocabulary as is found in the climactic section of Joshua 8. As for 20:39, the use of הפך there may be a case of backward-harmonisation so that the same verb is used to describe both the actual event and the earlier anticipation of it.

Finally, there is also the use of נבלה (folly) in Josh. 7:15 and Judg. 19:23,24; 20:6,10. Granted, these five occurrences of נבלה all fall

had a hand in the composition or redaction of the central section, then his decision to use the rare נתק in spite of the availability of alternative synonyms would argue more strongly for an attempt at conscious allusion to Joshua 8.

[80] פנה is used in 8:20, שוב in 8:21, and הפך in 8:20.

[81] פנה is used quite consistently in 20:40,42,45,47. Even in the rest of the epilogue, פנה appears to be the verb of choice to convey the idea of turning or turning around (cf. 18:21,26; 19:26).

[82] The only other occurrences of הפך in Judges is in 7:13 in the central section, where it appears once in the Hithpael as 'tumble', and once in the Qal to mean 'overturn'.

outside the account proper of the two military campaigns. But what is noteworthy is that all these occurrences of נבלה refer to events that directly or indirectly led to the launch of both campaigns. In Josh. 7:15, נבלה refers to Achan's looting of the devoted things. This act indirectly resulted in Israel's initial defeat at Ai, and hence, the necessity of a second attempt to take the city in Joshua 8. In Judg. 19:23,24 and 20:6,10, נבלה refers to the sexual perversity of the citizens of Gibeah and the ensuing crime that eventually forced the rest of Israel to fight against Benjamin. As these are the only instances where נבלה is used in either book, what this seems to suggest is that the author of the epilogue of Judges may have intended to create a link with Joshua also through the use of this marked term, so that both the campaign against Ai and the one against Benjamin are seen as directly or indirectly caused by the commitment of a נבלה.

But other than a shared plot and shared vocabulary, the two accounts also share the use of a special rhetorical technique, namely, that of alternating perspectives to heighten dramatic tension at the climax.

In recent years, much has been written about the literary unity of the account of the campaign against Benjamin in Judges 20. Contrary to a popular belief that repetitions and dislocations found in the account betray a crude combining of two distinct accounts of the same events,[83] Revell and Satterthwaite have argued that the overall textual integrity of the Judges account can actually be maintained if one views apparent repetitions and dislocations as a special rhetorical device aimed at presenting the same events from two or more perspectives.[84] But while the more elaborate use of this technique in Judges 20 has drawn the attention of scholars, it has gone relatively unnoticed that a briefer use of the same technique is also found in Joshua 8.[85]

[83] Burney, 447; Soggin, 1987:293–94; Schneider, 277. Amit (1998:350 n. 45) even calls it "faulty editorial work"!

[84] Revell, 417–33; Satterthwaite, 1992:80–89.

[85] This lack of awareness may be due partly to the brevity of the interchange, and also to the fact that some English translations such as the NIV and the NJB give the Hebrew disjunctive at the beginning of Josh. 8:21 a direct causal nuance with the addition of 'for'. This gives the impression that 8:21 follows directly from 8:20. But while the Hebrew disjunctive can indeed provide parenthetical information to explain the action in a previous clause (cf. 1 Sam. 9:15; 2 Sam. 18:18, and indeed, the final clause in Josh. 8:20, which explains the inability of the men of Ai to flee in any direction), it generally does not convey direct causality in the way these two English translations render it.

Upon closer examination, it seems clear that Josh. 8:20 and 8:21 are records of the same chain of events from two different perspectives. Both verses begin with the sighting of the smoke going up from the city (ראה ... עלה עשן העיר), and both end with the turning around of the Israelite contingent against their pursuers. But while 8:20 records the events from the perspective of the men of Ai (the הנה clause highlighting their surprise, followed by a statement of their inability to flee in any direction), 8:21 records the same events from the perspective of Joshua and his men (their immediate understanding of the significance of the smoke, and hence, the description of the ambush's capture of the city as if it were actually witnessed even though that could not have happened in reality). Furthermore, the two perspectives are given in immediate succession, and the transition from one to the other is marked by a disjunctive clause at the beginning of 8:21 introducing the subject of the new perspective: "Now Joshua and the Israelites . . . (ויהושע וכל־ישׂראל)".

Perhaps because this alternating of perspective in Josh. 8:20–21 is very brief, with only one verse dedicated to each perspective, its effect is not as noticeable as the more elaborate version found in Judges 20. But nonetheless, it shares the same rhetorical technique as Judg. 20:36b–41.

For like Josh. 8:20 and 8:21, Judg. 20:36b-39a and 20:39b–41 also share the same beginning and end: the false defeat of the Israelite troops marks the beginning of both perspectives, while the turning around (הפך) of the men of Israel (איש ישׂראל) upon their enemy marks their respective ends. But whereas 20:36b–39a record the events from Israel's perspective (stating the rationale behind their retreat, the action of the ambushing party, the prior arrangement for the ambushing party to send up smoke once the city is taken, and the anticipated response of the Israelite troops to turn around once the smoke is seen), 20:39b–41 records basically the same events from Benjamin's perspective (their interpretation of the Israelite retreat, the הנה clause highlighting their surprise to see the smoke, and their sense of terror and doom at the actual turning around of the Israelite troops). Again, the two perspectives are given in immediate succession, and the transition from one to the other is also marked by a disjunctive clause in 20:39b introducing the subject of the new perspective: "Now Benjamin . . . (ובנימן)".[86]

[86] Notice that although another disjunctive is also found towards the end of the

It should also be pointed out that in both cases, this description of the same events successively from two perspectives heightens the dramatic tension, thus marking the climax of both narratives.

Thus, with the two accounts sharing the same plot, using the same highly marked vocabulary at roughly the same point in the narrative, and employing the same rhetorical technique to heighten dramatic tension at their respective climaxes, there is little doubt that the author of the epilogue of Judges was intentionally alluding to the campaign against Ai.

But while the two accounts indeed share many features in terms of the way they are presented, there are also clearly discernible differences. The first of these concerns the different outcomes of the respective campaigns.

Within the larger context of the book, it seems clear that the campaign against Ai in Joshua 8 is considered a significant success. For not only does it represent an important step in the fulfilment of YHWH's promise to give Israel land west of the Jordan (Josh. 1:1–5),[87] the success of this campaign and the campaign against Jericho also became the reference point for the nations as they began to take Israel seriously as a threat to their own security.[88] This too, seems to represent fulfilment of YHWH's promise in Deut. 2:25 that reports of Israel's victories would instil fear and anguish in the nations. If so, it is hard to view the outcome of the campaign against Ai as anything but positive: Israel's success in destroying the city and its inhabitants is exactly as events should unfold.

second perspective in 20:41 with ואיש ישׂראל, that disjunctive does not, however, indicate a shift of perspective back to the men of Israel. This is seen in that the narrative sequence resumes after the disjunctive with the men of Benjamin still being the subject of the following consecutive clause. On the other hand, when the perspective shifts, a new narrative sequence begins with the subject of the following clauses usually aligned with the subject of the new perspective. Thus, the ואיש ישׂראל clause of 20:41 merely serves to highlights the action of the men of Israel from the perspective of Benjamin in a vivid way. They took their eyes off the battle for a brief moment to look at the smoke, and when they looked back, the men of Israel had already turned in battle.

[87] Jericho and Ai represent the first two victories west of the Jordan as Israel sought to take possession of the land YHWH promised their forefathers.

[88] According to Josh. 9:3, it is Israel's successes at Jericho and Ai that motivated the Gibeonites to seek a treaty. And according to Josh. 10:1–2, it is the destruction of Ai plus the Gibeonite surrender that led directly to the united campaign of the five kings against Israel.

But the same can hardly be said with regard to the outcome of the campaign against Benjamin. For whereas the victory over Ai is immediately followed by the gathering together of the victors before YHWH for covenant renewal (Josh. 8:30–35), the victory over Benjamin is also followed by a gathering together of the victors before YHWH, albeit to mourn and complain about the demise of one of their tribes (Judges 21). Thus, even though the two campaigns, using the same military strategy, basically delivered similar results, one led to an affirmation of faith, while the other, to soul-searching and regret. What then, accounts for this significant disparity in outcome?

In the process of answering this question, one is led to yet a second difference between the two accounts, namely, the degree of YHWH's involvement in the respective campaigns. For while YHWH's direct involvement in the campaign against Ai is unmistakable at every level, the same cannot be said about the campaign against Benjamin.

In the campaign against Ai, YHWH is presented as the one who devised the ambush strategy. In Josh. 8:8, after Joshua had given preliminary instructions to the Israelites, his added command for them to act according to the words of YHWH (כדבר יהוה) seems to indicate that it was not Joshua himself but YHWH who initiated the ambush strategy.

Furthermore, as the strategy was being carried out during the battle, and the men of Ai took the bait and started pursuing the fleeing Israelites, at the critical juncture in 8:18, the narrative reports YHWH's direct instructions to Joshua to hold out his javelin as a signal for the fleeing troops to turn around. What this seems to show is that not only was YHWH responsible for initiating the strategy, He was also responsible for dictating the precise timing in the execution of that strategy.

And that is not all. At the end of the narrative when plunder was taken, there is yet another explicit reference in 8:27 to YHWH's instructions regarding the disposition of livestock and plunder.

The cumulative effect therefore, is that YHWH is seen as directly involved at every stage of the campaign: at the planning stage, during its execution, and in its aftermath.

In contrast, in the narrative of Israel's campaign against Benjamin, the report of YHWH's involvement is much more muted. As Boling points out, the fact that Israel employed the ambush strategy only on their third attempt to engage the enemy suggests that the strategy may have been prompted tardily only by the memory of Joshua 8.[89] As such, the strategy probably did not directly originate from YHWH.

As for the battle itself, although YHWH was undeniably credited with striking the Benjaminites before Israel in Judg. 20:35, yet that is the only mention of YHWH throughout the entire battle account. As that statement seems to be an anticipatory summary of the whole battle and not a part of the on-going narrative of the battle itself, one suspects it may have been provided more as an overall theological statement in response to YHWH's promise in 20:28 rather than an actual description of the specific involvement of YHWH during the battle.[90] If so, one can argue that, unlike the account of the Ai campaign, no specific act within the account of the campaign against Benjamin is actually attributed explicitly to YHWH's direct guidance or involvement.[91]

Of course, that is not to say that YHWH was entirely uninvolved in the campaign against Benjamin. After all, one cannot overlook the fact that YHWH did promise to give the Benjaminite into the hands of Israel in 20:28. But even there, the promise of victory did not come until Israel inquired of YHWH for the third time. And the fact that Israel had to suffer two crushing defeats even after following YHWH's instructions from the first two inquiries is without parallel in Hebrew Scripture. In light of this, it is not unreasonable to suggest that the key to understanding the whole episode may actually lie in one's ability to make sense of what happened at the three oracular inquiries. And here, a case can be made that the issue primarily concerns the identity of Israel's opponent at war.

For in contrast to the Ai campaign, where the citizens of Ai can properly be looked upon as an enemy because they stood in the way

[89] Boling, 1982:237.

[90] Admittedly, the distinction is a fine one, and deserves further exploration. But the point is that in certain narratives, YHWH's actions form part of the narrative and YHWH is treated as a character playing a crucial role in advancing the plot (e.g. Josh. 10:11; Judg. 4:15; 7:22; 1 Sam. 7:10; 14:15). In such cases, the focus is on specific acts of YHWH as a part of His direct involvement. In contrast, there are times when YHWH's action on behalf of His people is reported in a summary statement that is not a part of the narrative proper, and hence, does not advance the plot (e.g. Josh. 10:42; Judg. 4:23; 9:56–57; 1 Sam. 7:13; 14:23). In such cases, the focus is more on the fact of YHWH's involvement and the statement is often more a theological summary rather than a description of any specific act.

[91] Hudson (49,65) in fact speaks of God as 'absent' in Judges 20.

of Israel inheriting the promised land, in the campaign against Benjamin, Israel's opponent was actually a tribe of Israel, and hence, a 'brother', even if this brother had just committed a נבלה. And such a distinction is not insignificant.

Furthermore, this distinction was apparently not lost on the Israelites either. In his article, Satterthwaite notes that the Israelites, having commenced their campaign against Benjamin with firm resolve at the outset, almost lost that resolve after two initial defeats.[92] This loss of resolve is most clearly seen in the progression of the three questions Israel addressed to YHWH at the beginning of each attempt to engage Benjamin in battle.

Here, Satterthwaite is no doubt correct in noting the increasing poignancy of the questions, evident in the use of "my brother (אחי)" on the second and third day plus the raising of the possibility of ending the campaign on the third. But through this progression, one can also sense that the Israelites were becoming increasingly aware that their opponent's identity might have been a major issue.

On the first day when the Israelites inquired of YHWH, all they were concerned about was who should go first in battle. Here, the opponents are referred to in 20:18 only as "sons of Benjamin (בני בנימן)", and the fact that the Israelites should fight them was not even questioned in the least.

But in the second inquiry after their first defeat, the Israelites now refer to their opponents as "sons of Benjamin, my brother (בני בנימן אחי)" in 20:23. It is as if their initial defeat had brought a new awareness that going up against their brother with malignant intent might have been the very thing that had brought defeat. After all, as one discovers later in 21:1,5,7, the Israelites had apparently taken a solemn oath to commit every town in every tribe to this battle. Furthermore, from a second oath not to give Israelite daughters in marriage to any Benjaminite, it seems that Israel had every intention of disowning Benjamin from the very beginning.[93] For the lan-

[92] Satterthwaite, 1992:82.

[93] Although Judges 21 did not make clear when exactly these oaths were made, it is reasonable to think that they were made before the first battle. For the oaths seem to display a confidence and determination that fits well with Israel's initial frame of mind, before that confidence began to wane with each successive defeat. Besides, if they were indeed thinking about putting an end to the whole enterprise by the time they made their third inquiry, it would be unlikely for such an oath to have been made then or any time after that.

guage of the oath in 21:1, "No man among us will give his daughter to Benjamin as wife (איש ממנו לא־יתן בתו לבנימן לאשה)", echoes YHWH's command in Deut. 7:3 regarding the Canaanites that "You shall not give your daughter to his son (בתך לא־תתן לבנו)". Thus, one can argue that the Israelites were in fact prepared to treat Benjamin as if they were one of the non-Israelite nations.

Of course, with their initial defeat, the Israelites probably started having second thoughts about this strategy. That probably explains why in the second inquiry, instead of asking who should be the first to go, they now emphasised the brotherhood of Benjamin,[94] and even began asking if they should go at all.

But YHWH answered in the affirmative, so out they went again. But surprisingly, this resulted in another crushing defeat. By then, the Israelites were probably beginning to worry that YHWH's command for them to go represented not so much His approval of their campaign, but rather, His attempt to punish them for harbouring malignant intent against their brother. Thus, they made a third inquiry before YHWH, this time with the addition of "or shall I cease (אם אחדל)" after similarly referring to the Benjaminites as "my brother" in 20:28.[95] It is almost as if they were desperately drawing YHWH's attention to the real possibility of putting an end to the campaign altogether.

This may also explain why this time, they preceded their inquiry with fasting, burnt offerings, and peace offerings. This is presumably to convey an urgent desire to be restored to YHWH's favour, if indeed that favour had already been lost.[96]

---

[94] This belated emphasis on Benjamin as a brother has, of course, been already pre-empted by the narrator's use of the same term in 20:13.

[95] Other noticeable differences between the way Israel approached YHWH the second and the third time also convey an increasing desperation. These include the use of 'all' to modify 'sons of Israel', plus the additional 'all the people' for greater emphasis on pan-community involvement. And instead of "they cried before YHWH until the evening (ויבכו לפני־יהוה עד־הערב)" in 20:23, the description in 20:26 is now more involved: "they went to Bethel and cried and remained there before YHWH and fasted that day until evening (ויבאו בית־אל ויבכו וישבו שם לפני יהוה ויצומו ביום־ההוא עד־הערב)".

[96] Taken separately, 'to fast (צום)', 'burnt offering (עלה)', and 'peace offering (שלם) do not necessarily offer definitive insight into the motives of the Israelites. For while the present context clearly precludes עלה from being a celebratory offering (cf. 1 Sam. 6:14), עלה can, however, be offered either as an accompaniment to a petition for divine intervention in a time of need (cf. Judg. 11:31; Jer. 14:12), or as an atonement for sin (cf. Lev. 1:4; 16:24). And although שלם is usually offered as an

Therefore as one can see, the progression of the three questions seems to suggest a growing awareness on the part of Israel of who their opponents were, and that their identity as a brother might necessitate a re-evaluation of their original plan of action. In fact, by the third inquiry, Israel was sounding distinctly as though they were begging to be relieved of their prior commitment to war.

But if the Israelites were beginning to waver in their commitment to fight against the Benjaminites, YHWH was not. Hence, as the Israelites brought the matter before Him for a third time, YHWH finally granted His long-delayed promise of victory as He told them once again to go.

But why is this promise of victory granted at this point? Unfortunately, the text offers no clear explanation. While the need to punish Gibeah for committing a נבלה and the rest of Benjamin for supporting them seem obvious, how much Israel's fasting and weeping also became a factor remains unclear. Lest one is tempted to conclude that the granting of victory reflects YHWH's satisfaction with Israel's response, the lack of direct involvement on the part of YHWH in the subsequent battle account as noted earlier should give pause to such a conclusion.[97] For if anything, the lack of specific involvement attributed to YHWH in the lengthy battle account seems

---

expression of thanks (Lev. 7:12), the fulfilment of a vow (Lev. 7:16; 22:21), or during the Feast of Weeks (Lev. 23:19), it can also be understood simply as a general concluding sacrifice (based on the Piel of the root) or a symbol of forgiveness and peace with God when offered after the עלה (see discussion in *HALOT* and *TWOT*). As for צום, while it is generally practised in times of grief and mourning (1 Sam. 31:13; 2 Sam. 12:21–23), it can also signal repentance (1 Sam. 7:6; 1 Kgs. 21:27). But although numerous possibilities exist in interpreting each of the three items, taken together in the present context, it seems to signal steps taken to restore damaged relationship with YHWH (see Cundall, 1968:203; Boling, 1975:286; Block, 1999:560). After all, as Wenham (68) points out, divine displeasure is certainly implied in the first two defeats of the Israelites under the hands of the Benjaminites.

[97] If this is true, then Begg's assertion (329–30) that similarities between Joshua 8 and Judges 20 are meant "to further inculcate one of the Deuteronomist's key lesson, i.e. at any and all moments of Israel's history, defeat can be reversed when Israel turns to YHWH and YHWH renews His support" may not necessarily reflect the intention of the author of the epilogue. Incidentally, Boling (1982:236) also holds a similar view that the didactic value of the two accounts is to "let the point be made that there is no defeat of Israel that cannot be at last turned around if YHWH is truly allowed to take command". But as is being argued in the present chapter, the allusions to Joshua in the prologue and epilogue of Judges are consistently ironic. Therefore it is highly unlikely that the present allusion to Joshua 8 in fact serves to reinforce positive Deuteronomistic themes.

to reduce the role of YHWH almost to that of a spectator not unlike the reader. It is almost as if, having promised victory, YHWH took a step back to see what Israel would do with it, and to find out whether insights gained from the two prior defeats would cause them to act differently towards their brother than what they had originally planned.[98]

Unfortunately, they did not. Possibly dismissing their earlier fears as mere paranoia once they received YHWH's promise of victory, the Israelites ended up following their original plan of action.

That Israel did not moderate their dealings with Benjamin in spite of their earlier reference to Benjamin as אחי can be seen in several ways. First, the use of הכה . . . לפי־חרב in Judg. 20:37,48 is significant. As has already been pointed out, the phrase, which is also used in Josh. 8:24, seems closely related with the concept of the חרם as it is often used interchangeably with חרם itself.

But while the application of חרם may indeed be appropriate with respect to Ai since it was mandated for cities belonging to the foreign nations occupying the land (Deut. 7:1–4; 20:16–18), there is no basis for its application to fellow Israelites other than for idolatry (Exod. 22:19; Deut. 13:13–19) or illegal appropriation of devoted objects (Deut. 7:26; Josh. 6:18). Since Benjamin's crime, heinous though it may be, was neither, that makes Israel's חרם-style actions against Benjamin excessive and inappropriate.

Thus, consistent with their vow not to give their daughters in marriage to any Benjaminite, the Israelites had continued in war to treat Benjamin as if they were one of the non-Israelite nations.

But not only was Benjamin treated as a non-Israelite nation, it was treated even more harshly than the non-Israelite enemies at Ai. For while in the Ai campaign, 12,000 men and women from Ai were slaughtered, in the campaign against Benjamin, 25,000 armed warriors alone were killed, not including additional civilian casualties from the various Benjaminite towns. That makes the Benjaminite casualty at least more than double the casualties of Ai.[99]

---

[98] Although some might object to the idea of an omniscient God having to test His people to find out what is in their heart, such a concept is, however, not foreign to Old Testament narrative tradition. Gen. 22:1–14; Exod. 16:4; Deut. 8:2,16; Judg. 2:22; 3:4 all speak of YHWH testing His people to find out where their allegiance lies.

[99] Whether or not the biblical numbers in both accounts represent the actual number of casualty is as yet unclear. Boling (1975:285) suggests interpreting each

Furthermore, while at Ai, the city alone was burnt and made into a permanent heap of ruin, in the battle against Benjamin, the Israelites did not just set fire to Gibeah, the offending city, but also to all the Benjaminite towns they came across (20:48). And while livestock and other plunder were spared at Ai, in Benjamin, all the animals and everything else were struck with the sword under חרם-style slaughter (20:48).[100]

Thus, not only had Israel not treated Benjamin with the compassion of brothers, they even dealt with them more harshly than they did to the non-Israelite enemies at Ai. No wonder then, that while the Israelites at Ai had reason to celebrate with covenant renewal after they disposed of an enemy according to YHWH's instructions, the Israelites who fought against Benjamin were left to mourn the consequence of their own action as they gave in to excessive vindictiveness in dealing with a brother.[101] And by alluding extensively to the Ai campaign and showing the exact same actions leading to celebration at Ai but mourning in Benjamin, the author of the epilogue has in fact highlighted once more the lack of discernment of a generation who knew only to superficially copy past strategies of success without understanding how to appropriately apply them in their own context.

---

number in the text as two sets of numbers that have been fused together: one representing the number of military unit and the other, the total number of men involved. These numbers, according to Boling, have been fused together by the Masoretes who misunderstood them, thus giving exceptionally large numbers that may not correspond to the actual number of people involved. But regardless of whether Boling's interpretation is correct, the point is that the casualty for Benjamin is still significantly greater than that of Ai.

[100] While no passage directly suggests that what is included in the חרם is in proportion to the degree of wickedness or the extent of danger posed, this can nonetheless be inferred from a passage like Deut. 20:10–18, where the women, children, and livestock in distant cities are spared, but everything in nearby cities are required to be completely destroyed. Thus, one can argue that the complete destruction of everything in Benjamin suggests that to Israel, Benjamin was looked upon as a most serious threat or the worst type of enemy.

[101] The irony is that in 21:3, the Israelites actually tried to pin the blame for their own disastrous course of action onto YHWH, who, as has been argued, has not been portrayed as being directly involved in the battle.

4. *Allusion to Israel's successful attempt at dealing with potential transgressors in the account of her unsuccessful attempt to deal with Benjamin*

Another allusion to Joshua is also found in Judges 20. Here, however, the allusion rests more on similarity of plot and attendant circumstances than on direct linguistic correspondences,[102] even though such correspondences do exist.

In Joshua 22, Joshua sent the two and a half tribes back to their inheritance east of the Jordan. As the tribes reached Geliloth near the Jordan, they built an altar on the border of Canaan on the Israelite side (22:9–10). When the rest of Israel heard about it, the whole assembly (כל־עדה) gathered (קהל) at Shiloh ready to go to war against the two and a half tribes for their illegitimate cultic practice (22:11–12). But they decided to first send a delegation to the eastern tribes to clarify matters. The delegation consists of Phinehas, son of Eleazar the priest, as well as ten leaders, each the head of a family division from the respective tribes (22:13–14). They went with words of firm rebuke (22:15–20), but also a conciliatory offer to share the land with the tribes if they were dissatisfied with their own land (22:19). The conflict was defused when the eastern tribes clarified what turned out to be a misunderstanding (22:21–29). A potential civil war was thus avoided.

In Judg. 19:29–20:17, a similar sequence of events also took place but with a very different outcome. The Levite whose concubine was raped and murdered in Gibeah cut her up into twelve parts and sent them to the various tribes (19:29–30). Upon seeing the grisly sight, an assembly (העדה) of Israelites gathered (קהל) at Mizpah armed and ready to go up against Gibeah (20:1–2). Having heard the story from the Levite in person (20:3–7), the Israelites were convinced of Gibeah's guilt (20:8–11). They then sent a delegation of unspecified men throughout Benjamin to relate their demand for the wicked men of Gibeah to be turned over for execution (20:12–13). But Benjamin refused, and thus, a civil war began (20:13–17).

Several parallels between the two accounts can be found. To begin, in both narratives, a gathering (קהל) of an assembly (עדה) of Israelites

[102] Niditch (1982:374) describes Judges 19–20 as "a thematic companion piece" to Josh. 22:10–34.

(בני ישׂראל) is reported. What is noteworthy here is that the verb קהל, which often occurs in the Hiphil in a causative sense, is found only three times in Joshua (18:1; 22:12) and Judges (20:1), all of which are in the Niphal.[103] As for עדה, while it is more extensively used in Joshua in the sense of an assembly or a congregation,[104] the word is found only four times in Judges in reference to the gathering together of Israel as a nation.[105] Incidentally, all four instances occur in the epilogue of the book (20:1, 21:10,13,16) and all refer to the same assembly of Israelites that gathered together to deal with the problem of Gibeah and Benjamin. In other words, while עדה and קהל seem more widely used in Joshua, in Judges, they seem highly marked and are restricted only to Judges 20 and 21. In particular, since the only times the two words are used in tandem in Joshua and Judges are in Josh. 18:1; 22:12, and Judg. 20:1, a case can be made that this unique combination in Judg. 20:1 may represent a deliberate attempt to allude to a similar gathering described in Joshua 22.

This appears even more likely when one considers the similar contextual circumstances under which the assemblies of Israelites were gathered. In both cases, the gathering was in response to what was considered blatant sinning within the community. In fact, while it is explicitly stated in Josh. 22:12 that the whole assembly of Israel had gathered to go to war against the perceived offenders, the same is also implied in Judg. 20:1–2, where those gathered are said to be armed with swords.

Furthermore, in both cases, a delegation was sent to the offending party, and in each case, the question posed is similarly phrased using the formula: מה + definite noun + adjectival use of זה + אשׁר + verb + ב + personal noun/pronoun. Thus, while the question in Josh. 22:16 is "What is this trespass that you committed against the God of Israel? (מה־המעל הזה אשׁר מעלתם באלהי ישׂראל)", in Judg. 20:12, the question is "What is this evil that has been tolerated among you? (מה הרעה הזאת אשׁר נהיתה בכם)".

But in spite of the above parallels, discernible differences can also be detected. First, while the delegation sent in Joshua 22 from Shiloh consisted of representatives from Israel's leadership seeking a mutually

[103] קהל as a noun is also found in Josh. 8:36 and Judg. 20:2; 21:5,8.

[104] Josh. 9:15,18,19,21,27; 18:1; 20:6,9; 22:12,16,17,18,20,30.

[105] The word is also used once in Judg. 14:8 to refer to a swarm of bees.

satisfactory resolution to the problem, the men sent in Judges 20 from Mizpah, who went with a message of uncompromising demand, were not identified. Thus, while the former at least reflects a willingness of Israel's leadership to consider the other side's grievance, the message of the latter reflects a verdict already reached on the basis of a one-sided testimony. This means that the Gibeathites have effectively been denied a fair chance to present their version of events. Could this lack of fairness and tact be at least partially responsible for Benjamin's decision to side with the indefensible Gibeathites? If so, what this allusion to Joshua 22 seems to draw attention to is that, the sin of Gibeah notwithstanding, the rest of Israel must also bear part of the responsibility for plunging the nation into civil war.

But other than subtly drawing attention to Israel's responsibility in the civil war, the allusion, once established, also serves to bring out other important contrasts.

In the Joshua account, the gathering of Israelites at Shiloh to deal with the potential cultic violation of the eastern tribes seems to establish Shiloh as the place where cultic purity of the nation is jealously guarded. Granted, in Judges, the crime of Gibeah did not involve a cultic violation, nor did the gathering of Israelites take place at Shiloh. But what is of interest here is that the other episode also found in the epilogue of Judges does involve a cultic violation. In fact, in 18:31, Shiloh is explicitly mentioned when the idols of Micah at Dan are contrasted with the house of God in Shiloh.

This seems to raise the following question. If the gathering of the tribes at Mizpah to deal with the crime against the Levite and his concubine is indeed warranted, then why was there no similar gathering to deal with the idolatry of Micah and Dan?[106] After all, in Joshua 22, the gathering at Shiloh was to safeguard Israel's cultic purity. But now, the very issue that incited collective action in the previous generation no longer seems to elicit the same kind of response in the new generation. Instead, what excited national outrage was

[106] In fact, as Wadsworth (15) points out, Pseudo-Philo's midrashic account seems to question how it can be that Israel started a war on account of the outrage done to the Levite's concubine, but was apparently unmoved by a greater outrage: Micah's apostasy. In the eyes of Pseudo-Philo, this apparently explains the lack of success Israel had against the Benjaminites at the initial stage of the civil war. Similarly, Amit (1998:352) also expresses puzzlement that the united assembly of Israel had not dealt with the idolatry of Micah and the Danites.

now a sensationalised report of a crime against individuals. This is not to say, of course, that the heinous crime against the Levite and his concubine did not warrant some kind of collective intervention by the tribes. But in contrast, the complete lack of any intervention on the part of Israel to deal with the idolatry at Dan shows a clear shift of priorities in the collective psyche of the new generation. Thus, if Shiloh had indeed stood for the safeguarding of cultic purity in the generation of Joshua, in Judg. 18:31, it is portrayed almost as helplessly looking on as idolatry took hold at Dan.

But that is not all. At the end of Judges after the war against Benjamin had been fought and won, Shiloh again came into play. In their attempt to find wives for the remnants of Benjamin, the leadership of Israel ordered the killing of all at Jabesh Gilead except for its virgins, who were then brought to the camp at Shiloh. Then they also sanctioned the forcible abduction of more young women, this time, even young women who were celebrating a feast of YHWH (חג־יהוה)[107] at Shiloh. Thus, instead of being the place where cultic purity was defended, Shiloh now became the place where sexual purity was taken away from innocent young women against their will. And what is most ironic is that this leadership-sanctioned violation of Israelite women actually began as an attempt to avenge the sexual violation of the Levite's concubine by the Gibeathites. In this way, the leaders of Israel are actually portrayed as endorsing the perpetration of the very same crime that outraged them in the first place. The absurdity of the situation, coupled with the inability of Shiloh to defend even the sexual purity of its own virgins, let alone the cultic purity of the whole nation, therefore highlights the depth of decline not only of Shiloh, but also of the entire generation during the period of the judges.

Concluding Observations and Implications

From the above discussion, it can be seen that a strong case indeed exists for some kind of compositional unity between the prologue

[107] This is probably a reference to the Feast of Tabernacles as this feast is most often referred to as חג־יהוה (Lev. 23:39) or חג ליהוה (Lev. 23:41; Num. 29:12). The dancing mentioned in Judg. 21:21,23 also seems to fit the atmosphere of rejoicing at this feast (Lev. 23:40; Deut. 16:14). Note, however, that both the Passover and Feast of Unleavened Bread are also described as חג ליהוה in Exod. 12:14; 13:6.

and epilogue of Judges. With respect to thematic unity, the discovery of unifying structural and bi-directional influences between the prologue and the epilogue seems to point strongly to the likelihood that the same author may have been responsible for the composition of both sections. But it is in the area of shared literary/rhetorical dependence on Joshua that the argument for compositional unity seems the strongest on account of the way events in Joshua are alluded to in the prologue and epilogue of Judges.

As has already been noted, all four instances where events in Joshua are alluded to in the prologue and epilogue of Judges seem to be ironic in that they seem to undercut the subject through discrepancies between the subject and the allusion. Thus, while the events alluded to in Joshua all seem to be examples of success or victory that are presented in a very positive light, the same can hardly be said of the alluding events in the prologue and epilogue of Judges. In fact, if victories are to be found at all in these events in Judges, they are superficial and temporary at best, often giving rise to further complications that ultimately end in dismal failure.

But what is most ironic here is that these alluding events that ultimately end in failure all have beginnings that echo the episodes of success they allude to in Joshua. In fact, one can say that these allusions to Joshua are almost designed to give an initial impression that a past moment of glory is about to be re-enacted. It is only as the narrative progresses that one realises that glory is not to be had after all. The net effect therefore, is that Israel is portrayed in the prologue and epilogue almost as desperately trying to recapture the past successes of their predecessors, only to fall miserably short because they knew only how to emulate the outward form of those successes without truly understanding the substance behind them.

Thus, possibly with Rahab and Jericho in mind, the house of Joseph sent spies to make a deal with an inhabitant of an enemy city, not realising that the conditions for offering חסד were not even present in the first place. Or hoping to find new territory to occupy for themselves, the Danites followed the tradition of commissioning spies to seek out new opportunities just as their predecessors had done. But the spies turned out to be of questionable character, and ended up leading their tribe not only into a new territory through the questionable use of force, but also into an unforeseen opportunity for idolatry. Or in dealing with errant brothers, the Israelites remembered how the threat of war by the whole assembly, conveyed to the erring party through a delegation, managed to bring about a satisfactory resolution in the past. But their lack of diplomatic skill in executing a similar attempt instead ended up bringing about a civil war. Then as they looked for a military victory, they meticulously copied a strategy successfully used in the past against Ai, all the while oblivious to the fact that strategies appropriately used against foreign enemies may not be equally appropriate when used against one's brothers. Thus, in all these, Israel is presented as having looked to and indeed even having emulated the outward forms of their predecessors' past successes. But for all that, they still failed, largely because they had not truly understood the substance behind previous successes, and therefore, could not appropriately apply them in the new context.

Incidentally, this highlighting of how far Israel had fallen when compared to her predecessors is not restricted only to the four instances where unrelated events in Joshua are alluded to in the prologue and epilogue of Judges. In at least two other episodes also referred to earlier in this chapter, the same theme is also discernible. First, the link in Judg. 1:19 to Joshua's assessment of the obstacle posed by the enemy's רכב ברזל in Josh. 17:18 also seems to bring out Judah's failure to live up to the expectations of the previous generation. Second, the contrast of the two pre-war pledges involving the giving or not giving of daughters in marriage in Judg. 1:11–15 and 21:1–23 also serves to bring out the lack of wisdom and discernment of the new generation of leaders as compared to the older generation represented by Caleb. In fact, one can also say that references in the prologue to the initial allotment of specific cities to specific tribes in Joshua 15–19 also highlight the failures of those tribes to fulfil what was originally considered an accomplishable mandate.

But if this interpretation is correct, it has significant implications in two important areas.

First, from the way Joshua is used in these two sections, one can advance a powerful argument for the dependence of Judges on Joshua rather than vice versa. For while there is every reason why the author of the prologue and epilogue of Judges would want to allude to episodes of success in Joshua as he wrote about Israel's subsequent failures, rhetorically speaking, there is simply no reason why the author of Joshua would want to allude to episodes of failure in Judges when he wrote about Israel's initial success in taking possession of the land. For by alluding to Israel's past successes, the author of the prologue and epilogue of Judges would essentially be placing two generations side by side for comparison. And in so doing, the deficiencies of the second generation would become all the more obvious as they are seen making blunders where their predecessors had succeeded under similar circumstances.

Second, the way Joshua is used in the prologue and epilogue also has significant implications for the compositional unity of the two sections. For not only is the extent of Joshua's influence on these two sections nothing short of remarkable,[108] there also seems to be a general unity of purpose behind the way Joshua is alluded to in the prologue and epilogue of Judges. In fact, one can say that the majority of references to Joshua appear to convey essentially the same overall message, and not once has that message been contradicted. This, therefore, argues so strongly for compositional unity between the two sections that one would not be overreaching to conclude that the same hand must have been responsible for the creation of both the prologue and epilogue of Judges.

[108] One would be hard pressed to find any other portion of significant length in Hebrew Scripture that is as predominantly influenced by another as what is being witnessed here. As the above discussion shows, references to Joshua in the two sections of Judges are absolutely pervasive. There is hardly an episode in the prologue and epilogue that is not in some way linked to Joshua!

CHAPTER THREE

ECHOES OF THE MAJOR JUDGES: LINKS BETWEEN THE EPILOGUE AND CENTRAL SECTION OF JUDGES

To write about links between the epilogue and central section of Judges presents no small challenge. For even a cursory survey of available literature will reveal that significantly more attention has been paid to the lack of continuity between the two sections than to links that tie them together, if such links indeed exist. Obvious disconnections between the two sections include the fact that in the epilogue, no mention is made at all of the judges who seem to dominate the central section. In their place, we find two stories involving Levites who heretofore have not been mentioned at all in the book. The cyclical framework of apostasy, oppression, crying out for deliverance, and the raising up of a deliverer that essentially organises the central section also no longer organises the epilogue. Instead, it is a new refrain: 'In those days, Israel had no king' that serves to bind the epilogue together into a unit.[1] Furthermore, if the central section is primarily concerned with deliverance from various external oppressions, the focus of the epilogue seems instead to be on spiritual, social and political chaos that were generated entirely from within. Taking also into consideration the fact that the two stories in the epilogue seem to disrupt the narrative flow of what is known as Deuteronomistic History,[2] and many are convinced that the epilogue

---

[1] Amit (1998:337–41), Becker (257–99), and Mayes (2001:253–54) do not even see the epilogue as one unit, but argue that Judges 19–21 (or Judges 20–21 for Mayes) actually represents a later redactional supplement to Judges 17–18. This seems to represent a further development of Noth's suggestion (1962:79) that the repetition of the refrain in 19–21 is redactional from 17–18 and thus not original to 19–21. In addition, Jüngling (245–84) argues that Judges 20 and 21 represent two later additions to Judges 19 in order to correct what was perceived to be unsatisfactory endings to the original story.

[2] Mayes (1985:14–15) for example, sees the chronological statement of Judg. 13:1 as covering also the period of the Samuel stories. The epilogue is thus seen as disrupting the continuity of Deuteronomistic History.

should be viewed as a redactional appendix[3] composed independently of the central section[4] and tacked on to it at a later date.

Obviously, not all scholars are in agreement with such an assessment. Veijola, for example, thinks that the epilogue in its current form is fully compatible with the literary structure and theological concerns of Deuteronomistic History, and is therefore more closely integrated into the central section than is generally recognised. He argues that Judges 17–21 represents part of a final cycle that commences after Samson, in which the evil Israel did (described in Judges 17–21) led to oppression in the hands of the Philistines (1 Samuel 4) and the subsequent rise of Samuel as the final judge.[5] But while Veijola's suggestion is indeed novel, it does not fit easily or naturally into the pattern through which the cycles are presented in the central section of Judges.[6] Besides, Veijola's argument does not proceed from the structure of the book in its current form, but rather, from the overall structure of Deuteronomistic History. Therefore as such, it presupposes full acceptance of Noth's hypothesis concerning the relevant books.

Others have taken a different approach to argue for a closer relationship between the major sections of Judges. Gooding, for exam-

---

[3] So referred to by J. Gray (239, 243). Moore (365) calls them "Two additional stories of the times of the Judges". Soggin labels them "Appendix on Various Themes" (1987:261), and thinks they have been put at the end of the book because they are concerned with the period before the monarchy (1987:163). Tollington (196) also agrees that the stories were later "appended as the conclusion of the book".

[4] Burney (xxxvii) and Moore (xxix–xxxii) date the stories back to very old sources resembling the most ancient parts of the Hexateuch. J. Gray (243) and Tollington (196) seem to agree, and think that these stories have been united and reinterpreted as they were appended by a post-exilic editor as a conclusion to the book. But Noth (1962:81–82) sees the polemics of Judges 17–18 as arising out of the royal Israelite sanctuary of Dan established by Jeroboam I, while Yee (152–55) sees Judges 17–18 as part of the propaganda to justify the reforms of Josiah. In any case, all these scholars seem to see a Sitz im Leben for all or part of the epilogue that differs significantly from that which gave rise to the central section of the book.

[5] Veijola, 24–29. A similar view is apparently held by Jobling (47–51), who also sees Judges 17–21 as representing one of the many gaps that are found between judges.

[6] In the cyclical pattern found in the central section, the evil committed by the people is usually reported briefly (3:7,12, 4:1, 6:1, 10:6, 13:1) rather than described in detail. Furthermore, this brief report is usually followed immediately by an unambiguous statement attributing the rise of the foreign oppressors directly to YHWH (3:8,12, 4:2, 6:1, 10:6–7, 13:1). But such a statement is lacking in Veijola's conception of the last cycle. These are but two of the problems Veijola's proposal faces.

[7] Gooding, 75–78. Granted, one of the 'double introduction' is found in 2:6–3:6, which technically, is counted as belonging to the central section of the book.

ple, attempts to establish connections between the major sections through a rhetorical analysis of the book's overall structure. But while the overall symmetry highlighted seems to support a unified composition of the book, that symmetry only links the 'double epilogue' to the 'double introduction', but not to the bulk of the central section.[7]

Likewise, Gunn and Fewell also try to argue from a literary standpoint that the narratives often labelled as later supplements in Judges 17–21 are in fact intimately connected with the preceding plot.[8] Yet again, all the examples cited merely connect events in the epilogue with those in the prologue of the book. Not a single example is cited that links the epilogue to the immediately preceding central section. This, therefore, begs the question: if literary and thematic links can only be found between the epilogue and the prologue of Judges (which, incidentally, is also considered a late addition) but not between the epilogue and the central section of the book, then what justification is there for the recent approach taken by so many to analyse the book as an integrated whole?

To be sure, literary and thematic links between the epilogue and the central section do exist, even though they may not be immediately obvious. Webb, in his groundbreaking study of Judges as an integrated work, has in fact noted a few such links in passing,[9] even though he calls them "reminiscences of events that have been narrated earlier in the book" and dismisses most of them as being "of only marginal significance thematically".[10] But are they indeed as insignificant as Webb thinks? This will be the subject of more detailed exploration in the present chapter.

In order to justify the following exploration so that it is not perceived as a biased and meaningless exercise undertaken solely to prove a point, it is perhaps first necessary to present a few preliminary observations that point towards the necessity of this exploration. And these observations begin with some unique features that characterise the narratives found in the epilogue.

---

[8] Gunn and Fewell, 120.

[9] So has Gunn (1987:106), who argues that the 'coda' does have strong thematic links with the rest of the book. Unfortunately, however, other than the link between Gideon's handling of the kingship offer and the refrain in the epilogue (1987:114–15), the other two cited by Gunn, namely, the link between the introductory formula in 17:1 and the outset of the Samson story in 13:2 (1987:107), and the link between story of Levite's concubine and Jephthah's daughter (1987:119), are only mentioned very briefly and not discussed in any detail.

[10] Webb, 1987:198–99.

That the narratives in the epilogue exhibit some unusual features that set them apart from the rest of the book has been noted by many. Indeed, Brettler speaks of "strange things" happening in "odd stories", and repeatedly characterises episodes in the epilogue as "bizarre", "absurd", and stretching notions of "historical probability".[11] Similarly, Boling also characterises Judges 19–21 as "an account that swarms with incongruities".[12] But just what exactly is it that makes these narratives in the epilogue so 'bizarre' and full of 'incongruities'?

To be sure, the incongruities Boling had in mind are probably redactional in nature,[13] while Brettler's concern seems restricted to the historical plausibility of the events.[14] But even from a literary standpoint in relation to plot and characterisation, the narratives seem full of inconsistencies, such that nearly all the main characters act in inexplicable ways and make decisions that appear self-contradictory and 'bizarre'.

Consider the following examples. In Judges 17, Micah and his mother appear to show a high regard for YHWH through their speeches. Yet, they seem entirely oblivious to the incompatibility of the idolatrous cult they set up with the central demands of YHWHism. Likewise, the Levite Micah ended up employing was supposed to draw his identity as a servant of the YHWH cult, and yet he seems to see no problem serving in a syncretistic cultic shrine that represents a significant compromise to YHWHism. The Levite in Judges 19 had apparently gone to great lengths to woo back the concubine who left him, but at the first sign of danger, seems to think nothing of sacrificing her to save his own hide. Why, then, did he bother to woo her back if she was so casually dispensable? And then there are the Benjaminites. Confronted with hard evidence of Gibeah's crime, the Benjaminites nonetheless inexplicably chose to side with the offenders, thus igniting a civil war that almost doomed the entire

---

[11] Brettler, 1989a:410, 412, 397.

[12] Boling, 1975:38.

[13] Boling, 1975:288. Soggin (1987:300–01) and Mayes (2001:253–55) have also commented on apparent redactional incongruities within these chapters, especially with regard to the incongruity between the implication of chaos in the refrain and the seemingly orderly process that led to the Benjaminite war.

[14] Brettler (1989a:397) asks, "Are we really to believe that Danite worship originated from a kidnapped cult image made from stolen silver, or that a concubine was dismembered and her parts were 'mailed' to all tribes of Israel, ultimately provoking civil war?"

tribe. Also not to be left out are the Israelites. Set against the context of their collective inability to dispossess the surrounding nations (1:19–35), the Israelites' united determination and unqualified success in almost annihilating one of their own is certainly most disquieting. From whence came this zeal that made them vow to do to their brother (21:1,7,18) what they were apparently unwilling to do to their supposed enemies (3:6)? And how does one justify a decision that seems to multiply six-hundredfold a crime the civil war was meant to rectify? Thus, even from a literary standpoint, these seemingly inexplicable behaviours and decisions repeatedly challenge our sense of 'what ought and ought not to be', and they are indeed nothing if not 'bizarre' and full of 'incongruities'.

And yet, what is most interesting is that tucked away inconspicuously within almost every single one of these bizarre episodes is an echo of a specific event that took place in the life of a major judge in the central section of the book. True, some of these echoes are connected by no more than a specific word or phrase, while others seem to depend exclusively on plot parallels to make the connection. But tenuous as they may initially seem, the connections are nonetheless there. And until each of them has been carefully examined and their collective significance duly considered, they should not be dismissed too quickly as being only of marginal value.

Therefore, in the following section, events in the epilogue and the echoes that link them to their counterparts in the central section will be carefully examined. Only after all cases have been examined will conclusions be drawn as to whether or not these links collectively provide further insight towards an overall understanding of the book and the strategies used for its composition.

Links between 'Bizarre' Episodes in the Epilogue and the Major Judges

1. *The idolatry of Micah echoes the idolatry of Gideon*

The epilogue of Judges begins with the episode of Micah, whose theft of his mother's eleven hundred shekels of silver eventually led to the crafting of an idol,[15] which was then placed in a household

[15] The terms פסל ומסכה are probably best interpreted as a hendiadys, which, as Block (1999:480 n. 19) suggests, refers to "a carved image overlaid with molten

shrine already containing אפד and תרפים. But what seems at first glance to be an account of one family's fall into idolatry gradually takes on greater significance as Danite spies on a mission to seek an inheritance for their tribe came upon Micah's house. This chance encounter eventually resulted in the Danites robbing Micah of his cultic objects as they migrated northwards, so that the very idol that ensnared Micah and his family ended up ensnaring the entire tribe of Dan.

In light of the overall plot, it seems clear that the focus of the narrative in Judges 17–18 is on the spread of idolatry and cultic anarchy in Israel. That this is so is further supported by the fact that the unifying elements that link the different episodes of the narrative together are the various idolatrous cultic objects: פסל (17:3,4; 18:14,17,18,20,30,31), מסכה (17:3,4; 18:14,17,18), אפד (17:5; 18:14,17,18,20), and תרפים (17:5; 18:14,17,18,20). Furthermore, the two characters whose presence is found almost throughout the narrative also turn out to be Micah, the one responsible for the crafting of the cultic objects, and the Levite, his idolatrous priest. But what is most curious here is that in these initial episodes, the characters who were primarily responsible for commissioning the idols are actually portrayed as YHWHists, albeit YHWHists who seem totally oblivious to the glaring incongruity between their professions of faith and their actions.[16]

Take Micah's mother, for example. Upon discovering that the thief of her eleven hundred shekels of silver was her son, she immediately invoked a blessing in the name of YHWH (17:2). She then decided to consecrate the returned silver to YHWH in an act of apparent piety (17:3), and yet totally failed to see the glaring incongruity of consecrating that money for the making of a carved image overlaid with molten metal (פסל ומסכה).[17]

---

metal". This, according to Boling (1975:256), would explain the singular form of the following main verb in 17:4. Their appearances in 18:17,18 as two distinct objects are explained by Soggin (1987:275), Noth (1962:72 n. 12), and Boling (1975:256,264) as a misunderstanding by later scribes, thus resulting in the separation of the two terms as they are repeated from 17:3,4.

[16] Although in Judges 17, the focus is mainly on Micah and his mother, yet the same incongruity also applies to the Levite. For he too, proclaims with confidence YHWH's blessing in 18:6, while all the time, he was serving as the illegitimate personal priest of Micah's idolatrous cult.

[17] Incidentally, prohibition against the crafting of פסל is explicitly stated in the second commandment of the Decalogue (Exod. 20:4; Deut. 5:8), while the making

The same is also true of Micah. Having met the sojourning Levite and discovered his identity, Micah immediately employed him as his priest (17:10). His declaration of confidence that YHWH will hence be good to him (17:13) was apparently based on a not-entirely-incorrect recognition of the propriety of Levitical priesthood. But still, he completely failed to see the impropriety of setting up an idolatrous cult at his own home.

Such incongruities in the characterisation of Micah and his mother in these initial episodes thus cry out for some sort of explanation. And yet none is provided within the narrative to account for such bizarre actions.

Interestingly, such inexplicable incongruities seem to echo a similar episode in the central section of the book. Admittedly, the links between the two episodes are subtle, yet a credible case can be made for the presence of conscious allusion in the epilogue to the earlier episode.

As has been noted above, some of the most prominent elements that seem to unify the narrative in Judges 17–18 include the four terms for idolatrous cultic objects repeated throughout the narrative. Of the four, פסל and מסכה are clearly used in a pejorative sense throughout Hebrew Scripture, and the term תרפים is also linked to idolatry or non-YHWHistic practices in 1 Sam. 15:23, 2 Kgs. 23:24, Ezek. 21:26, Hos. 3:4, and Zech. 10:2.[18] אפד, on the other hand, does have a positive function within the YHWH cult. In fact, all references to אפד in the Pentateuch are to a special priestly garment,[19] and in 1 Sam. 2:28, 14:3, 21:10, and 22:18, the term also refers to a piece of garment worn by those in priestly offices.[20] Interestingly,

of מסכה, first associated with the golden calf in Exod. 32:4,8 and Deut. 9:12,16, is also clearly forbidden in Exod. 34:17 and Lev. 19:4. In fact, the crafting of either, said to be detestable to YHWH, heads the list of curses announced on Mount Ebal in Deut. 27:15.

[18] It is not entirely clear what exactly תרפים refers to in Genesis 31 and 1 Samuel 19, and what function these objects serve in the context of those narratives. Dan (102–05), referring to a Hasidic folktale from Pe'er Mi-Qedoshim about the MaHaRaL of Prague, thinks the folktale provides parallels to Rachel's theft of the תרפים in Genesis 31. He thus argues that the תרפים in question may be a magical object that would enable pursuers to find the pursued. The connection, however, seems speculative.

[19] Exod. 25:7; 28:4,6,12,15,25–28,31; 29:5; 35:9,27; 39:2,7,8,18–22; Lev. 8:7.

[20] In 1 Sam. 20:10, the אפד was apparently not being worn by Ahimelech the priest when he was speaking to David. But this may only be due to the unexpected arrival of David at a time when the priest was not on active duty.

the young Samuel under the apprenticeship of Eli (1 Sam. 2:18), and David, as he was bringing the ark back to Jerusalem (2 Sam. 6:14; 1 Chron. 15:27), are also said to have worn a linen ephod (אפוד בד), even though neither was serving in a priestly capacity. Yet the texts seem to offer no condemnation of either in the matter.

Other than being a special priestly garment, the אפד is apparently also used as a cultic object that aids in the making of oracular inquiries. David repeatedly used it when making inquiries of YHWH in 1 Sam. 23:6,9 and 30:7, but this practice is again not condemned in the relevant texts.[21]

In light of all this, one can say that the use of אפד in a pejorative sense as an idolatrous cultic object is actually quite uncommon. In the seven possible cases where the word is so used in Hebrew Scripture, other than Hos. 3:4,[22] the remaining are all found in Judges. Furthermore, of the six instances in Judges, five occur in the narrative involving Micah and the Danites in Judges 17–18. That

[21] In fact, commenting on 1 Sam. 23:6–13, Hertzberg (1964:191) points out that the Lord's will is clearly brought into the centre of the picture through these acts of inquiry, and that in this episode, David, as the instrument of the Lord's will, is actually presented in a particularly attractive light.

[22] Even here, it is debatable whether the word is in fact used in a pejorative sense as an idolatrous cultic object. True, in Hos. 3:4, it is used in conjunction with תרפים, as is the case in Judg. 17:5; 18:14,17,18,20. But it is by no means sure that the three pairs in Hos. 3:4, consisting of six items Israel is said to do without (אין) for many days, are all meant to be seen as undesirable. While the second item in the second and third pair, sacred stone (מצבה) and teraphim (תרפים), are undoubtedly pejorative, the first item in these two pairs, sacrifice (זבח) and ephod (אפוד), are both words that can take on either a positive or negative connotation. Adding to the complication is the fact that both items in the first pair, king (מלך) and ruler (שׂר) seem inherently neutral. Therefore it is possible to argue that what the three pairs of six items represent in Hos. 3:4 is the loss of political autonomy (no מלך or שׂר) and the cessation of any religious life, be it a form of worship that is approved (זבח and אפוד) or disapproved (מצבה and תרפים). This, incidentally, seems to be supported by Wolff (62), who notes that with the three pairs of negation, legitimate as well as illegitimate contact is prevented. If so, the second and third pair in the list should be understood as essentially synonymous, each conveying the idea of total religious quarantine through the pairing together of opposites by means of merism. This seems to find further support in that Hos. 3:3, which is the symbol for which 3:4 serves as the interpretation, also speaks of the necessity of many days of sexual quarantine before normal relationship can be restored. Here, Andersen and Freedman (306) note that the woman's abstinence from sex is both with regard to her lovers (the Baals) and her husband (YHWH). This again seems to suggest the pairing together of opposites in a case of merism. If this interpretation of Hos. 3:3–4 is indeed correct, it would leave the six instances in Judges as the only ones where אפוד is used negatively to refer to an idolatrous cultic object, a point also noted by Auld (1989:258).

leaves Judg. 8:27 regarding Gideon's אפד as the only other time in the book where אפד is found and used in the same negative sense to refer to an idolatrous cultic object. Since none of the other three terms for idolatrous cultic objects occur anywhere else in Judges outside of Judges 17–18,[23] one cannot help but suspect that a conscious attempt is being made to link the Micah episode to the Gideon episode through this unusually negative use of אפד.[24]

This suspicion is further confirmed in several ways. First, while the episode involving Gideon's אפד conveys vital information that adds to the overall portrayal of Gideon, the mention of Micah's אפד seems redundant and non-essential from the standpoint of the overall plot. For although McMillion may well be right in noting that the mention of the אפוד ותרפים serves ironically to ridicule the senseless multiplying of cultic objects,[25] his subsequent observation that the four terms were narrowed down to three in 18:20, and eventually

---

[23] It is debatable whether the same term פסל is found in Judg. 3:19,26, where Ehud is said to have first turned back at הפסילים and later passed through them again as he escaped homewards. Medieval Jewish commentators like Rashi and Kimhi, as well as Targum Jonathan, all render the term 'quarries' instead of 'idols' (Rosenberg, 22), but this is dismissed by Lindars (1995:143) as a likely attempt to avoid the impression that the Israelite company had gone to an idolatrous shrine. Soggin (1987:51) and Cundall (1968:77) think that the term may be referring to the stones set up by Joshua at Gilgal as recorded in Josh. 4:19–24, but Block (1999:165) thinks it would be highly unusual for the author to be referring to the commemorating stones for such a sacred moment in the nation's history with a term as pejorative as הפסילים. Block himself thinks that the term should probably be taken in its normal sense as idols, with the two references in 3:19,26 meaning to show how Israel had come to accept such pagan symbols as a part of their own religious landscape. But such an interpretation does not explain why the text apparently gives the impression that הפסילים serve as some kind of boundary marker beyond which Ehud felt he had left the danger zone of enemy territory. For the same reason, the suggestion of J. Gray (263) that הפסילים are inscribed stones recording a vassal treaty also seems unconvincing. Burney (71) thus takes הפסילים as some kind of sculpted boundary stones analogous to the Babylonian kudurru stones, marking the limit of Moabite territory. Another possible interpretation is also offered by Lindars (1995:143), who agrees with Ehrlich that הפסילים may well be a place name, the definite article not withstanding. Lindars thinks this may be why the narrator felt no need to elucidate it, since this place near Gilgal may be well known to his audience. In spite of the profusion of possible solutions, many agree that a definitive answer to the problem may not be possible (Amit, 1998:186; Lindars, 1995:143). In light of this uncertainty, and the fact that most proposed solutions do not take the term in 3:19,26 in its normal sense of 'idol', one should perhaps refrain from linking the term with פסל.

[24] This is also hinted at by Amit (1990:8 n. 9).

[25] McMillion, 233–34.

to only the פסל in 18:30–31 underscores the fact that the central issue is really about the corruption of worship in general and not about the individual cultic items.[26] In fact, within the narrative, the mention of אפוד ותרפים adds no extra significance that is not already conveyed by the mention of פסל ומסכה. Thus, the hypothetical removal of אפוד ותרפים from the narrative altogether would not have detracted from the overall plot by one bit. On the contrary, their introduction into the narrative in 17:5 seems somewhat forced and entirely unmotivated by plot necessity, and one cannot help but suspect that אפד was probably introduced into the narrative solely as a link to the Gideon episode, while תרפים was consciously paired with אפד to ensure that the latter is understood negatively.

But second, a deliberate attempt to link the narratives concerning Micah and Gideon is also most likely in that plotwise, the stories seem to share certain bizarre elements. If, as mentioned before, the glaring incongruity between the actions and professions of Micah and his mother seems bizarre and inexplicable, then interestingly, the same incongruity between action and profession is also found in Gideon.

In Judg. 8:22, Gideon is offered some kind of kingship by the Israelites. He promptly declines in 8:23, claiming that neither he nor his sons will rule over the people because YHWH is the one who rules over them.

But just as in the case of Micah and his mother, no sooner had Gideon made a profession of faith that seems to confirm his identity as a YHWHist, he immediately acted in the way of a pagan idolater. In the very next breath, Gideon asked the people each to donate a gold earring, which he then made into an אפד, a cultic object that became a snare not only to himself and his family (8:27), but also to 'all Israel', just as Micah's idols not only became a snare to himself and his family, but also to the tribe of Dan.

But if the episode concerning the creation of Micah's idols is indeed consciously linked to the episode of Gideon's idolatry through shared incongruities and the use of אפד in the same unusually negative sense, then what is the purpose of such a connection? Curiously enough, while the parallel between the two episodes seems sufficiently apparent, the allusion to Gideon ultimately offers no more insight

[26] Ibid., 234.

into the psychology of Micah and his mother than their incongruities manage to shed light on Gideon. The actions of the protagonists in both cases are equally bizarre and inexplicable. Thus, in the end, all the parallel shows is that although bizarre, the incongruity between action and profession demonstrated by Micah and his mother is not unique after all, since the exact same tendency has also been displayed by one of Israel's judges.

2. *The Levite's violation of practically every Levitical regulation echoes Samson's violation of practically every Nazirite regulation*

If the actions of Micah and his mother seem puzzling in light of the YHWHistic sentiments they openly expressed, then so is the behaviour of the Levite. For to a reader familiar with regulations concerning Levites, what this Levite did comes across as a violation of all that a Levite should stand for.[27]

First of all, Levites, as a special class within Israel, were given exclusive responsibility of taking care of objects associated with the YHWH cult (Num. 1:50–53). At the initial stage of the nation's history, this would include the Tabernacle as well as all portable furnishings that were associated with it. They were also entrusted with the responsibility of assisting the priests in carrying out their cultic duties (Num. 3:5–10), and were possibly also responsible for teaching the Law (Deut. 33:10).[28] Because of their cultic responsibilities, they were not given an inheritance of land in the same way other Israelites were, but would receive as their inheritance the tithes presented to YHWH by the rest of Israel (Num. 18:21–24; Deut. 18:1–2). In addition, the tribes were also constantly reminded not to neglect the material needs of the Levites living among them, but to include them when they show charity towards the aliens, fatherless and widows (Deut. 12:12,18,19; 14:27–29; 16:11,14; 26:11–13).

---

[27] Admittedly, the portrayal of Levites in Hebrew Scripture is fragmentary. Hence, many questions remain regarding how exactly they function within the YHWH cult. In fact, there is even debate about whether according Deuteronomy, all Levites are priests (See Emerton, 129–38) or whether only a minority of them was given priestly rights (Wright, 1954:325–30; Abba, 257–267; Duke, 193–201). But although many aspects about the Levites seem to lack clarity, there does seem to be enough information to provide a rough picture of what is expected of them, as the following discussion shows.

[28] The function of Levites as teachers of the Law is argued by Wright (1954:329), who also cites 2 Chron. 17:7–9; 35:3; Neh. 8:7–9 as support.

As for a place to live, Levites were given special towns from within the inheritance of the other tribes (Num. 35:1–5; Josh. 21:1–42). If they chose to move from one of these towns, they were guaranteed employment and a means of livelihood at the main sanctuary, where they would serve in the name of YHWH (Deut. 18:6–8).

In light of these Levitical stipulations, the situation of the Levite in Judges 17 becomes somewhat curious. To begin, he was described as living within the clan of Judah in Bethlehem (17:7,9), yet Bethlehem was not one of the Levitical towns (Josh. 21:9–16). So why had he been living there? In addition, he was in search of a place to stay where he would be able to find employment and a means of livelihood (17:8,9; 18:4). But why did he not go to the main sanctuary and serve there with his fellow Levites in the name of YHWH, since employment and livelihood were guaranteed there?

But perhaps most damning of all is the Levite's consent to serve as a priest in Micah's household shrine. For first of all, a Levite's cultic responsibility is supposed to be in connection with the main sanctuary.[29] Besides, the explicit prohibition in Deuteronomy 12 against worshipping anywhere else apart from the place of YHWH's own choosing[30] renders Micah's household shrine illegitimate. Being someone whose very identity implies intimate associated with the cult, the Levite should have known this. And yet, he seems content to serve in this illegitimate shrine.

Second, the Levite should also have known that in the YHWH cult, only descendants of Aaron could assume the priesthood (Num. 3:10; 18:1–7). But as the author eventually disclosed (Judg. 18:30), this particular Levite was not a descendant of Aaron, but of Moses.[31] Therefore as such, he had taken upon himself a position he had no right to take in the first place.

But worst of all, Micah's household shrine was one that housed a מסכה (17:3,4; 18:14,17,18). This, in itself, is a great irony because

---

[29] The items they were entrusted to care for were all sacred items connected with the Tabernacle (Num. 1:50–53; 3:7–8,21–37; 4:1–33; 18:6).

[30] Wilson (83–84) argues that the entire epilogue is in fact an explication of the final refrain, the second part of which (everyone did what was right in his own eyes) is drawn directly from Deut. 12:8 to focus on cultic impropriety (75–76).

[31] Although a suspended נ in the MT may turn the name from Moses to Manasseh, the original reading as Moses seems supported by the versions. Weitzman (449–60) thinks that the נ was probably added not only to shield Moses from the taint of idolatry, but also to discredit Manasseh, the first high priest of a Samaritan temple, by fusing his figure with that of the corrupt Jonathan.

according to Exod. 32:25–29, the Levites had at one point demonstrated such zeal for YHWH that they were willing to kill their brothers, friends, and neighbours for worshipping a מסכה (cf. Exod. 32:4,8). But by consenting to serve Micah's מסכה, this Levite had in fact turned his back on an honour that had once distinguished his people from the rest of Israel.[32]

In light of all these, the question, therefore, is, "Why did he do it?" Why did this Levite violate almost every regulation and tradition that defined him as a Levite, even though as grandson of Moses, he, of all people, should have known better? Unfortunately, the text seems to provide no clue.

And yet, the recklessness with which this Levite violated all the Levitical regulations seems to find a parallel in the life of a major judge, Samson.

To be sure, Samson was not a Levite. Yet, the narrative made it quite clear that he was consecrated as a Nazirite from birth (13:5,7).[33] Samson himself admitted as much in 16:17. In this respect, both Samson and the Levite were among those who had been set apart for YHWH.

But if Samson had indeed been set apart as a Nazirite, he certainly never acted like one. In fact, one can even say that, much like the Levite in Judges 17–18, Samson had violated almost every stipulation that defined his special status.[34]

---

[32] Could the Levites' act of loyalty at Sinai form the basis upon which the tribe was set apart for YHWH? Hebrew Scripture never made any explicit connection between the two, but this is nonetheless a tantalising conjecture, given the fact that a similar zeal of Phinehas for YHWH's honour became the basis upon which he and his descendants were rewarded with a covenant of lasting priesthood (cf. Num. 25:10–13). If the Levites' zeal in Exodus 32 indeed forms the basis of their consecration for YHWH, then the decision of the Levite in Judges 17–18 to serve Micah's מסכה would represent an even greater violation of his Levitical calling, for that would mean a turning back on the very thing that gave him his identity as a Levite in the first place.

[33] Admittedly, Wharton (57–60) and others have argued that mentions of the Nazirite vow in 13:5,7 represent later additions to the narrative. Yet what Wharton is really questioning is not so much whether Samson was in fact a Nazirite, but merely whether references to the Nazirite vow in 13:5,7 are original to the birth narrative. For Wharton seems to think that references in 13:5,7 were added later to harmonise with 16:4ff, and in particular, with 16:17. The authenticity of Samson's self-identification as a Nazirite in 16:17 is, however, never in dispute.

[34] Bal (25) and Marais (127) also see Samson as repeatedly transgressing his Nazirite status. Exum (1983:31) and Andersson (179), however, dispute the suggestion that Nazirite rules play a significant role within the narrative: Exum, because

For according to Nazirite regulations in Numbers 6,[35] there are three main stipulations that a Nazirite must observe during his entire period of separation unto YHWH. Two of these are directly mentioned in Samson's birth narrative. The first, which the angel of YHWH communicated explicitly to Samson's mother in Judg. 13:4, is abstinence from יין and שׁכר (Num. 6:3–4).[36] The second, also mentioned by the angel in Judg. 13:5, is against the cutting of hair by a razor (Num. 6:5). Finally, there is the prohibition against contact with dead bodies, since that would render one ceremonially unclean (Num. 6:6–8). This last stipulation, however, is not explicitly referred to in Judges 13.[37] Yet in the course of the narrative, Samson is shown to have violated all three stipulations related to his Nazirite status.

The most explicit violation, which also happens to be the one most significant to the plot of the narrative, is the shaving off of his hair. Granted, the shaving was not portrayed as a voluntary act Samson himself undertook, but was imposed upon him unawares by Delilah while he was asleep on her knees (16:19). Yet, it was Samson himself who disclosed to Delilah the secret concerning the source of his strength,[38] and this, in spite of every indication that Delilah would

there was no explicit censure of Samson for any of his actions, and Andersson, because the supposed rules of cleanliness were never mentioned within the narrative. For critiques of Exum's and Andersson's views, see n. 48 below and Wong, 2006b: forthcoming.

[35] Blenkinsopp (1963:66) seems to imply that Judges 13 is dependent on Numbers 6 when he speaks of changes to the formulation of the Nazirite vow in Judges 13 from what is found in Numbers 6.

[36] Exum (1983:44 n. 30) argues that in the Samson narrative, the prohibition against drinking wine and other strong drink, as well as against eating any unclean food, is directed only at the mother and not specifically at the child. But the immediate context makes it clear that the reason she needed to observe these regulations was because of her pregnancy (13:5). For the child she would carry was to be a Nazirite to YHWH from the womb (מן־הבטן) and not just from birth, as some English translations have it. Thus, if the mother needed to observe these regulations for the sake of the child inside her, the implication is that these regulations would be of paramount importance for the child as well since they had to be safeguarded for his sake even before he was born.

[37] One wonders, however, whether this stipulation has not been recast into the present prohibition against unclean food in 13:4. See n. 49 below for more discussion of the matter.

[38] How Samson's words in 16:17 are to be interpreted is admittedly controversial. Crenshaw (1974:498) seems to think that it implies Samson's awareness that "his great strength resides within *him*, rather than upon the sudden stirring of God's spirit". Margalith (229) also sees in Samson's words evidence that his supernatural powers reside inherently in his locks. But by explicitly linking his hair with his iden-

use such information against him.[39] In this respect, Samson was ultimately responsible for his hair being cut off.

Samson's other two violations of his Nazirite vow are less obvious,[40] and thus one is left with the impression that this theme of vow violation has been largely ignored between the opening and final episodes of the narrative.[41] However, hints of such violations are actually present even in the central chapters of the narrative.[42]

---

tity as a Nazirite, Samson may in fact be demonstrating a real understanding of the essential connection between the uncut hair and his identity of being a Nazirite. For according to Num. 6:18–20, the shaving off of a Nazirite's hair is considered an indication that the period of separation is over, and hence, the end of one's status as a Nazirite. If so, what Samson was saying could be that his strength is connected with his special status as a Nazirite set apart to YHWH, and this status is inextricably connected to the state of his hair. Therefore, the shaving off of his hair would signal an end to this special status, and with it, also an end to his supernatural strength. Thus, even Wharton (61), who disputes the originality of the reference to the Nazirite vow in 13:5,7, concedes that in the text as it currently stands, fidelity to Samson's calling, as signified by the keeping of Nazirite obligations, "is the true key to Samson's God-given strength".

[39] It is somewhat of a mystery why Samson would disclose such vital information to Delilah when three time already, she has shown her intention to subdue him using information he had given to her about himself (see Ackerman, 35). This prompted numerous attempts by scholars to psychoanalyse Samson. Crenshaw (1974:498) for example, speaks of Samson interpreting Delilah's desire to gain power over him as a desire to keep him for herself. Vickery (71) sees Samson as someone hurt by past betrayals and thus "profoundly in need of someone to trust". Alter (1990:53) thinks that Samson is inherently excited by and drawn to the threat of danger. Webb (1987:169) and Greene (72) speculate that behind Samson's self-betrayal was a desire to "be done with fighting the Philistines and settle down with the woman he loves": in other words, a desire to be "like any other man". Intriguing as these suggestions may be, the text actually gives no support whatsoever to any of these conjectures.

[40] Niditch (1990:613) claims that the other aspects of the Nazirite vow, apart from the hair, are not the interest of the Samson writer.

[41] See, for example, Eissfeldt, 81–87; Exum, 1981:25 n. 1; 1983:33.

[42] See, for example, Blenkinsopp, 1963:66; Crenshaw, 1979:129; Greenstein, 1981b:251; Greene, 60,64–65; Gunn, 1992:232–33. Gunn (1987:118) claims that "the Nazirite vow permeates the narrative", and Freeman (147) also speaks of Samson violating various Nazirite taboos on the basis of the expectations set up in Judges 13. Here, it should be noted that the prohibitions against strong drink and unclean food actually receive more prominence in the birth narrative than the prohibition against the cutting of hair, since the former two are each repeated at least three times (13:4,7,14) by the various characters within the narrative, while the prohibition against the cutting of hair is only mentioned once in 13:5. Thus, one cannot help but wonder why these prohibition against wine and unclean food would be given such prominence at all in the birth narrative, if their violations are indeed not referred to anymore in the rest of the narrative as some seem to think. For that would render a significant part of the birth narrative irrelevant to the story as a whole.

With regard to the violation of the prohibition against יין and שׁכר (Num. 6:3–4), it is perhaps not insignificant that Samson is reported in 14:10 to have prepared a מִשׁתה.[43] While a wedding celebration is perhaps to be expected under the circumstances, the fact remains, however, that a משׁתה is very often associated with wine and drinking.[44] In fact, the word is explicitly used at least six time with יין[45] and twice in 1 Sam. 25:36 and Jer. 51:39 with שׁכר.[46] It is also used with other words related to fermented drink and its consumption, such as with שׁמר twice in Isa. 25:6 and with שׁתה in Gen. 26:30, Job 1:4, and Jer. 16:8.

In the particular case of Samson, Greene further observes that the mention of the משׁתה in Judg. 14:10 is followed immediately by כי כן יעשׂו הבחורים. This suggests to Greene that Samson's behaviour in this matter was likely the same as any other man's, thus making it most probable that Samson himself would have been involved in the drinking.[47] Thus, the language of 14:10 suggests that Samson had indeed violated the abstinence component of his Nazirite vow.[48]

---

[43] The word also appears in 14:12,17.

[44] While Greene (64) is right to point out that the word emphasises through its root שׁתה the drinking component of a feast, his suggestion that the word choice is deliberate is perhaps overstating the case. For it seems that other than the rare כרה, which only occurs twice in 2 Kgs. 6:23, משׁתה is the only word used in Hebrew Scripture to indicate a non-religious feast or banquet. For a religious feast, the word commonly used is חג. This predominant use of משׁתה for non-religious feasts probably reflects the fact that in days before a wide variety of beverage choices were available, celebratory feasts were mainly characterised by the copious consumption of wine and fermented drink. That such drinks can induce feelings of euphoria probably makes them especially suitable for such occasions. In fact, one may even say that to have a celebratory feast without wine and related beverages would be an inconceivable notion to an ancient Israelite. Thus, since few other words have been used in Hebrew Scripture to designate such feasts, Burney's translation (342) of משׁתה as "a drinking bout" in Judg. 14:10 is probably unwarranted. But that wine and fermented drink were involved is almost certain.

[45] Esth. 5:6; 7:2,7,8; Isa. 5:12; Dan. 1:16. The reference to משׁתה in Esth. 1:5 is obviously also associated with יין in view of 1:7,10, and the same can be said of Esth. 5:4,5 in view of 5:6, and Esth. 5:8,12,14; 6:14 in view of 7:2,7,8.

[46] Although it is the adjective שׁכר that appears in 1 Sam. 25:36 and the Hiphil verb form that appears in Jer. 51:39 rather than the noun שׁכר as in Judg. 13:4,7,14, the words are nonetheless from the same root and are related to intoxicating drink and being drunk.

[47] Greene, 65.

[48] Incidentally, some have questioned whether violations of Samson's Nazirite vow are implied in the mention of the feast and the incident involving the lion's carcass in Judges 14. In particular, Exum (1983:31–32) rejects Blenkinsopp's suggestion (1963:66) that these two incidents speaks of "an implicit repudiation of the

As for violation of the prohibition against defilement from contact with dead bodies, this original stipulation in Numbers 6 seems to have been recast into a new prohibition previously not associated with the Nazirite vow. This concerns the prohibition against eating anything unclean (Judg. 13:4,7,14).[49] But in the end, whether it is

---

vow", arguing instead that it cannot be demonstrated that these anecdotes have the Nazirite vow in mind since Judges 14 neither identifies Samson as a Nazirite nor provides any indication that it regards his actions as infractions of the vow. But a prominent stylistic feature of Judges is that the book seldom offers explicit and direct appraisals of its characters' actions anyway. After all, Exum herself has elsewhere negatively evaluated Gideon's hesitation (1990:416–17) and his treatment of the uncooperative towns (1990:418), Jephthah's human sacrifice (1990:422–23) and his dealing with the Ephraimites (1990:422–23), Micah's idolatry (1990:426), the Danites' ruthlessness (1990:426), the Levite's opportunism (1990:426), the baseness of the second Levite and his host (1990:428), and the decision of the elders of Israel (1990:431). And in none of these is any explicit condemnation to be found directly in the text either. This does not mean that Exum is wrong in evaluating these incidents negatively. On the contrary, she may well have been right on target. But what this does mean is that in a book that has consistently displayed remarkable subtlety and restraint in its evaluation of the actions of its characters, it is not necessarily illegitimate to read between the lines, provided that there are good contextual reasons to do so. To insist on explicit confirmation from the text in every single case before an interpretation is accepted would render a book like Judges almost impossible to interpret. See also n. 177 below for further comments on subtlety as one of Judges' main stylistic features.

[49] Admittedly, the suggestion that the prohibition against eating anything unclean may be a recasting of the original prohibition against contact with dead bodies is largely conjectural. It is based primarily on the following observations. First, since Samson's killing of the lion with his bare hands is directly attributed to the Spirit of YHWH coming upon him (14:6), it may prove challenging for the author to harmonise it with YHWH's requirement in Numbers 6 against coming into contact with dead bodies. Second, if the primary issue in the prohibition against contact with dead bodies is one of ritual defilement (Num. 6:7), then the new prohibition against eating unclean food would in some way preserve the essence of the original prohibition. Third, the phrasing of the prohibition against eating anything from the grapevine mentioned in Judg. 13:14 (מכל אשר־יצא מגפן היין לא תאכל) echoes very strongly the language used in Num. 6:4 (מכל אשר יעשׂה מגפן היין . . . לא יאכל). This seems to suggest that the author was indeed familiar with the original Nazirite requirements in Numbers 6. Fourth, by reporting how Samson ate the honey taken from the lion's carcass, the author did present Samson as having violated the explicit prohibition of 13:4,7,14, a prohibition relevant to the immediate context of the narrative. But the fact that the very same act can also be viewed as a violation of the original prohibition against contact with dead bodies in Num. 6:7 seems to suggest once again that the author was very much aware of the original prohibition not mentioned in the narrative. Indeed, it almost seems as if this convergence of both violations in one single act was designed to cover both possibilities, so that regardless of whether it is the prohibition specifically mentioned in Judg. 13 that is in view, or the original prohibition some would come to expect but is not specifically mentioned in the narrative, the sequence of events would still yield the same result. In light of the above observations, one has reason to suspect that the prohibition

the Numbers 6 stipulation against contact with dead bodies or the Judges 13 stipulation against eating unclean food that is in view seems unimportant. For in recounting how Samson scooped out with his hands honey he found in a lion's carcass and ate it, the author of the story had effectively made sure that either way, Samson is presented as having violated a key injunction associated with his calling as a Nazirite.[50]

Thus, much like the Levite in Judges 17–18 who managed to violate almost every regulation that defined his special status as a Levite, Samson also managed to violate almost every regulation that defined his special status as a Nazirite. Unfortunately, other than this outward parallel, neither episode makes any attempt to shed further light on the other. But by portraying the Levite as someone who, like Samson, has also violated nearly every essential stipulation of his special calling, the author of the epilogue has shown that the bizarre and shocking behaviour of the Levite was not unprecedented.

3. *The Danites doing what was right in their own eyes echoes Samson going after what was right in his own eyes*

In Judges 18:1, the Danites are brought into the narrative about Micah and his idols as their search for a permanent inheritance led them to cross paths with Micah.

Admittedly, what the Danites did to secure for themselves an inheritance does not immediately strike one as being as bizarre and incomprehensible as some of the other actions portrayed in the epilogue. Yet, that they applied the ban[51] to a peaceful and unsuspecting people living far away from anyone else is nonetheless disturbing behaviour that requires some kind of explanation.[52] But again, while

---

against eating unclean food may indeed represent a deliberate recasting of the original prohibition in order to circumvent a theological problem inherent in the text.

[50] Andersson (165) disputes this by suggesting that maybe the narrator's purpose in mentioning the eating of the honey without telling his parents is to clarify that no one but Samson's wife knew the answer to his riddle. But in light of Soggin's comment (1987:240–41) that "even for someone who was not a Nazirite, the honey would have been impure, since it came from a corpse (Lev. 11:24–40)", it is hard to imagine that a Jewish audience would focus only on the secrecy issue when it comes to Judg. 14:5–9 but entirely overlook the more obvious issue of defilement.

[51] Here, the word חרם is not actually used in the narrative about the Danites. However, as has already been noted (see pp. 43–46), the language nonetheless suggests an application of the חרם.

[52] The illegitimacy of the Danites' annihilation of Laish has been argued by

it seems that no explicit explanation can be found within the context of the narrative itself, a subtle link can nonetheless be detected which hints at some kind of parallel with an earlier episode concerning Samson.

This allusion to Samson can be detected through the following clues. First, both episodes share a few prominent place-names. In the Samson narrative, the exploits of Samson are introduced by a reference to YHWH's Spirit stirring in Samson במחנה־דן בין צרעה ובין אשתאל (13:25). Interestingly, the Danites' exploits also seem to be intricately tied to צרעה ואשתאל as these are the cities from which the spies were sent, to which they returned to report their findings, and from which the tribe's warriors set off again to claim their inheritance (18:2,8,11). In fact, other than two references in Joshua (15:33, 19:41), and a further reference associated with Samson's burial place in Judg. 16:31, these are the only times in Hebrew Scripture that the two cities are mentioned together.[53] As for מחנה־דן, other than in 13:25, it is also mentioned in 18:12 as the place where the Danite warriors first set up camp as they proceeded northwards towards Laish. Incidentally, these also happen to be the only two times מחנה־דן is mentioned in Hebrew Scripture.[54] Thus, it seems that all three place-names are found together in close proximity only in the Samson narrative and in the narrative of Danite migration in the epilogue of Judges. This, therefore, argues strongly that these place-names are use as a rhetorical devise linking the episodes together.[55]

McMillion (239–40), while Satterthwaite (1993:80) also characterises the "sacking of Laish" as "an atrocity not sanctioned by God".

[53] צרעה is mentioned by itself in Judg. 13:2 as the place where Samson's father was from, as well as in 2 Chron. 11:10 and Neh. 11:29. But אשתאל is not mentioned anywhere else on its own in Hebrew Scripture. Note also that הצרעתי והאשתאלי is also found in 1 Chron. 2:53, while הצרעתי is mentioned on its own in 1 Chron. 4:2.

[54] The debate about whether the two מחנה־דן represent the same place is succinctly summarised by O'Connell (215). Indeed, it is possible that the term מחנה is being used differently in 13:25 and 18:12, with the former as part of a proper name and the latter simply as a common noun. But if this is the case, it would only strengthen the argument that מחנה־דן is being used deliberately as a rhetorical link between the two episodes, since it is highly unusual for two places that do not share the same proper name to be referred to in exactly the same way.

[55] This is also suggested by Bauer (2001:5.4), although Bauer's conclusion is debatable that Judg. 18:12 is prior and that Judg. 13:25 was added later as a polemic against the Danites to highlight the fact that the Spirit of YHWH did not come upon them in מחנה־דן as He did on Samson.

But other than significant place-names, the two episodes also share certain plot parallels. For example, in the Samson episode, the mention of צרעה ואשתאל is immediately followed by the report of Samson seeing a Philistine woman in Timnah and wanting to take her as wife. This somewhat parallels the situation in which the Danites found themselves. For while Samson's seeking of a wife can, in a sense, be seen as a matter concerning future progeny, the same is true of the Danites' attempt to seek a land inheritance, since the future survival and continuation of the tribe would be at stake if there was no land to sustain them.

But the similarities between the two episodes go even further. In Samson's case, his decision to take the Philistine woman is based primarily on what he saw. This is made amply clear not only in that his attraction is first introduced by the verb ראה (14:1), but also by the fact that in asking his parents to get her for him, he again based his request on his 'having seen' (ראיתי) the Philistine woman (14:2).

Incidentally, this same theme of acting on the basis of seeing is also found in the Danite episode. Having made a short stop at Micah's house on the way to find land inheritance, the five spies finally arrived at Laish, where the same verb ראה is used to describe their initial discovery of a people who were living peaceful and unsuspecting lives (18:7). Shortly thereafter, as the spies returned to their people to report their finding, their urging of their brothers to take immediate action is again based on their 'having seen' (ראינו) the good land and the unsuspecting people (18:9). Thus, both in the Samson and in the Danite episodes, what the protagonists saw is quickly followed by attempts to persuade others to act on the basis of their earlier sightings.

But that is not all. In Samson's case, his being guided by what he saw is further emphasised when his choice of woman was questioned by his parents. In response, Samson answered, היא ישרה בעיני (14:3), an assertion repeated again by the narrator in 14:7.

But the phrase 'right in one's eyes' (ישר בעיני־) is also echoed repeatedly in the refrain found in the epilogue of the book: איש הישר בעיניו יעשה (17:6; 21:25). Admittedly, this part of the refrain actually does not appear explicitly in the episode concerning the Danites. However, it must not be overlooked that the short form of the refrain, בימים ההם אין מלך בישראל, in fact brackets the episode of Danite migration in 18:1 and 19:1.[56] And even though the short form of the refrain lacks the second half of the full formula איש הישר בעיניו יעשה, the repeated occurrences of the full and short refrain in relatively close proximity makes it likely that readers would automatically supply the ellipsis whenever they encounter the short refrain.[57] If so, one can indeed argue that just as Samson's desire to marry the Philistine woman he saw (ראה) expresses his being ruled by what is 'right in his own eyes (ישר בעיני)',[58] so the Danites' decision to annihilate the peaceful and unsuspecting citizens of Laish on the basis of what their spies saw (ראה) is equally a concrete example of how the tribe as a whole did what was right in its own eyes (הישר בעיניו יעשה).[59]

But there may yet be one more parallel between the two episodes. In the Samson story, Samson's choice of the Philistine woman whom he has just seen (ראה) was questioned in 14:3 by his parents, whose words seem to imply that taking a woman from among their own people as wife would have been preferable to taking a foreign woman.[60]

---

[56] To be sure, the majority of scholars such as Dumbrell (23–24), Amit (1990:5), Exum (1990:427), O'Connell (239), and McMillion (237) are in agreement that the refrain serves primarily as a transitional device that concludes the previous episode and introduces the next. Thus, strictly speaking, the presence of the shortened refrain in 18:1 and 19:1 is not primarily to serve as a 'bracket' for the Danite episode. But it is nonetheless noteworthy that the episode is transitioned from the preceding episode and joined to the next by this particular refrain.

[57] Writing about the short refrain in 18:1, Amit (1990:6) argues that "the device of repetition and the contiguity of the two statements (i.e. the long and short refrain) cause the reader to assign to the partial repetition the significance of the entire statement, and the reader thinks of the days without a king as that period in which 'every man did what seemed right in his own eyes.'" Noth (1962:80 n. 30), Wilson (74), McMillion (232,237), and Mayes (2001:242) also argue that the audience would naturally remember the full refrain even though its second half is not repeated in 18:1 and 19:1.

[58] Incidentally, Judg. 14:3,7 and the full refrain (17:6; 21:25) are the only times the phrase ישר בעין occurs within the book.

[59] An interesting suggestion by Fokkelman (1992:43–44) is that the ellipsis of the refrain in 19:1 may actually be deliberate so that what is left out in the short refrain is explored in the following story of the rape of the concubine. The permission given by the host to the Gibeathites in 19:24 to do to her what is good in their eyes (הטוב בעיניכם) thus serves as a concrete illustration that fills out the ellipsis. But if such a possibility can indeed be entertained concerning the ellipsis in 19:1, then cannot a similar possibility also be entertained for 18:1, whereby the story of the Danites taking what looked good to them actually serves as a concrete illustration that fills out a similar ellipsis?

[60] Thus, Bal (76) characterises Samson's desire as "illegitimate" because the woman was a foreigner.

Of course, how the parents' words are to be evaluated precisely in this context is a matter of some debate, especially in light of the narrator's immediate comment in 14:4 that Samson's parents had been ignorant of YHWH's involvement behind Samson's choice. Therefore it is not immediately clear whether Samson was justified in making that choice or whether his parents' evaluation of the matter was correct.

In considering this matter, however, the following factor must be borne in mind. While the narrator's comment can indeed be construed as a defence of Samson's choice, the fact remains that had that choice been readily recognisable as appropriate and the parents' reaction as misguided, the comment would not have been necessary in the first place. Therefore, the very fact that the narrator needed to insert a special comment at this point suggests that the parents' perspective would have constituted the normal and expected viewpoint.

This is further substantiated by the following facts. First, the characterisation of Samson's parents is generally very positive in the preceding episode of his birth. Granted, many have noted that Manoah is portrayed as somewhat of an obtuse, comic character who takes a secondary role to his wife in the birth narrative.[61] But even so, both parents are presented as essentially devout YHWHists. In fact, as Soggin points out, "the Israelite family portrayed here is somewhat idealised, the home of ancient virtue in sharp contrast with the general sexual and ethical disorder of the protagonist".[62] For this reason, Soggin further suggests that the objection of "Samson's pious parents" in 14:3 to their son's desire to take a Philistine wife is to be understood as taking place under an "ideal framework of a believing and practising family".[63]

Second, in the introduction of the central section in Judges 3:5–6, intermarriage with the surrounding non-Israelite nations is spoken of

---

[61] Exum, 1980:58; Alter, 1983:124; Block, 1999:397.

[62] Soggin, 1987:236.

[63] Ibid., 237. Incidentally, this seems to represent a far better understanding of the parents' objection than that of Block (1999:425), who argues from silence that because the parents did not explicitly mention anything about YHWH's command or Samson's Nazirite status, their objection was purely cultural and ethnic and had nothing to do with covenantal issues. Block even suggests that the parents might find acceptable a wife from the surrounding Canaanites as long as she was not Philistine!

negatively in connection with idolatry. And although the Philistines are not explicitly listed in 3:5, their being mentioned in 3:3 as one the nations left to test Israel suggests that intermarriage with the Philistines is to be regarded as no different from intermarriage with the sons and daughters of any of the other foreign nations.

Third, the majority of scholars seem to be in agreement that Samson's repeated involvement with undesirable women, of which the Philistine woman is one, is generally to be evaluated negatively in the context of the book. In fact, there is a view not unpopular among scholars that Samson is to be looked upon as symbolic of Israel as his lust for foreign and inappropriate women is seen as analogous to Israel's love for idols.[64]

Thus, taken together, the above facts suggest that the readers are expected to identify with the parents' objection. In fact, this could well be why the narrator felt it necessary to supply an editorial comment in 14:4 to explain the situation further.

But still, what is the point of this editorial comment? If it is indeed not meant to be an endorsement of Samson's choice and an invalidation of his parents' objection, another possibility is to see it as an attempt to exonerate Samson by clearing him of ultimate responsibility. But such an interpretation is also not without difficulties. For in the process of absolving Samson, the responsibility for his sin will have rested squarely on YHWH instead. And as Greene points out, the notion of YHWH leading Samson into sin in order to save the nation would present a significant theological problem not only for the modern reader but also for the ancient audience.[65]

But perhaps there is a third way to look at this. As Chisholm points out, although 14:4 may suggest YHWH having directly caused Samson to make the choice he did, the language used does not restrict one to such an interpretation. In fact, it is possible to understand the verse as asserting that YHWH had allowed Samson to follow his desires because He could still use the situation to accomplish His goals.[66] A possible parallel would be Joseph's interpretation of his brothers' actions in Gen. 45:5–8; 50:19–20. For in the context

[64] Gros Louis, 161; Greenstein, 1981b:247–53; Webb, 1987:200–01; Wilson, 78–79; O'Connell, 223–24.
[65] Greene, 64.
[66] Chisholm, 107–08.

of Genesis, God is certainly not presented as approving of the brothers' wicked deeds. Yet He allowed those deeds to happen, and even used them to accomplish deliverance for Jacob's family.

But if Joseph's interpretation of his brothers' action can indeed serve as an analogy for interpreting the editorial comment in Judg. 14:4, then the point of the comment is not so much to justify Samson's choice as it is to explain how such an apparently undesirable choice could still lead to a relatively positive outcome as some of Israel's enemies were struck down in the process.[67] In this case, the objection of Samson's parents would remain valid, and Samson's choice of marriage partner on the basis of what he saw would be regarded as an inferior choice in light of the available alternative of choosing from among his own people.

But if Samson's choice on the basis of what he saw is indeed presented as an inferior choice, then in a way, the same can also be said of the Danites' choice. For while the city Laish which the spies saw indeed represented an easy target, the fact remains that this was not the inheritance originally assigned to the tribe by lot in the presence of YHWH (Josh. 19:40–46,48). And not only is this fact subtly referred to in 18:1, it is also implied in 1:34–35 of the prologue, which in turn alludes to Josh. 19:40–48. In fact, in Josh. 19:47, Dan's northern conquest is presented as the tribe's own 'Plan B' in light of their failure to claim the inheritance originally allotted to them under 'Plan A'. Therefore, for both Samson and the Danites, one can say that their respective search for mate and land to guarantee the perpetuity of their future has gone beyond the choices originally prescribed by YHWH in favour of what they saw (ראה) that looked 'right in their eyes'.

But if the above parallels between the two episodes can indeed be sustained, what then is the point of such a link? Does one episode serve to throw additional light on the other by further illuminating the possible motives of the protagonists? Unfortunately, it does not seem so. For parallels notwithstanding, each episode seems to offer little additional insight into the other with regard to why the pro-

[67] Note also that throughout the narrative, Samson is repeatedly portrayed as wanting to form marriage/sexual alliances with the Philistines. In view of this, the editorial comment may actually be drawing attention to the fact that it was really YHWH and not Samson who was actively seeking to deliver Israel from her Philistine oppressors.

tagonists chose to act the way they did. Therefore, if the Danites' decision to attack an isolated and peaceful settlement on the basis of what they saw (ראה) seems to demand some kind of explanation, the only quasi-explanation available here is that such things are not unprecedented. For one of Israel's judges also had a history of allowing what he saw (ראה) govern his choices, and as a result, an inferior choice was made.

4. *The Levite's wooing and abandoning of the concubine echoes Samson's wooing and abandoning of his wife*

The second of two major narratives comprising the epilogue of Judges opens in Judges 19 with an episode concerning another Levite. This Levite was from the hill country of Ephraim, and had travelled to Bethlehem of Judah in order to woo back[68] a concubine who had acted unfaithfully by leaving him and returning to her father's house.[69] Having succeeded in wooing her back, he then set off for home with her and his servant, making it as far as around Jebus by nightfall. Not willing to spend the night in a non-Israelite city, the Levite and his company journeyed on to Gibeah in Benjamin, where they finally received hospitality from an old Ephraimite after a significant wait at the city square. But as they were enjoying their evening meal,

[68] דבר על־לב, found eight times in Hebrew Scripture, can certainly connote 'to woo', as Gen. 34:3 and Hos. 2:16 seem to suggest. Otherwise, as used in Gen. 50:21; Ruth 2:13; 2 Sam. 19:18; Isa. 40:2, it simply means 'to speak kindly or with encouraging words'.

[69] Here, some uncertainty exists regarding how זנה is to be understood in 19:2. While the normal sense of the verb is 'to play the harlot', and hence, to act unfaithfully, some, on the basis of the LXX translation with ὀργίζομαι in Codex Alexandrinus, have suggested a different root underlying זנה meaning 'to be angry'. This will be dealt with in greater detail in the following discussion. But for now, to those who object to taking זנה in the normal sense because the penalty against the adulteress would have been death (Lev. 20:10), it should be noted that the word may have been used figuratively rather than literally. Indeed, as Boling (1975:274), Bal (81–82), and Tsang (449) point out, since Israelite law did not allow for divorce by a woman, the very act of the concubine walking out on her husband may have been sufficient for her to be regarded as having acted unfaithfully, and hence, having committed adultery. The Hebrew text is therefore interpretive in that the second clause of 19:2 beginning with ותלך מאתו may be explicative of the preceding clause ותזנה עליו פילגשו. Such a use of the consecutive verb form is not uncommon, and according to Waltke and O'Connor (551–52), it is found also in Ruth 2:3 and Exod. 2:10, where both examples also involve a series of two or more consecutive clauses in which the last in the series is explicative of the immediately preceding one.

wicked men of the city came pounding on the old man's door demanding that the Levite be handed over so that they could have sex with him. The host tried to reason with the men, offering instead to sacrifice his own daughter as well as the Levite's concubine. When the offer was rejected, however, the Levite took matters into his own hands and shoved his concubine out of the door, whereupon she was raped all night until dawn. When the Levite woke up the following morning, he found his concubine lying at the doorway unconscious, presumably dead. He then put her on his donkey and went home. After he got home, he cut her into twelve pieces and sent them to the tribes of Israel. This resulted in a collective outcry, which eventually led to a civil war between Benjamin and the rest of Israel in which the tribe of Benjamin was almost annihilated.

This is undoubtedly a bizarre story, not only because of the incredible wickedness of the citizens of Gibeah, calculated to remind one of Sodom and Gomorrah,[70] but also because of some inexplicable behaviour of certain central characters of the story. Among these is the puzzling behaviour of the Levite towards his concubine.

When, at the beginning of the story, one sees the Levite making the journey from the hill country of Ephraim to Bethlehem in Judah just to woo back his concubine, one naturally assumes that, for whatever reason, her presence is desired. This is especially so in light of the explicit suggestion that her departure to her father's house was the wrong thing to do: an act of unfaithfulness.[71] Thus, the Levite's willingness to make the journey for the sole purpose of wooing her back in spite of her error hints at how important she must have been to him.

And yet, as the story progresses, especially to the point when the Levite's welfare was threatened by the wicked men of Gibeah, the Levite's treatment of the concubine suddenly turns appallingly callous. Indeed, Niditch notes that as the Levite prepares to sacrifice his concubine to a violent mob to save himself,

> . . . the language conveys the unconsidered swiftness with which he gives her up and the harshness, 'The man seized his concubine, and made her go out to them outside.' She is cast from that safe world

[70] The similarities between the two narratives have been noted by Culley (1976: 56–59), Lasine (38–41), Niditch (1982:375–78), Block (1990:326–41), Matthews (1992:3–11), and Penchansky (77–88).

[71] This again assumes that the normal sense of זנה is accepted. See n. 69 above.

> to the hostile outside by force. He has not discussed the matter with her; he does not relate to her. There is no communication between them. His only attempt to speak with her comes the next morning when she lies dead at the door.[72]

Lasine comments further on the Levite's reaction after he found her dead the following morning:

> He opens the doors and comes out 'to go on his way' (19:27). Considering the circumstances, the fact that he came outside for the purpose of 'going on his way' is bizarre. The dry, factual tone of the narrative shows that the Levite is acting as though nothing at all had happened the night before, when in reality he had thrown his concubine out to a rabid mob in order to save himself, and perhaps, his host's daughter. The reader must immediately wonder: 'What was he doing all night, while she was being raped and abused? He's acting as though he had a good night's sleep and is cheerfully looking forward to their continued journey.' . . . The Levite's insensitivity reaches absurd proportions when the narrator turns his attention back to him, after describing the woman's posture. The Levite says to her, 'Up, let's get going' (19:28). For him to talk to her as though she were not only alive but ready to continue their journey is totally absurd. He acts as though he were in a hurry to get on the road to beat the morning traffic.[73]

But all this callousness from one who has just travelled all the way from the hill country of Ephraim to Bethlehem to woo back this very concubine? Why bother in the first place if indeed he intends to treat her as an object of so little worth? Surely, here is an incongruity in the characterisation of the Levite that cries out for some kind of explanation. Yet none is forthcoming from the text.

Interestingly, the puzzling behaviour of the Levite seems once again to echo a similar episode in the central section of the book, that of Samson's attempt to woo back his wife[74] in Judg. 15:1–8. While admittedly, the two episodes share very little in terms of vocabulary, there are, however, several plot parallels that immediately strike one as analogous.

First, both narratives begin with the protagonist going to the house of his in-law with the expressed purpose of winning back an estranged

---

[72] Niditch, 1982:370.

[73] Lasine, 44–45.

[74] Although Samson may not have consummated the marriage with the nameless Philistine woman, who was subsequently given to another, she is nonetheless referred to as אשתו in 15:1.

spouse.[75] Thus, while in 19:2–3, the Levite went to his concubine at her father's house in order to 'speak to her heart (דבר על־לבה)', in 15:1, Samson went to his wife, presumably still living at her father's house, with a gift of a young goat.

Second, both narratives end with the woman in question having come to a violent death. While the Levite's concubine was raped to death (19:25–28), Samson's wife was burned to death along with her father (15:6).

Third, in both narratives, the protagonist then uses the death of the spouse as justification to call for (19:29–20:7) or exact (15:7–8) revenge, even though in reality, it was the action of the protagonist himself that had directly or indirectly caused that death. In the case of the Levite, he was directly responsible for his concubine's death because it was he who threw her to the rabid mob outside (19:25).[76] As for Samson, although his role in his wife's death was not direct, it was nonetheless his burning of the Philistines' grain fields, vineyards, and olive groves that drove them to seek revenge by burning to death his wife and her father (15:4–6). Thus, both protagonists were demanding revenge for horrific deaths that they themselves were partially responsible for.

But while the above three points provide the clearest parallel between the two narratives, there are also a couple of significant albeit not exact correspondences in plot that are worth highlighting. First, in both narratives, the death of the woman can be traced ultimately to a demand for sex. In the case of the concubine, trouble first came when the wicked men of Gibeah came and demanded in 19:22 that the Levite be brought out so that they may 'know him (נדענו)'. As for Samson, his explicitly stated intention of going into his wife's chamber (אבאה אל־אשתי החדרה) in 15:1 also suggests that he had sexual activity in mind.[77] This demand for sex thus becomes

[75] This parallel between the two episodes is also noted by Matthews (1989:250).

[76] Incidentally, this fact is conveniently left out by the Levite when he reported to the tribes about what happened in 20:4–7.

[77] Admittedly, the expression בוא אל followed by a person does not in itself necessarily suggest sexual activity, although it can (Gen. 16:4; 29:21,23; 30:3,4; 38:2,8,9,16,18; Judg. 16:1; Prov. 6:29). Nor does חדר necessarily suggest the bridal chamber or bedroom, although again, it can (Exod. 7:28; 2 Sam. 4:7; 13:10; Song 1:4; Joel 2:6). But taken together in the current context, it seems clear that Samson's desire to enter into his wife's chamber is to consummate the marriage by having sex. Why else would her father refuse and offer instead to give him the younger

the catalyst in each case that sets into motion a chain of events that finally results in death for both women.

Second, the initial demand for sex in each case was refused by a father figure, who not only justified his refusal, but also offered a substitute that was subsequently rejected. In the case of the Levite, as soon as the wicked men of Gibeah made their demand, the host went out to the men and urged them not to do such a vile and disgraceful thing because the Levite was his guest (19:23). Instead, he offered to bring out his own daughter and the Levite's concubine, and gave them permission to mistreat the women in whatever way they desired (19:24). But the offer was rejected by the men, who were unwilling to listen (19:25). In Samson's case, his demand to go to his wife was also denied by the father, who explained to Samson that the daughter in question had already been given to another because he thought Samson hated her (15:2). Instead, he offered Samson the younger and supposedly more attractive daughter (15:2). But this was rejected by Samson, who then used the incident as a justification for getting even with the Philistines (15:3).

Granted, for the last two points, the plot correspondences are not perfect since in the Levite's case, the ones demanding sex are a third party, while in Samson's case, it is the protagonist himself. But this discrepancy notwithstanding, the occurrence of all five parallels in both narratives in the exact same order points to some kind of conscious literary dependence.

That this is so can further be seen in that while all the aforementioned plot features seem integral to the Samson narrative, some of the same features seem superfluous in the narrative concerning the Levite and his concubine. For example, within the larger narrative of Judges 19–21, the episode concerning the Levite and his concubine seems to serve primarily to provide the cause that explains Israel's civil war with Benjamin.[78] If so, then within the episode found in Judges 19, it is really the atrocity of the Gibeathites causing the death of the concubine that is the central focus of the story. This means that what took place before the commencement of the Levite's return journey to the hill country of Ephraim is really of minor

daughter, if all Samson wanted was to talk, or visit, or conduct business of a non-sexual nature with her?

[78] Indeed, Fokkelman (1999:87) understands the function of Judges 19 mainly as fuse for Judges 20–21.

significance. Therefore, for all intents and purposes, the episode could have started with something like: "There was a Levite who travelled with his concubine and his servant from Bethlehem in Judah to the hill country of Ephraim. When they came near Jebus, the day was almost gone. . . .", and nothing of significance to the overall plot of larger narrative would have been lost. As the narrative stands in its current form, however, the detail about the Levite's previous relationship with his concubine and the lavish description of the time he spend at his in-law's house seem curiously irrelevant to the overall plot. In fact, the father-in-law is not even mentioned again. Not only so, as the narrative stands, the impression given that the Levite cared greatly about the concubine also introduces a sense of incongruity in light of the way he later treated her.

Granted, one may argue that the lavish hospitality scenes at the in-law's home are relevant in that the showing of hospitality or the lack thereof does constitute a minor theme that serves to further highlight the chaos and lawlessness of the period.[79] But even so, this still does not explain why the information explaining the separation between the Levite and his concubine has to be given. After all, a man visiting his in-law with his wife or concubine does not require special justification. Thus, the information given in 19:2–3 really seems altogether superfluous, so much so that one suspects its presence in the narrative is solely for the purpose of providing a more complete plot parallel with the Samson episode in 15:1–7. After all, with the Levite presented as making the journey to Bethlehem to woo back the estranged concubine at her father's home, the two narratives would have been presented as effectively sharing plot-wise a similar beginning, middle, and end.

But if this is indeed the case, then it might also help solve an interpretive problem in 19:2. As has been noted earlier, there has been some debate as to how זנה is to be understood in 19:2. Most commentators seem to favour taking the word to mean 'to be angry' over 'to play the harlot',[80] despite the fact that such a meaning for

[79] Lasine, 37–39. Jüngling (294) even sees the hospitality theme as the main theme in the Judges 19 narrative. But this is based on Jüngling's belief that Judges 20 and 21 actually represent later additions that originally did not follow from Judges 19.

[80] Cundall (1968:193); Boling (1975:273–74); Soggin (1987:284); Niditch (1982:366); Block (1999:523).

זנה is otherwise unattested elsewhere in Hebrew Scripture.[81] The reasons for such a preference are as follows.

First, זנה meaning 'to be unfaithful' or 'to play the harlot' is elsewhere never followed by the preposition על, as is the case in Judg. 19:2. Second, two ancient versions seem to support an alternative meaning. For the MT תזנה עליו in 19:2, LXX[A] has ὠργίσθη αὐτω (she was angry with him), while Targum Jonathan has ובסרת עליוהי (she despised him).[82]

While the use of על with זנה is admittedly a difficulty that has no easy solution, the evidence from the versions is not straightforward. Concerning the LXX[A] translation, even Boling acknowledges that the Hebrew behind it is not entirely clear.[83] This is because ὀργίζομαι is normally and consistently used to render the Hebrew phrase חרה־אף (Judg. 2:14,20; 3:8; 6:39; 9:30; 10:7; 14:19), and it is hard to see how this can be confused with זנה. Boling and Block both suggests a possible scribal error in the Hebrew as זנח is wrongly transcribed as זנה in the MT,[84] even though Block promptly dismisses this as less likely than the alternative of retaining the Hebrew and recognising a second root for זנה as 'to be angry'.

What is most curious here, however, is the fact that scholars are so ready to support the LXX[A] and possibly the Targum readings in spite of the paucity of other manuscript support for them. One suspects that the real reason behind this is really not so much because of textual evidence but because the MT reading presents certain difficulties regarding logic and plausibility.[85] Cundall and Matthews, for example, both state that 'she was angry with him' is more plausible than 'she played the harlot against him' because the penalty

---

[81] *HALOT*, probably after Driver, lists 'to be angry' as the meaning of a homonymous root for זנה. This is based primarily on the Akkadian root zenū, which can mean 'to be angry' or 'to hate'. It is believed that 'to hate' has eventually developed into the meaning 'to be apostate', and hence, the meaning 'to be unfaithful' in Hebrew for זנה. But the meaning 'to be angry' is preserved in a homonymous root which shows up in Judg. 19:2 as 'to feel repugnance against'. But not only is this doubtful because the questionable case in Judg. 19:2 represents the only instant where such a root is allegedly found, as Erlandsson (99) and Ringgren (105) respectively point out, the Akkadian root zenū may not even be related to זנה, but instead, to זנח in Hebrew, which means 'to reject, exclude'.

[82] Smelik, 607.

[83] Boling, 1975:274.

[84] Ibid.; Block, 1999:523.

[85] This point is also emphasised by Bal (82–83).

for adultery was death (Lev. 20:10).[86] Boling too, finds it strange that the woman would become a prostitute and then run home.[87] Bohmbach further adds that under such circumstances, the father would surely not welcome her back and provide a place for her for some four months because of the supposed shame she would bring.[88] Similarly, Soggin's preference for 'she was angry at him' is probably also based on logical considerations. After all, he notes that the Levite's behaviour seems to suggest that the responsibility of the matrimonial crisis lay with the husband, and that in view of how glad the concubine and father-in-law were to be reconciled, the quarrel could not have been very serious.[89] All of these considerations seem to go against the possibility that the concubine has in fact been unfaithful.

But what if the author's point is precisely to present her as unfaithful?[90] For if, as has been argued, 19:2–3 was penned solely for the sake of providing a parallel to the Samson episode in 15:1–7, then the concubine's unfaithfulness would in fact provide a perfect parallel to Samson's wife, who was estranged from Samson precisely because she had, in a sense, been unfaithful to him by betraying his secret to her people. In fact, Samson's words in 14:18, "Had you not ploughed with my heifer, you would not have solved my riddle" makes it clear that he sees himself as having been betrayed, and that accounts for his angry departure from her. Thus, by taking זנה in the normal sense of the word as 'to be unfaithful' in 19:2, the parallel with 15:1–7 is actually strengthened.[91] There is therefore no need to go out of one's way to find justification for supporting the LXX^{A} reading.[92]

---

[86] Cundall, 1968:193; Matthews, 1992:7.

[87] Boling, 1975:273.

[88] Bohmbach, 90.

[89] Soggin, 1987:284.

[90] Note again that this unfaithfulness does not have to be in the literal sense of having committed adultery. If the unfaithfulness merely refers to her having run away for an undisclosed reason, then much of the logical objections raised above by the various scholars would no longer be an issue.

[91] Such an understanding would thus constitute an argument against Bal's position (83–88) that the 'unfaithfulness' is in fact an offence against the concubine's father rather than against the Levite.

[92] That reading, as well as the Targum reading, can in fact be accounted for by suggesting that the translator had misread זנה for זנח. To smooth out the sense of the verse, the translator of the Targum thus interpreted 'to reject him' as 'to despise him' (well within the semantic range of זנח), while the translator of the LXX^{A} explained it as 'to be angry with him'. Incidentally, the translation of LXX^{B} as

But assuming that a plausible case has been made for the conscious allusion of Judges 19 to the Samson episode in Judges 15, what then is accomplished by such an allusion? Unfortunately, as in the previous incidents, the allusion to Samson in this case again contributes little in terms of providing additional insight into the bizarre and inconsistent behaviour of the Levite towards his concubine. The only message the parallels seem to convey is that the Levite's behaviour, though bizarre, was perhaps not unprecedented after all. For one of the judges of Israel has likewise acted in a very similar manner.

5. *Benjamin's surprisingly incongruent decision to support the guilty Gibeathites echoes Ehud's surprisingly incongruent use of deception*

In the aftermath of the rape and subsequent death of the concubine, the Levite took the concubine home and cut her up into twelve parts, sending them presumably to each of the twelve tribes of Israel in an attempt to rally support to avenge the injustice done. Judges 20 then opens with a gathering of all the tribes of Israel, with the exception of Benjamin, at Mizpah, where a quick investigation was made into the circumstances leading to the horrific crime. The Levite was then called upon to give an eyewitness account of what happened.

Admittedly, the Levite's testimony was not exactly an accurate reflection of the events as they happened. As many have pointed out, the testimony the Levite gave in 20:4–7 consists of clear discrepancies when compared with the actual account of the events in 19:22–28.[93] These discrepancies in the testimony were undoubtedly self-serving, intending to cast the Levite in a more favourable light as the danger he faced was exaggerated and the role he played in sending the concubine out to her death was left out. But that notwithstanding, the overall guilt of the Gibeathites in the rape and subsequent death of the concubine was not in dispute.

Upon hearing the Levite's testimony, the Israelites 'rose as one man' and decided to go up against Gibeah to exact justice for the crime committed. But this was not before the tribes decided to first send representatives to Benjamin demanding that the guilty party be

---

ἐπορεύθη ἀπ' αὐτοῦ (she went away from him) may also be based either on an interpretive misreading of זנה as זנח or on an attempt to explain the precise sense of זנה.

[93] J. Gray, 382; Polzin, 201; Niditch, 1982:371; Lasine, 48–49; Tsang, 466–67; Block, 1999:554; Schneider, 267.

handed over. In so doing, the Israelites appear to have at least shown proper deference to tribal-political protocol. Moreover, the explicit reason given in 20:13 for demanding that the guilty party be handed over, namely, for them to be put to death so that the evil can be purged from Israel (נבערה רעה מישׂראל), is a legitimate one, not to mention that Benjamin, being a part of Israel, would also stand to benefit from such a purging.

Yet in a most bizarre turn of events, not only did Benjamin refuse to turn over the guilty party, they did the opposite by rallying to the defence of the Gibeathites,[94] gathering their troops at Gibeah in order to fight against the rest of Israel. In fact, this show of solidarity by the Benjaminites towards the Gibeathites is further highlighted by the fact that seven hundred[95] chosen Gibeathites ended up joining the Benjaminite contingent as active participants.

But in light of the obvious guilt of the Gibeathites, why did the Benjaminites decide to side with Gibeah against the rest of Israel?[96] Unfortunately, no explanation appears to have been given in the text. Yet a subtle allusion to one of the judges may actually shed some light on the matter.

In reporting the Benjaminites' solidarity with the Gibeathites as they prepared for war, it is specifically mentioned in 20:16 that seven hundred Benjaminites within their contingent are 'restricted in the right hand (אטר יד־ימינו)'. Furthermore, these left-handers were also said to be able to sling a stone at a hair and not miss.

Here, several things should be noted. First, in the larger context of the account of the civil war that immediately follows, there is no further mention of stone-slingers in the ensuing battle. This, of course, does not necessarily mean that the stone-slingers did not play a role

[94] This, according to Amit (1998:338–39, 343–44), portrays Benjamin as acting in an exceptional way and in opposition to biblical norms, thus reflecting their distorted values.

[95] There is a textual problem in 20:15–16 that makes it unclear as to whether the number 700 actually occurs only once (the versions), referring either to the number of Gibeathites or the number of left-handed slingers, or whether it occurs twice (MT) referring respectively to both groups. As this textual problem is extremely complicated and does not appear to alter the facts that some Gibeathites did join the Benjaminite contingent and part of the Benjaminite contingent consisted of left-handed slingers, I will simply note the problem at this juncture without pursuing it any further.

[96] Indeed, Soggin (1987:282) remarks that the Benjaminites could have just handed over the guilty ones and justice would have taken its course.

at all, for there seems to be evidence elsewhere to suggest that stone-slinging can be an important part of Israelite warfare.[97] In spite of this, however, in the description of the battle that follows, the emphasis seems to be on the sword as the principle weapon, as חרב appears seven times within the battle narrative.[98] In fact, the entire Benjaminite and Israelite contingent are characterised specifically in 20:15,17 as איש שלף חרב. What this suggests, therefore, is that from a rhetorical perspective, the mention of the stone-slinging ability of the seven hundred left-handed Benjaminites is actually superfluous in relation to the following battle narrative. The superb marksmanship of these stone-slinging left-handers is therefore most likely brought up primarily to clarify that their left-handedness is not to be construed as a liability but as an asset. To that end, they may even be presented as somewhat of an elite force even though this does not appear to have any direct plot relevance in the context of the battle narrative.

But even so, the question still remains as to why the left-handedness of these seven hundred warriors needs to be brought up in the first place. For like the detail about their stone-slinging ability, the left-handedness of these Benjaminite warriors appears to have no particular relevance in the context of the battle narrative. For no further mention was made of them in the rest of the narrative, such that for all intents and purposes, the entire reference to the seven hundred left-handed, stone-slinging Benjaminites in 20:16 can be left out altogether and the plot would not have suffered in the slightest. Why then, was this seemingly pointless piece of information included at this point in the narrative?

To answer this question, a second thing one needs to note is that the specific language used to describe the left-handedness of these Benjaminite warriors is highly unusual. Normally, one would expect some form of שׂמאל to be used to indicate left-handedness, as that would seem the most direct way. Indeed, such a form is used in 1 Chron. 12:2 as well as in Judg. 3:21, where Ehud's left-handed activity is described with: וישלח אהוד את־יד שׂמאלו.

But in Judges 20:16, these Benjaminites are described as אטר יד־ימינו, an obscure expression that, incidentally, has only been used one other time in Hebrew Scripture: to describe another Benjaminite,

[97] Cf. 2 Kgs. 3:25; 2 Chron. 26:14; Zech. 9:15.
[98] Judg. 20:15,17,25,35,37,48.

Ehud, in Judges 3:15. In fact אטר is such a rare word that its precise meaning is still uncertain, as it is found as an adjective only in Judg. 3:15 and 20:16 and as a verb only in Ps. 69:16. Taking into consideration the immediate context, the verb in Ps. 69:16 is generally understood to mean 'to close' by comparison with the Arabic cognate *ʾatara* (meaning 'to fence around'). The adjective is then generally taken to mean 'bound' or 'restricted'.[99] But even if this meaning is accepted, there is still a great deal of debate with regard to what exactly the phrase אטר יד־ימינו refers to. Here, commentators seem almost equally divided into those who take the phrase to refer to a physical handicap,[100] ambidexterity,[101] or left-handedness.[102]

But regardless of what this highly unusual phrase refers to exactly, the fact that it is used only twice in Hebrew Scripture, both in the same book and both referring to people from Benjamin, seems to argue strongly for a case of conscious allusion. That the use of the phrase in 3:15 is original and is being alluded to in 20:16 also seems a reasonable inference, since the phrase in 20:16, and indeed, that whole verse, seems unmotivated by plot necessity and is inexplicable within its immediate context. Thus, if it can be shown that the use of the phrase in 3:15 is in fact rhetorically significant, then a case can be made that 20:16 depends on 3:15.

So, is the use of אטר יד־ימינו in 3:15 rhetorically significant in its immediate context? The answer appears to be in the affirmative, since in the immediately preceding epithet, Ehud is identified as a Benjaminite (בן־הימיני), thus allowing ימין in the two consecutive epithets to form a significant wordplay.

To be sure, the suggestion of wordplay is dismissed by Lindars as an example of over-interpretation.[103] Nonetheless, it should not be

[99] Not all subscribe to such an interpretation. Kornfeld (105–07) argues that אטר is derived from the Akkadian *ētēru* 'deliver', thus taking the phrase in Judg. 3:15 to mean that Ehud is capable of saving with the right hand. But as Lindars (1995:141) rightly points out, this does not make sense in the context of the Ehud story, and should therefore be rejected as a viable interpretive option.

[100] Alonso-Schökel, 148–49; Soggin, 1987:50; 1989:96–97; Webb, 1987:131; Chalcraft, 183; Handy, 236; Tsang, 116.

[101] Rösel, 1977:270; Halpern, 40–43; Block, 1999:161.

[102] Boling, 1975:86; Dexinger, 268–69; Marais, 92; Jugel and Neef, 46–47. This position is apparently also supported by medieval Jewish commentators such as Rashi and Kimchi, as translated by Rosenberg (21,162) and reported by Dexinger (269) and Lindars (1995:141).

[103] Lindars, 1995:141. Here Lindars specifically cites Soggin (1987:50, 1989:97)

overlooked that the use of the gentilic form here is somewhat unusual. For in Hebrew Scripture, the normal way to refer to Benjaminites is through the collective בנימין or the epithet בני בנימן. In fact, out of over seventy cases where someone from the tribe is referred to, in only about ten or so is the gentilic form used.[104]

Furthermore, it is also noteworthy that it is apparently in the gentilic form of the tribe name that the original composite nature of the name Benjamin is preserved. For in Gen. 35:18, when the name בנימין is first coined by Jacob, it was in response to a name originally given by Rachel to her son at her deathbed. To reflect an awareness that she would die giving birth to her son, Rachel named the boy בן־אוני (son of my trouble). But his father Jacob renamed him בנימין (son of the right hand),[105] presumably to reflect this son's favoured position in his eyes.[106] But this act of renaming, which essentially left intact the first element of the original name but changed only the second, testifies to the composite nature of the name as it was first given. Of course, over time, as the etiology of the original name faded in significance, the composite form gradually came to be regarded as an indivisible unit. This is most clearly seen in the frequently-occurring בני בנימן, where the initial בן־ of the original composite form is no longer open to inflection, thus making it necessary to introduce a separate בן in construct relationship with the name to express 'sons of Benjamin' or 'Benjaminites'.

---

and Boling (1975:86), but others who also see an intentional wordplay between the two epithets include Auld (1984:148), Ogden (1991:410–11), Handy (236), Amit (1998:179), and Marais (92).

[104] In the book of Judges, בנימין is used 17 times (Judg. 5:14; 20:17,20,25,35(x2), 36,39,40,43,44,46; 21:1,6,14,17,18) and בני בנימן 19 times (Judg. 1:21(x2); 20:3,13(Qere),14,15,18,21,23,24,28,30,31,32,36,48; 21:13,20,23) to refer to someone from the tribe of Benjamin. Only twice (3:15; 19:16) is the gentilic form used.

[105] Auld (1984:148) sees the etiology of the name as a reference to Benjamin being located south of their relatives in Ephraim. But Boling (1975:86) sees this southerly connection as a later tradition, thus favouring a reference to the right hand as a more accurate reflection the original etiology. It should also be noted that although the tribe name is outwardly identical to a group of semi-nomadic southerners known as the Yaminites attested in Mari, Malamat (1989:34–35) sees no connection between the two.

[106] The idea of the right hand being related to favour can be seen in Gen. 48:12–20, where both Jacob and Joseph were apparently aware of the significance attached to being blessed with the right hand versus the left. In Hebrew hymnic literature too, it is well established that the right hand of YHWH is often a reference to His strength and salvation (Exod. 15:6,12; Pss. 20:7; 21:9; 60:7; 63:9; 89:14; 98:1; 118:16).

But for some reason, the composite nature of the original name Benjamin seems to have been preserved in the gentilic form of the tribe name. This is seen primarily in that in gentilic forms, the first element of the name is open to regular inflection as if it were a regular construct chain.[107] Thus, while the gentilic singular appears as בן ימיני,[108] the plural appears as בני ימיני.[109] Furthermore, in the four instances where the gentilic form appears with the definite article as בן־הימיני,[110] the placement of the article is also consistent with the way articles are normally placed in composite construct-chain names.[111] Moreover, the composite nature of the tribe name as preserved in the gentilic appears to be so fluid that in 1 Sam. 9:1, it even allows for the replacement of the first elements of the composite name בן־ with the semantically similar idiomatic expression בן־איש,[112] thus resulting in the form בן־איש ימיני.[113]

In any case, considering how two relatively rare epithets, namely, the gentilic בן־הימיני that seems to preserve the etiological root of the name Benjamin as 'son of the right handers'[114] and the obscure אטר יד־ימינו that expresses left-handedness in a round-about way as restriction of the right hand, are used in succession to characterise Ehud, a case can certainly be made that a wordplay is fully intended, the objections of Lindars notwithstanding. But if so, then the use of

---

[107] Normally, one would not expect etiological components of a proper name to display variable internal inflection, as the whole name is generally taken as a fixed unit.

[108] 1 Sam. 9:21; Ps. 7:1; 1 Chron. 27:12 (Qere).

[109] Judg. 19:16; 1 Sam. 22:7.

[110] Judg. 3:15; 2 Sam. 16:11; 19:17; 1 Kgs. 2:8.

[111] See Waltke and O'Connor, 245, and Joüon, 518. Other such examples include אבי העזרי in Judg. 6:11,24; בית הלחמי in 1 Sam. 16:1,18; 17:58; 2 Sam. 21:19; בית האלי in 1Kgs. 16:43.

[112] The expression בן־איש is also similarly used in Lev. 24:14 and 1Sam. 17:12, where it is immediately followed by gentilic forms, and in 2 Sam. 1:13; 20:23; 1 Chron. 11:22.

[113] In 2 Sam. 20:1 and Esth. 2:5, the form איש ימיני also appears, reflecting either the replacement of the בן־ with another word in roughly the same semantic range, or a form similar to בן־איש ימיני in 1 Sam. 9:1, but with the semantically redundant בן־ having dropped off. Another somewhat unusual occurrence is also found in 1 Sam. 9:4, but there, McCarter (174–75) argues that ארץ־ימיני in the MT actually represents a toponymic corruption.

[114] One wonders if this may indeed be an example of what Bar Efrat (270) refers to as a conscious reviving of fossilised expressions through the restoration of full stylistic value so as to hint at an original meaning.

אטר יד־ימינו in 3:15 is in fact rhetorically significant in its immediately context. This, therefore, makes it all the more likely that the otherwise unmotivated use of the same phrase in 20:16 is an attempt at a conscious allusion to 3:15.

But still, what is the point of the allusion? To answer this question, one must go back to the Ehud narrative to discover what exactly the rhetorical significance is of the wordplay involving בן־הימיני and אטר יד־ימינו.

In this regard, most commentators seem to agree that the main point of the wordplay is to show Ehud, the left-handed 'son of the right-handers', to be an unlikely choice for a hero.[115] But while Ehud being an unexpected choice for a hero is undoubtedly conveyed by the punning epithets, one wonders if such an explanation is sufficiently precise to capture the full force of the wordplay. After all, that Ehud was an unlikely choice for a hero is precisely because a 'son of the right-handers' is expected to excel in his right hand. Yet this בן־הימיני is אטר יד־ימינו!

Here, the extremely rare אטר, often translated as 'bound' or 'restricted', seems to connote some sort of deficiency.[116] Thus if Ehud was an unlikely choice for a hero, it is precisely because he seems to have fallen short in the very area that is supposed to define his core identity as a 'son of the right-handers'.

But if the point of the wordplay is indeed to highlight a 'falling short' in a core area of one's identity, then assuming, as Bar-Efrat does, that "in general, no information is included in the exposition which does not have a definite function in the development of the action",[117] can one not further extend this sense of 'falling short' and see it as subtly foreshadowing certain of Ehud's actions in the ensuing narrative? In this, one is reminded particularly of Ehud's use of deception to facilitate his assassination of Eglon, King of Moab.

[115] Sternberg (332), for example, writes that given the cultural associations of right vs. left, the normative circumlocution "radicalizes . . . our wonder at God's choice of such an ill-omened deliverer." Auld (1984:148–49), commenting on the pun, also highlights what an "improbable assailant" Ehud was for the Lord to use. Klein (1988:37) writes that Ehud as "an unlikely choice is immediately suggested". And Andersson (36) remarks that "God's using remarkable and unexpected heroes when saving Israel is a common motif in OT that appears over and over again in the book of Judges".

[116] Hence some actually argue that Ehud was handicapped in the right hand.

[117] Bar Efrat, 114.

That deception was used repeatedly by Ehud[118] is a fact commentators generally do not dispute.[119] In fact, Culley even uses the Ehud narrative as a typical illustration of a sub-genre known as 'deception story',[120] while Webb points to deception as having played an "absolutely central role" within the narrative.[121] What is controversial, however, is how this use of deception is to be evaluated.

On the one hand, Webb, among others, argues that the "grotesquely comic character of the story makes moral judgements irrelevant".[122] He also asserts that Ehud being YHWH's chosen saviour who has been raised up makes his deceptions "providentially directed and guaranteed".[123] A similar position is also held by Amit, who sees YHWH as essentially behind Ehud's actions.[124] Chalcraft likewise argues that Ehud's deception is only 'potentially deviant' and does not reflect negatively on his character because its target is the 'out-group' who is "a deserving victim of maltreatment".[125] These commentators therefore see little cause for concern with respect to the use of deception, and generally maintain that Ehud should legitimately be viewed as the hero of the story.[126]

On the other hand, however, there are also others who, on moral grounds, are far less comfortable with Ehud's tactics. Among these, Klein is especially vehement in her criticism of Ehud, attributing his deception and trickery to an apparent unwillingness to rely on YHWH.[127] She also asserts that YHWH was absent from Ehud's

---

[118] These include taking advantage of his left-handedness to hide his dagger on the right thigh, attempting to gain Eglon's trust through his role as a tribute-bearer, deliberately cultivating a sense of mystery by first leaving and then turning back after having crossed the border, consciously misleading Eglon with his ambiguous word choice, falsely invoking God's name to arouse Eglon's curiosity, and turning Eglon's trust into an opportunity for assassination.

[119] Boling (1975:88) calls Ehud's actions a "single piece of diplomatic treachery". Block (1999:160) calls Ehud a "master of deceit". O'Connell (85,91–92) and Tsang (116) also commented on Ehud's use of deceptive tactics.

[120] Culley, 1974:177–78; 1975:5,7–9.

[121] Webb, 1987:130–31.

[122] Ibid., 131.

[123] Ibid., 132.

[124] Amit, 1989:98–99,120–21; 1998:172–73,178,181.

[125] Chalcraft, 183–84.

[126] In fact, Miller (116) comments that "the story clearly portrays the setting in which Ehud acts as false or inverted, such that killing the host was not only appropriate, but honourable".

[127] Klein, 1988:46. Polzin (160) also thinks that Ehud is not portrayed as particularly likeable, coming across in the narrative as "repugnant, deceitful, and cruel".

actions because he elevated ends over means.[128] O'Connell, commenting not so much on Ehud's use of deception but on his invoking of YHWH's name in the subsequent battle, likewise leaves open the possibility that Ehud's actions may not have been viewed entirely positively. For O'Connell, however, such an evaluation is not immediately obvious from the text. Rather, it is only "the subsequent growing concern of the Judges compiler/redactor with the leadership qualities of Israel's deliverers" that leads him "in retrospect, to inquire whether Ehud's characterisation as a self-promoting saviour is an intended nuance".[129]

Such negative evaluation of Ehud is categorically rejected by Andersson as 'disturbing' as he considers them clearly going against the 'norm of the story' had the story been properly read as an autonomous literary unit rather than as an extract from a larger text.[130] In particular, Andersson's objection focussed on the fact that alleged support for negative readings of the text are often drawn from themes imported into the narrative from the larger context. But what if an argument can be made from within the Ehud narrative to support a less-than-positive reading?

Consider again the wordplay between בן־הימיני and אטר יד־ימינו. Understood in its narrowest sense, the wordplay undoubtedly highlights the surprising choice of a 'son of the right-handers' who turns out to be 'restricted in the right hand'. But if the element of surprise rests on the fundamental incongruity between Ehud's restriction in the right hand and his core identity as a 'son of the right-handers', then is it not possible to see this incongruities as being applied at a deeper level to hint at another set of incongruity equally significant with respect to the plot, namely, the incongruity between Ehud's use of deceptive tactics to assassinate, and his core identity as a deliverer raised up by YHWH?

What is being suggested here is that rhetorically, the wordplay that introduces Ehud in the exposition may actually have a more significant role to play with regard to his characterisation than is generally recognised. Instead of simply highlighting Ehud's left-handedness, the incongruity revealed by the wordplay may carry deeper

[128] Klein, 38.
[129] O'Connell, 97–98.
[130] Andersson, 48–49.

symbolic significance in portraying Ehud as someone whose actions and choices are liable to fall short of the standard expected of him on the basis of who he is.[131] Thus, if the choice of Ehud is surprising, it is surprising not only because his restriction in the right hand obviously fell short of the norm expected of a 'son of the right-handers', but also because the tactics he used likewise fell short of the standard expected of a deliverer raised up by YHWH.

In relation to this, one can perhaps point to two further observations that may provide some support to such an interpretation.[132] The first is the general observation that in ancient Near-Eastern cultures, left-handedness was often considered peculiar and unnatural.[133] In fact, in his discussion of the Sumerian-Akkadian text "Enlil and Ninlil: The Marriage of Sud", Civil refers to a polarisation commonly found in Mesopotamian didactic and ritual texts where opposing ethical implications are associated with the respective sides of the two hands: the right is regarded as pure, and the left, impure.[134] To be sure, this observation on its own may not be significant enough to bear upon the interpretation of Ehud's left-handedness. But given that the rare אטר, which seems to be intentionally chosen to describe Ehud's left-handedness, also conveys a sense of deficiency, one wonders if the negative connotation usually associated with left-handedness may not have been deliberately preserved and subtly worked into the ensuing plot of the narrative.[135]

---

[131] That the wordplay may carry a deeper symbolic significance should not be immediately dismissed. After all, even at the most superficial level, the surface incongruity is largely symbolic rather than real. For surely in reality, no one would expect all Benjaminites to be right-handed simply because they are descendants of Benjamin, 'son of the right hand'. Thus, that this 'son of the right-handers' should be restricted in the right hand is surprising only because the incongruity is readily understood as operating on a symbolic level. In other words, the issue here is not so much whether the wordplay should be understood symbolically, but how far that symbolism extends.

[132] There is actually a third argument that seems to lend further support to this somewhat negative interpretation of Ehud's use of deception, and it has to do with possible inter-biblical allusions made to Ehud in the negative portrayal of Joab in 2 Sam. 3:27 and 20:8–10. For detail of this argument, see Wong, 2006a: forthcoming.

[133] Boling, 1975:86. Feldman (184) even sees this as a possible explanation for Josephus' omission of all mentions of Ehud using his left hand in his retelling of the story.

[134] Civil, 46–47.

[135] In this respect, although Miller's interpretation (114) of Ehud's 'restriction in the right hand' as a physical defect may be disputed, his observation that "a dys-

The second observation is more directly related to the text, and has to do with the interpretation of another phrase found in the immediately context. Here, one notices that in the exposition section of the Ehud narrative, two disjunctive clauses in 3:16–17 interrupts the overall flow of the narrative. The first disjunctive gives a detailed description of the חרב Ehud made for himself, while the second focuses on the physical build of Eglon King of Moab. Commentators are generally in agreement that the two clauses provide vital information relevant to the ensuing plot of the narrative. But while it gradually becomes clear as the plot unfolds why information about the length of the weapon and the size of its intended victim is previewed,[136] the significance of the double-edged blade remains less obvious. And although numerous plausible explanations have been advanced,[137] the text itself offers no clarification.

Taking a different approach, however, Good understands the relevance of the double-edged blade primarily in terms of its symbolic value. Noting that the usual term for the business edge of a sword is literally 'mouth (פה)', he sees irony in the way the word is used in conjunction with Ehud's 'message': Ehud's cryptic words are double-edged like his sword.[138]

In the same vein, Handy also notes that 3:15–16 seem to play upon the deception both with the hand and with the double-mouthed blade. In fact, he even wonders whether an idiom exists in Hebrew for 'double-talk' that is related to 'double-mouthed'.[139]

While neither Good nor Handy went any further to explore this link between Ehud's sword and his words, such a link, however, is worth pursuing for the following reasons. First, there has always been a close connection between חרב and the group of words that are

functional right hand in those days was almost certainly taken as a mark of other defects" is something worth bearing in mind.

[136] The relative shortness of the sword coupled with the enormity of its intended victim is apparently what allowed the sword to be sunk completely into the king's belly, such that it did not need to be removed in the aftermath of the assassination (3:21).

[137] These include Lindars' suggestion (1995:142) that a double-edge is particularly suitable for a straight plunge rather than a hacking stroke, Amit's suggestion (1989:108, 1998:182) that a double-edge is effective for quick action, and Alter's suggestion (1981:39) that a double-edge is lethal through a quick thrust.

[138] Good, 33–34.

[139] Handy, 240.

associated with mouth and speech. For not only is חרב often described as having a mouth (פה)[140] or mouths[141] that can be opened (פתח)[142] to devour (אכל)[143] or be satiated (רוה),[144] words and speech are also often characterised as being like the חרב.[145]

But second, and more importantly, in the narrative itself, Ehud did in fact rely on the deceptive use of words with double meaning to accomplish his mission. While Eglon was probably led to lower his guard because he understood the דבר־סתר from אלהים to be a secret oracle from some god he recognised,[146] Ehud knew, however, that the דבר־סתר from אלהים he was about to deliver was none other than the secret weapon he had brought on behalf of YHWH. In this respect, the דבר Ehud was referring to may have been the חרב he brought, the equation of one with the other made even more obvious in that while the secret דבר had two meanings, the hidden חרב had two mouths (שני פיות)!

But if the דבר־סתר capable of double meaning was indeed, for Ehud, none other than the hidden weapon with two mouths, and the hidden weapon with two mouths indeed needed the דבר־סתר with a double meaning to create an opportunity for its deployment, then is it not possible to understand the reference to the חרב with שני פיות in 3:16 as a subtle anticipation of Ehud's use of deceptive words to accomplish his goal?[147] And if, as Alter believes, every detail in the exposition of the narrative in 3:15–16 contributes to a clear understanding of just how Ehud's mission was accomplished,[148] then

[140] The idiomatic phrase for 'edge of the sword' is לפי־חרב. See Gen. 32:26; Exod. 17:13; Deut. 13:16; Josh. 6:21; Judg. 1:8; 1 Sam. 22:19; 2 Kgs. 10:25.

[141] Judg. 3:16; Ps. 149:6; Prov. 5:4.

[142] Ps. 37:14; Ezek. 21:33.

[143] Deut. 32:42; 2 Sam. 2:26; 11:25; 18:8; Prov. 30:14; Isa. 1:20; 31:8; Jer. 2:30; 12:12; 46:10,14; Hos. 11:6; Nah. 2:14.

[144] Isa. 34:5; Jer. 46:10.

[145] Speech-related words that are compared to or described as חרב include לשון (Pss. 57:5; 64:4), פה (Isa. 49:2), שן (Prov. 30:14), חך (Prov. 5:3–4), שפה (Prov. 5:3–4), and בטה (Prov. 12:18). Furthermore, in Ps. 59:8 and Job 5:15, the חרב is also said to come forth from the פה.

[146] While most commentators are aware of the double meaning in Ehud's use of דבר in 3:19–20, it is Handy (236–37) who points out that even the use of אלהים may be a case of double meaning. For while Ehud may have had YHWH in mind as he thought about the deployment of his secret weapon, his deliberate avoidance of the divine name may be intended to fool Eglon into thinking that the divine oracle was from some other god.

[147] This is also briefly suggested by McCann (44).

[148] Alter, 1981:38.

would it not be far more satisfying to take the reference to the double-edged blade as foreshadowing the tactics Ehud would use, rather than to come up with possible explanations for that detail that have little overt support from the text?

But if the description of Ehud's weapon in the exposition indeed turns out to have symbolic significance in foreshadowing his verbal duplicity in the ensuing narrative, then it is likely that the description of Ehud's physical attributes through the wordplay involving ימין also functions similarly in hinting at the surprising tactics he would use. Taken together therefore, the unexpected left-handed 'son of the right-handers' wielding a double mouthed weapon would constitute a fitting symbolic introduction to an incongruously deceptive deliverer who would attempt an assassination with the help of verbal double entendres.[149]

But even if it is true that the point of the wordplay between אטר יד־ימינו and בן־הימיני in 3:15 is to hint at the incongruity between Ehud's tactics and his core identity as a deliverer from YHWH, how would this be relevant in the context of 20:16, where the same אטר יד־ימיני appears again? Especially since the significance of the phrase in 3:15 is derived primarily from a wordplay that is not repeated in the context of Judges 20, to what extent can one argue that the use of the phrase in 20:16 might carry similar rhetorical implications as in 3:15?

Admittedly, a comparable wordplay to the one found in 3:15 does not appear in 20:16. But significantly, those described as אטר יד־ימינו in 20:16 are also Benjaminites. And although it is true that in the immediate context of Judges 20, the more conventional בני בנימן is used rather than the rarer gentilic form as is in 3:15, in 19:16, the rarer gentilic form בני ימיני is in fact used to describe the Gibeathites, who, according to 20:14–15, joined the Benjaminite contingent as active participants.

But the important thing is, simply because no overt wordplay is found in the immediate context of 20:16 does not mean that a similar rhetorical function as that found in 3:15 must automatically be ruled out. For if the rhetorical significance of the wordplay involving אטר יד־ימינו in 3:15 is understood primarily in relation to someone of Benjaminite origin, then when this phrase is applied subsequently

[149] Incidentally, Marais (93) thinks that this kind of foreshadowing adds suspense to the story, as information is often given at a stage in the narrative where it seems unnecessary, only for their full implications to become relevant at a later stage.

also to others of Benjaminite origin, one can conceivably dispense with the wordplay and the same rhetorical force could still be understood by a reader who has already grasped the significance of the phrase in the earlier context. Thus, when Benjaminite warriors are described in 20:16 as אטר יד־ימינו, a reader who already understands that phrase as hinting at some kind of deviation from or falling short of an expected norm when applied to Ehud the Benjaminite would probably understand the phrase as implying the same thing in 20:16. If so, the characterisation of an elite force within the Benjaminite contingent as אטר יד־ימינו[150] may indeed be a subtle hint that the Benjaminites' decision to go to war against the rest of Israel in defence of their obviously guilty fellow-tribesmen is in fact something that falls short of the expected norm and is therefore incongruous with their core identity as Israelites.

But even assuming that the use of אטר יד־ימינו in association with Benjaminites in 20:16 indeed hints at incongruous behaviour that falls short of an expected norm, no explanation is offered to account for such behaviour. For the only thing the allusion to Ehud shows is that the Benjaminites in Judges 20 were displaying the same propensity as Ehud of acting incongruously with respect to their core identity. But just as no clear explanation has been offered to account for Ehud's surprising choice of tactics, so no clear explanation has been offered to account for the Benjaminites' surprising choice of alliance. What the allusion does point to, however, is that the bizarre behaviour of these Benjaminites in Judges 20 is no isolated incident when it comes to Benjaminites. For another Benjaminite, a judge of Israel, no less, has also displayed the same propensity to act in a way that falls short of the expected norm.

[150] That אטר יד־ימינו is not applied to the entire Benjaminite contingent is probably out of logical necessity, as it would seem unrealistic if not downright unbelievable to suggest that the entire Benjaminite contingent of 26,000 are left-handers. Thus, an elite force of stone slingers, which does not figure at all in the ensuing narrative, is introduced specifically to serve a representative role. By presenting them as the best of the Benjaminites, they are thus qualified to represent the whole tribe. The deviance associated with them as implied in their description as אטר יד־ימינו is therefore associated with the whole tribe by extension.

6. *The harshness with which Israel dealt with Benjamin in war echoes the same harshness with which Gideon and Jephthah dealt with their fellow Israelites*

With the Benjaminites refusing to hand over the guilty party but instead, gathering warriors in preparation for war, the rest of Israel also mustered their troops in response. Battle soon ensued, and perhaps not surprisingly, the rest of Israel won decisively. What is surprising, however, is the level of united determination and degree of harshness with which the Israelites dealt with their brother Benjamin in the course of battle. This comes across especially clearly when this determined harshness against a brother is viewed in the context of Israel's consistent failure to deal similarly with their foreign enemies throughout the book.[151]

In the prologue, for example, after some initial successes in which the חרם was applied to Canaanites in Zephath (1:17) and possibly Jerusalem (1:8),[152] the rest of the prologue is followed by a series of לא־הוריש's which characterises almost every tribe of Israel.[153] As a result of their collective failure to dispossess and destroy[154] the nations, YHWH indicated through His messenger in 2:3 that He would no longer dispossess them before the Israelites.

With the nations now cohabiting with the Israelites, the Israelites soon started developing more intimate relationships with them. Thus, according to 3:6, the Israelites "took their daughters for themselves as wives, and gave their daughters to their sons (יקחו את־בנותיהם להם לנשים ואת־בנותיהם נתנו לבניהם)", a description that certainly seems to echo the prohibition in Deut. 7:3: "You shall not give your

[151] Webb (1987:192) actually notes that part of the horror of the Benjaminite war account is that "the war is prosecuted with a determination and a thoroughness surpassing anything evidenced in Israel's war with the Canaanites anywhere in Judges".

[152] For Jerusalem, the use of הכה . . . לפי־חרב is possibly intended as synonymous with חרם. For a brief discussion of the relationship between the two terms, see p. 37.

[153] Tribes specifically mentioned include Judah (1:19), Benjamin (1:21), Manasseh (1:27), Ephraim (1:29), Zebulun (1:30), Asher (1:31–32), and Naphtali (1:33). But in 1:28, this failure is applied to Israel as a whole, thus probably including tribes not specifically mentioned in the immediate context.

[154] Although הוריש is often translated as 'to drive out', Lohfink (1983:14–33) argues that the verb actually connotes 'to destroy'. Thus, what is at issue is not the expulsion of the nations but the destruction of them, which Israel had failed to accomplish.

daughter to their son and you shall not take their daughter for your son (בתך לא־תתן לבנו ובתו לא־תקח לבנך)". As this prohibition against inter-marriage is immediately explained in Deut. 7:4 as a necessary precaution against apostasy, it perhaps comes as no surprise that the report of Israel's violation of this prohibition in Judges 3:6 is followed immediately by a report of the resulting apostasy: "and they served their gods".

This apostasy in turn sets into motion the ensuing cycles in the central section of the book, where in anger, YHWH handed Israel over to the surrounding nations to be oppressed. In her distress, Israel cried out to YHWH, who then raised up judges to deliver them from their enemies. But once a particular enemy was gone and the land enjoyed rest for a period, the cycle would start again with another round of apostasy, followed by another oppressor, another judge, another deliverance, and yet another round of apostasy once peace has been restored.

But what is noteworthy here is that even as YHWH raised up judges to deliver His people, a tension persisted between the judges and the people in that the judges' efforts to rid the nation of oppressors did not always receive full support from the people. This is seen over and again in the accounts of the various judges. In the song of Deborah, for example, it is revealed that at least four of Israel's tribes did not participate in the war against Jabin and Sisera (5:15b–17). And when Gideon pursued Zebah and Zalmunna, the kings of Midian, the towns of Succoth and Peniel also refused to give aid (8:4–9). According to Jephthah in 12:2–3, the Ephraimites refused to lend a hand even when he called upon them to help fight the Ammonites. And when Samson slaughtered some Philistines, the men of Judah actually took the side of the Philistines and came looking for Samson in order to tie him up and hand him over to the enemy (15:11–12). What all these seem to show, therefore, is a picture of the Israelites not entirely acting in unity with their judges even as the judges tried to deliver them from their oppressors.

But surprisingly, the unity and determination that seem lacking in Israel's struggle against foreign oppressors now appeared in full display as the Israelites prepared to take on one of their own. Indeed in the narrative surrounding the battle against Benjamin, Israel's unity is repeatedly highlighted with descriptions such as כל־בני ישראל in 20:1,7,26, כל שבטי ישראל in 20:2,10; 21:5, and כאיש אחד in

20:1,8,11.[155] Of the three phrases, the first two have hitherto not been used anywhere else in the book in relation to any action taken by Israel,[156] while the third has only been used once in 6:16 in the context of a promise of YHWH. This portrayal of unity is further conveyed by the use of קהל (20:1,2; 21:5,8) and עדה (20:1; 21:10,15,16) to describe the assembling together of the entire congregation of Israel in the events leading up to and in the aftermath of the conflict with Benjamin. Although both these terms appear frequently in the Pentateuch and Joshua in connection with the gathering together of all Israel in unity, neither is used in Judges except in these last two chapters. Taken together, therefore, the picture painted in Judges 20–21 is one where Israel, albeit minus Benjamin, was displaying a unity hitherto unseen in the book as they tried to deal with their erring brothers.

But not only does this emphasis on unity contrast sharply with the apparent lack thereof elsewhere in the book in relation to dealing with foreign oppressors, the actual strategies used by the Israelites to deal with Benjamin also seem to be ones that should have been applied to the surrounding nations but were not. Consider the oath against inter-marriage with any Benjaminite, for example. While Judg. 3:6 suggests that Israel had apparently failed to observe the prohibition of Deut. 7:3 against inter-marriage with the nations, according to Judges 21, they actually took a similar oath prohibiting themselves from giving their daughters in marriage to any Benjaminite. The actual language of the oath, איש ממנו לא־יתן בתו לבנימן לאשה (21:1), with variations in 21:7,18, echoes both the prohibition in Deut. 7:3 against giving Israel's daughters to the sons of the surrounding nations (בתך לא־תתן לבנו) and the report of Israelite non-compliance in Judg. 3:6 (ואת־בנותיהם נתנו לבניהם). Thus, the tough stance originally commanded by YHWH against the nations is now applied by the Israelites to their brothers. The irony is that while the Israelites did not observe YHWH's prohibition regarding inter-marriage with

155 W. Nelson (59 n.22) also notes that the triple reference to the unity of the nation in Judg. 20:1,8,11 represents the first time all Israel has acted in unison since Judges 2.

156 כל־בני ישׂראי does appear twice in the book, but only in connection with the message of YHWH being spoken to 'all the sons of Israel' in 2:4, and with 'all the sons of Israel' being oppressed by the Philistines and Ammonites in 10:8.

the nations, they now did all they could to avoid violating their own oath not to inter-marry with Benjamin.

Then consider also what is practically the application of the חרם on the Benjaminites. Although the word חרם never actually appears in the battle narrative of 20:29–48, there are, however, sufficient hints to suggest that the חרם was in fact intentionally applied.[157]

First, the description of the war employs language usually associated with the application of the חרם.[158] Second, it also records the systematic annihilation of all living things including animals (20:48), and the burning of cities (20:48), both of which are commonly associated with the application of the חרם.[159]

Finally, as has been pointed out earlier, the whole narrative of the Benjaminite war makes strong allusion to the campaign against Ai in Joshua 8. But in 8:26, the Ai campaign is explicitly said to represent an application of the חרם.[160] The strong analogy between

---

[157] Boling (1974:41–42) speaks of the conflict as an "intra-Israelite application of the herem". Exum (1990:430) also categorises the war as amounting to 'a holy war', thereby probably suggesting that an application of the חרם is implied.

[158] See p. 37 for a brief discussion of הכה . . . לפי־חרב as a possible synonym for חרם.

[159] For the systemic annihilation of living things including animals in a חרם situation, see Deut. 13:16; Josh. 6:21; 1 Sam. 15:3. For the burning of cities in a similar situation, see Deut. 13:17; Josh. 6:24.

[160] Admittedly, Josh. 8:26, which is the only instance where חרם is mentioned in the narrative of the Ai campaign, is missing in the LXX. But that does not automatically mean that the verse is a MT plus. First, although the LXX of Joshua 8 is consistently shorter than what is found in the MT, some of the shorter readings may in fact be LXX minuses rather than MT pluses. Indeed, Butler (78) argues that the significant omission of whole clauses in 8:11–12 and the entire 8:13 from the LXX is a result of attempts at harmonisation. A contradiction in number with 8:3 may have lead to the deliberate omission of parts of 8:12, while a desire to portray the encampment as positioned opposite to the ambush to the east of the city (cf. 8:11 LXX) may have led to the intentional omitting of references to the encampment being set to the north in 8:11,13. Second, where MT-pluses seem obvious in Joshua 8, the pluses often represent either logical or theological amplifications (e.g. 8:7, where a traditional formula promising victory from YHWH may have been added), or attempts at harmonising with information presented elsewhere in the text (e.g. 8:2, where ולמלכה may have been added to harmonise with the mention of the king of Jericho in the same verse, and 8:8, where the entire clause about burning the city with fire may have been inserted to harmonise with 8:19). But 8:26 does not fit the above categories. Rather, 8:26 introduces an additional function for the holding out of the javelin that has hitherto not been hinted at elsewhere in the narrative. In fact, it is precisely because this new information is so unexpected and so far removed from the last mention of the javelin in 8:18 that the verse seems awkward in its present location. Besides, the verse also presents a logical difficulty as it implies that Joshua's hand was held out with the javelin the

the two campaigns therefore suggests that the same may also have been intended as Israel took on their brother Benjamin.

But if this is true, then the situation is ironic in that while the Israelites were unsuccessful in applying the חרם to the nations around them as they should,[161] they enjoyed great success applying the חרם to their own brothers.

All in all, therefore, the impression conveyed is that not only were the Israelites displaying more unity and determination against their brothers than they ever did against their enemies and oppressors, they were also much more ready and willing to deal harshly with their brothers in a way they never did towards the nations around them. This raises the question, "Why?"

Unfortunately, once again the text appears to be silent when it comes to offering an explanation for the Israelites' harsh treatment of their own as compared to their apparent inability or unwillingness to deal similarly with their foreign oppressors. Upon closer reflection, however, one realises that this is actually not the first or the only time this has happened. In fact, on two separate occasions in the central section, two of Israel's judges have also conducted themselves similarly, treating their fellow countrymen more harshly than they did their foreign oppressors.

The first involves Gideon. As Gideon and his men were in pursuit of the two Midianite kings, Zebah and Zalmunna, they requested material support from two Israelite towns, Succoth and Peniel. Upon their refusal to help, Gideon threatened to deal with them harshly when he returned in victory. So, after Gideon eventually captured the two Midianite kings, he returned to settle score with the two uncooperative towns. He first punished the elders of Succoth with desert thorns and briars as he had previously promised in 8:7. Then

---

whole time he was actively leading the counter-attack and the subsequent slaughter (cf. 8:21,24b in the LXX, where Joshua is the subject of the main verb). The omission of 8:26, then, actually makes for a much smoother reading and bypasses a logical difficulty. If that is true, one can argue on the basis of lectio difficilior that the omission of 8:26 in the LXX represents an attempt at smoothing out the narrative by leaving out a difficult verse that is not essential to the overall plot. Alternatively, a much simpler solution is to see the LXX omission as nothing more than a case of homoioteleuton, where 8:26 has been accidentally left out as the ending of 8:25 is confused with the identical ending of 8:26. Either way, there does not seem to be sufficient justification to dismiss 8:26 as a late redactional supplement added by the MT.

[161] Cf. Deut. 7:1–5; 20:16–18.

he also tore down the tower of Peniel as he said he would in 8:8. But in addition, 8:17 also notes that Gideon killed the men of Peniel, an act that went beyond what he had earlier threatened to do.

Significantly, this killing of the men of Peniel is followed immediately by a report on Gideon's interrogation and execution of the two Midianite kings. In the course of the interrogation, Gideon learned that the two kings had killed his blood brothers at Tabor. Gideon's response, however, is revealing. He told the two kings that had they spared his brothers at Tabor, he would have spared them in return (8:19). That Gideon actually entertained the possibility of not killing the two kings right after he had just killed a townful of Israelite men for not supporting him in his pursuit of the kings certainly reflects poorly on Gideon. For it shows a willingness on the part of Gideon to treat his own people much more harshly than he was prepared to treat the leaders of Israel's foreign oppressors.

The second incident involves Jephthah. In the account of Jephthah's dealing with the Ammonites who were oppressing Israel at the time, there is a lengthy section in which the back-and-forth diplomatic wrangling between Jephthah and the Ammonite king is reported in detail (11:12–28). This detailed reporting of diplomatic wrangling is somewhat curious, since it neither advances the plot nor results in diplomatic success. As Gunn astutely observes, Jephthah's "elaborate exercise in diplomatic rhetoric" merely "ends with the narrator's laconic observation that 'the king of the Ammonites did not listen to Jephthah's words'".[162] Given that the dialogue with the Ammonite king had accomplished practically nothing, the narrator could have omitted all that detail and simply given a summary report of the attempt, and narrative would not have suffered at all. Why, then, did the narrator go to all that trouble preserving the entire exchange, especially since nothing of significance to the plot appears to have been conveyed through the dialogue?

To be sure, those who see words or 'opening of the mouth' as a special theme of the Jephthah narrative may well regard the preservation of the dialogue between Jephthah and the Ammonite king as thematically significant.[163] Yet from a slightly different perspective, it is also possible to view this detailed reporting of the exchange as an

[162] Gunn, 1987:116.

[163] See Webb, 1987:73–75; Exum, 1993:131–36; Marais, 119.

attempt to offer an explicit contrast with the way Jephthah handled his dispute with the Ephraimites in 12:1–6. For in contrast to the patient and elaborate effort he took to present his case before the Ammonite king,[164] when dispute arose between him and the Ephraimites who felt slighted in not being invited to join in the war, Jephthah's response was terse and uncompromising. At least the Ammonite king was given opportunities to reply to Jephthah's charges, and military campaign was launched only after the king had put an end to diplomatic discourse. In the case of the Ephraimites, however, Jephthah apparently did not give his fellow Israelites a chance to answer his rebuttal. Instead, the impression given by the text is that Jephthah called his men together and launched an attack against the Ephraimites almost as soon as he rebutted their initial charge (12:4).[165] And as a result, 42,000 Ephraimites were killed in the ensuing battle (12:6).

What this seems to show is a stark contrast between how Jephthah dealt with Israel's foreign oppressors and how he dealt with his fellow Israelites. However one may evaluation the complaints of the Ephraimites and their motives, the fact remains that the Ephraimites were a part of Israel who desired to take part in a military campaign against a foreign oppressor. But Jephthah, who had previously displayed a capacity for patient diplomacy when he so desired, chose instead not to extend to his fellow countrymen the same patient diplomacy he had extended to their foreign oppressors. And in so doing, he too, like Gideon before him, dealt with his brothers with more harshness than he did with his enemies.

In the end, do the actions taken by Gideon and Jephthah shed any more light on the action taken by the Israelites against Benjamin in the final chapters of the book? Unfortunately, no. Yet what they do show is that this bizarre harshness displayed by the Israelites against their brothers was not unprecedented, for their judges have also displayed the same tendency on different occasions.

---

[164] Webb (1987:55) argues that the words of Jephthah to the king are uncompromising and are thus not words of a man desperate for peace. In fact, Webb thinks those words may even contain veiled threats. But even if this is true, the fact remains that at least Jephthah did engage in extended diplomatic dialogue with the Ammonite king before taking up military action against him.

[165] Exum (1990:423) also noted that in marked contrast to Gideon before him and to his own lengthy negotiation with the Ammonites, Jephthah did nothing to prevent fighting with the Ephraimites.

7. *Israel's rash oath that doomed some of their virgin daughters echoes Jephthah's rash vow that doomed his virgin daughter*

After the war with Benjamin had been fought and won, the elders of Israel suddenly found themselves facing an unexpected problem. They had been so successful in annihilating the Benjaminites that they suddenly realised they were in danger of wiping out the tribe altogether. Apparently, the entire Benjaminite population had been killed off in the aftermath of the war (20:48), such that the six hundred Benjaminite warriors who had escaped were the only ones left of the tribe. And to compound the problem, the oath the Israelites had taken at the beginning of the war not to give any of their daughters to Benjaminites as wives now came back to haunt them, as there were no more Benjaminite women left for the survivors to take as wives. Thus, unless some kind of solution is found, even the remaining Benjaminite survivors would be destined to die without being able to produce another generation of Benjaminites.

In order to prevent the extinction of one of the tribes of Israel, the elders then searched for a way to provide wives for the Benjaminite survivors without breaking their oath. They discovered that the town of Jabesh Gilead had not sent warriors to fight in the Benjaminite war. As they had previously sworn an oath to put to death any who refuses to participate in the war, they decided to send men to annihilate the town of Jabesh Gilead. All the virgins, however, they would spare, so that these could be given to the Benjaminites as wives. But that still left them two hundred women short. So, the elders came up with another idea to meet the challenge. Noting that an annual festival would be taking place shortly in Shiloh where girls would come out dancing by the vineyards in celebration, the elders thus authorised the remaining Benjaminites not yet provided with wives to go and each carry off for himself one of the dancing girls. This way, they would be able to circumvent their oath because technically, the girls would not have been 'given' to the Benjaminites in marriage.

Now considering what started the war in the first place, the decisions of the elders of Israel were certainly most bizarre. For while the war was initially started to avenge the rape and subsequent death of one Israelite woman, the Levite's concubine, the two acts authorised by the elders to provide wives for the Benjaminites basically amounted to the rape of six hundred virgins of Israel. For the two hundred virgins at Shiloh were certainly abducted against their will, and the same can also be said of the four hundred from Jabesh Gilead, whose lives were spared only so that they could be handed over to the Benjaminites as wives. Thus, in the process of avenging one rape, the avengers actually ended up authorising two acts that led to a further six hundred rapes just to compensate for their over-zealousness in seeking what was supposed to be just retribution![166] How does one even begin to account for such bizarre and incomprehensible decisions? Unfortunately, the text provides no overt explanation.

But here again, like the other episodes in the epilogue already discussed, there appears to be a subtle link back to one of the judges in the central section of the book. This time, the allusion is to Jephthah and the vow he made that eventually resulted in the sacrifice of his daughter.

The fact that the narrative of the elders' decision in Judges 21 alludes to Jephthah and his vow can be seen in several ways. To begin, both involve a rash vow or oath made prior to a war, with the devastating effects of the vow/oath felt only after the respective wars have been won.

Admittedly, in the Jephthah narrative, what Jephthah did in 11:30, referred to again in 11:39, is that 'he vowed a vow (וידר נדר)', whereas in the narrative involving the Israelite elders, it is נשׁבע 'to take an oath' that is repeatedly used in 21:1,7,18. Yet, the two words are by and large synonymous. In Ps. 132:2, for example, נשׁבע and נדר are used as a synonymous pair in a parallel bicolon, both apparently referring to the same vow/oath David took before YHWH. Furthermore, in Num. 30:3, the two words are also used synonymously in a law that seems to have specific relevance to the two narratives in question. For Num. 30:3 dictates that regardless of whether a man has vowed a vow to YHWH or taken an oath (ידר נדר ליהוה או־השׁבע שׁבעה), the word he has given must not be broken, but that he must do 'according to all that came out of his mouth (ככל־היצא מפיו)'. This, incidentally, seems to be the precise situation

[166] Bal (71) observes that the victim of Gibeah is 'avenged' by the extension of the category of virgin victims. In addition, that the retribution the Israelites sought was far from 'just' in the first place is also hinted at by Soggin (1987:281), who notes that the utter disproportion between the crime and the punishment is not without irony.

in both narratives, with the phrase 'according to that which came out of your mouth (כאשׁר יצא מפיך)' even found explicitly in 11:36.

In any case, not only is the unbreakable pre-war vow/oath with post-war significance common to both narratives, there are also similarities with regard to how the victims of the vow/oath are described. Here, it should be noted that the unintended victim of Jephthah's vow, namely, his daughter, is characterised primarily in two ways. First she is repeatedly referred to as בת both by Jephthah (11:35) and by the narrator (11:34,40). Then she is further presented as a virgin, as her בתולים is referred to both by herself and the narrator in 11:37,38. In fact, in 11:39, she is also described as 'not having known a man (לא־ידעה אישׁ)'.

What is significant here is that in the narrative concerning the elders' decision, the same two main characterisations are also used respectively of the two groups of virgins who fell victim to a rash oath. First, the virgins of Shiloh are twice referred to in 21:21 as בנות־שׁילו, a description that certainly connects them with Jephthah's daughter.[167] Not only so, but the fact that they were actually involved in dancing (מחלות) when they met their fate, innocently oblivious to the oath that would soon doom them, is almost an exact echo of Jephthah's daughter (בת), who also came out dancing (מחלות) to meet her father, innocently oblivious of the vow that would soon doom her. As מחלות is only used twice in the book of Judges and on these very occasions, a case can certainly be made that some kind of conscious allusion is intended.[168]

But if the virgins of Shiloh mirror Jephthah's daughter in that both were portrayed as innocent, dancing daughters when they met their fate, the girls of Jabesh Gilead also mirror Jephthah's daughter with regard to their virginity. For not only are they referred to in 21:12 as נערה בתולה, a phrase that reminds one of the בתולים of Jephthah's daughter, they are also described with the same לא־ידעה אישׁ that characterises Jephthah's daughter in 11:39. In fact, like the

[167] Note that such a description of the virgins of Shiloh coming from the mouths of the Israelite elders also renders the elders father figures. This, therefore, strengthens the parallel with Jephthah, whose role is primarily that of a father in the episode concerning his daughter. Thus, in both cases, daughters are doomed by their fathers' words.

[168] In addition, the closely related polel fs participle המחללות is also found in 21:23. Since this is the only time this form occurs in Judges and it is also used of the daughters of Shiloh, it further strengthens the case for conscious allusion.

use of מחלות, the clause לא־ידעה איש also occurs only twice in the book of Judges and on precisely these two occasions.

What all this seems to point to is conscious artistic design in the way the narrative of the elder's decision in Judges 21 is linked to the earlier Jephthah narrative. For four significant descriptions used to characterise the victim of Jephthah's rash pre-war vow seem neatly divided into two pairs, with each pair being applied exclusively to one of the two groups of women who also fell victim to a similar rash pre-war oath. Thus, even if Soggin and Boling are right in suggesting that the two episodes concerning the women of Jabesh Gilead and Shiloh were originally independent episodes that have now been united by the common theme of "bringing women in to reconstitute the tribe of Benjamin",[169] one can still argue that the bringing together of these two episodes in its present form is far from a random decision, but involves conscious literary design so that the episodes are reworked to echo the incident about Jephthah's daughter.[170]

Unfortunately however, even if the narrative of the elders' decision in Judges 21 is carefully reworked to echo the incident about Jephthah's daughter, the allusion seems not to have shed any light on why the elders ever allowed what they did to happen. All it seems to points to is that if the elders' decision was indeed bizarre, it is at least not unprecedented because a similarly bizarre conclusion involving rash vows has happened before in the life of one of Israel's judges.

Significance and Implications of Links

Having examined the above seven cases where allusions to narratives about the judges are identified, some concluding observations are now in order.

---

[169] Soggin, 1987:300, Boling, 1975:294.

[170] The alternative, of course, is to claim that it is in fact the Jephthah narrative that is the later composition and that it represents an amalgamation of the two narratives in Judges 21. But this is unlikely, as the four descriptions in question all seem integral to the Jephthah narrative, whereas the metaphorical use of בת in Judg. 21:21, as well as the somewhat superfluous mention of נערה בתולה in 21:12 seem non-essential in their respective contexts. Therefore it is far more likely that these terms were deliberately incorporated in the Judges 21 narrative to mirror the Jephthah story rather than the other way around. This is not to mention that critical scholars are generally in agreement that the epilogue of Judges is significantly later than the material in the central section of the book.

While each of the above allusions may indeed be of little more than marginal value when taken individually, collectively, they seem to offer significant new insights into how the book was put together and how it should be read. But to justify a collective approach to these allusions, one must first highlight again some of the distinctive features shared by all seven allusions.

First, all these allusions seem to occur at particular points in the epilogue where the characterisation of the various protagonists appears most bizarre. Taken together, it almost seems as if these allusions were placed deliberately at strategic points in the narratives to provide some sort of bearing for the readers as they navigate strange and turbulent waters.

Second, in terms of the way these allusions function, they seem to display a surprising uniformity. For all of them seem to draw the readers back to parallel episodes in the lives of the major judges, such that the judges are shown to have acted in a similarly bizarre manner as the protagonists encountered in the epilogue.

Finally, while all these allusions seem to establish definite links with specific episodes in the lives of the major judges, whoever scattered these links throughout the epilogue never drew directly upon them to provide overt explanations for similar happenings in the epilogue. In fact, he seems utterly content merely to establish various parallels without further comments or explanations, thus displaying much faith in the ability of his readers[171] to understand the point he was making once they pick up the key connections and notice the pattern that emerges.

With all seven allusions sharing the above distinctive features, one is thus amply justified in taking these allusions together as a collective whole. Moreover, although some of these allusions could conceivably be added to the original composition at a later date, since they only involve words or phrases that appear somewhat superfluous to the overall plot of their respective narratives,[172] the rest seem too deeply integrated into the narrative structure to be secondary.[173]

---

[171] This is especially so in light of Sternberg's observation (270) that this essentially opaque presentation of a paradigm through an inductive approach carries significant risk of being missed either in whole or in part.

[172] The reference to the 'left-handed' Benjaminite contingent in Judg. 20:16, for example, or the mention of the 'ephod' in 17:5; 18:14,17,18.

[173] These include the 'seeing' of the Danites, the various plot parallels that link the death of the concubine with that of Samson's wife, and the oath of the Israelite leaders.

Thus, unless one is prepared to argue that allusions with such uniformity of purpose actually arise independently from different hands during different stages of redaction, it makes far better sense to see all the allusions as originating from a single source that was responsible for crafting and placing them at strategic points during the compositional phase of the epilogue.[174] This source should therefore be properly referred to as the 'author' of the epilogue.

But there are a few important ramifications of such an understanding. To begin with, if all these allusions are indeed integral to the original composition of the epilogue, such that together, they form a significant part of the rhetorical strategy of its author, then to the extent that they make frequent references to the major judges in the central section, they point to a more intimate relationship between these two sections at a compositional level than has generally been assumed. For as has already been noted at the beginning of this chapter, the general consensus is that there is no literary relationship between the epilogue and the central section of Judges at the compositional level, that the epilogue is a totally independent literary unit that has been artificially tagged on to the central section by some late redactor, and that as such, it represents an intrusion into a continuous narrative known as 'Deuteronomistic History'. But

[174] As for the argument of Amit (1998:337–41) and Mayes (2001:253–54) against compositional unity of the epilogue, it should be noted that it is based primarily on a positive interpretation of the actions of Israel's leaders in Judges 20–21. They argue that the leaders' actions demonstrated a strong, centralised rule, something that is incompatible with the apparently negative view of Israelite leadership expressed in the refrain. But as has already been pointed out, the actions taken by Israel's leadership in Judges 20–21 are anything but positive, as their overzealous attempt to remedy a personal injustice actually precipitated a national crisis and led to even greater injustices. If so, then no contradiction actually exists between the narrative in Judges 20–21 and the refrain, for the leaders of Israel would also have been counted among those who did 'what was right in their eyes'. As for Jüngling (275–80), although he recognises that the actions sanctioned by the leaders can be construed negatively, yet he argues that these decisions were nonetheless made unanimously. Therefore as such, they do not fit the description 'every man did what was right in his eyes'. But perhaps here, Jüngling is taking the idea of individualism implied in 'every man' too literally. For if the decision of the Benjaminites to fight against the Israelites and the decision of Jabesh Gilead not to join the war are also considered contrary to the refrain because they were made with a certain degree of consensus by those involved (276), then one can potentially argue that even the actions of the wicked Gibeathites in Judges 19 do not fit this refrain, since the wicked townsfolk apparently also acted in one accord. This would leave the elderly host and the Levite as the only ones whose actions fall under the criticism of the refrain in 21:25. And that is a reading I doubt even Jüngling would endorse. Thus, the various arguments against the compositional unity of the epilogue do not hold up.

if these allusions to the major judges are in fact integral to the original composition of the epilogue, then if nothing else, one would at least have to concede that the epilogue as it now stands was not composed entirely independently of the central section, but may in fact have been composed with the narratives of the central section in mind as the author of the epilogue creatively tried to establish links between the two sections through the use of the various allusions.

But if this is indeed the case, then the current placement of the epilogue immediately after the central section may not have been the act of unjustified appending as it is so often assumed to be. For even if one grants it for the sake of argument that the central section had at one point circulated independently without the epilogue, whoever gave the book its current form must have done so intelligently on the basis of the links that connect two sections together, and not just clumsily by artificially binding together two unrelated documents on the basis of a common historical timeframe.

But one can go even further. For not only does the current placement of the epilogue after the central section make sense in light of the pattern of allusions that connects the two sections together, one can even argue that from its very inception, the epilogue was never meant to be read as an independent work, but as a commentary on the judges that serves as a conclusion to the central section. Consider the following.

As has already been pointed out, each of the allusions in the epilogue seems to refer back to a parallel episode in the life of a major judge. As a result, the major judges are shown to have acted in an equally bizarre manner as the protagonists encountered in the epilogue. But still, what is the point of this literary strategy?

To be sure, through the allusions, the bizarre episodes in the epilogue are shown to be not quite as unprecedented as one might initially think. But in creating them, the author of the epilogue has actually managed in one brilliant stroke to redirect the focus of the reader back to the lives of the major judges. For each of the narratives in the epilogue is so bizarre that collectively, they almost seem calculated to shock. But imagine that, in the process of being thus shocked, the reader suddenly realises that each example of shocking behaviour actually has a precedent somewhere else earlier in the book. This would force the reader to go back and re-evaluate the earlier narratives, such that if the bizarre nature of the earlier acts has somehow been overlooked in a relatively straightforward reading of the stories, such acts would now be processed again and be seen for what they really are.

In other words, the allusions to the major judges scattered throughout the epilogue are not really there to shed further light on the events found in the epilogue; they are there primarily to shed light on the prior acts of the judges. What this means is that, severed from the central section, the allusions in the epilogue would have lost the primary significance of their existence and ended up as curiosities that further compound the incomprehensibility of the bizarre narratives. This suggests, therefore, that the epilogue was actually composed as a continuation of the central section, and was never meant to be read independently of it.

In fact, one wonders if the failure to recognise this may not have been the very reason why events in the epilogue have so often confounded so many. For acceptance of the critical position that the epilogue of Judges is generally unrelated to the central section has pre-disposed scholars to seek meaning for the epilogue by and large from within the epilogue itself. This has perhaps blinded them from seeing that the events of the epilogue are actually most meaningful only when understood in relationship to the narratives in the central section.

But still, what messages do these narratives intend to convey? Certainly, by showing that the bizarre acts in the epilogue have all found precedents in the lives of the judges, the author has managed to cast the judges in a very uncomplimentary light. For by showing them to have engaged in the same sort of unprincipled behaviour that characterises the various protagonists in the epilogue, the judges are essentially portrayed as being no better than characters that are consistently derided in the epilogue.[175]

But that would still be somewhat of an understatement. For while the various protagonists in the epilogue are mostly nameless, thus perhaps signalling that they could potentially be anyone within the

---

[175] That a derisive tone is used to describe many of the characters and events in the epilogue has been noted by many. Gunn (1987:119), for example, comments on the sardonic way the narrator describes the opportunistic Levite in Judges 18. McMillion (234) has also commented on the narrator's ironic ridiculing of Micah's senseless multiplying of cultic objects. As for the Levite in Judges 19–20, Lasine (44–46) has pointed out how his reaction to his concubine's death is depicted as ludicrous.

general population,[176] the judges, however, were leaders specially raised up by YHWH. As such, the judges were expected to lead the nation by setting the right examples. And yet, if their actions were indeed examples, they have been atrocious examples. Is it any wonder, then, that chaos seems to rule in almost every episode in the epilogue?

In fact, one can even argue that without the author of the epilogue actually coming out and stating it as such, it is nonetheless possible to see the entire epilogue as no less than an indictment of the judges. For if the allusions to the judges scattered throughout are indeed meant to link each of the bizarre episodes back to a major judge, then perhaps the primary purpose of the links is collectively to suggest some kind of cause-effect relationship between the judges' actions and the cultic, moral, and social breakdown witnessed in the epilogue. For if indeed the actions of the judges serve as precedents for all that happens in the epilogue, then in a way, the events narrated in the epilogue really represent nothing more than the worst of the judges served up in one concentrated dose. And to the extent that anyone should be horrified at what he reads about in the epilogue, that someone should eventually come to the realisation that these are exactly the sort of things that Israel's leaders have been allowing to happen in their own lives all along. Thus, if society is shown to have broken down completely by the time one reaches the epilogue, the allusions imply that the breach actually originated all the way from the top.

What one is witnessing here, in other words, is a master storyteller at work, one so skilful in his art that he managed to find a way to convey his assessment of the events he was narrating without actually having to resort to a single direct evaluative comment.[177]

---

[176] Hudson (59–60) argues that anonymity in the epilogue of Judges is used primarily to 'universalise' the characters and to show loss of identity and personhood. While some sort of universalisation may indeed be implied by the anonymity, Hudson's statement that this is meant to portray "every Levite, every father-in-law, every host, every single man within that society" as committing "such barbaric atrocities 'from Dan to Beersheba' (20:1)" is surely overstating the case. A more reasonable position would be to understand the anonymity as indicating that similar acts could potentially be committed by anyone anywhere in a society where 'every man does what is right in his own eyes'.

[177] Incidentally, if one has to pick one aspect of style that characterises Judges, this would probably be it. For the book as a whole is surprisingly devoid of direct evaluative comments. In a way, this may be precisely what opens up the various

Instead, through the use of subtle allusions by means of key-word associations, puns, and plot parallels, he has left hints here, there, and everywhere, so that those who read the text with careful attention will be rewarded with his unique perspective regarding the events he has taken such care to narrate.

From all this, therefore, one has to conclude that the epilogue of Judges is not a later appendage to a book it does not originally belong. On the contrary, it must have been conceived as a continuation of the central section of Judges even at its very inception, and may indeed hold the interpretive key to understanding the unspoken assessment of the judges and of the era. But if this is indeed the case, then not only does this understanding hold potentially significant implications with regard to the validity of the Deuteronomistic History hypothesis, it also has the potential of providing full justification to an integrative reading of the book. For such a reading would no longer constitute an 'artificial' reading,[178] but would in fact reflect the underlying intention of the book's 'author' in putting the book together in its current form.[179]

narratives to such a wide variety of possible interpretations, thus making the book so controversial.

[178] This, in fact, seems to be one of Andersson's (58–60) implicit criticisms of Amit's method, since she concedes that the book was formed in an almost boundless redactional process, and yet claims that the book has a coherence that allows it to function as a meaningful literary text in its current form.

[179] These issues will be explored in greater detail in the final chapter of this study.

CHAPTER FOUR

PROLOGUE AS PARADIGM: LINKS BETWEEN THE PROLOGUE AND CENTRAL SECTION OF JUDGES

Although consisting only of 41 verses, the prologue of Judges (1:1–2:5) has generated much debate from a historical-critical perspective. Such debate revolves around two main areas. On the historical front, it concerns whether the conquest account in Judges 1 presents a more reliable picture than the somewhat idealised account in Joshua 10–12.[1] On the literary front, there are also a couple of problems for which no consensus has been reached. One concerns the source behind the conquest accounts in Joshua 13–19 and Judges 1, whether dependency exists, and if so, the direction of dependence.[2] The other involves the redactional history of the prologue, whether it has internal unity, and how it is connected to what precedes in Joshua and what immediately follows in the introductory framework to Judges' central section in 2:6–3:6.[3]

Although it does not fall within the mandate of the present chapter to examine these critical issues, a simple observation can nonetheless be made. Even from a cursory survey of the issues cited, it is obvious that when it comes to the prologue of Judges, there is far more interest in its relationship with Joshua than there is in its relationship with the central section of the book. In fact, Auld once commented that discussion of Judges 1 has become "something of an appendix to discussion of the book of Joshua",[4] as the critical position generally assumes no immediate or contextual connection between the prologue and the central section of Judges.[5] Yet is this perceived disconnection between the two sections accurate? This will be the focus of the present chapter.

---

[1] Moore, 7–8; Wright, 1946:105–14; Rösel, 1988:121–35; Callaway, 53–84; Younger, 1994:207–27.

[2] Auld, 1975:261–85; Mullen, 1984:33–54; Lindars, 1995:42–73; Younger, 1995:75–92.

[3] O'Doherty, 1–7; Brettler, 1989b:433–35; Rösel, 1980:342–50, 1999:49–58.

[4] Auld, 1975:262.

[5] This is noted by O'Doherty (1–2) and Mullen (1984:34–35).

Under critical scholarship, the prologue of Judges is generally viewed not as a unified document but as a "collection of miscellaneous fragments of varying dates and varying reliability".[6] Such a conclusion is reached by and large on the basis of perceived historical and literary inconsistencies within the section, as well as contradictions with material that is considered part of Deuteronomistic History.[7]

Yet by focusing almost exclusively on the redactional process through which the prologue arrives at its current form, perhaps not enough attention has been paid to the rhetorical concerns of the section as a whole and to its relationship with the rest of the book. Thus, a different approach may be needed.

Assuming that whoever was responsible for the final form of the prologue and its placement at the beginning of the canonical text did not put the section together unthinkingly but purposefully, it is perhaps worthwhile to examine the section not from the perspective of its redactional history, but from the perspective of its overall rhetorical structure, in order to discover the section's main rhetorical concerns. Once these concerns are discovered, they should then be compared to the rhetorical concerns of the central section, to see if any correspondence exists. If significant correspondence in fact exists, then it is possible that the two sections are more closely related than has hitherto been assumed.

Rhetorical Structure of the Prologue

As it currently stands, the prologue of Judges is by and large structured as one continuous narrative. This is seen in that the narrative is basically presented through a continuous series of consecutive verb forms from 1:1 to 1:26[8] with only minor interruptions.[9] Be that as

---

[6] Wright, 1946:109. This is also echoed by Auld (1975:275–76) and Mullen (1984:34).

[7] This position is best exemplified by Auld (1975:261–85) and Lindars (1995:3–73), and is also reflected in Weinfeld (1993a:388–400), although the primary concern of the latter is to demonstrate the pro-Judah stance of the final redactor.

[8] The verbal consecution is halted in 1:27–33 because these verses consist predominantly of negated clauses which cannot continue the verbal consecution by virtue of the presence of the negative particle לֹא.

[9] Of the interruptions, four disjunctive clauses in 1:10,11,23,26 are intrusive epexegetical notes. As for the disjunction in 1:21, even had the fronting of the direct object to clause initial position not taken place, the verbal consecution would still

it may, from a rhetorical standpoint, it is nonetheless possible to discern at least two major types of narration intertwined within this continuous narrative.

As scholars of poetics have pointed out, it is possible to distinguish between narratives that serve primarily to report and summarise, and those that are descriptive and 'scenic'.[10] Bar-Efrat distinguishes the two primarily by whether narration time is significantly shorter than (report narrative) or roughly corresponds to (scenic narrative) narrated time.[11] Both Alter and Bar-Efrat further consider the use of dialogue and direct speech as a characteristic of scenic narratives.[12]

On this basis, the prologue of Judges seems to consist of a straight report-type narrative punctuated by mini scenic narratives.[13] Webb, Block, Klein, and Niditch[14] have all identified three such mini-narratives in the episodes concerning Adoni-Bezek (1:5–7), Achsah (1:12–15), and Luz (1:23–26).[15] However, if the use of direct speech

---

not have continued since the negative particle לא would inevitably break any verbal consecution. As for the remaining disjunctives, the clauses in 1:16,22 seem to be supplying supplementary information, while the one in 1:8 seems to be circumstantial or synchronic. The disjunctive in 1:25 seems to be primarily for contrastive emphasis. But other than 1:8, none of the above has produced a significant break in the narrative, as the verbal consecution simply continues after these minor interruptions. The only real break in the narration comes after 1:8, where the opening disjunctive of 1:9 seems to introduce the beginning of a new narrative sequence.

[10] Licht (29–30) actually identifies four modes of narration, of which straight (reporting) and scenic narratives are the first two. The other two Licht calls 'description' and 'comments', and they correspond respectively to the two categories Bar-Efrat (146–47) calls 'depictions' and 'interpretations, explanations, and evaluations'. According to Bar-Efrat, these are characterised by the stopping of narrative time flow. Incidentally, Licht's 'comments' are also found in the prologue of Judges in the form of epexegetical notes and supplemental remarks introduced by disjunctive clauses.

[11] Bar-Efrat, 150–51.

[12] Alter, 1981:63–87, Bar-Efrat, 149–50.

[13] This has also been noted by Block (1999:78), who calls these two types of material in Judges 1 "annalistic chronicles focusing on military achievements", and "anecdotal reports of personal affairs".

[14] Webb, 1987:119; Block, 1999:78; Klein 1989:12–13; Niditch, 1999:196. Note that although Klein speaks of the Adoni-Bezek episode as one of the expositional narratives along with the Achsah episode, she somehow fails to include it with the Achsah and Luz episodes as she classifies the latter two as dramatised expositional narratives.

[15] Webb (1987:119) includes 1:4 also as part of the Adoni-Bezek narrative, 1:11 as part of the Achsah narrative, and 1:22 as part of the Luz narrative. Block (1999:78) likewise includes 1:11 as part of the Achsah narrative. I, however, see 1:4,11,22 as part of the report narrative that lead into the corresponding mini scenic

does serve as a marker for scenic narratives, then one would have to include the opening episode concerning Israel's inquiry and Judah's invitation of Simeon (1:1–3) as well as the final episode concerning the angel of YHWH (2:1–5) also as scenic narratives. There would thus be a total of five such mini scenic narratives within the prologue.

In most cases, the mingling of report and scenic narratives represents nothing out of the ordinary. In fact, the use of both modes of narration to tell a story would probably constitute the biblical norm.[16] However, given the relative shortness of the prologue, the presence of five distinct mini scenic narratives dealing with apparently unrelated subject matters raises questions regarding their rhetorical function within the prologue.

This is especially so in light of the fact that, perhaps with the exception of the opening and final episodes, the other mini-narratives seem neither necessary nor helpful with regard to the construction of a unified argument for the prologue. One is in fact at a loss to explain why these and not other episodes are singled out to receive the scenic treatment. For example, why provide scenic details only about Adoni-Bezek and not leaders of other conquered cities? Why include a domestic scene featuring Achsah in the midst of a conquest report? And why tell only the story behind the conquest of Bethel and not stories behind the conquest of other cities?[17] Viewed from the perspective of the prologue's internal logic, the choice of these episodes for scenic treatment seems random and puzzling. In fact, instead of enhancing the flow of the overall narrative and bringing the central concern of the prologue to the fore, the presence of these mini-narratives actually disrupts the narrative flow and renders

narratives. There is admittedly no hard and fast rule for determining where a scenic narrative begins when it grows out of surrounding report narratives. In this particular case, however, the fact that 1:4,11,22 seem to constitute an integral part of the report on Israelite military action seems to tilt the balance in favour of them being part of the report narrative that launches the respective scenic narratives.

[16] Bar-Efrat (150) actually considers it impossible to tell a story over an extended period of time by the scenic technique alone. Report narratives are necessary to convey continuity and communicate information about developments over a longer period of time. Licht (30) also maintains that the various modes of narratives are practically always combined.

[17] Block (1999:102) speculates that the reason for the insertion of the anecdote is "surely to be found in Bethel's special place in Israelite tradition and history." But surely, Jerusalem occupies at least an equally significant place if not more so in Israelite tradition and history. Why then is the report of its conquest in 1:8 not likewise elaborated on?

the overall argument of the prologue opaque. As this seems to evince poor skill on the part of the narrator according to Licht's two essential qualities of a narrative, namely, aesthetics and the conveyance of information,[18] is it any wonder then, that the prologue is frequently regarded as having been clumsily cobbled from unrelated fragments?[19]

But perhaps a better explanation exists for the presence of these mini-narratives than simply the incompetence of the final redactor. Perhaps these mini-narratives do in fact serve a definite rhetorical function.

In seeking to understand what this possible rhetorical function may be, it is of interest to note that each of the five mini-narratives seems to contain scenic details that link them to other narratives and sections within the book.[20] A few of these have already been discussed in some detail in an earlier chapter. Of these, the linking of the two military campaigns at the beginning and end of Judges through similarly worded oracular inquiries and the identical selection of Judah, as well as the contrast between the giving of Caleb's daughter in marriage and the not giving of Israel's daughters in marriage to any Benjaminite, represent direct links between specific episodes in the prologue and epilogue of the book. As for the account of the conquest of Luz/Bethel, although it is not directly linked to any other specific episode within the book, its allusion to the conquest of Jericho in Joshua 2 and 6 nonetheless shares the same rhetorical strategy employed elsewhere in the epilogue to highlight the failures of the generation of the judges as compared to successes of the previous generation.

As for the mini-narrative concerning the angel of YHWH in 2:1–5, it has also been pointed out earlier that this episode is rhetorically linked to the final episode in Judges 21 in that both concern weeping at Bethel/Bokim over diminishing national fortunes.[21] Admittedly, such a link does not really require the full scenic treatment as found

---

[18] Licht, 12.

[19] Wright, 1946:109; O'Doherty, 2; Auld, 1975:275–76; Mullen, 1984:34.

[20] The fact that these mini-narratives contain motifs which recur at significant points in the rest of the book has been noticed both by Webb (1987:119) and Younger (1994:217 n. 39). However, when it comes to the exact episodes being linked and the rhetorical significance of such links, my understanding is slightly different from theirs especially regarding the Achsah episode and the conquest of Luz/Bethel. For details of my understanding of these episodes, refer to my earlier discussion on pp. 42–46; 51–55.

[21] See pp. 40–42.

in Judg. 2:1–5, since the actual speech of the angel does not play a role in forging a link between the two episodes. However, YHWH's words spoken through the angel do represent one of the two occasions in the prologue where YHWH's speech is directly reported. The other occasion is in the opening episode where YHWH's reply to Israel is quoted in 1:2. That being the case, one can argue that the direct speeches of YHWH in the opening and closing episodes of the prologue in fact form a kind of inclusio. This is further confirmed by the fact that in the opening episode of the prologue, it is YHWH's words that set into motion the series of military actions that follow, whereas in the closing episode, YHWH's words represent an evaluation of the series of military actions just reported.

Moreover, the direct reference to YHWH's covenant (בריתי) in 2:1, the rebuke directed against Israel for not obeying Him (ולא־שמעתם בקלי) in 2:2, and YHWH's decision not to rid the nations from before them in 2:3, are all themes that are picked up and reiterated in the introductory framework for the central section in 2:20–21.[22] In this respect, one can say that the specific words of YHWH reported directly in the scenic narrative of 2:1–5 are in fact thematically linked to the introductory framework of the central section and anticipate events that are to come.

Finally, with regard to the mini-narrative concerning Adoni-Bezek, it will simply be noted for now that Adoni-Bezek's confession also provides significant links to the narrative concerning Abimelech in Judges 9. Further discussion of these links as well as their rhetorical function within the book will be presented in the next chapter.

But what is significant here is that while the presence of the five mini-narratives seems inexplicable purely from the perspective of the internal logic of the prologue, when viewed in light of the thematic links they forge with the rest of the book, their presence does seem to serve a definite rhetorical function. In fact, given their somewhat intrusive presence within the prologue, one may even argue that their presence in the prologue is solely for the purpose of establishing rhetorical links with subsequent sections and episodes within the

[22] Granted, the word for ridding the nations in 2:3 is the Piel of גרש, while it is הוריש in 2:21. But the two verbs seem largely synonymous as they both imply the same action when applied to the nations in relation to the conquest. Compare, for example, Exod. 33:2 and Josh. 3:10; Josh. 24:18 and Judg. 11:23; and Pss. 80:9 and 44:3.

book, and not for elucidating the internal argument of the prologue itself. If this is indeed the case, then the presence of these mini-narratives actually argues for the current form of the prologue being composed specifically as an introduction to Judges rather than it having had a prior existence and a different function before it assumed its current role.[23]

But still, is there an underlying argument to the prologue? If so, what is it? In trying to answer these questions, it seems reasonable to assume that if the mini-narratives were indeed included for the sole purpose of establishing thematic links with other narratives and sections of the book, then the underlying argument of the prologue, if it exists, should be sought from the remaining material outside of the mini-narratives. And sure enough, once the prologue is stripped of the mini-narratives, what emerges is a surprisingly lucid and relatively coherent conquest report as follows:[24]

> 1:4 And Judah went up and YHWH gave the Canaanites and Perizzites into their hands. So they struck down ten thousand men at Bezek. 1:8 Then the men of Judah did battle in Jerusalem and captured it. They struck it with the sword while they set the city on fire. 1:9 Afterwards, the men of Judah went down to fight against the Canaanites living in hill country, the Negev, and the lowland. Judah went against the Canaanites living in Hebron (formerly called Kiriath Arba) and struck down Sheshai, Ahiman, and Talmai. 1:11 They then went from there against those living in Debir (formerly called Kiriath Sepher).[25] 1:17 Then Judah went with Simeon their brother and struck down the Canaanites living in Zephath, destroying it and renaming the city Hormah. 1:18 But Judah did not capture Gaza, Ashkelon, and Ekron with their surrounding areas.[26] 1:19 As YHWH was with Judah, they took possession of the hill country. But they did not dispossess those living on the plains because they had iron chariots. 1:20 When Hebron

[23] This view of Judges' prologue as having a prior existence and a different function is most recently advocated by Brettler (2002:94–97), who sees Judg. 1:1–2:10 as originally an appendix-like conclusion to the book of Joshua that has been inadvertently associated with Judges. However, Brettler does allow for certain modifications to have taken place before the block of material was re-cast as an introduction for Judges.

[24] Translation my own.

[25] Although 1:16 is not one of the mini-narratives, it is nonetheless also left out of this rendition of the conquest report as it very likely represents supplemental information that is included solely in anticipation of the introduction of Heber the Kenite in the Deborah-Barak episode in Judges 4.

[26] For arguments for the adoption of the LXX reading here over the MT, see Wong, 2005:95–98.

> was given to Caleb in accordance with the words of Moses, he dispossessed the three sons of Anak from there. 1:21 But the men of Benjamin did not dispossess the Jebusites living in Jerusalem, so that the Jebusites lived with the men of Benjamin in Jerusalem until this day. 1:22 Now the house of Joseph also went up against Bethel. YHWH was with them. 1:27 But Mannaseh did not take possession of Beth-Shan or Taanach or Dor or Ibleam or Megiddo along with their surrounding area, as the Canaanites were determined to live in that land. 1:28 When Israel was strong, they put the Canaanites into forced labour, but they did not utterly dispossess them. 1:29 Nor did Ephraim dispossess the Canaanites living in Gezer, so that the Canaanites lived in their midst in Gezer. . . .[27]

A careful examination of this narrative at the "core" of the prologue reveals that structurally, the narrative is organised along two distinct trajectories. First, there is a geographic trajectory that moves roughly from south to north according to the location of the tribes as their military exploits are reported. The account thus begins with Judah and Simeon, the two southernmost tribes, and proceeds northwards to Benjamin. This is followed by a report concerning the two Joseph tribes north of Benjamin, with their collective accomplishments reported first, followed by the individual exploits of each of the two tribes. The narrative then resumes its northward move through Zebulun, Asher, and Naphtali, and finally concludes with the relocated tribe of Dan at the northern tip of the land.

Along with this south-to-north geographic trajectory is also a corresponding downward trajectory that represents the decreasing ability of the tribes to take full possession of their land. As Younger has showed, this deteriorating trend is mainly communicated in four-stages focusing on the cohabitation arrangements of the Canaanites in relation to the Israelites.[28]

In the initial stage where Judah and Simeon belong, there is no explicit mention of Canaanites living among these two tribes. Instead, the two tribes are presented as being somewhat successful in dispossessing the surrounding nations to take possession of their land. But in the second stage from Benjamin to Zebulun, it is repeatedly stated in 1:21,27,29,30 that Canaanites were living (ישׁב) with (את) or among (בקרב) the tribes.

---

[27] The rest of the chapter from 1:30 to 1:36 basically follows unchanged from the current canonical text.

[28] Younger, 1994:219–20. A similar progression is also mentioned by Webb (1987:99).

The situation worsens in the third stage as Asher and Naphtali are described in 1:32,33 as living among the Canaanites (וישב בקרב הכנעני ישבי הארץ) instead of the Canaanites living among them. This gives the impression that the Canaanites have now become the dominant power over Asher and Naphtali.

In the final stage, nothing is explicitly said about cohabitation between Dan and the Canaanites. It is stated, however, that the Amorites had confined (לחץ) Dan to the hill country and not allowed them to come into the plains. This seems to suggest that Dan could not even take a foothold in Amorite territory, let alone being able to settle among the Amorites. Indeed, as Webb notes, Dan is here presented as being allowed to live only at a distance from its allotted land.[29]

Regarding these two trajectories, a few more observations can be made. First, it seems that these two trajectories are meant to be viewed not independently, but as an integrated whole. This is seen in that both trajectories have the exact same beginning and end points (Judah and Dan), with the exact same intervening data being used in the same order to construct them. This, in fact, is what allows Younger to present both trajectories together in a single diagram to highlight their relationship with one another.[30] The following is a modified version of Younger's diagram, with the labels changed to reflect my characterisation of the trajectories.

Given that this sophisticated structural arrangement encompasses practically the entire conquest report, from a rhetorical standpoint,

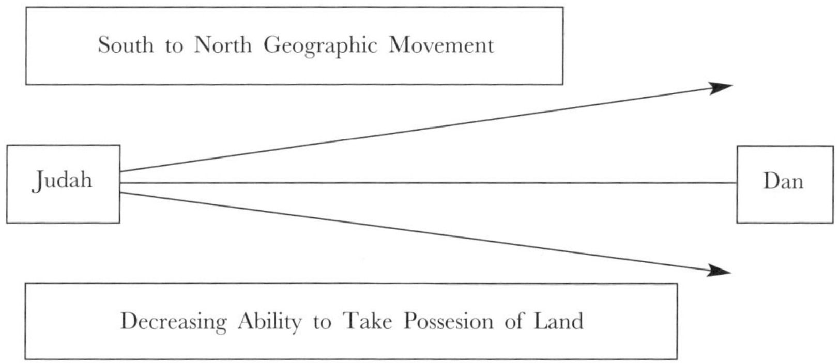

[29] Webb, 1987:99.
[30] Younger, 1994:217.

one can claim that the main argument of the prologue is therefore reflected in this very arrangement. Thus, if one is to give a one-sentence summary of this structural arrangement, it is: "The ability of Israel's tribes to take possession of their land decreases as one moves from south to north."

But this leads to a second observation, which is that the above statement most likely represents only a literary reality and not an actual political-historical reality. In other words, the adoption of this particular arrangement of material in the conquest report in Judges 1 may have been motivated more by a specific rhetorical purpose than by historical accuracy.

Two pieces of evidence can be cited to support such an understanding. First, the entire schema summarised as "The ability of Israel's tribes to take possession of their land decreases as one moves from south to north" immediate strikes one as being too neat to be an accurate reflection of actual historical reality. For historical reality is almost inevitably messy, and therefore does not readily lend itself to orderly schematisation. This is why Younger characterises Judges 1 variously as "a highly stylised account", "a deliberate geographically-arranged narration", and a figurative account utilising "an artificial geographic arrangement".[31] Mullen likewise calls it a "literary summary", suggesting further that the artificial organisation of the narrative indicates that "historical concerns were at best secondary to the narrative".[32]

Second, a careful examination of the schematised arrangement in Judges 1 also reveals a minor discrepancy when compared with information presented elsewhere within and outside the book. This discrepancy involves the placement of Dan at the end of the integrated trajectories.

Admittedly, for Dan to be placed at the end of the geographic trajectory is, at first glance, not inappropriate since its northward migration is already anticipated in Josh. 19:47, and would subsequently be recounted in much greater detail in Judges 18. Once having thus migrated, Dan did in fact become the northernmost tribe.

[31] See Younger, 1995:76 and 1994:227.

[32] Mullen, 1984:53,43. Note, however, that the artificial organisation Mullen speaks of is not the same arrangement as the one suggested here. For Mullen refers to a much simpler threefold division of the prologue into concerns about the southern tribes (1:1–21), the northern tribes (1:22–36), and the messenger at Bokim (2:1–5). But the point being made is essentially the same, that a schematised presentation of events reflects more of a literary concern than a historical one.

Similarly, for Dan to be placed at the end of the trajectory depicting the tribes' decreasing ability to take possession of their land is also not inappropriate. After all, from the allotment narratives in Joshua 15–19 and the comment in Judges 18:1, one can reasonably infer that Dan was the only tribe that needed to seek an inheritance outside its original allotment because of its inability to take possession of its land portion.

But while Dan's position along each trajectory is not misplaced when the trajectories are considered separately, taken together, it gives an impression that is somewhat at variance with reality presented elsewhere. For while Dan seems to fare the worst among the tribes when it comes to its ability to dispossess the nations and take possession of their land, that lack of success only applies to its military exploits before its northward migration when it was still a southern tribe.[33] As Judges 18 shows, however, Dan's military exploits in the north in connection with its migration was in fact a resounding success, testified to by its ability to completely annihilate the citizens of Laish. This means that while Dan being the northernmost tribe and Dan being the least successful of the tribes are both technically true at different stages of its history, they are not true at the same time. Yet this placement of the tribe within the integrated schema gives the impression that diachronic realities have somehow been merged into a single synchronic event.

From these two observations, a case can be made that the schema in question is primarily literary in nature. This does not mean that any possibility of historicity is thereby automatically excluded. After all, as Younger has shown, Assyrian summary inscriptions, which seem to display genre parallels with the conquest report in Judges 1, are often also arranged according to artificially schematised geographic orientation. In the second annalistic section, for example, Assyrian campaigns that were conducted through a span of four to five years have also been telescoped into a single-year presentation in deference to the author's literary purpose.[34] Yet certainly, no one would consider these inscriptions fanciful or unhistorical. What characterises both the Assyrian summary inscriptions and the conquest

[33] The territory originally allotted to Dan in Josh. 19:40–46 clearly consists of southern cities surrounded by the territories of Ephraim, Benjamin, Judah, and the Philistines. See Aharoni et al., map 107.

[34] Younger, 1994:208–12.

report in Judges 1 is simply that a specific literary purpose has been given the highest priority in the composition and arrangement of the accounts.[35]

But still, the following questions beg asking. Why did the author/redactor of Judges 1 choose to shape his conquest report through this particular literary schema? And what is so significant about this particular arrangement? Interestingly, the answer to these questions may well be found in the observation that this schema depicting a deteriorating trend as one moves geographically from south to north actually mirrors the arrangement of material in the central section of the book.

That the narratives in the central section of Judges are basically arranged according to the same south to north geographical trajectory has not gone unnoticed. In fact, numerous scholars have commented on the fact that the south-to-north arrangement of the narratives in the central section according to the judges' tribal affiliation more or less mirrors the order of the tribes found in Judges 1.[36] Younger even sees the south-to-north arrangement in Judges 1 as a literary device to foreshadow the geographic orientation of the judges in 3:7–16:31.[37] Brettler also sees the geographic correspondence between the two sections as proof that some sort of redactional unity exists for the book as a whole.[38]

Similarly, that the narratives in the central section of Judges generally follow a downward trajectory reflecting some sort of deterioration

---

[35] To demonstrate that the literary purpose is given a high priority in the composition not only of Judges 1 but also of the whole book, Malamat (1976:154) notes that, with the exception of the Philistines in the Shamgar and Samson narratives, there is no duplication of the enemy or tribal affinity of the judges within the book. Malamat thinks that this absence of duplication raises the possibility that, in selecting the stories in the book, the compiler "wittingly restricted his choices so as to obtain a paradigmatic scheme of Israel's wars in the pre-monarchical period."

[36] Dumbrell, 25; Gunn, 1987:105; Globe, 1990:239; Younger, 1994:216; 1995:80; Block, 1999:59; Brettler, 2002:110. Furthermore, although never explicitly affirming a connection between the geographical arrangement of Judges 1 and the central section of the book, Webb (1987:132) nonetheless seems to acknowledge some formal interdependence with regard to the geographic arrangements of the two sections. This comes across most clearly when he speaks of Ehud appropriately coming after Othniel solely on the basis of his tribe Benjamin having come after Judah as in Judges 1.

[37] Younger, 1994:216, 1995:80.

[38] Brettler, 2002:110.

has also not gone unnoticed.[39] Lilley, for example, notes the steady deterioration throughout the central section and considers the theme of the book as one of increasing failure and depression.[40] Hudson, Wenham, and Dietrich see the book as chronicling a national decline that spirals downwards to reflect a rapidly disintegrating society.[41] O'Connell, Exum, and Gunn believe that the central section highlights progressive decline in the character of the judges, which in turn illustrates the chaos and hopelessness of the time.[42] In fact, Exum even connects the deterioration in the central section with that in the prologue by noting that the book as a whole mirrors the increasingly negative pattern found in Judges 1.[43]

But as widely as it is accepted that the central section basically follows a downward trajectory, this downward trajectory has surprisingly not been demonstrated in a systematic and comprehensive way. Granted, Exum did attempt to back up her assertion about the increasingly problematic character of the book's protagonists by embarking on a survey of the very protagonists in question.[44] But while she by and large succeeds in showing how most of the major protagonists do display questionable character traits, she has not addressed how such questionable character traits represent some kind of deterioration from one protagonist to another. To be sure, she speaks of Barak's hesitation being magnified in Gideon,[45] but other than this, it is unclear how Samson represents a step-down from Jephthah, or how Jephthah represents a step-down from Gideon in the process of deterioration. In other words, the comparative aspect that would justify her characterisation of the book's protagonists as "increasingly" problematic is simply lacking.

The same can be said of several similar discussions of the book. Like Exum, Wenham and Gunn have also pointed out a few isolated

[39] Admittedly, many of the following comments refer to this deterioration as something that characterises the book as a whole rather than just the central section. But since the central section constitutes almost three quarters of the book, any comment that applies to the book as a whole can reasonably be understood as also characterising the central section of the book.

[40] Lilley, 98–99,102.

[41] Hudson, 50; Wenham, 52; Dietrich, 2000:316–17.

[42] O'Connell, 266, Exum, 1990:411, Gunn, 1987:104.

[43] Exum, 1990:413.

[44] Ibid., 413–31.

[45] Ibid., 416.

examples of sequential deterioration,[46] but fail to provide more comprehensive proof to substantiate their claims that a downward trajectory exists for the book as a whole. For many others, that the book depicts a trend of progressive deterioration is simply considered self-evident, such that hardly any attempt is even made to show how it is so.[47]

In light of this deficiency, it seems both worthwhile and necessary at this juncture first to set forth systematically and in detail the evidence for progressive deterioration in the central section of the book. This will ensure that before any conclusion is drawn concerning the relationship between the prologue and central section, it will have been sufficiently well established that it is indeed appropriate to speak of the central section as being arranged according to some kind of downward trajectory.

Progressive Deterioration in the Central Section

Admittedly, it is no simple task to demonstrate that the narratives in the central section follow some kind of downward trajectory. This is primarily because the material in question consists by and large of narratives of the exploits of different individuals. Since each of these narratives has its own unique plot line, as a whole, they do not immediately lend themselves to easy comparisons.

Fortunately, as Gros Louis points out, there appears to be sufficient coherence to these narratives such that incidents and elements in one narrative are often echoed in the others.[48] Likewise, Gunn also notices that the narratives throughout the book share common themes and are linked to each other through associative connectors such as

---

[46] For example, Wenham (61) draws attention to the fact that Gideon's treatment of his uncooperative countrymen represents a more violent response than Deborah and Barak's rebuke. He also notes (62) how the cyclical framework has spiralled downwards, such that by the time of Jephthah, the nation's graver sin had resulted in God becoming more reluctant to help. Gunn (1987:113–14) also comments on how for the Samson cycle, the people no longer address God out of oppression like they did in previous cycles, thus making the Samson story climatic within the cyclical framework.

[47] A notable exception is Schneider (xii, 287), who made it one of her main tasks to demonstrate progressive deterioration throughout the book. Although she does offer more substantial treatment of the matter than most, the fact that her book is a commentary means that her evidence for deterioration is inevitably scattered throughout the book, thus making it difficult to see the big picture at a glance. The impact of her argument is hence significantly reduced.

[48] Gros Louis, 157.

motifs and wordplay.[49] In fact, to Gunn, such motif parallels not only serve a formal cohesive function, but also invite comparative evaluation by drawing attention to similarities and contrasts in situations and characters.[50] If this is true, then it is only natural that one should look for evidence of progressive deterioration in the central section by focusing on recurring motifs that are found in the narratives of two or more judges. This means that much of the following exploration will essentially be thematic in nature.

Before embarking on this thematic exploration, it is necessary first to point out that the very idea of progressive deterioration running through the central section is one that is actually rooted in an explicit statement in the text. In delineating the cyclical pattern that characterises Israel during this period in the introduction to the section, the narrator explicitly affirms in 2:19 that with the death of each judge, the people returned to behaviour even more corrupt[51] than their fathers. Here, the use of the comparative מן in ישׁבו והשׁחיתו מאבותם makes it quite clear that the cyclical pattern described in 2:10–19 is not simply a series of stagnant recurrences, but follow a downward spiral.[52] Each generation is thus portrayed as comparatively more corrupt than the generation before it. In fact, one suspects that it is primarily on the basis of this very statement that scholars feel justified in speaking of the narratives in the book as depicting some sort of downward spiral,[53] even though few have actually attempted to show how this deterioration systematically manifests itself in the narratives that follow.

But is the deterioration implied in 2:19 in fact traceable through the narratives in the central section of the book? The answer appears to be in the affirmative as this deterioration can be seen manifesting itself thematically in the following five areas.[54]

---

[49] Gunn, 1978:104,105.

[50] Ibid., 106.

[51] *HALOT*, citing Müller (259), classifies the use of the Hiphil of שׁחת as "internally factitive", thus meaning "to behave corruptly". Note the typographic error in *HALOT*. The proper page number for the citation of Müller should be p. 259 and not p. 295.

[52] The same use involving שׁחת and מן to indicate worsening degrees of corruption is also found in Ezek. 16:47; 23:11.

[53] Gooding (72), Webb (1987:158), and Marais (88) all speak of the cycles as degenerative primarily on the basis of 2:16–19.

[54] In this respect, the following discussion would constitute a rebuttal to the assertion of Rofé (31) that the editing of the stories in the central section is unaware of the degeneration mentioned in 2:19.

1. *Deterioration traced through the judges' decreasing faith in YHWH*

The first area where some sort of deterioration is discernible involves the decreasing faith of the judges in YHWH. This theme first comes up in the Barak narrative in Judges 4 as Barak is considered the first of the hesitant judges.[55]

In 4:6–7, YHWH issues a command to Barak through Deborah, telling him to gather together ten thousand men from Naphtali and Zebulun to go up against Sisera in battle. Barak was specifically promised victory as YHWH would give Sisera into his hands (ונתתיהו בידך). Barak, however, answered that he would only go if Deborah would go with him.

While the author has chosen not to disclose what motivated Barak to answer thus, it is nonetheless clear that Barak's answer had not met with YHWH's approval. For the honour that would have gone to him had he obeyed unconditionally would now go instead to a woman as YHWH sells Sisera into her hands.

Admittedly, the text has not made clear what exactly it is about Barak's answer that displeased YHWH. However, a couple of observations may provide some insight. First, the message of YHWH came through Deborah, who was introduced in 4:4 as a prophetess (נביאה). This seems clearly to establish both the messenger's credentials and the authenticity of the message. Second, the fact that YHWH had promised to give the enemy into Barak's hands (ונתתיהו בידך) should also engender faith. After all, in the preceding narrative, the very idea that YHWH has given the enemy into Israel's hands (כי־נתן יהוה את־איביכם . . . בידכם) was used by Ehud as a war-cry to rally the troops (3:28). But here, in spite of YHWH's explicit promise, which incidentally, was absent in the Ehud narrative, Barak acted with hesitation. This seems to suggest a lack of faith in YHWH.

But if Barak's faith in YHWH was indeed wanting, this weakness seems even more pronounced in the portrayal of the next judge, Gideon. In the first half of the Gideon narrative, one is reminded of this weakness in almost every scene.

When Gideon was first introduced, he was addressed by the angel of YHWH as a mighty warrior (גבור החיל) and commissioned to go "in this strength of his (בכחך זה)" to deliver Israel (6:12,14). As Gros

[55] Marais, 101.

Louis comments, "To such an announcement, and from an angel, we would expect an awed response. But Gideon, like Barak, is not convinced."[56] Instead, he responded by emphasising how lowly (דַּל) and insignificant (צָעִיר) he and his clan were. When YHWH then reassured Gideon of His own presence and of Gideon's ability to strike down the Midianites, Gideon then asked for a sign. Only when fire flared from a bare rock was he convinced. But even so, his subsequent actions continued to betray a faith insufficient to overcome his fears.

The first task entrusted to Gideon was the demolition of his father's altar to Baal and the Asherah pole beside it. However, because he feared (ירא)[57] his family and the men of the town (6:27), he only carried out the task at night.[58] When the townsfolk discovered what happened the next morning and demanded his death, Gideon was spared only when his father came to his defence. Gideon himself, however, was strangely absent even though the scene does end with him being renamed Jerub-Baal.

We next witness in 6:34 that the Spirit of YHWH had come upon Gideon (ורוח יהוה לבשׁה את־גדעון), and in response, he blew a trumpet and summoned his troops. But this is followed immediately by another display of doubt as Gideon asked for further signs to confirm his commission.[59] And this time, even one miraculous sign was insufficient to give him the assurance he needed, as he had to request a follow-up sign to confirm the first one.

Then on the night of the decisive victory, YHWH appeared to Gideon, telling him to launch an attack on the Midianites. But before Gideon was to do so, YHWH, well aware of Gideon's habitual lack of faith, actually took the initiative to offer him one final assurance. Interestingly, this assurance is presented in 7:10 as an option, to be

---

[56] Gros Louis, 152.

[57] It should be noted that in Hebrew Scripture, and especially in the Psalms, fear (ירא) is very often contrasted with trust (בטח), and in particular, trust in YHWH. See, for example, Pss. 27:3; 56:4,5,12; 91:2,5; 112:7.

[58] O'Connell (155) sees this unwillingness to confront the foreign cult openly as a sign of Gideon's lack of confidence in YHWH. For more insight into the rhetorical significance of this episode, see Wong, 2006c:540–44.

[59] Note that although Amit (1998:227) finds Gideon's lack of confidence surprising after his possession by the Spirit and the mustering of the army, she does not consider it a weakness or a lack of faith. In this regard, Amit departs from Block (1999:272–73), Exum (1990:417–18), Tanner (158,159), and O'Connell (150,163), all of whom see Gideon's doubt as a weakness or a lack of faith.

exercised only if Gideon is afraid (ואם־ירא אתה). Therefore, had Gideon trusted in the promise YHWH made to deliver Israel when He reduced Gideon's troops from 22,000 to three hundred (7:7), that extra trip down to the enemy camp would not have been necessary. That Gideon did make the trip in the end thus reveals his apprehension regarding the impending battle.

From these various instances, one gets the impression that the lack of faith that first surfaces in Barak seems to have intensified in Gideon. For while the hesitation Barak displayed in response to YHWH's calling seems to be an isolated incident, with Gideon, he seems to have shown a pattern of uncertainty about YHWH's calling and promises in spite of repeated reassurances from YHWH.

This theme of lacking of faith in YHWH continues to show up in the next major judge, Jephthah. In his case, this lack of faith manifests itself most clearly in the vow he made immediately prior to the battle against the Ammonites.[60]

Now an interesting observation about Jephthah's vow is that, like Gideon's requests for signs, the vow was also made after an explicit statement (11:29) that the Spirit of YHWH had come upon him (ותהי על־יפתח רוח יהוה).

Concerning this, Exum writes, "Since the spirit comes upon Jephthah just before he vows a sacrifice to YHWH in return for victory, it might be argued that he utters his ill-fated vow while under its influence. . . . If not a tacit acceptance of the vow, this act nevertheless implicates the deity in the terrible events that follow."[61] Such an interpretation, however, is somewhat curious, especially in light of the close parallel between this incident and the tests of the fleece in the Gideon narrative.

Structurally, the two incidents are presented almost as exact parallels of each other. Both begin with a statement of YHWH's spirit coming upon the judge (6:34a, 11:29a), followed immediately by a report of the judge making a significant move towards a showdown with the enemy. In Gideon's case, he blew his trumpet and suc-

---

[60] I am indebted to Professor Nicolas Wyatt for drawing my attention to an Ugaritic parallel in KTU1.14, where King Keret made a vow (ydr, cf. וידר in Judg. 11:30) to the goddess Athirat on his way to war, and eventually suffered for it. But unlike Jephthah, who suffered for making the inappropriate vow, Keret was punished for failing to keep his.

[61] Exum, 1990:422. The same point is also made by Exum elsewhere (1989:66).

cessfully summoned his troops from the various tribes (6:34b–35), while in Jephthah's case, he advanced against the Ammonites (11:29b).[62] These acts, following immediately after statements about YHWH's Spirit and being described using consecutive verb forms, should naturally be understood as representing the direct consequences of the coming of YHWH's Spirit. These are then followed by reports of the judges' direct speeches to YHWH, each introduced with ויאמר and opened with a conditional clause beginning with אם (6:36, 11:30). The critical issue here is how these speeches are to be interpreted.

Admittedly, Exum's stipulation of some kind of causal relationship between the coming of the Spirit of YHWH and Jephthah's vow is not impossible, as the consecutive forms introducing the vow can certainly be understood as consequential. But it is also possible to understand ויאמר and וידר in both the Gideon and the Jephthah incidents as logically contrastive or adversative[63] to what precedes, since the direct consequence of the coming of YHWH's Spirit has already been reported in the judges' military actions. If so, both the requests of Gideon and the vow of Jephthah can in fact be viewed as having been uttered in spite of the coming of YHWH's Spirit rather than as a result of it. A possible translation for the two verses would then be "And yet, Gideon said to God . . ." for 6:36, and "And yet, Jephthah vowed a vow to YHWH, saying . . ." for 11:30.

As a matter of fact, Exum actually seems to understand Gideon's requests along this line. In her discussion of Gideon's fearful, hesitant nature, she comments, "YHWH's spirit comes upon Gideon and afterwards he wants assurance".[64] This seems to suggest that Exum indeed sees Gideon's requests as another example of his apprehensive fear. But Exum is apparently also aware of the parallel

[62] Webb (1987:61) thinks that Jephthah's passing from Gilead to Manasseh and back to Gilead again in fact parallels Gideon call-up of volunteers. If so, one can say that in both cases, the presence of the Spirit of YHWH was responsible for motivating the judges to make concrete preparation for war.

[63] See *GKC*, 327, sect. 111e, Joüon, 641, sect. 171f, and Waltke and O'Connor, 550, sect. 33.2.1d. The best example of this use of the consecutive form is Gen 32:31, where Jacob declared that he saw God face to face "and yet" his life was spared (ותנצל נפשׁי). Incidentally, the consecutive form ותכבד in Judg. 1:35 may also fit this category, since the report of the hand of the house of Joseph being heavy upon the Amorites clearly contrasts with the immediately preceding statement of the Amorites' ability to limit the Danites to the hill country. Judg. 1:35 therefore gives precedent to this particular use of the consecutive form within the book.

[64] Exum, 1990:417.

between this and the Jephthah incident, which she would interpret differently in the same article. In an attempt to harmonise her treatment of the two incidents, Exum asks what the connection might be, if any, between animation by the Spirit and the subsequent revelation of Gideon weakness of character.[65] But to this question, Exum provides no answer, perhaps because it is inherently problematic to claim as she did with Jephthah that Gideon's tests were requested under the influence of the Spirit. For that would make the Spirit the instigator of doubt about YHWH Himself. So, to justify the different approaches she took in interpreting two similarly structured incidents, Exum writes, "To be sure, Gideon's test and Jephthah's vow are different matters and serve different functions."[66] But is that really true? For the two incidents may not be that different after all if both indeed function primarily to highlight the judges' common lack of faith in spite of the special presence of YHWH's Spirit.[67]

But even so, does Jephthah's vow represent some sort of deterioration from Gideon's requests? A case can perhaps be made.[68] For while Jephthah is certainly not presented as being habitually fearful the way Gideon was, his vow nonetheless seems to betray a desperation that exceeded that of Gideon. After all, Gideon's need for assurance, even though coming in the form of narrowly specified tests (6:36–40), merely involved a piece of wool fleece. But with Jephthah, the stakes are considerably higher because his vow potentially involved a human life. And as it turns out, a human life was in fact the price he eventually had to pay.

To be sure, much has been written about whether the language of Jephthah's vow refers only to an animal or also includes the possibility of a human sacrifice.[69] Concerning this, Exum is certainly

---

[65] Ibid., 418.

[66] Ibid., 417.

[67] Trible (1981:61–62; 1984:93–116), Gunn and Fewell (115) and Römer (1998:29–30) also see Jephthah's vow, uttered after YHWH's Spirit came upon him, as signalling a lack of faith. Webb (1987:63–64) further points out that the use of the emphatic infinitive נתון with the imperfect in the vow (thus, "if you will indeed give the Ammonites into my hands") in fact expresses Jephthah's insecurity regarding whether or not YHWH will reject him.

[68] For a different reason than that argued below, Bal (107) also hints at some kind of deterioration from Gideon to Jephthah. To Bal, whereas Gideon acted and came out with an offering before he demanded anything, Jephthah only made a verbal promise and showed no evidence of good faith before the vow was actually carried out.

[69] See, for example, Marcus, 1986:13–18; Webb, 1987:64, Robinson, 334–38.

correct in pointing out that the question is in fact moot because the one who came out to meet him in the end and who was subsequently sacrificed turned out to be human.[70] Furthermore, that Jephthah must have been aware of the potential implications of his vow can be seen in that, had he never considered the possibility of a human sacrifice, he would not have responded the way he did when he saw his daughter coming out to meet him. He would instead have greeted her gladly and simply looked around for the first animal. Thus, even though Jephthah most certainly did not make the vow expecting it to be his own daughter that would be sacrificed, he nevertheless must have been fully aware of the possibility that the sacrifice could be human. And to make such a high-staked vow on the brink of battle certainly betrayed the fear gripping him even as he advanced against the enemy. In this respect, one can argue that Jephthah's lack of faith in fact represents a form of deterioration from Gideon: if not in frequency, then at least in the intensity of his fear.

As for Samson, the final judge, a case can also be made that he too, displayed a lack of faith in YHWH. And the incident involved also happens to display certain parallels with the Gideon and Jephthah incidents just mentioned.

In 15:14b, a similar statement of the Spirit of YHWH coming upon the judge is again reported (ותצלח עליו רוח יהוה). This is also followed by a report of the judge's engagement with the enemy. In this case, the ropes on Samson's arm becoming like burnt flax and Samson being able to strike down a thousand Philistines with the jaw bone of an ass (15:14c–15) are surely to be seen as direct consequences of the Spirit's presence. This is then followed by a direct quote of Samson's boast, which leads to an etiological note (15:16–17). But in 15:18, a second speech of Samson is reported, and this time, it is addressed directly to YHWH. And in a development that parallels Gideon and Jephthah, it is again through the judge's first direct speech to YHWH after the coming of His Spirit that the judge's lack of faith becomes most evident.

In the case of Samson, it is the onset of a great thirst after his engagement with the enemy that prompted him to address YHWH directly and for the first time since the beginning of the narrative

[70] Exum, 1989:67; 1990:422.

about him. And the brief speech basically represents a complaint against YHWH. To be sure, Samson began by acknowledging that it was YHWH who had given a great deliverance into his hands. But the words that follow almost amount to an accusation that YHWH is not beyond negating the great deliverance He just gave. How is this so?

As Exum points out, Samson's words in 15:18 begin and end with the motif of giving into the hand.[71] In the first half of his speech, Samson acknowledged that it was a great deliverance (את־התשועה הגדלה) that YHWH had given into his hand (נתת ביד־עבדך). As Samson was the only person in danger in the immediate context, the deliverance he spoke of was obviously his own, and from the hands of the Philistines. But by asserting in the second half of his speech that he would die of thirst and hence fall into the hands of the uncircumcised (ונפלתי ביד הערלים), Samson was essentially implying that he would fall back into the hands of the very people from whom he had just been delivered. If that indeed came to pass, then the "great deliverance" spoken of in the first half of his speech would effectively have been negated completely.

To be sure, Samson's clever reference to his falling back into the hands of the Philistines may indeed have been a blatant attempt to "bait" the deity, as Exum puts it.[72] After all, whether or not he would fall back into the hands of the Philistines is in reality a moot point if, by then, he had already died of thirst as he claimed he would. Thus, for Samson to phrase his request to YHWH for deliverance from thirst in such a manipulative way after he just experienced "a great deliverance" from the Philistines certainly says something about his lack of faith in the God who has just delivered him.[73] And to the extent that Samson's lack of faith was displayed right after he had experienced YHWH's great deliverance, whereas Gideon's and Jephthah's lack of faith came before they experienced any victory, one can argue that the faith of Samson compares unfavourably

[71] Exum, 1981:23.

[72] Ibid. Also see Exum, 1983:41.

[73] This view of Samson's prayer is in marked contrast to Greene's (69). For Greene sees Samson's prayer as an expression of faith that contrasts with the murmuring of the wilderness generation in similar circumstances. But Greene's view of Samson as a new Israel, faithful precisely where old Israel was not, does not fit with the overall portrait of Samson in the rest of the narrative.

with that of Gideon and Jephthah. In this respect, Samson's lack of faith may indeed be seen as a form of deterioration from Gideon and Jephthah.

2. *Deterioration traced through the increasing prominence of the judges' self-interest as motivation behind their actions*

A second area where progressive deterioration is discernible is in the increasing prominence of the judges' self-interest as motivation for their action. This self-interest first becomes noticeable in the narrative about Gideon.

In 7:18, where Gideon gives instructions to his men prior to their attack on the Midianite camp, the battle cry specifically given was, "For YHWH and for Gideon (ליהוה ולגדעון)". The inclusion of Gideon's name in this battle cry is somewhat unexpected. After all, in 3:28, when Ehud rallied his troops to take on the Moabites, his battle cry only focused on the fact that YHWH has given their enemies into their hands (כי־נתן יהוה את־איביכם את־מואב בידכם).[74] Similarly, in 4:14, Deborah's battle cry[75] also focused on YHWH giving Sisera into Barak's hands as He goes ahead of Barak (כי זה היום אשר נתן יהוה את־סיסרא בידך).

Moreover, in the context of the Gideon narratives, the inclusion of Gideon's name in the battle cry may also be significant in that in the immediately preceding episode, YHWH had just made Gideon reduce the size of his troops "in order that Israel may not boast against me saying, 'my own hand has delivered me (7:2).'" In the end, however, after the battle was fought and won, the credit for victory would still be misplaced as the Israelites then offered Gideon kingship because "you have delivered us from the hands of Midian (8:22)". In light of these developments, one has to wonder if Gideon's inclusion of his own name in the battle cry was indeed appropriate,[76]

---

[74] Schneider (51) likewise sees Gideon's sharing of the victory with God in 7:20 as deterioration from Ehud's explicit affirmation that it was God who was responsible for victory.

[75] Although according to the text, Deborah's words were spoken specifically to Barak, yet in the context of ten thousand men being present with them ready for war (4:10), Deborah's public proclamation to one who is their commander-in-chief can certainly be viewed as a battle cry that functions to rally the troops for battle.

[76] Marais (112) sees Gideon's inclusion of his own name as turning on YHWH. Wenham (126) also notes that the addition of "for Gideon" in the battle cry is out of kilter with God's expressed wish that only He should be glorified in the victory.

and whether or not this act was at least partially responsible for the subsequent misguided offer of kingship to him.[77] Thus, the way Gideon shaped the battle cry may indeed betray a subtle promotion of self-interest even as he appears to be fighting for YHWH.

But if the matter still seems somewhat ambiguous regarding whether or not self-interest had come into play in Gideon's battle cry, the picture seems much clearer in the episode concerning Gideon's pursuit of the two Midianite kings.

After reporting the death of two Midianite leaders Zeeb and Oreb, the narrator next recounts Gideon's pursuit of two fugitive Midianite kings in 8:4–12. During this pursuit, Gideon twice sought help from two Israelite towns, Succoth and Penuel, and on both occasions, he was refused. So, after the two kings were captured, Gideon returned to Succoth and Penuel to punish the two towns for their refusal to help.

Up to the point where Gideon punished the elders of Succoth with thorns and briers in 8:16, the reader's sympathies may well have lain with Gideon since the towns' refusal to help their leader who was in pursuit of the nation's enemies seems inexcusable. But subsequent revelation calls for re-evaluation. If the report in 8:17 that Gideon killed the men of Penuel raises suspicion that something was amiss, the immediately following dialogue between Gideon and the two kings in 8:18–21 seems to confirm that Gideon's self-interest may indeed have been the true motivation behind his pursuit of the two kings.

In 8:18, Gideon inquired about the men the kings killed at Tabor. And when he received confirmation that those killed were indeed his blood brothers, he decided not to spare the kings. But the possibility Gideon raised of sparing the two kings is in itself problematic in several ways. First, notwithstanding Block's speculation that Gideon

---

Although Block (1999:282) thinks that Gideon's addition of his own name to the battle cry seems innocent enough, he also comments that "in light of what follows in chap. 8, one wonders if the narrator does not intend some ambiguity here."

[77] Exum (1990:419) hints at a connection between Gideon's battle cry and Israel's subsequent kingship offer. Webb (1987:152) further makes the interesting observation that the offer of kingship to Gideon may have been his own making because he had been acting more and more like a king from the moment he crossed the Jordan. If true, this means that Gideon may have been harbouring kingly ambitions even far in advance of the official offering of kingship to him. The question, then, is whether including his name in the battle cry might have represented the first sign of such ambitions.

may not have meant what he said,[78] the narrator seems to present Gideon as being serious when he raised the possibility of sparing them had they spared his brothers earlier. After all, Gideon's statement is preceded by an oath formula involving the personal name of YHWH (חי־יהוה).[79] But if Gideon's statement is taken at face value, this raises a second problem, which is that there seems to be no precedent for sparing foreign enemy leaders in war.

Already within the book of Judges, one can find examples of enemy leaders being executed when captured in war. Adoni-Bezek in 1:7 is one example, and Sisera could potentially be another, even though strictly speaking, he was not executed by an Israelite judge. But the fact that Barak pursued Sisera after the destruction of Sisera's forces, coupled with Deborah's prophecy that the honour would not be Barak's because Sisera would be handed over to a woman, suggests that had Barak caught up with Sisera before Jael killed him, Barak would have executed Sisera himself.

But the tradition of not sparing enemy leaders, and particularly kings, goes back even further. In Numbers 21, Sihon and Og were both struck down and killed. In the conquest accounts in Joshua, it has also been repeatedly mentioned that various enemy kings were put to the sword and killed. In particular, the language of Joshua 11:17 seems to suggest that many of these kings were first captured and then executed. This is confirmed by the accounts of how the king of Ai (Josh. 8:23,29) and the five Amorite kings (Josh. 10:16–18, 22–27) met their deaths. Moreover, if 'putting to the sword (הכה... לפי־חרב)' indeed suggests a חרם-styled execution as was argued earlier,[80] then the deaths of the kings of Makkedah (Josh. 10:28), Libnah (Josh. 8:29), Hebron (Josh. 10:36), Debir (Josh. 10:39), Hazor (Josh. 11:10), and the royal cities (Josh. 11:12) may also fit this pattern. In fact, not a single case can be found in the conquest narratives where a captured enemy king is spared.[81]

---

[78] Block (1999:294–95).

[79] Block (1999:295) actually considers the oath "an empty exploitation of the divine name in violation of the Third Commandment" for the sake of impressing his captives. But this is pure speculation as there is absolutely nothing in the text or in the surrounding context that would support such an understanding. On the contrary, an oath taken on God's life employs the strongest and most binding language available, thus reflecting the seriousness with which the oath was taken.

[80] See the brief discussion on p. 37.

[81] Not only so, but later in the period of the monarchy, Saul's sparing of the

All this seems to suggest that Gideon had no basis to even consider sparing the two Midianite kings. And the fact that he ended up not sparing them does not make the point moot, because it reveals an underlying error in Gideon's reasoning.

This leads to the third problem with Gideon's statement. Even though Gideon eventually did kill the two Midianite kings, his words nevertheless reveal that the action he took was motivated primarily by personal vengeance rather than a concern to rid the nation of foreign oppression. And this realisation is especially troubling when viewed in the context of his heavy-handed punishment of the two cities that refused to help. For in light of his statement to the two kings, one suddenly realises in retrospect that his punishment of the elders of Succoth and his killing of the men of Penuel may well be motivated also by personal vendetta rather than a sense of righteous indignation for their refusal to help YHWH's cause. Thus, as it turns out, all the time one thought Gideon was pursuing the two kings in the interest of national welfare, he may actually have been pursuing a personal agenda.[82]

But there may still be one other incident where Gideon's actions appear to be motivated by self-interest, and it is related to Israel's offer of kingship.

Strictly speaking, Israel's offer of kingship to Gideon is not presented as something engineered by Gideon. However, as has already been mentioned, the inclusion of his own name in the battle cry may have been a calculated move to raise his own personal profile, thereby making himself a natural candidate should the people ever consider having a king. What is worth further consideration though, is Gideon's response to the people's offer.

On the surface, Gideon gave a theologically sound reason for rejecting the people's offer of kingship, declaring that it is not he or his sons but YHWH who rules over them. Indeed, many take Gideon's answer at face value and interpret it as a recoiling from the impiety

Amalekite king Agag in 1 Samuel 15 also became the immediate cause of his rejection as king. And later still, Ahab's sparing of the Aramean king Ben-Hadad in 1 Kgs. 20:29–43 also resulted in severe judgement from YHWH.

[82] Webb (1987:151) thinks it is a personal vendetta which Gideon has been prosecuting with such ruthless determination in the Transjordan. Wenham (321) also notes that Gideon's pursuit of the two kings is not presented as a normal follow-up victory in the field but a campaign of revenge.

of the offer.[83] However, Gideon's subsequent behaviour raises suspicion and suggests that a different interpretation is possible.

To be sure, many have pointed out that subsequent to his refusal of the kingship offer, Gideon actually acted every bit like a king.[84] To begin with, there is the accumulation of wealth reported in 8:24–26. Significantly, the list of items he acquired through the collection from the people includes pendants and purple garments worn by the Midian kings, as well as the chains that were on their camel's necks, something already mentioned earlier in 8:21. Even if some of the trinkets were melted along with the other gold rings and ornaments to make the golden ephod, the kingly garments would certainly have been preserved. In fact, Fokkelman argues that the exact inventory of spoils listed after the weight of gold reflects Gideon's point of view, thus underlining Gideon's greediness and his obsession with royalty.[85] Commenting especially on the earlier report of Gideon taking the ornaments off the camels of the Midian kings after he had executed them, Fokkelman writes,

> Our first reaction to this paratactic sentence structure is mystification: what is the point of the weird detail about the ornaments when Gideon is bagging the biggest prize of all? Is the writer justified in mentioning the taking of the crescents on the same level as the execution? My answer would be that he is: these baubles represent Gideon's fascination with royalty, and form the first indication that he will be mesmerized by their material glamour. The narrator has promoted them to a position equal to that of the execution, because they represent the field of vision of the grasping Gideon and are the objects of his obsession.[86]

But other than the accumulation of wealth, there is also the multiplying of wives and concubines reported in 8:30–31, which, together with the accumulation of wealth, are specifically prohibited in the kingship regulations set out in Deut. 17:17.

Finally, it is also reported in 8:31 that Gideon named his son Abimelech, which means "My father is king".[87]

---

[83] Webb, 1987:152. See also Lindars, 1965:322; Wilson, 80; Gros Louis, 155; Mullen, 1993:149; Amit, 1998:97.

[84] See, for example, Jobling, 67; Gunn, 1987:114; Wenham, 121; Fokkelman, 1999:129.

[85] Fokkelman, 1999:147–48.

[86] Ibid., 148.

[87] Admittedly, the name can be taken to mean "The (Divine) King is my father",

Concerning this, it is perhaps noteworthy that in the majority of cases in Hebrew Scripture, the naming of a son is by the mother and not the father.[88] In fact, there are less than ten cases where a father is explicitly said to have named his son, and in most of these, a reasonable explanation can be deduced from the text. Jacob, for example, is said to have given Benjamin his name in Gen. 35:18, but this is only a case of renaming after Rachel already gave the boy a name before her death. Moses is also said to have named his son Gershom in Exod. 2:22, but the name is immediately explained in the text as reflecting the particular circumstances of Moses and not of his wife. In Gen. 5:3, Adam is said to have named Seth, but this represents only a summary statement. In the actual account of Seth's birth in Gen. 4:25, it is Adam's wife who is specifically said to have given Seth his name. In Gen. 16:15 and 21:3, Abraham is said to have named Ishmael and Isaac respectively, but in reality, the two names were already pre-ordained by YHWH in 16:15 and 17:19 before the boys' respective births. As for the naming of Esau and Jacob, it is actually not entirely clear who named the boys since the MT of Gen. 25:25–26 seems to vacillate between 3ms and 3mp verb forms, while the versions are split.[89] That leaves Seth's naming of Enosh in Gen. 4:26 and Lamech's naming of Noah in Gen. 5:29 as the only remaining cases where the father named the child instead of the mother. But in both these cases, the mother is not mentioned at all in the immediate context.

---

which would then be an expression of piety. But as Block (1997:362; 1999:304) argues, in view of Gideon's self-serving behavior, the name seems rather more likely to reflect Gideon's egotism than faith in YHWH. Besides, in Ancient Near-Eastern culture, divine fatherhood often constitutes part of kingly legitimation (cf. Ps. 2:7).

[88] Seth is named by Eve in Gen. 4:25, Moab and Ammon by their mothers in Gen. 19:37–38, the twelve sons and one daughter of Jacob named by Leah and Rachel in Gen. 29:29:32–35; 30:6,8,11,13,18,20,21,24; 35:18 (though the verb in 29:34 is 3ms in the MT and 3fs in the versions), Er, Onan, and Shelah by Shua in Gen. 38:3–5 (though the verb in 38:3 is 3ms in the MT and 3fs in the versions), Perez and Zerah by Tamar in Gen. 38:29–30 according to the versions, Moses by the Pharaoh's daughter in Exod. 2:10, Samson by his mother in Judg. 13:24, Samuel by Hannah in 1 Sam. 1:20, Solomon by Bethsheba in 2 Sam. 12:24 according to the Qere reading, Jabez by his mother in 1 Chron. 4:9, Peresh by Maacah in 1 Chron. 7:16, Beriah by his mother in 1 Chron. 7:23 according to the versions, and Emmanuel by his mother in Isa. 7:14.

[89] The LXX, Vulgate, and Peshitta have 3ms forms throughout, while the Targum and Samaritan Pentateuch have 3mp forms throughout. Incidentally, there is one case in Ruth 4:17 where community naming is apparently involved, so the 3mp verb forms in Gen. 25:25–26 should not be dismissed outright.

In light of all this, it is significant that Judg. 8:31 clearly states that it was Gideon who gave Abimelech his name even though the mother, Gideon's concubine, is also mentioned within the verse. Can it be then, that the narrator is specifically using this incident to hint at Gideon's personal ambition?[90] If so, then Gideon's rejection of the kingship offer may not be all it appears. No wonder then, that Block titles the section on 8:22–27 in his commentary "Gideon's Sham Rejection of Kingship".[91] Davies even argues that Gideon's words should be understood as an acceptance couched in the form of a pious refusal.[92] But regardless of whether Davies is right or not, the point is that, in spite of Gideon's verbal rejection of the kingship offer, his actions betray the fact that he may well be pursuing a personal agenda even as he judged Israel until his death.

But if Gideon's self-interest indeed seems to have been a motivating force behind much of what he did in the second half of the narrative about him, Jephthah's blatant self-interest is discernible right from the start.

At the opening of the narrative, the reader is told that the Ammonites came to make war on Israel. The elders of Israel then came to Jephthah, inviting him to be their commander (קצין) at war. Jephthah, however, brushed off their initial offer, and it was not until they revised the offer, agreeing to make him head (ראש) over all Gilead if he would fight the Ammonites, that Jephthah appeared interested.

In discussing Jephthah's negotiation with the elders, scholars generally agree that the main area of contention between the two parties concerns the leadership position being offered to Jephthah.[93] Although according to 10:18, Israel's leaders had already agreed to make whoever would lead them into battle against the Ammonites

---

[90] Indeed, Fokkelman (1992:33–34; 1999:130) and Marais (114) think the name Abimelech reflects Gideon's underlying kingly ambition. Ogden (1995:302), on the other hand, thinks that Abimelech was clearly misnamed in light of Gideon's rejection of the kingship offer because Abimelech was not in any sense the "son of the king". But Ogden may have missed the point of the irony here.

[91] Block, 1999:296.

[92] Davies, 154–57. This possibility is also raised by Gunn (1987:114).

[93] Webb, 1987:52–53; Exum, 1989: 73–74; Craig, 78–81; Wenham, 63. Marcus (1989:96–100; 1990:105–13), however, argues that the bargaining was not primarily about leadership position but about Jephthah's legal right to be reinstated as a legitimate adopted son. Willis (34–35) also suggests that what Jephthah was after was reinstatement into the clan, as he had earlier been disinherited.

head (ראש) over all Gilead, the elders' initial offer to Jephthah in 11:6 was only the position of military commander (קצין). It was only after Jephthah rebuffed this initial offer that they revised it and made it head over all Gilead. In this respect, the elders were clearly portrayed as opportunistic as they were apparently hoping to get away with offering Jephthah less than what had already been agreed upon among Israel's leaders.

But if the elders were opportunistic, so was Jephthah, who managed to take advantage of their desperation to exact what he wanted out of the negotiations. From this, one can see that Jephthah's action was dictated primarily by self-interest. For the nation, after all, was facing a crisis, and unlike Gideon, Jephthah did not seem to be harbouring any doubt at this stage about his ability to bring about some kind of deliverance. In fact, Jephthah's confidence in his own ability can be seen in that while the elders' revised offer in 11:8 never made victory a condition for making him head over all Gilead, Jephthah actually imposed that condition on himself voluntarily in 11:9. But in spite of his realisation that the nation was in dire straits and that he could be the one to deliver them, the impression one gets from his dialogue with the elders is that he was interested in playing the role of deliverer only if he could be made head over the people. In this respect, Jephthah's political ambition is not unlike Gideon's, except that while Gideon still couched his personal ambition in a pious rejection of an offer of kingship, Jephthah did not even bother to hide his personal agenda. Rather, he made it front and centre in his negotiations with the elders. Unlike Gideon, who at least showed some concern for the welfare of the nation in his dialogue with the angel of YHWH, Jephthah never once expressed any such concern.

Interestingly, Jephthah's political ambition may also have played a role in the vow he made. Although I admit to generally viewing any attempt to psychoanalyse biblical characters with scepticism, a reasonable case has nonetheless been made by Webb that Jephthah's vow may have been prompted by concerns for his personal stake in the war.[94] Webb points out that the opening words of the vow, "If you will indeed give the Ammonites into my hand (אם־נתון תתן את־בני עמון בידי)" echo the key condition in his bargaining with the elders, "If... YHWH gives them before me (אם . . . ונתן יהוה אותם לפני)", and

[94] Webb, 1987:63–64.

in so doing, brings Jephthah's personal stake in the outcome of the war directly into focus again. Webb speculates that while Jephthah spoke only of the interest of Israel publicly and officially in his negotiation with the Ammonite king, privately, his mind works on his own interest. He writes,

> Jephthah has everything to lose if the battle goes against him, not least his life (see 12:3), but also his position in his clan and tribe, and that clearly means a great deal to him. Formerly an outcast, he is now 'head and commander of all the inhabitants of Gilead.' But if he loses the war, the whole cycle of rejection will begin again. If Yahweh rejects Jephthah now, so too will Jephthah's people—again.[95]

If Webb is right, then even in the matter of his fateful vow, the fear that drove Jephthah into making the vow essentially has to do with self-interest.[96]

As for Jephthah's battle with the Ephraimites, it can be also argued that, like Gideon's treatment of the two uncooperative towns and his execution of the Midianite kings, Jephthah's slaughter of 42,000 Ephraimites basically represents an act of personal vendetta. Indeed, Jephthah's reply to the Ephraimites' accusation hints at this, for not only does the preponderance of first person singular references suggest that he has taken a very personal view of things,[97] his counter accusation is also essentially a personal one. The Ephraimites were accused in 12:2–3 of not saving him personally (ולֹא־הוֹשַׁעְתֶּם אוֹתִי) from the hands of the Ammonites so that he had to take his life into his own hands (וָאָשִׂימָה נַפְשִׁי בְכַפִּי) as he crossed over to fight them.

But if Jephthah had indeed taken a personal view of things, then contrary to what Exum thinks,[98] it is actually not surprising at all that he did not try reasoning with the Ephraimites the way he did with the Ammonite king. And to the extent that the battle with the Ephraimites represents an act of personal vendetta, his slaughtering of 42,000 Ephraimites certainly marks a significant deterioration from Gideon's killing of a mere townful of men in Penuel.

---

[95] Ibid., 64.

[96] Incidentally, Gunn (1987:117) also makes a similar point, arguing that it is perhaps the insecurity of the rejected "son of Gilead" that goads Jephthah to play hostage to fortune in order to secure the victory and headship over his rejectors.

[97] Within the two verses, one can find one occurrence of the independent first person singular pronoun אֲנִי, seven occurrences of the 1cs suffix (four times attached to nouns, twice to prepositions, and once to a direct object marker), and five 1cs verb forms.

[98] See Exum, 1989:75.

But it is not until one gets to Samson that the deterioration hits bottom. For even though with Jephthah, one can argue that almost every single action he took was privately motivated by self-interest, at least publicly, his negotiation with the Ammonite king and the subsequent war against the Ammonites appear to be in the interests of Israel. But when it comes to Samson, there is not even one single incident where he appears to be acting consciously for the interest of YHWH or Israel. For throughout these narratives, Samson is shown to have struck down Philistines on four separate occasions. Yet in every single one of them, he is presented as acting only out of his own personal vendetta. That Israel's oppressors, the Philistines, ended up suffering is something that came about only as an unintended by-product of Samson's revenge. In fact, if anything, Samson is presented as being only too eager to be associated with the Philistines via his interest in their women.[99] If it were not for the fact that things had turned out wrongly on a number of occasions, Samson would not even have been acting against the Philistines at all.

In the first incident where Samson struck down thirty Philistine men in Ashkelon, the reason for doing so can be traced back to his losing a bet with his Philistine wedding companions at the wedding feast (14:19). On that occasion, Samson teased his wedding companions with a riddle, setting as the price for the bet thirty linen garments and thirty sets of clothes. His wedding companions, unable to solve the riddle, threatened his wife with death, so that in order to save herself and her household, she coaxed the riddle's answer out of Samson. Perhaps partly out of anger that he had lost unfairly, and partly out of the need to obtain thirty sets of clothes, Samson, prompted by YHWH's spirit, went down to Ashkelon and struck down thirty Philistines, taking their clothes to pay for the lost bet. But what is noteworthy here is that had Samson not lost the bet, he would not have thought about striking down the Philistines.

Some time later, Samson again attacked and slaughtered many Philistines (15:8), but this time, it is in response to their burning his wife and father-in-law to death. But even this chain of events started innocently enough. Some time after he went away in a huff after his disastrous wedding, Samson returned to his father-in-law's place wanting essentially to consummate the marriage.[100] Upon being turned

[99] Wilson (78) also notes that Samson seeks not to oppose but to establish the most intimate of relationships with the enemy.

[100] See discussion on p. 106 n. 77 regarding Samson's intentions.

down by the father-in-law, who told him that the wife had already been given to one of his Philistine wedding companions, Samson then considered himself justified to act against the Philistines. So he burned their grain and vineyards and olive groves. When the Philistines found out it was Samson who had destroyed their entire harvest, they took revenge by burning to death his wife and father-in-law. And that was when Samson reciprocated by slaughtering the Philistines.

In this matter, what is important to note is that Samson's motivation in slaughtering the Philistines was essentially personal vendetta and had nothing to do with the Philistines' oppression of Israel. In 15:7, Samson stated that it was because the Philistines had acted thus (תעשׂון כזאת) in killing his wife and father-in-law that he would take revenge against them (נקמתי בכם). In other words, this slaughter of the Philistines would also not have taken place had the Philistines not burned Samson's wife and father-in-law to death. Thus, like the previous occasion, Samson's action against the Philistines largely represents a reaction against the turn of events on a personal level rather than a principled resistance against a national foe.

The third instance where Samson struck down a thousand Philistines with the jawbone of a donkey (15:15) follows more or less the same pattern. As a result of his previous slaughter, more Philistines came to Judah to capture Samson so as to exact revenge. The men of Judah, eager to avoid conflict with their overlord, then went to apprehend Samson themselves and turned him over to the Philistines. It was thus basically in self-defence that Samson struck down the thousand Philistines with the jawbone of a donkey, an act probably having more to do with self-preservation than national deliverance.

Finally, in Samson's last act which saw him destroying the temple of Dagon together with all who were in it including himself (16:29–30), again his motivation mainly has to do with personal vendetta. In his last prayer to YHWH in 16:28, Samson made it clear that the strength he asked for was so as to exact revenge upon the Philistines for his two eyes (ואנקמה נקם־אחת משתי עיני מפלשׁתים). Thus once again, Samson is shown to have acted out of self-interest rather than national interest.

From these four instances, one can see that from beginning to end, notwithstanding the fact that he did end up killing a significant number of Philistines, not even once did Samson act out of concern for the welfare of the nation. As Wilson notes, even when he defeated the enemies of God's people decisively, it was always because he has a score to settle or for self-defence, but never with clear intent to save his people.[101] As someone who was supposed to have judged Israel (15:20, 16:31), Samson is thus the most self-focused of all the judges.

3. *Deterioration traced through decreasing participation of the tribes in successive military campaigns*

A third and more obvious area where a progressive deterioration can be traced is the decreasing participation of the tribes in their judges' military campaigns. While some have wondered if the judges' sphere of leadership may have been more local than national,[102] the fact remains that many of the military campaigns within the book are presented as involving numerous tribes. But as the narratives move along from judge to judge, there is a discernible decrease in tribal participation.

In the Ehud narrative, although individual tribes are not named, 3:27 nonetheless gives the impression that all the tribes participated in the war against the Moabites. This is seen in that those who followed Ehud into war are described as 'Israelites (בני־ישׂראל)'.[103]

In the Deborah-Barak narratives, Zebulun and Naphtali were specifically mentioned in 4:10. But from Deborah's song in Judges 5, it seems that other tribes also participated. Specifically, Ephraim (5:14a), Benjamin (5:14b), the western half of Manasseh (5:14c),[104]

---

[101] Wilson, 78. Globe (1990:244) and Wenham (64–65) also make similar observations.

[102] See, for example, Burney, xxxiv; Moore, xxxix; Soggin 1976:175.

[103] Despite doubts expressed by Mayes (1969:355–56) and others as to whether the tribes of Israel took concerted military action together as a nation during the period of the judges, Block (1988:41–42) points out that the frequency of the name Israel is actually higher in Judges than in any other book in Hebrew Scripture, including Exodus to Joshua, where the nation is purportedly operating as a unit. Thus, if nothing else, the Israel of this period is at least presented as one nation.

[104] The text actually cites the clan of Makir rather than the tribe of Manasseh. However, according to Gen. 50:23 and Num. 26:29, Makir is a son of Manasseh, and the clan is counted as belonging to the tribe. But the land inheritance of Manasseh consisted of two separate portions: one east of the Jordan, and the other, west. Cundall (1968:98) and Boling (1975:112) both understand the reference to Makir as representing the clans of Manasseh west of the Jordan. For although Josh. 17:1–6 seems to suggest that all Makirites received land east of the Jordan, Josh. 13:31 suggests that only half the sons of Makir actually received land in the east. For the rest of the Makirites, their inheritance probably lay west of the Jordan. Since the mention of Gilead in 5:17a (see following footnote) likely includes the Manassites who have settled east of the Jordan, the reference to Makir in 5:14c probably refers to those who have settled in the west. The use of Makir rather than Manasseh may be because the two halves of the tribe took different stances with regard to participation in the war.

and Issachar (5:15a–b) are said to have joined the other two tribes, while Reuben (5:15c–16), the eastern half of Manasseh and Gad (5:17),[105] Dan (5:17b), and Asher (5:17c) are criticised for their non-participation. The city of Meroz is also singled out in 5:23 to be cursed for its refusal to help in the war. Thus, out of the ten tribes mentioned,[106] five and a half tribes appear to have participated while four and a half had not.

In the following narrative concerning Gideon, Manasseh, Asher, Zebulun, and Naphtali are clearly identified in 6:35 as tribes participating in the war against the Midianites. Ephraim was called out subsequently in 7:24 and the tribe also ended up playing a significant role. In contrast, two cities, Succoth (8:4–7) and Penuel (8:8–9) refused to help when Gideon was in pursuit of the two Midianite kings. As a result, both cities were severely punished for their lack of cooperation. Thus, one can count five tribes that participated in Gideon's military campaign, half a tribe fewer than those who joined Deborah and Barak. The number of cities specifically singled out for refusing to help also increased from one in Deborah's song to two in Gideon's case.

In the narrative of Jephthah's war against the Ammonites, tribal participation is further reduced. The impression given in the narrative is that Jephthah's campaign by and large involved only the

[105] There is some uncertainty as to how one is to understand the reference to Gilead. Technically, Gilead is a geographic designation covering the mountainous area east of the Jordan. In relation to the tribes of Israel, it would have constituted the area allotted to the half tribe of Manasseh and the tribe of Gad. Because of this, Burney (142), Moore (155), Auld (1984:159) and Block (1999:233) all see the reference to Gilead as a substitution for Gad since otherwise, Gad would have been the only non-southern tribe not represented in the roll-call in 5:14–18. This understanding is also supported by readings in the Peshitta and in some LXX manuscripts. On the other hand, Num. 26:29 and Josh. 17:1 indicate that Gilead is also the name for an eponymous clan belonging to Manasseh that received land east of the Jordan. In light of the fact that another clan of Manasseh is already mentioned in 5:14c (see previous footnote), one can argue that Gilead in 5:17 must therefore be a clan designation that serves to balance Makir by presenting the different stance of the two halves of Manasseh east and west of the Jordan. But perhaps the above two options need not be mutually exclusive. By referring to Gilead, the author of the song may have had in mind both the tribe of Gad as well as the half-tribe of Manasseh east of the Jordan. After all, both were primary occupants of the geographic area known as Gilead. If both had taken the same stance with regard to participation in the war against Sisera, then it is perhaps easier to simply group the two together under a shared geographic designation.

[106] The other two tribes not mentioned in the roll call are Judah and Simeon. Given that the battle with Sisera was fought in the northern location at Taanach by the Waters of Megiddo (5:19), the two southernmost tribes were probably not expected to actively participate.

Gileadites and possibly those from Manasseh west of the Jordan. Depending on whether Gilead is taken to be a reference to Gad, or to the half tribe of Manasseh east of the Jordan, or to both, and whether the reference to Manasseh in 11:29 is to the half tribe west of the Jordan, one can count at most two tribes being involved in the campaign against the Ammonites. And whether the Ephraimites were indeed not called as they claim in 12:1, or refused to go to Jephthah's rescue as he claims in 12:2, the fact remains that they were not involved in the war. In fact, if Jephthah's version of events is closer to the truth, it would mean that whereas it was only individual cities that had refused to help in the campaigns of previous judges, it is now an entire tribe that openly refused to help.

But if Jephthah's war against the Ammonites indeed involved only one or two tribes, Samson's exploits against the Philistines was basically only a one-man affair. In fact, after Samson slaughtered the Philistines who had burned his wife and father-in-law to death, three thousand men from Judah came to apprehend him so that they could hand him over to the Philistines. Thus, from the military campaign of Ehud in which all Israel participated, a point has now been reached where not only did the tribes not participate in support of their leader, one of them actually sided with the enemy against him.

4. *Deterioration traced through the judges' increasing harshness in dealing with internal dissent*

As the tribes became increasingly unwilling to participate in their leaders' campaigns and internal dissent became more frequent, the judges' responses to such dissent also became increasingly harsh.

When Barak and Deborah fought against Sisera, four and half tribes refused to participate. Although this refusal is not mentioned in the narrative portion of the account, it is highlighted in Deborah's song. In fact, a case can be made that the main purpose of the song is not so much to celebrate a victory as many have assumed,[107] but to serve as a polemic against the various tribes and cities for their non-participation.[108]

---

[107] Moore (127), J. Gray (221), Hauser (1987:265,279–80), Stager (224,232), and Block (1999:184,212–13) are among many who classify the song as a celebration of Israelite victory in battle.

[108] Vincent (81) has already noted that the song of Deborah appears not merely to be a war or victory ballad, but also a text that pays tribute to those who did

In any case, while the refusal of these tribes and cities to participate merely resulted in a verbal rebuke in Deborah's song, even though it is a strong rebuke that involves the calling down of curses, as the narrative of the judges continues, the response to internal dissent would gradually increase in harshness.

In his attempt to fight against the Midianites, Gideon also faced internal dissent. The Ephraimites' complaint that he had not called them earlier to join the battle was handled graciously by Gideon, who pacified them by emphasising the honour they received for killing the two Midianite leaders. But the towns of Succoth and Penuel were not quite so fortunate.

To be sure, a marked difference exists between the situation concerning the Ephraimites and that concerning Succoth and Penuel. The complaint of the former was merely that they were not given the opportunity to get involved earlier, whereas the problem with the latter two was that they refused to get involved. That being the case, perhaps the difference in approach Gideon used to deal with the two situations is justified.

Nonetheless, while Deborah and Barak merely rebuked the tribes and cities for their non-participation, Gideon exacted physical punishment.[109] And while punishing the elders of Succoth with thorns and briar seems to be a fair punishment since it was probably they who made the decision not to help, the killing of the men of Penuel comes across as excessively harsh. This is especially in light of the fact that 8:8 presents Penuel as having answered Gideon in exactly the same way the men at Succoth did (ויענו אותו אנשי פנואל כאשר ענו אנשי סכות).

But if Gideon's treatment of the men at Penuel seems excessively harsh, then Jephthah's treatment of the dissenting Ephraimites is even more so. At least with Succoth and Penuel, it is clear that they had refused to provide help when requested. With the Ephraimites, however, one is not even sure what exactly the offence was. For one, the Ephraimites' complaint against Jephthah is presented as essentially no different from an earlier complaint they made against Gideon. In 12:1, they asked why they were not called (ולנו לא קראת)

---

what they should and warns those who did not. But for further argument of this understanding of the song, see Wong 2007: forthcoming.

[109] Wenham (61) calls this the first occasion of civil war in Judges. Given the fact that the two towns are not specifically reported as having fought back, it may be a slight overstatement to call it a civil war. That distinction should perhaps be reserved for Jephthah's war with the Ephraimites.

to join Jephthah (ללכת עמך) to fight against the Ammonites (להלחם בבני־עמון), whereas in 8:1, they questioned why they were not called (לבלתי קראות לנו) when Gideon went to fight against the Midianites (הלכת להלחם במדין). Since the vocabulary used in the two questions is substantially the same, the questions are therefore presented as arising from essentially the same concern.

Granted, the degree of agitation on the part of the Ephraimites seems to have upped a notch against Jephthah, for their complaint was accompanied by a threat to burn down his house over his head. And to be sure, their complaint was disputed by Jephthah, who countered with an entirely different picture of what happened. According to Jephthah, he did call to them, but it was they who did not come to his rescue (ולא־הושעתם in 12:2 and אינך מושיע in 12:3).

Admittedly, the narrator has left things somewhat ambiguous. Having presented both the Ephraimites' and Jephthah's version of events, he seems to have made no effort to clarify for the reader which of the conflicting versions more closely approximate the truth. Thus, it is not at altogether clear whether the Ephraimites were indeed not called to join, or whether they were called but refused to go to Jephthah's rescue.

But regardless of which version of events is true, what is important here is that the similarity in phrasing of the two complaints launched by the Ephraimites against Gideon and Jephthah invites comparison between them. And while Gideon at least took a conciliatory tone with the Ephraimites, Jephthah's response was harsh and uncompromising.

The fact of the matter is, even had the Ephraimites failed to go to Jephthah's rescue as Jephthah claimed, the subsequent slaughter of 42,000 Ephraimites would still be an excessive and unwarranted punishment for failure to cooperate. But if the Ephraimites were indeed never called to participate as they claimed, then Jephthah's slaughter of 42,000 simply because they complained and issued a personal threat might constitute an abuse of the military power at his disposal. And to the extent that one may be horrified by Gideon's killing of the men of Penuel, Jephthah's much larger scale slaughter of his fellow countrymen for an offence similar to Penuel's certainly highlights a progressive deterioration when it comes to excessive harshness with which the judges dealt with internal dissent.

5. *Deterioration traced through YHWH's increasing frustration with His people as the cyclical pattern breaks down*

The final and perhaps most significant theme through which progressive deterioration can be traced is the breakdown of the cyclical framework that structures the narratives of the major judges.

It is generally recognised that the narratives of the major judges follow a cyclical pattern first introduced in a framework passage in 2:10–19. Although minor differences in interpretation exist regarding the number of stages that make up each cycle,[110] as well as how the stages are characterised precisely,[111] for the purpose of the present study, each cycle is seen to consist of five distinct stages.[112] They are: 1) Israel did evil in the eyes of YHWH, 2) YHWH, in anger, sold Israel into the hands of her enemies, 3) Israel cried out to YHWH[113] in distress, 4) YHWH raised up deliverers to defeat the enemies, and 5) the land had rest.[114]

---

[110] Boling (1975:74), Mullen (1984:35), Soggin (1987:43), Exum (1990:411–12) and Schneider (32) basically see a four-stage cycle characterised roughly as apostasy-oppression-distress-deliverance. Gros Louis (1974:143), Fokkelman (1999:137), and Gunn (1987:104–05), on the other hand, see the cycle as comprising six stages. These scholars all include the land having rest as the final stage, but while Gros Louis and Fokkelman distinguish between God's anger and His raising up of oppressors, Gunn sees the raising up of deliverers and defeat of the oppressors as distinct stages. Although Lindars (1995:100) identifies nine elements in the framework that are repeated subsequently in one form or another in the judges narratives, these are basically linguistic correspondences that are not to be construed as distinct stages of a cyclical history.

[111] For example, while Gros Louis (1974:143), Jobling (137–38 n. 7), and Schneider (32) see Israel as repenting in the third stage, Mullen (1982:191), Exum (1990:411–12), and Block (1999:153,159,253) are emphatic that Israel is merely presented as crying out for help, and not as repenting. This understanding seems to be supported also by Greenspahn (1986:392–94) and Brueggemann (108–09). Incidentally, if this second understanding is correct, then the arguments of Beyerlin (1963:2–5) and Guillaume (21–22) that the schema in 2:11–19 represents a critique of the framework introducing each of the judges cycles is not sustainable because there would be no material difference in the theology of the two: both would be testifying to YHWH's deliverance on the basis of pity and not repentance.

[112] This fives-stage cycle is also held by Amit (1998:36).

[113] Israel's crying out to YHWH is not specifically mentioned in the introductory framework. In 2:15, the Israelites were merely said to be in great distress (ויצר להם מאד). However, since the crying out (צעק/זעק) that recurs in the various judges narratives (3:9,15; 4:3; 6:6,7; 10:10) is presented in 10:9–10 as a direct response to their great distress (ותצר לישׂראל מאד), that crying out can perhaps be understood as implied in the introductory framework.

[114] The land having rest (ותשׁקט הארץ) is also not specifically mentioned in the introductory framework, even though it is repeated at the end of many of the judges

Although these five stages seem to recur with some regularity in the narratives of the major judges, these recurrences are not presented as static repetitions.[115] First, it has already been made clear in the framework in 2:19 that after the death of each judge, the people returned to ways even more corrupt than their fathers. This suggests that some kind of deterioration is in play with every recurrence of the cycle.[116] Second, as the narratives move from one major judge to another, the cyclical framework actually breaks down, thus confirming the statement of 2:19 that the cycles represent downward spirals. But how exactly does this breakdown of the cyclical framework manifest itself?

To be sure, the first two stages of the cycle seem quite stable and are found in each of the judges narratives. Each begins with a note that Israel did evil in the eyes of YHWH (3:7,12; 4:1; 6:1; 10:6; 13:1),[117] followed by a report of YHWH giving them into the hands of different enemies (3:8,12; 4:2; 6:1; 10:7; 13:1). For the next two stages, however, subtle variations appear that hint at a progressive deterioration.

In the Othniel and Ehud narratives, Israel's cry to YHWH is immediately followed by a report of YHWH raising up a deliverer to save them (3:9,15). In the Barak narrative, the same pattern is also implied, as Israel's cry is immediately followed by the introduction of Deborah, through whom YHWH commissioned Barak to deliver Israel from the hands of Sisera (4:3–7).

But this pattern is disrupted at the beginning of the Gideon cycle. When Israel cried out to YHWH because of the oppression of the Midianites, instead of immediately reporting the raising up of a deliverer, the text reports YHWH sending a prophet to rebuke the people

---

narratives (3:11,30; 5:31; 8:28). But the introductory framework does refer to the deliverance of the judges as lasting as long as the judges lived (2:18), and it is significant that the rest the land enjoyed is also explicitly linked to the lifetime of the judges in 3:11 and 8:28. Thus, one can perhaps look upon the land having rest as the continued manifestation of the judges' deliverance.

[115] Lilley, 97–99.

[116] Schneider (xii) points out that the Israelites do not begin each cycle at the same place each time, but that each cycle shows a generation beginning yet lower on the scale of legitimate behaviour than the previous generation had.

[117] Mullen (1993:154), however, argues that even the apostasy deteriorates as the narratives continue. He notes that whereas in 2:13, the people were worshipping the "baals" and "ashtaroth", by 10:6, they were also worshipping the gods of Aram, Sidon, Moab, Ammon, and Philistia.

for their disobedience (6:7–10).[118] The impression here is that having responded readily to the people's cry on the previous three occasions only to see them lapsing back into apostasy after each deliverance, YHWH is no longer content to come to their rescue so readily. The raising up of a deliverer is thus preceded by an open rebuke, thereby showing YHWH's displeasure with His people's cyclical lapses.

But the rebuke did little to halt the people's sinful pattern. Thus, after yet another lapse into apostasy following the deliverance through Gideon, YHWH's frustration with His people became even more evident at the beginning of the Jephthah cycle.

This time, when Israel cried out under the oppression of the Ammonites and made a show of repentance, rather than sending

[118] In light of the absence of Judg. 6:7–10 in the Qumran scroll 4QJudg[a], perhaps a brief defence of the integrity of the text at this point is in order. Although Auld (1989:263; 1998:123), Trebolle Barrera (1989:238; 1995:162), Tov (344–45) and Ulrich (6) consider the absence of 6:7–10 in 4QJudg[a] proof enough that the passage in question must have been a late addition to Judges as critical scholars have long suspected, further consideration of the matter reveals that things are not as simple as they seem. To begin, the exact stage during which Judg. 6:7–10 became part of the existing Gideon narrative is still debatable. If the passage is indeed part of the primary Deuteronomistic composition as Noth (1991:73–76), Boling (1975:34–36), and others maintain, then when Tov (344) speaks of 4QJudg[a] as possibly reflecting an earlier edition of the book before the passage in question had been added, that earlier edition can only be a pre-Deuteronomistic edition. But this is unlikely, as no other manuscript evidence of a pre-Deuteronomistic text is extant. Rather, what fits better with the scenario presented by Tov is the position of Veijola (43–48; 100–14), O'Brien (88 n. 21,24), and R. Nelson (1981:43–53) that sees Judg. 6:7–10 as part of a later updating of the primary Deuteronomistic composition. But while it is possible that what is reflected in 4QJudg[a] is indeed an earlier or even the original version of the Deuteronomistic composition, the absence of other corroborating evidence makes this only one possible option. Had other fragments of the same scroll been found that show passages similarly considered late also missing from their immediate contexts, such as a fragment of Judges 10 in which 10:6–16 are missing, then the case for 4QJudg[a] reflecting an earlier edition of Judges would have been much stronger. But as it is, the point made by Hess (124–25) is a valid one that in view of the limited size of the fragment that makes it impossible to see the larger context from which 4QJudg[a] is derived, reservation is called for regarding any hypothesis about the fragment. In fact, Hess (125–27) has presented what seems to be a credible option by suggesting that the omission may have to do with scribes inserting, omitting, or moving sections corresponding to the later Masoretic parashoth divisions for their own purposes, be it liturgical or otherwise. Besides, what, if any, relationship exists between 4QJudg[a] and 4QJudg[b] may also have some bearing on the issue, as the latter contains passages (Judg. 19:5–7; 21:12–25) that most critical scholars regard as belonging to the latest stage of the book's redaction. Thus, until further evidence can be found to clarify the matter, Judg. 6:7–10, which, after all, does seem to have direct literary connection and relevance to its immediate context (Schneider, 102), will be treated as an integral part of the text.

another prophet, YHWH Himself rebuked His people directly. Reminding them of the numerous times He had saved them in the past, YHWH basically called the people's bluff, accusing them of forsaking Him (ואתם עזבתם אותי)[119] and telling them that He would no longer save them. They were told instead to go and cry out to the gods they now worshipped (10:10–14). It was only after the people grovelled further and took concrete action to rid themselves of their idols that YHWH, exasperated[120] by their misery,[121] finally gave in (10:15–16). But the exchange between YHWH and Israel shows that the relationship between them had significantly deteriorated, so much so that YHWH's deliverance, even though it eventually came, is presented as being granted only with reluctance. Is it any wonder then, that by the time one arrives at the Samson narratives, Israel did not even bother to cry out to YHWH anymore,[122] but instead acted as though they were content to serve their oppressors (15:11)?

But Israel's crying out to YHWH is not the only stage of the cycle to have eventually gone missing. The rest the land is said to have enjoyed at the end of earlier cycles is also no longer found in the Jephthah and Samson cycles. And while Israel at least still managed to subdue the Ammonites under Jephthah (11:34), with Samson, the Philistines were not fully subdued. This is seen not only in that the prophecy concerning Samson at the beginning of the cycle merely speaks of him as "beginning" to deliver Israel from the hands of the Philistines (13:5), but also in that the Philistines continued to oppress Israel well after Samson's death. In fact, it was not until David's reign that the Philistines were decisively subdued (2 Sam 8:1).

[119] Since YHWH's rebukes in 2:2, 6:10 only mentioned Israel's refusal to obey (ולא שמעתם בקולי), can this accusation of forsaking (עזב) also be understood as signalling further deterioration in the relationship between YHWH and His people?

[120] Webb (1987:46–48) argues for an understanding of קצל as exasperation mainly on the basis of 16:6, where the word refers to Samson's reaction to Delilah's nagging.

[121] Polzin (177) interprets the misery (עמל) as referring specifically to Israel's "troubled effort" in attempting to secure YHWH's help. Webb (1987:47) thinks that Israel's importunity can indeed be included, but the word is probably used mainly to sum up Israel's condition as described in 10:8–9.

[122] Although it has been observed that 10:6–8 seems to serve as an introduction to both the Jephthah and Samson narratives, yet the crying out to YHWH reported in 10:10 seems to represent a response specifically to the Ammonite oppression mentioned in 10:9.

From these observations, one can see that the progressive deterioration so evident throughout the central section also applies to the cyclical framework. For not only were the people becoming more and more corrupt with each passing generation, YHWH's increasing reluctance to respond to their cries also suggests that their cries were becoming increasingly perfunctory and manipulative, until finally, they did not even bother to cry out anymore for deliverance. In addition, even the deliverers, whose deteriorating personal quality is evident in the accounts of their exploits, are presented as being less and less able to bring about lasting deliverance. Thus, at the end of the Samson narratives, not only were the enemies not dealt any crushing blow, the land was also deprived of rest.

Prologue as Paradigm for the Central Section

From the above discussion, one can see that the material in the central section has also been arranged to highlight some sort of progressive deterioration. In fact, Block presents the major judges cycles graphically as follows:[123]

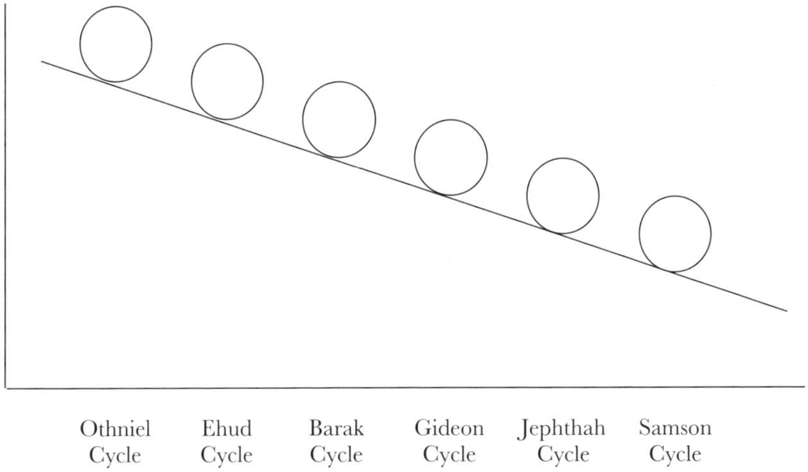

[123] Block, 1999:132.

But if this view of the central section is indeed valid, then a case can be made that the prologue of Judges in fact functions as a paradigm for the central section.

First, both the prologue and the central section are arranged roughly along a south-to-north geographic trajectory beginning with Judah and ending with Dan. Second, in both sections, this south-to-north geographic trajectory also seems to coincide with a simultaneous downward movement signifying deterioration. Thus, while the prologue moves from Judah, the most successful tribe, to Dan the least successful tribe with respect to their ability to take possession of the land, correspondingly, the central section moves from Othniel, the judge from Judah who is presented as nearly perfect, to Samson, the judge from Dan who is a "caricature of all that was expected of a judge".[124] In this respect, the structure of the prologue anticipates a similar arrangement in the central section.[125]

If this is the case, then for all intents and purposes, the diagram presented earlier[126] depicting the twin trajectories in the prologue may in fact work equally well as a graphic summary of the central section once the captions are appropriately modified. Thus, if the main argument of the prologue can be summarised as "The ability of Israel's tribes to take possession of their land decreases as one moves from south to north", then the main argument of the central section can similarly be summarised as "The spiritual state of Israel's people and leaders decreases as one moves from south to north."

But not only does the rhetorical structure of the prologue mirror the overall arrangement of the central section, even its idiosyncratic peculiarity finds parallel in the latter. As has been pointed out

---

[124] Wenham, 119. Brettler (1989a:405) also acknowledges that the geographic pattern in the central section needs to be joined with observations concerning the behaviour of the major judges as they move from south to north. Brettler (2002:111) notes further that as the narratives in the central section moves north, the judges' behaviour becomes more and more questionable.

[125] Exum (1990:413) and Younger (1994:223, 1995:80) both commented on how an increasingly negative pattern found in Judges 1 is mirrored in the book as a whole. Likewise, Block (1999:83) points out that the author has deliberately arranged and shaped the conquest report in Judges 1 to reflect the moral and spiritual decline evident in the rest of the book. Wenham (55–56) also makes a similar point that the organising principle seen in the prologue anticipates the arrangement of the core of the book.

[126] See p. 151.

earlier,[127] the placement of Dan along the trajectories in the prologue is somewhat problematic in that diachronic realities seem to have been merged into a single synchronic event. What this means is that if the downward trajectory depicting progressive deterioration is in fact primary, then Dan's position as the last tribe along the geographic trajectory is out of place. For it was the Dan before its northward migration that was the least successful with regard to its ability to dispossess the nation and take possession of their land. The Dan that emerged as the northernmost tribe, on the other hand, is a tribe that finally succeeded in dispossessing Laish and taking it as its own.

Interestingly, a similar geographical displacement involving Dan is also found in the central section where pre-migration events taking place in the south occupy a schematic position that implies a northern association. By this, one is referring to the exploits of Samson, the Danite judge, at the end of the judges cycles.

Even a cursory survey of the geography of the Samson narratives reveals that the exploits of Samson basically took place in the south. For the beginning and end of Samson's life are associated with Zorah and Eshtaol (13:1,24, 16:31), the very cities in the south from which the tribe Dan is said to have migrated later in 18:2,11 of the epilogue. Thus, the people Samson had to deal with, be it foreign power (the Philistines) or fellow Israelites (the Judahites), were all essentially southerners. This therefore places the events in the Samson narratives at a time before the tribe collectively moved northwards to occupy Laish.

But if the judges cycles are indeed arranged to highlight progressive deterioration as the tribal affiliation of the judges moves from south to north, then the same sort of geographic displacement has also taken place with regard to the Samson narratives as it has with regard to the placement of Dan in the conquest report in the prologue. For in both cases, events associated with Dan that took place in the south are actually placed within a specific rhetorical schema that anticipates the tribe's eventual settlement in the north, even though the actual settlement has yet to be reported in the book.

Surely, this almost exact parallel between the prologue and the central section not only with respect to overall structure, but also to

[127] See pp. 152–153.

peculiar details, cannot be simply coincidental. Rather, it lends support to Younger's claim that the geographic arrangement of the tribal episodes in Judges 1 actually foreshadows the geographic orientation of the judges cycles in Judges 3–16.[128] In fact, Globe even uses this structural foreshadowing as one of the main arguments for Judges 1 being an integral part of the final version of the book.[129]

But if Judges 1, and by extension, the prologue itself, indeed foreshadows the cycles by previewing a key structure of the central section, then can one legitimately speak of it as a paradigm for the central section?

To answer this, one must first consider the rhetorical relationship between the prologue and the passage often looked upon as the introductory framework to the judges cycles in 2:11–23. After all, it is this introductory framework that is most often looked upon as the paradigm that sets the pattern for the rest of the central section.[130]

But as has already been pointed out, the cyclical pattern described in the introductory framework actually breaks down. This is why Gunn speaks of the framework as establishing a norm that can then be undermined,[131] while Hudson speaks of the narrator as "slowly and methodically disintegrating his own patterns, stories, and characters."[132] Concerning this, Exum comments,

> Although we are led to expect a consistent and regular pattern, what happens is that the framework itself breaks down. . . . I take it as a sign of further dissolution. The political and moral instability depicted in Judges is reflected in the textual instability. The framework deconstructs itself, so to speak, and the cycle of apostasy and deliverance becomes increasingly murky.[133]

But if the cyclical pattern introduced in the framework is indeed unstable and deconstructs itself, can that pattern still be legitimately considered a paradigm?[134] Furthermore, to the extent that the cyclical

[128] Younger, 1994:216, 1995:80.

[129] Globe, 1990:237–38.

[130] See Gros Louis, 1974:142–44; Boling, 1975:74; Soggin, 1987:43–44; Mullen, 1993:132–33; Lindars, 1995:98,100; O'Connell, 58–59; Amit, 1998:154–55.

[131] Gunn, 1987:105.

[132] Hudson, 53.

[133] Exum, 1990:412.

[134] This is actually one of the issues that persuaded Marais (90–91) against taking 2:6–3:6 as a paradigm for the rest of the book. To Marais, a paradigm should provide a constant pattern that repeats itself. But in the case of 2:6–3:6, not all

pattern is itself subjected to the forces of progressive deterioration introduced earlier, does that not make the pattern of deterioration the overriding paradigm?[135] Thus, it is actually the pattern of progressive deterioration that reigns as the prime organisation principle that structures both the prologue and the central section, including its introductory framework. And while the cyclical pattern introduced in the framework indeed provides paradigmatic structure to a significant part of the central section, it is at best only a secondary paradigm, one that is itself subjected to the overriding paradigm of progressive deterioration.

If this view of the deterioration pattern as paradigm for the both sections is indeed valid, then it carries significant implications regarding the redactional relationship between the prologue and the central section. For one, the use of the same deterioration paradigm to structure both the prologue and the central section makes it extremely unlikely that the prologue could be a literary composition independently conceived and totally unrelated to the central section.[136] Rather, it is far more likely that the conquest report that makes up the core of the prologue was composed expressly as an introduction to the central section, offering important structural clues that would guide the interpretation of the latter.

As for the mini-narratives in the prologue, it has already been argued that their presence is primarily to establish rhetorical links with subsequent sections and episodes in the book. If so, this further strengthens the case that the prologue as it currently stands probably never had an independent existence apart from the rest of the book, but was most likely composed specifically for the central section as its introduction.

Incidentally, the conclusion reached here about the relationship between the prologue and the central section is actually not dissimilar

elements of the paradigm are repeated in each of the judges cycles. Instead, history in the central section is presented as following a degenerative pattern.

[135] Thus, Lilley (101) argues that the literary structure of the book as a whole and the central section in particular is actually progressive and not cyclical.

[136] Moore (4) asserts that Judg 1:1–2:5 was not composed for the place it now occupies within the book, but is an extract from an older history of the Israelite occupation of Canaan which the editor abridged and adapted to his purpose. Mayes (1985:15–16) also speaks of the prologue and epilogue as independent of the central section, implying that their association with the central section happened somewhat by chance as a late editor saw in them useful illustrations of the moral and spiritual state of Israel in the period.

to the conclusion reached independently in the last chapter about the relationship between the epilogue and the central section. In both cases, evidence seems to argue strongly against the likelihood of the prologue or the epilogue of Judges ever having an independent existence apart from the central section. Instead, what is suggested is that the two peripheral sections were composed specifically to introduce and conclude the present form of the central section. Taking into consideration an earlier conclusion that the prologue and epilogue may in fact originate from the same hand, and a consistent position begins to emerge regarding the way the book may have been put together as a whole. But before this 'consistent position' is examined in greater detail in chapter six of the present work, one final thematic thread that seems to link all three sections of Judges together must first be explored.

CHAPTER FIVE

NO KING IN ISRAEL: UNDERSTANDING THE EPILOGUE'S REFRAIN

In the previous chapters, a case is slowly being built that the three major sections of Judges may in fact show a significantly greater degree of compositional unity that has heretofore been recognised. But in order for the case to be convincing, one must address the issue of alleged contrasting viewpoints within the book. After all, according to historical critical scholarship, internal inconsistency is one of the sure signs of multiple redactions since a unified piece of literary composition is expected to be internally consistent with regard to its viewpoints and perspectives.

When it comes to Judges, a major area of alleged inconsistency has to do with the book's implied attitude towards the monarchy that would eventually succeed the rule of the judges. In this matter, while there seems to be broad agreement especially among critical scholars that an anti-monarchical bias is present in the Deuteronomistic central section of the book,[1] when it comes to the epilogue, many are convinced that it actually reflects a positive view of the monarchy.[2] How then does one explain the coexistence of these seemingly opposite viewpoints if the book is indeed a unified piece of literary composition?

To answer this question, two things need to be noted. First, while the argument for an alleged anti-monarchical sentiment in the central section comes from a number of different episodes,[3] the alleged pro-monarchical sentiment in the epilogue seems to be based primarily on a plain reading of the refrain that repeatedly punctuates

---

[1] See, for example, Noth, 1991:77; Richter, 1963:320,336–39; Buber, 1967:69–76; Becker, 303–06. A notable exception is Veijola (115–22), who argues for a pro-monarchical stance in the basic Deuteronomistic redaction and attributes the anti-monarachic sentiments to the later DtrN.

[2] See, for example, Noth, 1962:80; Lilley, 100; Cundall, 1968:178–81; Webb, 1987:202–03; Tollington, 192,194–95; Mayes, 2001:242,255.

[3] Such as the negative portrayal of foreign kings throughout the section, Gideon's rejection of the kingship offer in 8:22–23, and the narrative about Abimelech's disastrous rule as king in 9:1–57, including the allegedly most anti-monarchical fable told by Jotham in 9:7–15.

the narratives in that section. The full formula of this refrain, which brackets the epilogue towards its beginning (17:6) and at its end (21:25), informs the readers that "In those days there was no king in Israel; every man did what was right in his own eyes (בימים ההם אין מלך בישׂראל אישׁ הישׁר בעיניו יעשׂה)." The reduced formula, which is found in 18:1 and 19:1, consists only of the first half of the full formula.

Second, although at first glance, the meaning of this refrain seems clear, yet a number of diverse interpretations have surfaced, thus betraying an underlying complexity to any attempt at understanding its true meaning.

In light of these observations, it seems that one possible route to exploring whether contrasting viewpoints are indeed present within the current form of Judges is to begin with an attempt at understanding what exactly the refrain is meant to convey. For if it turns out that the refrain is in fact not pro-monarchical as many seem to think, then the alleged inconsistency within the book will no longer pose a problem that stands in the way of understanding Judges as a unified piece of literary composition.

Does the Refrain Constitute Positive or Negative Comment?

In order to understand the meaning of the refrain, one of the first questions that need to be asked is how the refrain functions within the epilogue. In particular, one must determine at the outset whether the refrain is meant to be taken as a positive comment about the narratives in the epilogue or a negative one, whether it is intended to bring comfort or express lament.

In this regard, one of the few scholars to argue for a positive reading of the refrain is Boling. Taking the repeated statement of "no king in Israel" to mean that YWHW was still king,[4] Boling essen-

[4] Boling, 1974:41; 1975:273. Although Boling considers the refrain in 17:6 and 18:1 to have been penned by a Deutronomic redactor, while the refrain in 19:1 and 21:25 was penned by a later Deuteronomistic redactor, he apparently understands both redactors as using the "no king in Israel" formula to indicate that YHWH was still king. But in this, Boling seems less than consistent. For while he affirms in his 1974 article that 18:1a is intended to show how YHWH was in fact still king, in his commentary (1975:258), he reads the same statement as a lamentation of the lack of acknowledgement of YHWH's kingship in Israel. Now although

tially sees 21:25 as a call to affirm the high kingship of YHWH and for every man to do what is right as he discerns it.[5] Thus, with the exception of 17:6,[6] Boling generally understands the refrain in a positive sense.

According to this interpretation, the story of the migration of Dan, whose tribal name means 'judgement', illustrates how YHWH uses the tribe to judge Micah for his idolatry.[7] The migration itself is thus presented as "the providential solution to the problem of Micah's establishment".[8]

As for the narrative concerning the Benjaminite war, Boling sees the two initial drubbings of Israel in Judges 20 as YHWH's way to teach the people to get their questions in the right order and at the proper place of enquiry, so that old-style Israelite unity can be restored.[9] But the campaign itself is meant to represent Israel as doing everything right, even though they may have overdone it.[10] Even the attempt to find wives for the Benjaminites is viewed positively as the elders are portrayed as finally using their heads to come up with an ingenious plan to preserve Israel.[11] For Boling believes

---

these two views are not necessarily mutually exclusive, it is doubtful that both could have been intended by the refrain's author at the same time, since the former gives an inherently optimistic evaluation of the situation, while the latter, a decidedly pessimistic one.

[5] Boling, 1974:37. Boling (1975:293) acknowledges that in earlier editions, the formula might have been used negatively to depict Israel as having repudiated YHWH's kingship. But convinced that the formula in 21:25 was added as late as the Babylonian exile, Boling takes 21:25 to mean that the time has arrived once again for every man to do what was right without any sacral political apparatus to get in the way. In this respect, Boling's view is not dissimilar to that of Mendenhall (1973:27), who understands "what was right in his own eyes" as a description of self-determination and freedom from interference and harassment by the king's bureaucrats or military aristocracy.

[6] Boling, 1974:44; 1975:256. However, Boling never clarifies how his positive view of 18:1 (1974:41) is reconciled with what is an apparently negative use of the refrain in 17:6.

[7] Ibid., 1974:41; 1975:259.

[8] Ibid., 1975:258.

[9] Ibid., 1974:43.

[10] Ibid., 1974:47 n. 19.

[11] Incidentally, such a positive understanding of the final story is not unique to Boling. Amit (1998:337–41) and Mayes (2001:254) likewise understand the story as illustrating unity and the effective functioning of the tribal assembly to exercise control and deal with crime in a balanced and responsible way. The major difference between Boling, on the one hand, and Amit and Mayes, on the other, is that the latter two still hold to a negative understanding of the refrain in 21:25. The latter two therefore acknowledge a tension between the story and the refrain, and Mayes'

that, by then, Shiloh had reverted to old Canaanite traditions after the venerable amphictyonic centre was abandoned by YHWHists.[12] Thus, the abduction of desirable maidens at Shiloh represents the providential turning of an evil into an ingenious solution to save the nation. In fact, Boling thinks that it is only here at the end of the book that things are presented as at last being done for the right reason.[13]

But perhaps Boling is overly optimistic in his understanding of the final stories in Judges. After all, Boling's interpretation of Judges 21 depends a great deal on a negative evaluation of Shiloh. Yet evidence to support that evaluation is slim. Pointing to the fact that Shiloh's location is described in 21:19, Boling suggests that this specification of location must have been because the cultic centre had fallen out of use by then and was no longer visited by YHWHists.[14] It follows therefore that the celebration spoken of in 21:19 must be Canaanite.

But this negative interpretation of Shiloh is curious, especially since Boling himself concedes that the virgins of Jabesh Gilead were brought to Shiloh in 21:12 precisely because of Shiloh's "amphictyonic legitimacy".[15] Besides, Boling also concedes that yearly YHWHistic feasts were in fact still celebrated in Shiloh during the time of Elkanah in 1 Samuel 1.[16] Thus, if contrary to Boling's suggestion, the celebration at Shiloh in 21:19 was in fact YHWHistic and not Canaanite,

---

solution is to suggest that Judges 20–21 represent a secondary addition to the epilogue, while the refrain serves originally to summarise only the more negative stories of 17–19. It seems to me, however, that Amit and Mayes have entirely overlooked the fact that the elders' supposedly 'balanced and responsible' decision in fact resulted in the rape of six hundred innocent virgins. At least Boling tries to deal with this by casting doubt on the innocence of the virgins of Shiloh, as the following discussion shows.

[12] Boling, 1974:43.

[13] Ibid., 1975:293–94; 1974:47 n. 19.

[14] Ibid., 1974:43; 1975:293.

[15] Boling 1975:292. To be fair, Boling (1975:294) also thinks that the episodes concerning the virgins of Jabesh Gilead and the virgins of Shiloh were from different sources and were artificially brought together on account of thematic similarities. But even so, it would be strange for Boling's Deuteronomistic redactor to simply be throwing together two stories that presuppose vastly different settings for Shiloh without attempting to clarify the situation. This is especially since a clear grasp of Shiloh's situation in the second story is essential for that story to be understood as Boling does.

[16] Ibid., 293.

then the elders' decision to allow its virgins to be abducted can in no way be viewed positively.

Moreover, even had Boling succeeded in defending the abduction of the virgins of Shiloh, there still remains the incident involving the four hundred virgins of Jabesh Gilead. Since Boling has explicitly affirmed that the narrative in 21:6–12 elicits sympathy for Jabesh Gilead, and considers the city the only segment of Israel not guilty of overreacting,[17] it is hard to see how this incident could possibly cast the elder's decision in a positive light.

As for the story of Danite migration, even if YHWH did use the tribe to judge Micah for his idolatry, the fact that the tribe took Micah's idols with them and ended up perpetrating the same idolatry in their new found land certainly does not speak well of the Danites. To the extent that the scope of that idolatry has now expanded from an individual/family level to a tribal level, it is hard to see how this sorry episode can possibly be "the providential solution to the problem of Micah's establishment" that Boling makes it out to be.

What one finds, in other words, is that the stories punctuated by the refrain in the epilogue all turn out to be much more negative than Boling thought. If so, then Boling's interpretation of the refrain as some kind of rallying call for every man to do as the characters in the epilogue did, namely, what is right as he discerns it, is very much in doubt.

Besides, the second half of the full refrain may actually be formulated to evoke negative sentiments. After all, the clause "every man did what was right in his own eyes (איש הישר בעיניו יעשה)" is certainly evocative of Deut. 12:8,[18] where the similarly phrased "you shall not do . . . every man all that is right in his own eyes (לא תעשון . . . איש כל־הישר בעיניו)" is found. In that context, every man doing what is right in his own eyes is specifically prohibited as an inappropriate way for Israel to conduct her worship when she succeeds in taking possession of her land.[19] That the first occurrence of

[17] Ibid., 292.

[18] This, in fact, is pointed out by Veijola (15–17) to argue that Judges' epilogue must also be Deuteronomistic.

[19] Boling (1974:44; 1975:294), however, thinks Moses presented the mode of decision making where every man does what is right in his own eyes as appropriate prior to the conquest. But nowhere in Hebrew Scripture has Moses ever prescribed or defended such a mode of decision making. On the contrary, it seems that what

the full refrain in Judg. 17:6 comes immediately after the mention of Micah's private family shrine and between two reports of Micah's installation of illegitimate priests at that shrine seems to suggest that the author of the epilogue did in fact have Deut. 12:8 in mind when he penned the refrain. For what Micah was doing is precisely what Deut. 12:8 warns against.

Furthermore, it is worth noting that, in contrast to the prohibition against every man doing what is right in his own eyes in Deut. 12:8, the propriety of doing what is right in the eyes of YHWH (עשׂה הישר בעיני יהוה) is actually repeatedly emphasised not only within Deuteronomy 12 but also throughout the entire book.[20] A case can therefore be made that, just like "doing what is evil in the eyes of YHWH (עשׂה . . . הרע בעיני יהוה)",[21] "every man doing what is right in his own eyes (איש הישר בעיניו יעשׂה)" may also be formulated specifically to contrast "doing what is right in the eyes of YHWH". If so, this would effectively make "doing what is evil in the eyes of YHWH" and "every man doing what is right in his own eyes" complementary statements.

As it happens, just as "every man did what was right in his own eyes" is found in the full refrain that brackets the epilogue in 17:6 and 21:25, "the Israelites did what was evil in the eyes of YHWH" is also repeatedly found in the central section of Judges in 2:11; 3:7,12; 4:1; 6:1; 10:6; 13:1. If, as has been argued earlier in chapter three, the epilogue was indeed composed specifically as a continuation of the central section in order to provide commentary on the major judges, then the fact that the two seemingly complementary statements both happen to function as structural markers in their respectively sections may very well reflect artful design rather than mere coincidence. This would further vindicate the view that "every man did what was right in own his eyes" is simply a variation of "the Israelites did what was evil in the eyes of YHWH".[22]

---

is emphasised in Deut. 12:8 is merely that, in view of the centralisation of worship soon to take place, the people should no longer conduct their worship any place they see fit. To read anything more into the statement as Boling did would be reading too much into the text.

[20] Deut. 6:18; 12:25,28; 13:19; 21:9.

[21] Deut. 4:25; 9:18; 17:2; 31:29.

[22] See Wilson, 74–76; Lasine, 55 n. 19; Deryn Guest, 1997:255; McMillion, 235; Block, 1999:475–76; Wenham, 66. This interpretation of the second half of the refrain is further confirmed by Greenspahn (1982:129–30), who cites an almost identical Egyptian parallel also used negatively to denote anarchy.

If this is true, the implication is again that the refrain must have been intended as a negative comment rather than a positive one as Boling suggests. Thus, instead of it being a rallying call for every man to do what is right as he discerns it, it is far more likely that the refrain is meant to be a lament against pervasive anarchy in Israel in the absence of a higher authority.

Interestingly though, the fact that negative stories in the epilogue are negatively evaluated by the refrain has not stopped Dumbrell from assigning an overall positive function to the refrain. The approach Dumbrell takes, however, is drastically different from that of Boling.

Unlike Boling, Dumbrell clearly recognises that the refrain expresses negative evaluation of the events narrated in the epilogue.[23] But Dumbrell also disagrees with others who see in the refrain a not-too-subtle endorsement of the מלך as a solution to the anarchy depicted in the epilogue. Dating the redaction of the book to the exilic period on the basis of 18:30–31, Dumbrell argues that the refrain could hardly be read as a recommendation of human kingship since it was the failures and excesses of that very office that served as background for the continuous narration of Israel's chequered history in the Deuteronomistic corpus.[24]

Instead, Dumbrell sees the refrain simply as a descriptive summary of a period that is characterised by religious and social upheavals in the absence of a centralised political institution. But in spite of such upheavals and the lack of a strong authoritarian administration, Israel survived, preserved by the willing interventions of her God. As a result, the reality of a united Israel with which the book had commenced was left intact at its end. Thus, according to Dumbrell, what the refrain offered to the exilic community for whom the book was put together is the hope that, just as God had preserved Israel in the days of the judges when she had no king and every man was doing what was right in his own eyes, so too God would preserve the exilic community at a time when the nation surrendered to apostasy and had run out of political alternatives.[25]

There is, however, one major weakness to Dumbrell's interpretation, and it is that his whole argument basically rests on an exilic

[23] Concerning Judg 21:25, Dumbrell (31) writes that "there is no denial by the writer of the disordered political condition of the period and the blatant individualism which characterised it."

[24] Ibid., 29–30.

[25] Ibid., 31–32.

setting for the composition of the book's epilogue. Thus, if this alleged exilic setting is in doubt, so would Dumbrell's interpretation be.

To be sure, at first glance, "the captivity of the land (גלות הארץ)" in 18:30 does seem to be referring to the exile. But even this is not entirely without dispute. First, the phrase גלות הארץ is unusual. As Van Der Hart and O'Connell have pointed out, while place and national names such as Judah, Israel, Jerusalem, and Gilgal have been spoken of metonymously as being exiled,[26] the application of גלה simply to הארץ without further specification is unusual.[27] This, in fact, is what prompted both scholars to agree with those who suggest emending the text to read "the exile of the ark (גלות הארון)".[28]

But if the ark was really meant, then the event referred to in 18:30 can conceivably be the capture of the ark by the Philistines as reported in 1 Samuel 4–6. If so, Dumbrell's case for an exilic dating of the epilogue would be put in jeopardy.

But even if the reading גלות הארץ is accepted, there still remains a possibility that 18:30–31 could represent an editorial gloss added by a redactor at a substantially later date.[29] And even if 18:30–31 is seen as original and rhetorically integral to the text, it is still by no means sure that the captivity referred to is the exile of the southern kingdom in 586 BCE. As a matter of fact, most commentators actually see the captivity mentioned in 18:30 as referring to the exile of Dan by Tiglath Pileser III to Assyria in 734 BCE or the final deportation of the northern kingdom under Sargon in 722 BCE.[30] While Dumbrell also acknowledges this possibility, he states, however, that even if the comment does refer to the exile of the northern kingdom around 722 BCE, it would still undoubtedly be made at a much later date, quite possibly after the fall of Jerusalem.[31] But this is pure speculation. For the comment could have been made

---

[26] See, for example, 2 Kgs. 17:23; 25:21; Jer. 1:3; 52:27; Amos 5:5.

[27] Van Der Hart, 722 n. 7; O'Connell, 481.

[28] See Burney, 415; Blenkinsopp, 1972:77; Van Der Hart, 722–23 n. 7; O'Connell, 481–83. According to O'Connell (337 n. 61), the medieval rabbi Kimhi also sees the capture of the land as referring to the capture of the ark and its sequel.

[29] Moore (xxxii) and Noth (1962:83) seem to hold such a view. O'Connell (28) also considers 18:30b a possible scribal gloss.

[30] See, for example, Moore, 400; Burney, 415; J. Gray, 237, 371; Cundall, 1968:192; Boling, 1975:266; Soggin, 1987:278; Block, 1999:513; Schneider, 242. Such a view is apparently also supported by the medieval rabbi Rashi (see Rosenberg, 150).

[31] Dumbrell, 29.

any time after the fact, which means that if 18:30 indeed refers to the exile of Dan and the northern kingdom, it could conceivably be penned within the 130 years or so between the event itself and the fall of the southern kingdom.[32]

The fact of the matter is, a wide variety of opinions actually exist regarding the compositional/redactional setting for Judges as a whole, such that an exilic redaction is simply one of many options. Taking into consideration evidence found in the epilogue, scholars have argued for an implied setting of the book in the early Davidic era when David was still ruling from Hebron,[33] at the height of the Davidic/Solomonic reign,[34] during the reign of Josiah,[35] and in the post-exilic period when a post-exilic community was seeking the restoration of the monarchy.[36] That such widely diverse alternatives have been proposed by equally competent scholars reveals how immensely difficult it is to specify a redactional setting for the book with any degree of certainty. Thus, for Dumbrell to argue for his interpretation of the refrain primarily on the basis of a very specific view of the book's setting has effectively undermined the credibility of that interpretation. The likelihood that the refrain is meant to function as a positive encouragement for the book's target audience is therefore very slim at best.

To Whom Does the מלך in the Refrain Refer?

If the refrain, and especially the second half of the full formula, indeed represents a negative comment on some very negative stories in the epilogue, then what the first half seems to suggest is that things would not have been as bad had there been a מלך in Israel.

[32] The position of Yee (152–67), who favours a Sitz im Leben for the epilogue in the Josianic era, would be one such example.

[33] O'Connell, 305–42.

[34] Cundall, 1970:180. Note also that although they make no direct statements with regard to the redactional setting of the book as a whole, both Jüngling (245,278,291,294) and Mayes (1985:15–16) also see the setting of the epilogue's refrain as originating from the beginning of the monarchy and possibly during the reigns of David and Solomon. Mayes notes, however, that the final incorporation of the material in the prologue and epilogue into the book may have taken place much later.

[35] Yee, 152–67.

[36] Burney, 410–11; Tollington, 195.

This therefore raises the important issue concerning the identity of this מלך who could have prevented the nation from falling into chaos. Three alternatives have been suggested.

1. *A Judge*

The first is suggested by Talmon, who, noting the absence of any mention of the judges in the epilogue of the book, sees מלך as referring to none other than the judges so prominently featured in the central section. Arguing that judges in this period were essentially responsible for the same functions as those of subsequent Israelite kings, and citing 1 Sam. 8:5–6, where Israel's demand for a king (מלך) is specifically for the purpose of judging them (לשפטנו), Talmon asserts that the מלך spoken of in the refrain actually refers to the judges themselves rather than to the monarchical rulers who would eventually succeed them.[37]

Pointing to the mention of priests from the house of Moses and Aaron who were from the third generation after the Exodus,[38] Talmon sees the events being described in the epilogue as having occurred early in the period before any of the judges came onto the scene. Thus, the refrain is looked upon as a comment pertaining to the period after Joshua but before the emergence of the judges, when political and religio-cultic anarchy was widespread. But as the subsequent raising up of judges remedied that situation, the refrain thus amounts to an indirect praise for the rule of the judges.

The problem with Talmon's interpretation, however, is that his equating of מלך with שופט remains unconvincing. For even if מלך can indeed refer to a non-dynastic ruler, the plainest meaning of the word in Hebrew Scripture and in the book of Judges is that of a king. In fact, Abimelech, who is the only named Israelite to be called מלך in Judges (9:6), was certainly not cast in the role of one of Israel's judges. Besides, had the author of the epilogue intended to refer to the judges in the refrain, why not simply use שופט? Why use instead a term that would be sure to cause confusion?

Furthermore, if the narratives are indeed meant to laud the raising up of judges by showing how bad things were before they came along, then from a rhetorical standpoint, it makes far better sense

[37] Talmon, 44,47–52.
[38] Ibid., 47,52.

for these narratives to be placed at the beginning of the book leading up to the introduction of the judges rather at the end of the book. For these stories of anarchy effectively ends the book on a down note, and thus, would be a curious way to extol the rule of the judges.[39]

For the above reasons, Talmon's interpretation is thus not persuasive.

2. *A Human King*

The second alternative, supported by the majority of scholars, understands מלך as referring to the human kings who would eventually succeed the judges in ruling over Israel. And at first glance, there seem to be good reasons for such an understanding.

First, this understanding takes מלך at face value and interprets it in accordance with the most common use of the word in Hebrew Scripture: as a human king. Second, such an interpretation makes good sense if the refrain in 21:25 is seen as a transitional statement that both sums up the period of the judges and anticipates a period in Israel's history characterised by the rule of kings.

If so, then in view of the fact that the refrain seems to be lamenting the religious, social, and political chaos that prevailed during this period where every man did what was right in his own eyes, what the statement "In those days there was no king in Israel" seems to imply is that such chaos would not have occurred had Israel already embraced some form of monarchical rule. Seen as an apology for kingship,[40] the refrain is thus understood as an implicitly pro-monarchical statement.

But this understanding of the refrain is not without problems, one of which is that what is directly affirmed and indirectly implied by this interpretation jars with reality depicted elsewhere in the book. The narrative about Abimelech is a case in point.

---

[39] To be fair, Talmon (44–46) also agrees that the material in the refrain fits better at the beginning of the book with Judges 1 rather than at the end. In fact, he even surmises that that material was originally a continuation of the prologue, but was later moved to the end of the book due to the disproportional length of the narratives compared to the relatively short notes in Judges 1. But it is highly doubtful that a competent redactor would opt for such a transposition purely on the basis of narrative length, especially since, from a rhetorical standpoint, such a transposition would obviously undermine the alleged intention of the book's author to glorify the rule of the judges.

[40] See, for example, Buber, 78; Noth, 1962:80; Cundall, 1968:180; Jüngling, 292–93; Gerbrandt, 134.

To begin, if מלך in the refrain indeed refers to a human king, then the assertion that there was no king in Israel during this period is contradicted by the narratives in the central section of the book.[41] For there was in fact a מלך in Israel during the period of the judges, and his name was Abimelech.

That Abimelech is portrayed as מלך in Judges seems clear. For not only does the narrator use the denominative verb מלך in 9:6 to speak of his installation as king, within the story itself, Jotham also uses the same verb in 9:16,18 when he refers to that same event. In fact, regardless of whether Jotham's fable was directed against kingship in general[42] or just the specific way in which Abimelech became מלך,[43] the fable about the trees looking for a מלך to rule over them would have been contextually fitting only if Abimelech, like the bramble in the fable, had indeed been offered kingship by the Shechemites. Otherwise the only point of connection between fable and real-life situation would have been lost.

Furthermore, even though some regard Abimelech's kingship as merely local in scope, extending only over a city-state,[44] Maly notes that the unduly full account of the details of this incident is a strong indication of the importance with which this incident was regarded

[41] Admittedly, "those days" in the refrain may simply be referring to the period during which the events in the epilogue took place, rather than the entire period of the judges. But if the argument presented earlier in chapter three stands that the epilogue was composed specifically as a conclusion to the narratives in the central section, then "those days" would very likely be referring to the entire period rather than just the time frame bound by the events of the epilogue.

[42] According to Buber (75), Jotham's fable is the strongest anti-monarchical poem of world literature. Richter (1963:285), Dumbrell (28), Townsend (26), Jobling (72), Ebach and Rüterswörden (11–18), Soggin (1987:177–78) and Schöpflin (15–16,20–21) also see the fable as intrinsically anti-monarchical. In fact, Soggin thinks that in its original context, the fable represents a rejection of the whole institution of monarchy and not just some of its worst aspects.

[43] Moore (245), J. Gray (320), Maly (299–305), Cundall (1968:128), Boling (1975:174), Webb (1987:159), O'Connell (164), Amit (1998:106–07), Block (1999:321), and McCann (72–73), are among those who see Jotham's speech as a whole as directed more against the Shechemites and Abimelech than against monarchy as a form of government. In fact, Maly (304) observes, ". . . just as in the original fable there was no general condemnation of kingship itself, so, too, in the biblical adaptation there can be found no criticism, on principle, of the rule of a king. It is a criticism, rather, that is directed primarily against those who were foolish enough to anoint a worthless man as king, and secondarily, against the worthless king himself."

[44] Lindars (1965:318), Boling (1975:183), Fritz (129), Soggin (1987:180–81), and Mullen (1993:150) all deny that Abimelech ever ruled over Israel as a whole, but see him basically as a city-state king.

in Israelite tradition.[45] Considering also that Abimelech is specifically said to have governed Israel[46] for three years in 9:22,[47] and his followers are described as Israelites[48] in 9:55, a strong case can be made that his rule is intentionally depicted as more extensive than just a local rule.[49] If so, the Abimelech incident may have been intended to depict the first time the institute of kingship is experimented within an Israelite context.[50]

But not only does Abimelech's kingly rule contradict the refrain's assertion that there was no king in Israel during this period, the way Abimelech is portrayed also disputes the refrain's implication that chaos and anarchy would have been avoided had there been a king in Israel. For Abimelech is perhaps the most negatively portrayed character among named Israelites in Judges. In fact, he is the only named individual in the book of whom it is explicitly said that God took an initiative to cause his downfall (9:23–24,56).[51]

But what is of significance here is not just that Abimelech was wicked, but that the narrative about him seems calculated to resonate

---

[45] Maly, 305.

[46] Cundall (1968:127), seeing the extent of Abimelech's kingdom as limited, thinks ישראל should be understood in the same limited sense. But this argument is circular, and thus, unconvincing. Boling (1975:175), on the other hand, concedes that Abimelech did serve as governor (שׂר) of Israel for a while, but sees that as different from ruling as king. Admittedly, the verb שׂרר (9:22), which occurs only four times in the Qal in Hebrew Scripture, is not used explicitly with מלך as its subject. But its occurrence in a synonymously parallel colon with מלך in Isa. 32:1 suggests that the concept of governing does fall within the same semantic range as kingly rule. Considering that nowhere else in the Abimelech narrative is a separate office of שׂר mentioned, it is perhaps reasonable to understand שׂרר in 9:22 as some kind of a stylistic variant of מלך (9:8,10,12,14) or משׁל (9:2), thus speaking also of Abimelech's kingly rule.

[47] Fritz (129) and Soggin (1987:180) consider 9:22 a later interpolation. But even if this is true, there is still no denying that whoever added this statement wishes to present Abimelech's reign as being over all Israel and not just Shechem.

[48] Cundall (1968:136), Webb (1987:156) and Amit (1998:112) all see the איש־ישׂראל as referring to those who had supported Abimelech.

[49] Amit (1998:104) points out that Abimelech's anointment, following the murder of the other potential heirs, clearly indicates his intention to rule over all areas formerly under Gideon's influence. Likewise, Dietrich (2000:318) also sees Abimelech's power base as being over "large parts of central Palestine".

[50] Maly, 299; Webb, 1987:159. Even Soggin (1987:194) concedes that DtrN had portrayed the Abimelech incident as a first attempt to institute the monarchy in Israel.

[51] While in Samson's case, YHWH merely left him after he had his hair cut off (16:19–20), in Abimelech's case, God actually sent an evil spirit to stir up trouble between him and the Shechemites (9:23). It was even twice stated that this was in order to repay both parties for the wickedness they did in killing Gideon's seventy sons (9:24,56).

with a specific event in the epilogue. To show how this is so, one must first explore a prior link between the narrative about Abimelech and the one about Adoni-Bezek in the prologue.

Although superficial parallels between the Abimelech narrative and the Adoni-Bezek narrative are often noted,[52] such parallels have thus far not been fully explored. The most obvious parallel between the two is that, in both narratives, seventy victims are specified. But this in itself may not be all that significant as the number seventy, which appears in a number of different contexts throughout Hebrew Scripture, may simply be an idiomatic way of indicating 'a great many'.[53]

What is noteworthy, however, is that in both cases, the victims belong to the ruling class. In the case of Adoni-Bezek, his victims were seventy kings (מלכים), whereas in the case of Abimelech, his victims were his seventy half-brothers, who according to 9:2, are presented as having the right to rule over (משל) the people of Shechem. Not only so, but in both cases, the perpetrators themselves also belong to this same class. For although Adoni-Bezek is never explicitly called מלך, his title nonetheless suggests that he was ruler of Bezek. As for Abimelech, that he was son of Gideon, Israel's judge, and that his seventy half-brothers had the right to rule over Shechem also place him within the ruling class by virtue of family connection. The fact that he eventually managed to get all the nobles of Shechem to make him king only further underscores the importance of this family connection.[54] Thus, while in Adoni-Bezek, we have a Canaanite ruler brutally mutilating seventy Canaanite kings, in Abimelech, we have an Israelite king brutally murdering seventy of his brothers who stood in the way of his kingly ambition.

But there is a further point of significant parallel. In both narratives, divine retribution appears to be a key focus. In the case of Abimelech, that retribution is a primary theme of the narrative has been noticed by Boogaart, Janzen, and Webb.[55] Not only is divine

[52] Hamlin, 150–51; Webb, 1987:232 n. 14; Deryn Guest, 1997:257.

[53] Boling, 1975:55; Lindars, 1995:18. Fensham (1977:135) also sees the number as symbolic.

[54] It is important to recognise that the nobles of Shechem did not make Abimelech king simply because he was one of them, but also because he happened to be one of Gideon's sons. Thus, Abimelech's attraction as a candidate to rule over the Shechemites was both because he had political legitimacy and because he was one of their own.

[55] Boogaart, 49; Janzen, 33–37; Webb, 1987:156,158–59.

retribution twice specified by the narrator as the primary explanation for what happens within the narrative (9:24,56–57), but the unfolding of the plot also emphasises an exact correspondence between the wickedness of the protagonists and the retribution they eventually received.[56]

But the same two features are also found in the Adoni-Bezek narrative. For in 1:7, Adoni-Bezek himself offered an explanation for the misfortune that had befallen him, and just as in 9:24,56–57, the retribution of God (אלהים) is affirmed as the primary cause. Granted, the verb שׁלם in the Piel, used by Adoni-Bezek to speak of retribution, does not correspond exactly to שׁוב used in 9:56–57. But that the two verbs fall within the same semantic range when used of retribution is seen in that in four other times in Hebrew Scripture, the verbs are used synonymously in parallel cola.[57]

Moreover, not only did Adoni-Bezek affirm the fact of divine retribution, but the manner of that retribution, namely, the cutting off of his thumbs and big toes, also corresponds exactly to his prior cutting off of the thumbs and big toes of seventy kings. Thus the manner of retribution for Adoni-Bezek also parallels the manner of retribution for Abimelech in that the punishment is shown to perfectly fit the crime.

From these observations, one can argue that, rather than the parallels occurring by sheer coincidence, the two narratives may in fact be interdependent. Since the retribution theme in the Adoni-Bezek episode seems abruptly introduced and entirely unconnected with what goes on in the rest of the prologue, one can further argue that the Adoni-Bezek narrative may have been composed specifically to foreshadow the Abimelech narrative. In fact, given the geographic proximity between Bezek and Shechem,[58] one wonders if Adoni-Bezek may not have been chosen as the main protagonist just to accentuate the close connection between the two narratives, notwithstanding speculations about whether Adoni-Bezek is to be identified with Adoni-Zedek mentioned in Josh. 10:1–5.[59]

[56] See Boogaart, 48–53 for detailed discussion.

[57] Exod. 21:34; Deut. 32:41; Ezek. 33:15; Joel 4:4.

[58] See Aharoni et al., maps 57 and 87. Na'aman (45) even speculates whether Adoni-Bezek might not in fact be the king of Shechem!

[59] Auld, 1975:268–69; Soggin, 1987:21; Weinfeld, 1993a:391. However, both Mullen (1984:45 n. 47) and Na'aman (45) think that the Adoni-Bezek narrative represents a tradition distinct from that of Adoni-Zedek.

But still, what is the purpose behind this conscious link between the two narratives? Clearly, one function is to heighten the already negative evaluation of Abimelech. For by showing him to be in the same league as a Canaanite king, pursuing the same kind of action and inviting upon himself the same kind of retribution from אלהים, the author was in effect drawing attention to the Canaanisation of this Israelite ruler.

But further reflection reveals that Abimelech was not merely acting like a Canaanite king; he may in fact have outdone him. For while Adoni-Bezek's brutality was directed only at other kings unrelated to him, Abimelech's victims were his own half-brothers. And while Adoni-Bezek merely maimed his victims, Abimelech murdered his in cold blood. Thus, one cannot help but wonder if it is rhetorically significant that divine retribution is mentioned only once in the narrative about Adoni-Bezek (1:7), but twice in the narrative about Abimelech (9:24,56). Can this be one way of highlighting the gravity of Abimelech's offence? But regardless, this Canaanisation of Abimelech, and the fact that he may have even out-Canaanised the Canaanites, is what turns out to be the link that ties these two narratives to another narrative in the epilogue of the book.

Earlier in chapter three, it was noted that within the epilogue of Judges, there are numerous bizarre episodes featuring incomprehensible action with unspecified motives. It was also pointed out that many of these bizarre episodes actually echo specific events found in narratives of the major judges in the central section of the book.

As it turns out, other than the seven instances highlighted, there is an eighth instance where similar echoing may be found. But instead of alluding to a major judge, the allusion this time is to a different kind of Israelite leader: King Abimelech.

In Judges 19, a Levite journeys from the hill country of Ephraim to Bethlehem to woo back a concubine who had left him and returned to her father's house. Having succeeded in his mission, the Levite then set off for home with his concubine and servant, making it as far as the vicinity of Jebus by nightfall. Not willing to spend the night in a non-Israelite city, they journeyed on to Gibeah in Benjamin, where they finally received hospitality from an old Ephraimite residing in the city. But as they were enjoying their evening meal, wicked men of the city arrived, demanding that the Levite be handed over so that they could have sex with him. The host tried to reason with the men, but to no avail. Then the Levite took matters into his own hands and shoved his concubine out the door, whereupon she was raped all night and eventual died.

That this is a shocking story is beyond dispute. But one of the most shocking things is that the perpetrators of this heinous crime were actually Israelites. And it is precisely in this matter that the Canaanisation theme emerges again.

That the Gibeathites were consciously being compared to non-Israelites in Judges 19 can be seen in two ways. The first is that a Canaanite group, the Jebusites, is explicitly used as foil to highlight the wickedness of the Gibeathites. In the narrative, when the Levite and his party came near to Jebus at nightfall, the Levite's servant actually suggested spending the night there. But the suggestion was rejected by the Levite precisely because the Jebusites there were non-Israelites. The implication is that it would be dangerous to spend the night among people who are not part of the covenant community. Yet as it turns out, what awaited them at the Israelite town of Gibeah was actually far worse than what they ever imagined happening to them at the hands of the Jebusites.[60] And to the extent that dangers that are assumed to be associated with non-Israelites have not only been actualised but probably even exceeded by Israelites, the narrative seems to be drawing attention to the Canaanisation and even hyper-Canaanisation of Israel.

But there is a second way through which the text draws attention to this Canaanisation of Israel, and it is through an allusion to the narrative in Genesis 19 about Lot and the angels in Sodom.

That a striking similarity exists between the narratives found in Genesis 19 and Judges 19 has long been noticed by scholars.[61] There is, however, little consensus when it comes to the nature of that relationship or the direction of dependence between the two. While Niditch has put forward a case for the priority of the Judges narrative over the Genesis narrative,[62] Lasine's argument for the opposite seems more convincing.[63] Lasine's position is further bolstered by Block, who not only offers a thorough analysis of the two narratives

[60] Had the kind of danger they eventually encountered been even remotely considered possible at the hands of the Jebusites, the servant probably wouldn't have suggested staying at Jebus to begin with, nor would the Levite's answer be as mild.

[61] Von Rad (218); Culley (1976:58–59); Tollington (194).

[62] Niditch, 1982:375–77.

[63] Lasine, 1984:38–41.

in question, but also argues from rhetorical considerations that Genesis 19 is unlikely to be patterned after Judges 19 as it is difficult to see why the small Israelite settlement of Gibeah should have been afforded archetypal status such that Sodom would be depicted as an ancient day Gibeah.[64] Rather, Block points to the Canaanisation of Israel as a theme that could plausibly explain why the narrative in Judges 19 so unambiguously draws upon a well-known story from patriarchal traditions.[65] In the words of Block,

> By patterning the . . . climactic scene after Genesis 19, the narrator serves notice that, whereas the travellers had thought they had come home to the safety of their countrymen, they have actually arrived in Sodom. The nation has come full circle. The Canaanisation of Israelite society is complete. When the Israelites look in a mirror, what they see is a nation which, even if ethnically distinct from the natives, is indistinguishable from them with regard to morality, ethics, and social values. They have sunk to the level of those nations whom they were to destroy and on whom the judgment of God hangs.[66]

But if patterning the behaviour of the Gibeathites after the Sodomites and using the Jebusites as foil are indeed aimed at depicting Israel as having been thoroughly Canaanised and more, then it is important to recognise that this Canaanisation was in fact not unprecedented. For according to the narrative sequencing of the current form of the book, long before nameless Gibeathites acted out what may have been the worst of Canaanite depravity,[67] an Israelite king by the name of Abimelech had already shown that not only was he capable of behaving like a Canaanite king, he could even outdo them in brutality.

And this has special relevance with respect to the interpretation of Judges' refrain. For as mentioned before, those who take מלך in the refrain as referring to a human king implicitly understand the

---

[64] Block, 1990:326–341.

[65] Others who also argue for the dependence of Judg 19 on Gen 19 include Jüngling (291), Gage (371), and Matthews (1992:3–11).

[66] Block, 1990:336.

[67] The fact that in Israelite tradition, Sodom has come to represent the epitome of non-Israelite depravity can be seen in the following ways. First, in rebukes directed against Israel through the prophets, sinful Israel is often compared to Sodom to highlight her utter depravity (Isa. 1:10; 3:9; Jer. 23:14; Ezek. 16:48). Second, the destruction that befell Sodom as judgment for her sin is also spoken of frequently as the epitome of judgment that could befall a people (Deut. 29:22; Isa. 1:9; 13:19; Jer. 49:18; 50:40; Lam. 4:16; Amos 4:11; Zeph. 2:9).

refrain to be implying that the chaos and anarchy described in the epilogue would not have occurred had Israel had a king. But given that the only Israelite king found in the book is one whose embrace of Canaanised values and behaviour is exactly the problem that gave rise to the kind of depravity found in Gibeah, it is hard to see how the refrain can possibly be viewed as a recommendation of human kingship in Israel.[68]

Admittedly, that the Abimelech narrative seems to argue strongly against human kingship is no new revelation. In fact, the narrative has long been regarded as anti-monarchical.[69] But even so, many critical scholars continue to see little difficulty with taking an essentially pro-monarchical view of the refrain because they view the epilogue and the central section of Judges as independent works. In particular, many believe that the epilogue was appended to the book only after the central section had already been redacted as part of Deuteronomistic History. Thus, Buber, for example, sees the current form of Judges as basically consisting of two books, each complete within itself and each being edited from an opposing biased viewpoint: the first anti-monarchical, and the second pro-monarchical.[70]

But in light of the preceding discussion about the complex rhetorical links that seem designed to connect the Abimelech narrative with parallel narratives in both the prologue and the epilogue, the standard critical position such as the one expressed by Buber may no longer be tenable. For what these complex links show is that the prologue and the epilogue must have been composed with the Abimelech story in mind rather than having been composed independently of it. In this respect, this confirms the evidence already presented in earlier parts of the present study. Thus, if the prologue in general, including the Adoni-Bezek narrative, was indeed composed specifically to foreshadow events found in the central section of the book, and the bizarre episodes in the epilogue, including the Sodomite behaviour of the Gibeathites, were also composed with the narratives of the central section in mind to serve as an evaluative

[68] In fact, Maly (304–05) suggests that, if anything, the disastrous reign of Abimelech would influence people away from kingship. Marais (134–35), likewise, sees the Abimelech story as shattering the hopes for a monarchy.

[69] See, for example, Buber, 73–75; Peter, 10; Townsend, 25–26; Crüsemann, 32–42; Niditch, 1999:205.

[70] Buber, 68.

conclusion, then it would make little sense for the author of the epilogue to pen a refrain that expresses a sentiment directly opposed to the very material he was trying to conclude.

Besides, even if, for the sake of argument, one is to lay aside for the moment the negative portrayal of King Abimelech, a pro-monarchicical interpretation of the refrain would still be problematic when viewed in the larger context of Israel's historical traditions as found in the Former Prophets. For even the earliest redactional setting proposed for Judges places it no earlier than during the early reign of David.[71] This means unless one is prepared to push the redactional setting even further back to an even earlier date, one would have to at least take into consideration the reign of Saul when one attempts at interpreting the refrain.

Interestingly, there are a number of instances where the portrayal of Saul in 1 Samuel actually seems to parallel the portrayal of Abimelech in Judges. First, both are presented as being willing to resort to murder to eliminate leadership rivals. While Abimelech killed his seventy half-brothers on one stone (Judg. 9:5), Saul sought repeatedly to kill David (1 Sam. 18:11,17,21; 19:1,10,15; 20:31,33; 23:15; 24:12), and even massacred the priests and inhabitants of Nob (1 Sam. 22:17–19) for helping David. Second, Abimelech and Saul are the only two characters in Hebrew Scripture upon whom it is specifically said in Judg. 9:23 and 1 Sam. 16:14–16; 18:10; 19:9 that God sent an evil spirit (רוח רעה). Finally, the circumstances of their deaths also bear certain resemblances. Both Abimelech and Saul were severely injured in battle, and each asked his armour-bearer (נשׂא כליו) to kill them in order to avoid a greater humiliation (Judg. 9:54; 1 Sam. 31:4).

From these parallels, it seems possible to argue for some kind of dependent relationship between the two narratives. While it is never easy to determine the direction of dependence, from a rhetorical perspective, it seems more likely that the narrative about Saul is dependent on the one about Abimelech rather than vice versa. For by depicting Saul as a latter-day Abimelech, the author of Samuel would have immediately conveyed his negative evaluation of Saul to the readers even as they are led to view his ultimate downfall as a just retribution from YHWH, much like Abimelech's downfall was.

[71] O'Connell, 305–42.

Otherwise, it is hard to see what could possibly be achieved by depicting Abimelech as a forerunner of Saul. After all, the negative evaluation of Abimelech is already so explicit in the text that making him Saul-like adds almost nothing to the narrative other than perhaps giving him further legitimacy as a forerunner of the Israelite king.

But regardless of which direction the dependence goes, the link between Abimelech and Saul is decidedly uncomplimentary to either. And that makes it problematic for a pro-monarchical interpretation of Judges' refrain. For even if Judges was redacted within the golden age of Israelite monarchy when the monarchy could be viewed favourably, the only way the refrain could suggest kingship in general as a means of preventing the kind of atrocities found in the epilogue would be for the author completely to overlook the reigns of both Saul, Israel's first official king, and Abimelech, the first Israelite given the title 'king'. But given that the latter featured so prominently within the book as the only non-judge who ruled among the judges in Israel, such a scenario is highly unlikely.

And positing a late date for the epilogue or the final redaction of the book is no help either. For even if the epilogue is composed as late as the exilic or post-exilic era, as Dumbrell points out, given that it is the failures and excesses of the Israelites kings that were partly responsible for the exile, it is highly unlikely that any exilic author would actually be recommending kingship as a solution to Israel's problems.[72]

In other words, the main problem with a pro-monarchical understanding of the refrain is that give the history of monarchical rule in Israel, one is hard pressed to come up with a Sitz im Leben in which an unqualified endorsement of the institution would make sense.

And that may have been what prompted some scholars to suggest that the מלך referred to in the refrain is not a general reference to just any king, but a reference to an ideal[73] or Davidic[74] king.

---

[72] Dumbrell, 29–30. Likewise, Marais (135) also points out that if the book has a post-exilic setting, then any hope in the monarchy would have been deconstructed by Israel's history. This in fact is what led Block (1999:483) to endorse an anti-monarchical interpretation of the refrain, understanding it to mean "Israel did not need kings to lead them into idolatry since the people did it on their own."

[73] Hamlin, 151. The same is also implied by Davis (158,62) and Brettler (1989a:409).

[74] Buber (79), conscious of the anti-Saulite polemic in the immediate context, thinks that when it comes to the king referred to in the refrain, only the Davidic is to be understood throughout. Jüngling (295) also holds a similar position.

But if this is so, then why did the author not simply qualify the term explicitly? Given that מלך is already used prominently in the Abimelech narrative to which the epilogue alludes, one would have thought that the author of the epilogue would at least try to avoid confusion by qualifying the refrain along the line of אין מלך אמת בישראל, if he indeed intended the מלך to be referring to an ideal or Davidic king.[75] But as it is, no such attempt is made to provide the necessary clarity. This therefore raises the possibility that the author of the epilogue may never have intended מלך in the refrain to be understood as a human king in the first place.

3. *YHWH, the divine King*

This leaves a final alternative with regard to whom מלך in the refrain may be referring, and it is to YHWH, the divine King.

Admittedly, to understand מלך in the refrain as referring to YHWH is not an alternative that has been widely considered. Nonetheless, such an interpretation has much to recommend itself.

First, in the wider context, YHWH's kingship over Israel seems to be a tradition that was established relatively early.[76] In fact, three poetic texts in the Pentateuch generally considered early all speak of YHWH as Israel's king.

At the end of Moses' song in Exod. 15:18,[77] the eternal reign of YHWH is acclaimed (יהוה ימלך לעלם ועד). Here, although it has been argued from Ugaritic parallels and parallels with certain psalms that this kingship spoken of is YHWH's universal kingship,[78] the

[75] Compare this to 2 Chron. 15:3, where the prophet Azariah, speaking of a period in Israel's history generally identified as the period of the judges, qualifies his statement by saying that there was no "true" God (לא אלהי אמת).

[76] Townsend (21) argues that the idea of God as King has existed in other Near Eastern cultures even before Israel came into existence, and therefore, would not have been new to Israel. To Townsend, the kingship of God motif may even be Canaanite in origin.

[77] The dating of Exodus 15 is admittedly highly controversial and, according to Zenger (456–58), ranges from the 13th Century to the 5th Century BCE. However, the linguistic evidence presented by Robertson (147–55) seems to point towards Exodus 15 being the oldest among biblical Hebrew poetry. Robertson (155) thus suggests a 12th Century date for Moses' song.

[78] Cassuto, 177–81; Propp, 545–46. But even though water imagery abounds in the first half of the song, it should be noted that in the current context, the focus is not on YHWH's triumph over the rebellious sea, but on YHWH's deliverance of Israel using the sea as an agent.

immediate context seems to suggest that this kingship has particular relevance with regard to Israel. After all, in 15:16, Israel is specifically referred to as YHWH's people (עמך), a people whom He is said in 15:13,16 to have redeemed (עם־זו גאלת) and purchased/begotten (עם־זו קנית). And the fact that YHWH is presented in 15:13 as leading and guiding Israel to His own holy abode, and in 15:17 as bringing them in and planting them in the mountain of His inheritance, the sanctuary He established for His own dwelling, further establishes the special relationship between YHWH and Israel. In the context of this special relationship, YHWH's kingship in 15:18 should therefore be understood as having particular relevance for Israel instead of simply as a general statement of YHWH's universal kingship.[79]

In Num. 23:21,[80] YHWH is also presented as Israel's king, even though in the context of Balaam's second oracle, this assertion may only represent Balaam's perspective. In 23:21, after observing that no trouble is seen in Israel, Balaam states that YHWH was with His people, and was being greeted by them as their king. That מלך here is understood to be referring back to YHWH in the preceding colon is accepted by most commentators.[81]

In Deut. 33:5,[82] a reference is also made of YHWH becoming king in Jeshurun (ויהי בישרון מלך). Here, although YHWH is not explicitly stated as the subject of the verse, that He is the intended subject is recognised by the majority of commentators.[83] In fact, attributing the original setting of the poem to the public acclamation of YHWH's kingship over Israel at a tribal assembly, Seeligmann argues that מלך in 33:5 cannot refer to a human king because that

[79] Compare this also with Exod. 19:4–6, where, although YHWH's rule over all the earth is affirmed, it is His special election of Israel as His people that is in focus.

[80] Although the dating of Balaam's oracles is also much debated, on the basis of what is believed to be the same character Baalam being mentioned in the 8th Century BCE Deir ʿAlla Inscription, Milgrom (473–76) argues that the Balaam tradition may have preceded the 8th Century.

[81] G.B. Gray, 353; Milgrom, 321 n. 62.

[82] Again, the dating of the chapter as a whole is complicated, as parts of it seem to reflect sayings dating back to as early as the period of the judges, while other parts seem to reflect linguistic usage characteristic of a later date. On balance, however, Tigay (523–24) thinks that the poem as a whole was composed possibly during the time of Solomon or earlier in the united monarchy, or conceivably in the pre-monarchical period.

[83] Craigie, 1976:393–94; Mayes, 1979:400; Tigay, 322.

would be foreign to the subject matter of the poem.[84] Thus, to Seeligmann, the poem bears evidence to a theocracy in Israel before any human king ruled over the nation.[85]

But not only is the kingship of YHWH over Israel a tradition that in general seems to have been established relatively early in Israel, it can also be shown that the concept of YHWH as Israel's king is presented by the biblical authors as a concept very much alive during the period of the judges.

First, in the book of Ruth, which is set in the days when the judges rule (ויהי בימי שׁפט השׁפטים), the first character to be introduced is named Elimelech (Ruth 1:2). Although the precise meaning of the name is debated, Campbell thinks that for an Israelite, the name very likely means "The King (YHWH) is my god".[86] Alternatively, Block thinks the name could mean "My God (YHWH) is king".[87] Either way, the name would testify to an implicit acknowledgment of YHWH's kingship over Israel.

But this implicit acknowledgement of YHWH's kingship is also found within Judges itself. In Judg. 8:22–23, Gideon is offered kingship over Israel. Although it is true that מלך is never directly used either in the offer or the response, yet the use of משׁל in 9:2 that leads to Abimelech's eventually becoming מלך in 9:6, and the use of the same word in connection with David and Solomon's reigns in 2 Sam. 23:3 and 1 Kgs. 5:1 show that what is being offered is undoubtedly some form of kingship.

Gideon, however, rejected this offer. Regardless of whether his rejection is sincere or not, what is significant is that his response, which pitches the offer made to him against YHWH's right to rule over Israel, represents an implicit acknowledgement of YHWH's rightful kingship over Israel. This, incidentally, is also consistent with the perspective found later in 1 Sam. 8:7 and 12:12, where the people's request for a human king is interpreted by both YHWH and

[84] Seeligmann, 79,89.

[85] Ibid., 90.

[86] Campbell (52) sees the name as an authentic and typical name in Canaan prior to the time of the Israelite monarchy. See also Greenstein (1981a:203–04), who sees the name as a literary invention. But while Greenstein is right in pointing to the literary significance given to a number of names in Ruth, Campbell notes that the name Elimelech may be the only one in the story not having a symbolic meaning pertinent to the narrative.

[87] Block, 1999:625.

Samuel as a rejection of YHWH as king. What these incidents seem to show therefore, is that YHWH's kingship over Israel is at least presented as a reality well understood by Israel's leaders in the period immediately preceding the establishment of monarchy.

But even if this is true, all it does is to establish the possibility that the מלך in Judges' refrain can indeed refer to YHWH. Whether or not it actually does still needs to be determined from the immediate context and the larger context of the book. In the process of doing so, however, one question needs to be raised.

Supposing that מלך in the refrain is indeed to be understood as referring to YHWH, in light of what has just been said about YHWH's kingship being a concept that seems to be very much alive within Israelite tradition during the period of the judges, in what sense, then, can it be said that there was no מלך in Israel?

One possibility is to understand אין מלך בישׂראל as highlighting the fact that even though YHWH was the rightful king over Israel, He was not being honoured as such by His people.

In his commentary, Boling suggests that the use of the short refrain in 18:1 is meant to lament "the lack of acknowledgment of YHWH's kingship in Israel".[88] Similarly, Block understands אין מלך בישׂראל as a comment on Israel's rejection of theocracy.[89] After arguing that YHWH's kingship is assumed throughout Deuteronomy by virtue of it being structured after ancient Near Eastern suzerainty treaties,[90] Block sees the fourfold repetition of אין מלך בישׂראל in the epilogue as indicating that the nation no longer recognised anyone, not even YHWH, as king. The ensuing episodes in the epilogue thus provide the evidence of Israel's complete repudiation of YHWH's claim on their lives. Gunn and Fewell, citing YHWH's later comment to Samuel in 1 Sam. 8:7, likewise think that one can look back at the refrain in Judges in retrospect and see that there was indeed no king in Israel. For judging by the behaviour of the people, YHWH might as well have not existed.[91]

But this interpretation has more to recommend it. First, such an understanding of אין מלך בישׂראל seems to fit remarkably well with

[88] Boling, 1975:258.
[89] Block, 1999:59,476.
[90] See also Mendenhall (1955:24–50) for discussion of parallels between Israelite covenant tradition and Hittite suzerain-vassal treaties.
[91] Gunn and Fewell, 121.

the second half of the full refrain to offer up a coherent evaluation of the period of the judges. For as has already been pointed out earlier, the second half of the full refrain, 'every man did what was right in his own eyes (איש הישר בעיניו יעשה)', seems to echo a similar phrase in Deut. 12:8 that may have been designed to serve as a contrast to the Deuteronomic concept of doing what is right in YHWH's eyes (עשה הישר בעיני יהוה). If so, this would make 'doing what is right in one's own eyes (איש הישר בעיניו יעשה)' a virtual complement to the oft-repeated 'doing what is evil in the eyes of YHWH (עשה . . . הרע בעיני יהוה)' in the central section of the book, both essentially pointing to Israel's failure to do what was right in the eyes of YHWH.

But Israel' persistence in doing what was right in their own eyes but evil in YHWH's may only be a surface manifestation of a deeper, underlying problem, one that is expressed by the author of the epilogue as אין מלך בישראל. For if the manifestation of that problem is such that the people were choosing what was right in their own eyes over against what was right in YHWH's, then it seems only reasonable that the problem itself must have had something to do with Israel's fundamental relationship with YHWH. Thus, it would make perfect sense to understand the refrain אין מלך בישראל as referring to Israel's non-honouring of YHWH's kingship. After all, it is only when YHWH was no longer honoured as king and His will ignored that the people began living according to the standards they set for themselves. And the result was the chaos and anarchy so evident in the narratives in the epilogue.

But there is a second way in which this interpretation of אין מלך בישראל seems to fit well in context, and it has to do with the way YHWH is portrayed in the epilogue. For it has not gone unnoticed that in the epilogue, YHWH's role and involvement within the narratives has diminished significantly. Commenting on the story of Micah's idols and their subsequent fall into the hands of the Danites, Exum writes, "YHWH does not participate in the events of this story. The divine absence is especially noteworthy after an account (i.e. the Samson account) where YHWH had controlled everything from offstage."[92]

---

[92] Exum, 1990:426. The same point is also made by McMillion (237), who cosiders the absence of YHWH in Judg 17–18 all the more striking since He was an active participant in earlier parts of the book.

And YHWH's involvement has not increased substantially either in the second narrative about the Levite, her concubine, and the subsequent civil war. True, YHWH did speak to Israel on three occasions (20:18,23,28), but in none of them did He take the initiative. Rather, in all three, He spoke only in response to Israel's inquiry. In fact, in two of the three occasions, His simple two-word instruction for the Israelites to go up against Benjamin resulted in significant defeats for the Israelites rather than the expected victories. It is almost as if YHWH was simply telling the Israelites what they wanted to hear in order to keep them from bothering Him further.[93] It is only on the third occasion, after the Israelites had grovelled before Him with weeping and fasting and offering of sacrifices, that He finally gave them the promiseed victory they sought. Overall, therefore, the three exchanges give the impression that YHWH's involvement in Israel's affairs at this point was grudging at best.

As for specific actions which YHWH undertook on behalf of Israel in this portion of the epilogue, as has already been noted earlier, the attribution of victory to YHWH in the war against Benjamin in 20:35 is brief.[94] Considering how detailed the actual battle account is, that a one-sentence summary is the only mention of YHWH within the entire battle account makes the statement seem almost perfunctory. And other than 20:35, the only other statement about YHWH's action given by the narrator is 21:15, where YHWH is said to have made a gap among the tribes of Israel. But given that the Israelites had earlier tried to put the blame for the imminent demise of Benjamin on YHWH in 21:3, and that 21:15 actually begins with a resumptive statement recapitulating Israel's grief in 21:2,6, it is entirely possible that 21:15b in fact reflects Israel's perspective rather than the narrator's. If so, then the summary statement in 20:35 may have been the only statement the narrator made within the entire epilogue that remotely speaks of YHWH taking any action at all.

Regarding this absence of YHWH in the epilogue, Exum, who understands מלך in the refrain as referring to a human king, writes, "The concluding stories illustrate the depravity and anarchy of the

[93] Note Israel's incessant grovelling that so exasperated YHWH in Judg. 10:11–16.
[94] See pp. 64–65.

times, a time when there is no king but YHWH (8:23), whose beneficial guidance, it seems, cannot be assumed."[95] She further writes, "Judg. 21:25 suggests that this anarchy results from the lack of a king. But Israel has a king; YHWH rules over Israel. In Judges 17–21, YHWH's rule is ineffectual, either because YHWH does not intervene in events or because YHWH intervenes in ways that result in destruction rather than benefit."[96]

But if this supposedly ineffectual rule of YHWH, mainly on account of His absence, is indeed such a significant factor contributing to the chaos and anarchy found in the narratives in the epilogue, then the question that begs asking is: Why has YHWH so abruptly withdrawn Himself from Israel's affairs?

As it turns out, YHWH's withdrawal from Israel's affairs may not be as abrupt as initially thought. For even back in the central section, there already exists an episode where YHWH is portrayed as being on the verge of forsaking His people.

In Judges 10:9–10, one finds the Israelites crying out to YHWH in distress when they were oppressed by the Ammonites. But according to 10:11–14, YHWH was initially unwilling to deliver them. And the reason given in 10:13 for this unwillingness is that the Israelites had forsaken Him (ואתם עזבתם אותי) to serve other gods. In response therefore, YHWH too would forsake them.

What is interesting here is that other than in the introductory framework in 2:12,13, Judg. 10:6,10,13 are the only times עזב is used in the book to describe Israel's relationship with YHWH. Significantly, these three verses in Judges 10 also happen to represent respectively the narrator's evaluation of Israel, Israel's own admission of guilt, and YHWH's accusation against the people. The cumulative effect, therefore, is that Israel's forsaking of YHWH as her God is a fact beyond dispute.

Not surprisingly, it is also here, where Israel's forsaking of YHWH is no longer in doubt, that for the first time in the book, YHWH indicates that He was no longer willing to deliver them.[97] Even

---

[95] Exum, 1990:425.

[96] Ibid., 431.

[97] Note that according to 2:1–5,20–22, in response to Israel's disobedience (לא־שמע בקלי), YHWH merely refused to dispossess Israel's enemies before them. And while 2:14–15 indeed speak of YHWH handing Israel over to her enemies, 2:16–18 immediately speak of YHWH's provision of deliverance through the judges.

though 10:16 implies that YHWH ultimately relented on account of Israel's pathetic grovelling, the seed has already been sown for the kind of alienation between Israel and YHWH witnessed in the epilogue.

But if, in Judges 10, YHWH's unwillingness to intervene on Israel's behalf to deliver her is indeed brought on by Israel's prior forsaking of Him as her God, then it goes to reason that His non-involvement in the affairs of Israel in the epilogue may very well have been brought on by a similar rejection. This thus lends support to the interpretation that the oft-repeated first part of the full refrain, אין מלך בישׂראל, may indeed be speaking of the non-honouring of YHWH as king in Israel. For not only would such an understanding reveal the underlying problem behind the people's choice to do what was right in their own eyes, it would also go a long way towards explaining YHWH's absence from the narratives in the epilogue.

Interestingly, this understanding of אין מלך בישׂראל as referring to the non-honouring of YHWH as king in Israel actually finds support from an unexpected source: a message delivered by the prophet Azariah recorded in 2 Chron. 15:1–7.

In 2 Chron. 15:1, Azariah goes out to meet King Asa upon his return from a victorious campaign against the Cushites. The theme of his message, expressed in 15:2, is that YHWH would be with His people when they are with Him. To clarify what this means, Azariah then breaks down this theme into two complementary principles: If the Israelites seek Him, He will be found by them, but if they forsake Him, He will also forsake them. To demonstrate how the two principles work, Azariah then looks back to the nation's history in 15:3–6,[98] before finally closing his message with a word of exhortation for his contemporary audience in 15:7.

To establish the relevance of this passage to our understanding of the refrain in Judges, the first questions that need asking concern whether the historical illustration in 15:3–6 refers to an identifiable period in Israel's history, and if so, which period it is. Admittedly, the period referred to is not clearly defined. Instead, it was merely introduced with the ambiguous "for a long time (וימים רבים)". Even

[98] Admittedly, there is some uncertainty as to whether 15:3 refers to the past or to the future, especially since the verse in question has no finite verb. Although the LXX and the Vulgate suggest a future reference, most commentators see the verse as referring to the past. See Williamson, 267; Dillard, 120; Japhet, 719.

so, it seems possible to argue from clues within the text that a specific period of Israel's history was referred to.

First, that 15:3–6 most likely refers to one specific period in Israel's history rather than a number of diverse eras can be seen in that the remote demonstrative ההם in the second chronological marker of the section in 15:5 seems to point back to the ימים רבים mentioned in 15:3. This suggests that the events mentioned in 15:3–4 and 15:5–6 are by and large presented as having occurred within the same period in the nation's history. If so, then in spite of the somewhat cryptic description in 15:3, one may still be able to identify the period from clues found in 15:4–6.

In 15:6, Azariah speaks of God troubling Israel with every kind of distress (צרה), and this distress seems related to the crushing of nation upon nation and city upon city. In fact, according to 15:4, it may well be on account of this very distress (צרר) that Israel turned to YHWH and sought Him.[99] The situation presented here thus seems to parallel events in the period of the judges. For in Judges, Israel is also described in 2:15 and 10:9 as being in distress (צרר) as a result of YHWH allowing nations round about to oppress her. In fact, the accounts of the various judges testify to the fact that numerous nations and cities were involved in warfare with Israel. As a result of this distress, Israel also turned to YHWH and cried out for deliverance.[100]

Moreover, in connection with the turmoil with which God troubled Israel, 2 Chron. 15:5 also speaks of there being no safety in going out and coming in. Interestingly, this is also reminiscent of Judg. 5:6, where Deborah speaks of roadways ceasing to be fit for travel[101] in the days immediately before YHWH raised her up to deliver Israel.

---

[99] That the distress in 15:4 is recognised as the same distress spoken of in 15:6 is what caused some scholars to view 15:4 as misplaced and to suggest transposing the verse to a position following 15:6. However, both Williamson (268) and Japhet (720) argue against emendation in favour of preserving the original structure of the passage.

[100] In fact, when YHWH refused to deliver His people in 10:14 and asked them to go and cry out to their other gods for deliverance, the noun צרה is also used.

[101] Here, although חדל is most often used to refer to the cessation of a certain course of action (Gen. 11:8; Exod. 23:5; Ruth 1:18; 1 Sam. 12:23, 23:13; 2 Chron. 16:5) or a specific object ceasing to exist (Exod. 9:29; Ps. 49:8; Prov. 19:9; Isa. 24:8), the verb can also be used to refer to an object losing certain critical qualities. Thus in Job 19:14, for example, the use of the verb to describe Job's near-

Thus, although there was no significant verbal correspondence between the description of the period referred to in 2 Chron. 15:3–6 and the description of the era of the judges in the book of Judges, there seems to be sufficient parallels between the two to warrant identifying the period referred to in 2 Chron. 15:3–6 as the period of the judges.[102]

But if this is indeed the case, then what exactly does 2 Chron. 15:3 mean when the period is described as one when there is neither true God nor instructing priest nor the law? Interestingly, the answer may actually be found in the rhetorical structure of the passage.

While it seems clear that the citing of Israel's history in 2 Chron. 15:3–6 is meant to illustrate and validate Azariah's message, it still bears asking what exactly the illustration was illustrating. A close examination of the entire speech and the response it elicited seems to indicate that, rather than illustrating the overriding theme of YHWH being with His people when they are with Him (15:2a), the citing of past history was actually aimed at illustrating the two accompanying principles that say, "If you seek Him, He will be found by you, but if you forsake Him, He will forsake you (15:2b–c)."

That the whole episode comprising Azariah's speech and the people's response focuses on the seeking and finding of YHWH is clear in that this motif repeatedly crops up within the episode. For not only is this motif stated as a principle in 15:2 and emerges again in the historical illustration in 15:4, the actual seeking and the subsequent finding of YHWH as a part of the people's response is also recorded in 15:12,13,15.[103]

---

kinsmen does not mean in context that they died, but only that they have ceased to be near-kinsmen by no longer going near him. Thus, חדל in the context of Judg. 5:6 may also be taken to mean that roadways have ceased to be fit for travel rather than their having ceased to exist altogether. Furthermore, although the reason for this condition was not specifically stated in the text, one can surmise from the immediate context that it was because of the advance of enemy troops (5:8) that rendered the major roadways unsafe for travel.

[102] Myers (88), Williamson (267), Dillard (120), and Japhet (719) are among many who see the historical period referred to in 2 Chron. 15:3–6 as referring to the period of the judges.

[103] Here, the fact that דרשׁ is used in the statement of the principle in 15:2 while בקשׁ is used in the historical illustration in 15:4 should not be too much of an issue. After all, the two verbs are often used together synonymously in parallel cola in Hebrew Scripture. See, for example, Deut. 4:29; Judg. 6:29; 1 Chron. 16:11; Job 10:6; Pss. 24:6, 38:13, 105:4; Jer. 29:13; Ezek. 34:6; and Zeph. 1:6. Besides, both verbs are used interchangeably within the response section of 2 Chronicles 15, with

But if the seeking and finding of YHWH in past history as recounted in 15:4 is indeed meant to illustrate the actual outworking of the principle "If you seek him, He will be found by you", then what is the function of the rest of the historical illustration?

Granted, the verb עזב which dominates the complementary principle that says "If you forsake (עזב) Him, He will forsake (עזב) you" is not used in the historical illustration in 15:3–6. Nonetheless, it seems clear that the events recounted in 15:5–6 are meant to illustrate the "He will forsake you" part of this principle. For not only is the distress spoken of in 15:6 clearly attributed to God, the use of מהומה in 15:5 also implies a divine origin of Israel's turmoil. For of the twelve times מהומה is used in Hebrew Scripture, in ten of them, the turmoil spoken of is either explicitly said to be caused by YHWH or implied to be such from the context.[104] And while in half of those instances, this מהומה has to do with YHWH's judgment on the nations, in the other half, it speaks of YHWH's judgment on Israel. In fact, Deut. 28:20 even specifies that this מהומה would come as a consequence of Israel's forsaking (עזב) of YHWH. Thus, it seems beyond dispute that 2 Chron. 15:5–6 must aim at illustrating the part of the principle that speaks of YHWH forsaking His people as a result of their forsaking Him.

But if 15:4 is indeed meant to illustrate the seeking and finding of YHWH, while 15:5–6 is meant to illustrate YHWH's forsaking of His people, then where within the historical illustration is the part that illustrates Israel's forsaking of YHWH? After all, the principle given in 15:2c is "If you forsake Him, He will forsake you." That being the case, surely Azariah would not have detailed YHWH's forsaking of His people in history without at least making clear that it was only on account of Israel having first forsaken YHWH that YHWH decided to forsake them. If so, then one can reasonably conclude that what is left of the historical illustration, namely, the cryptically worded 15:3, must have been the part that speaks of Israel's prior forsaking of YHWH.

Hence, what is most likely meant by there being neither true God nor instructing priest nor the law for Israel is that, rather than speak-

---

דרשׁ being used in 15:12,13 and בקשׁ being used in 15:15 to speak of essentially the same act.

[104] The ten instances comprise Deut. 7:23; 28:20; 1 Sam. 5:9,11; 14:20; 2 Chron. 15:5; Isa. 22:5; Ezek. 7:7; 22:5; Zech. 14:13.

ing of the mere absence of these three things at some particular point in the history of Israel, 15:3 must be referring to the non-honouring of YHWH and instructing priest and the law in Israel during the period of the judges. After all, if 15:3–6 is indeed referring to the period of the judges as it is generally believed, then this may be the only way the verse would make sense. For in an era when YHWH was already known to Israel and both the priesthood and the law were well established, the only way YHWH and the law could meaningfully be absent from Israelite society would be for them to be absent from the perspective of a society that has chosen to ignore them. Besides, as indicated in 15:4, the fact that YHWH could still be sought and found when His people needed Him shows that the true God was not really absent in the absolute sense, but merely from those who did not honour Him. Thus, as Israel forsook YHWH during this period by honouring neither Him as the true God nor the law nor the priest who taught the law, in response, YHWH also forsook Israel and brought upon her all kinds of turmoil and distress, until she decided once more to seek Him.

If this is indeed how 2 Chron. 15:3–6 is to be understood, then it has a significant bearing upon the interpretation of the refrain in the epilogue of Judges: 2 Chron. 15:3 confirms an understanding of Judges' refrain that takes מלך as referring to YHWH rather than a human king. For by characterising the period as one when אין מלך בישׂראכל, the author of Judges' refrain may in fact be saying the exact same thing the author of Chronicles (or Azariah) was saying when he characterised the period as one when לישׂראל ללא אלהי אמת.[105] מלך in Judges's refrain, then, would simply be a divine epithet that is referentially equivalent to אלהי אמת in 2 Chron. 15:3.

[105] Note too, that this convergence of perspective does not even need to presuppose literary dependence. In fact, that there is very little linguistic correspondence between 2 Chron. 15:3–6 and Judges seems to point to two essentially independent compositions. But it is possible that a consensus evaluation of the period of the judges had already been well established within Israelite tradition, such that independently of each other, the author of Chronicles and Judges were both drawing from the same tradition as each spoke about the period in his own way.

CHAPTER SIX

COMPOSITIONAL STRATEGY AND RHETORICAL PURPOSE OF JUDGES

In the preceding chapters, rhetorical links that connect the major sections of Judges have been explored. It is therefore time to bring the results of these explorations together so that a comprehensive picture can emerge regarding the overall compositional strategy of the book.

Furthermore, in the process of doing so, one expects also to gain significant insight about the rhetorical purpose that guides the book's composition. This purpose, which allows one not only to grasp the central message of Judges, but also to see with greater clarity how the component parts interact to advance that message, will also be discussed in the present chapter.

Compositional Strategy of Judges

Before any attempt is made to uncover the overall compositional strategy of Judges, it is perhaps desirable to first review briefly some of the conclusions drawn in preceding chapters about the relationships between the major sections of Judges.

In chapter two, it has been argued that not only do specific episodes in the prologue and epilogue demonstrate significant thematic unity and progression, but the pervasive use of ironic allusions to Joshua in both sections to highlight the failures of the generation after Joshua also suggests that the same hand may have been responsible for the composition of both sections.

In chapter three, it has been shown that contrary to accepted wisdom, the epilogue may actually be intimately related to the central section as the bizarre behaviour of each of the epilogue's protagonist seems to mirror similarly bizarre behaviour displayed by one of the major judges in the central section. This suggests that rather than it being an unrelated appendage artificially attached to the central section, the epilogue may have been composed with the central section in mind to serve as an evaluative conclusion to the judges narratives.

In chapter four, it has been shown that the prologue introduces a progressive deterioration theme that also dominates the central section. Since this theme is developed in both sections along a similar south-to-north geographic trajectory, it is likely that the prologue is designed to be a paradigm for the central section so as to provide structural clues for the interpretation of the latter. This means that, rather than the two sections being independent compositions, the prologue may have been composed expressly as an introduction for the central section.

Incidentally, the above conclusions from the three chapters actually dovetail quite nicely into each other. For if the prologue and the epilogue are not composed independently of the central section, but specifically to serve as paradigmatic introduction and evaluative conclusion for the central section, then the idea that they may have originated from the same hand becomes all the more feasible.

Moreover, this compositional unity between the prologue and epilogue is further substantiated by a complex link discovered while considering the book's stance on kingship. This link, which connects all three sections of Judges, is constructed by first connecting the narrative of Abimelech with that of Adoni-Bezek through the common themes of brutality against seventy rivals and the eventual receipt of divine retribution. In so doing, Abimelech is effectively portrayed as being thoroughly Canaanised and more. This extreme Canaanisation theme then shows up again in the epilogue as the perversity of the Gibeathites is presented as a re-enactment of Sodom. Since this Sodom-like behaviour of the Gibeathites is bizarre and inexplicable in the same way that the behaviour of the other protagonists in the epilogue is bizarre and inexplicable, and since subtle allusions to Israelite leaders in the central section are almost inevitably found when the protagonists in the epilogue behave bizarrely and inexplicably, one can argue that the bizarre display of extreme Canaanised behaviour by the Gibeathites very likely alludes to a similar display of extreme Canaanised behaviour by Abimelech in the central section. If so, the Canaanisation of Abimelech may in fact be subtly presented as a precedent for the Gibeathites, just as the actions of the major judges are also subtly presented as precedents for the actions of the various protagonists in the book's epilogue.

What is especially interesting about this complex link, however, is that in order to present both Abimelech and the Gibeathites as thoroughly Canaanised and more, their respective behaviour needs to be set against that of Canaanite foils. While an obvious parallel is readily available for the Gibeathites in the account of the Sodomite incident in Genesis 19, for Abimelech, however, no comparable parallel exists outside Judges. This being the case, it may well be that the Adoni-Bezek account was included in the prologue solely to establish Abimelech's Canaanisation. This seems especially likely in view of two facts. First, the Adoni-Bezek account does not seem to fit naturally into the overall argument of the prologue,[1] and second, in spite of its extreme brevity, the account actually contains two significant parallels with the Abimelech narrative.

But if the inclusion of the Adoni-Bezek account in the prologue is primarily to establish the Canaanisation of Abimelech so as to create a precedent for the Canaanisation of the Gibeathites in the epilogue, and if this strategy of pointing back to the central section for precedent whenever a character in the epilogue acts bizarrely and inexplicably is a characteristic feature of the epilogue, then it follows that the same hand that composed the epilogue must have also played a significant role in shaping the prologue. Taken together with the other evidence already presented, it therefore seems indisputable that the same hand must have been responsible for the crafting of both the prologue and epilogue of Judges.

Here, it should be noted that although the above conclusions may have provided new insight into how the current form of Judges came into being, thus far, they are not incompatible with the essentials of Noth's theory regarding the Judges portion of DH. For even if the prologue and epilogue of Judges were composed by the same author to serve respectively as paradigmatic introduction and evaluative conclusion to the central section, there is still nothing to suggest that they cannot be post-Deuteronomistic compositions that were added to the central section when DH was divided into canonical books.[2] In fact, given all that has been said, one might even argue that the author of the prologue and epilogue was none other the one who divided DH into canonical books, and that out of his special interest in the period of the judges, he composed an introduction and a conclusion for the material he isolated out of DH in order to present his unique interpretation and evaluation of the period.

[1] Noth (1991:23 n. 2) actually calls the introduction of the Adoni-Bezek account "strangely abrupt".

[2] Ibid., 24.

But as intriguing as this scenario may be, another alternative exists that may provide even more satisfactory answers to questions concerning the compositional strategy of Judges. Consider the following.

When it comes to the material within the central section of Judges, one of the questions often raised but seldom satisfactorily answered is "Why these stories?" Gros Louis, for example, seeing parallels between Judges and the Odyssey, where the Homeric poet had a number of stories to draw on but judiciously selected those that went together to transform a travel tale into an epic, asks regarding Judges, "Why these heroes? Why these particular stories? Why in this particular order?"[3] Similarly, Brettler wonders whether there is any plausible historical or ideological background that would help explain why the author/redactor of the central section chose these particular stories and arranged them in this order.[4] For indeed, although one can see how some of the narratives seem to work well in conjunction with others to provide pattern and continuity, there are also narratives the inclusion of which seems perplexing.

Take the Abimelech narrative, for example.[5] In a section dominated by narratives of judges who were raised up by YHWH to deliver His people from foreign oppressors, why was the story of Abimelech included, since he was neither a judge nor did he deliver Israel from foreign oppressors?[6] Or consider the narrative about

[3] Gros Louis, 141–42. Although Gros Louis does try to answer these questions by exploring patterns and links between the narratives, he has only succeeded in showing how various narratives in the central section can be connected without explaining why these episodes are included in the first place.

[4] Brettler, 1989a:403–04. Here, Brettler (1989a:404–08) tries to answer the question by pointing to a polemic against the northern kingdom. But while this may explain why most of the judges are anti-heroes, it still does not explain why these particular stories were chosen.

[5] Note that according to Noth (1991:37), the Abimelech narrative is considered the work of Dtr and not a post-Deuteronomistic addition. In fact, Richter (1963:320) includes the Abimelech narrative as part of his Retterbuch that served as a source for Dtr.

[6] In Bluedorn's (30–49) survey, he shows that most attempts to explain the inclusion of the Abimelech narrative in Judges have failed to provide a satisfactory answer. Unfortunately, the answer Bluedorn himself provides proves equally unsatisfactory for two reasons. First, in spite of his attempt (273–80) to argue that the theological theme "YHWH versus Baalism" also pervades the rest of Judges, a natural reading of the text simply does not support his contention that this theme is a main concern in the book. Therefore, even if one grants it that the Gideon-Abimelech narrative is a polemic against Baalism, Bluedorn's interpretation would still fall under the same criticism he directs against others for not being able to

Jephthah's daughter. In a section where every episode about a major judge seems related directly or indirectly to Israel's foreign enemies and their idolatrous cultic influences, why was this personal and largely domestic episode included?[7] In fact, if one takes Judges 2:6–3:6 at the beginning of the central section as an encapsulation of the most salient features of the period and a preview of the narratives to follow, then the narratives about Abimelech and Jephthah's daughter seem almost like unnecessary digressions that could just as easily have been left out without detracting from one's overall understanding of the period. Thus, solely from the perspective of the internal logic of the central section, the inclusion of these narratives seems inexplicable and perplexing.

But what is most interesting here is that a different picture emerges if the material in the central section is viewed in light of what the author of the prologue and epilogue was trying to accomplish. For if the epilogue of Judges is indeed meant to serve as a subtle evaluation of Israel's leaders in this period as episodes in the lives of these leaders are echoed in the bizarre happenings of the epilogue, and if the prologue of Judges is likewise meant to introduce a deterioration paradigm that is progressively played out in the lives of the major judges, then between these two very specific purposes, one suddenly discovers that the inclusion of nearly every single episode in the central section can readily be accounted for, with the exception perhaps of the minor judges and the brief episode of Samson's exploits in Gaza in Judg. 16:1–3.

explain how the Abimelech narrative integrates with the rest of the book. But second, even Bluedorn's argument that the Abimelech episode is a polemic against Baalism fails to convince. For by insisting that the narrative is not about retribution for the crime and wrong-doing of Abimelech and the Shechemites but about Baal not being God (224,264) and punishment for idolatry (184–87,249), Bluedorn is actually imposing his theological reading over the narrator's explicit assertion in 9:23–24,56–57 that the main concern of the narrative is in fact focused on retribution for the murder, and not idolatry, committed by the protagonists.

[7] This may have been why Mayes (1977:317) considers the story of Jephthah's daughter an appendix to the original collection of traditions about Jephthah. For an intriguing explanation for the inclusion of this story from an unconventional reading of the text, see Bal's suggestion (21–28; 257, ns. 19–20) that Jephthah's daughter, together with Samson's wife and the Levite's concubine, represent three unnamed women who were killed by men. This, balanced by three other stories in the book of men killed by women for social reasons, is understood by Bal as an indication that the author of the book is sensitive to issues of power dissymmetry between men and women.

This therefore raises an interesting possibility. What if, instead of the author of the prologue and epilogue having composed those two sections to introduce and conclude an already substantially fixed collection of hero stories, it is actually the author of the prologue and epilogue who was responsible for choosing which of the hero stories to include in the central section in order to illustrate his specific purposes? After all, to have to compose an introduction and a conclusion to a substantial body of fixed text that already has its own purpose, and still be able to shape that introduction and conclusion such that rhetorical links are established with almost every single episode of that fixed text, is a challenge that even the most skilled of authors would find daunting. But if, on the other hand, an author with a clear and specific purpose is asked to select from a large pool of traditions only those that best illustrate his purpose, then that task becomes much easier and more manageable, and the end result would be an economical collection of narratives consisting only of those narratives that are relevant to his purpose and nothing else. In such a case, one would then expect each of the selected narratives to serve a definite function within the larger whole, much as what one finds here in Judges when the narratives of the central section are seen in light of the specific purposes of the prologue and the epilogue.

Under this theory, for example, the inclusion of the narrative of Jephthah's daughter can easily be explained. For not only would the uttering of Jephthah's vow contribute to the progressive deterioration theme already introduced in the prologue and is now being played out in the accounts of the successive judges, what eventually happened to Jephthah's daughter also constitutes a significant parallel with what happened to the virgins of Jabesh Gilead and Shiloh in the epilogue, thus providing precedent for the rash oath taken by Israel and its elders.

As for the Abimelech narrative, not only would its inclusion be justified by the link with the Adoni-Bezek narrative in the prologue to create precedent for the Canaanisation of the Gibeathites in the epilogue, but its presence would also help guide the interpretation of the refrain in the epilogue, so as to reduce the likelihood of it being misinterpreted as an implicit endorsement of human kingship.

But even so, how does one explain the inclusion of the minor judges and of Samson's exploit in Gaza in the central section, since these appear to have no direct rhetorical connection with the material in the prologue and the epilogue? Would the inclusion of these narratives not raise doubts about the validity of the present hypothesis?

Surprisingly, it would not. In fact, on the contrary, what appears to undermine this hypothesis actually turns out to provide further substantiation for it.

First, consider the brief narrative of Samson's exploit in Gaza recorded in Judg. 16:1–3. While the episode itself seems entirely unrelated to the purposes that have been identified for the prologue and the epilogue, in the context of the Samson narratives, it does seem to play a significant role. This is especially so if one embraces the popular interpretation of Samson as a microcosmic reflection of the nation itself. For as has been frequently pointed out, strong parallels do exist between Samson and Israel.[8]

To begin with, both Samson and Israel were set apart by YHWH. As Wilson further notes, in both cases, this special calling took place before 'birth'.[9] Greenstein thus sees Samson's Naziriteship as typifying Israel's covenant with YHWH.[10]

But in spite of this special calling, Samson could not resist the lure of foreign women,[11] much as Israel failed to resist the lure of foreign cults.[12] In fact, Samson's pursuit of the first of his many Philistine women is presented in 14:3,7 as going after 'what was right in his eyes', just as every Israelite is said in the epilogue to be doing 'what was right in his own eyes (17:6; 21:25)'.[13] Yet when Samson

[8] In fact, Greenstein (1981b:247–54) sees Samson as essentially an allegory that epitomises Israel, and considers the parallel between Samson and Israel as the central interpretive principle that allows one to understand the various aspects of the Samson saga.

[9] Wilson, 78.

[10] Greenstein, 1981b:247.

[11] Although the nationality of both the prostitute in Gaza and Delilah is never specified, it is reasonable to infer that they were Philistine. After all, as Gaza was Philistine territory, one would not expect to find an Israelite prostitute there. As for Delilah, her residence in what was most likely Philistine territory and her ready cooperation with the rulers of the Philistines seem also to suggest a Philistine identity.

[12] This parallel between foreign women and foreign cults becomes even more compelling when one takes into consideration that relationships with foreign women have often been linked in Hebrew Scripture to the adoption of foreign cults. See, for example, Num. 25:1–3; Deut. 7:1–4; Judg. 3:5–6; 1 Kgs. 11:1–6.

[13] Incidentally, 14:3,7 and the full refrain (17:6; 21:25) are the only times ישר בעין occurs in Judges.

cried out to YHWH in distress in 15:18, YHWH delivered him, just as He repeatedly delivered His people when they cried out to Him in distress.[14]

But in the end, when Samson, like Israel, has been enticed once too often, His source of strength left him, just as YHWH, the source of Israel's strength, eventually also withdrew Himself from intervening to deliver His people.[15] As a result, both Samson and Israel were eventually overcome and subdued by their enemies. In fact, according to Gros-Louis, even the blinding of Samson "seems to symbolise and crystallise the blindness of Israel. . . . Samson suffers literally the darkness which the Israelites suffer figuratively".[16]

But if Samson is indeed meant to serve as a figure for the nation Israel, then what seems like an insignificant episode in Judg. 16:1–3 suddenly takes on greater significance. For a key parallel between Samson and Israel is the repeated and almost compulsive involvement of each with things foreign and forbidden: whereas for Samson, it was foreign women, for Israel, it was foreign gods. But in trying to bring out Samson's compulsive involvement with foreign women, the Gaza episode becomes critically important. Not only is this because it would otherwise be difficulty to establish a pattern of repeated behaviour with only two examples, but also because out of the three episodes that chronicles Samson's involvement with foreign women, it is his dalliance with the prostitute at Gaza that most clearly reveals the true nature of his compulsion. After all, when Samson first pursued the Philistine woman in Timnah, his desire was to marry her. With Delilah, it is also explicitly stated in 16:4 that he loved (אהב) her. Thus, without the Gaza episode, one might easily have read the two narratives as merely chronicling Samson's misfortune in love.

[14] Admittedly, the verb used to describe Samson's crying out in 15:18 is קרא rather than זעק or צעק that is used repeatedly of Israel's crying out in 3:9,15; 4:3; 6:6,7; 10:10,12,14. But within Judges, especially in 4:6,10 and 12:1–2, the three verbs seem to be used interchangeable in the context of calling to arms. Besides, the use of קרא in 15:18 is surely related to the etiological note in 15:19, as the name עין הקורא would only make sense contextually if קרא is used to describe Samson's crying out in 15:18.

[15] Although this withdrawal of YHWH from delivering His people is not fully played out until substantially later in Israel's history, as has been noted earlier on pp. 182–84; 216–19, even within Judges, the increasing absence of YHWH from Israel's affairs is already noticeable.

[16] Gros Louis, 161.

But with the inclusion of the Gaza episode, the nature of Samson's compulsion becomes much clearer. As it turns out, it was not only love Samson was after, it was also quick sex with foreign prostitutes.[17] In fact, coming right before the narrative about Delilah, the Gaza episode actually deconstructs Samson's 'love' for Delilah by causing one to wonder what exactly the nature of that 'love' is. And in hindsight, the anger and frustration that drove Samson to burn the Philistines' harvest after he was denied access to his former wife's chamber (החדרה) also suddenly begins to make more sense.

But not only is this Gaza episode significant in terms of clarifying the true nature of Samson's compulsion, it is also significant from the perspective of the epilogue's purpose. For if the inclusion of this episode is indeed primarily to help establish the parallel between Samson and Israel, then this inclusion may actually reflect the same underlying rhetorical strategy as that used in the epilogue. For as has already been pointed out, one of the main rhetorical features of the epilogue is that almost all bizarre and inexplicable behaviour associated with its protagonists are subtly linked to analogous actions of one of Israel's leaders in the central section. Other than the fact that this particular link between Samson and Israel occurs wholly within the central section, it actually shares many of the same features found in links between narratives in the epilogue and the central section.

First of all, like the other links, the link between Samson and Israel is essentially one that connects the behaviour of Israelites in the general population with the behaviour of a prominent Israelite leader. Second, given that all Israel ever got out of her involvement with foreign gods was the wrath of YHWH and the resulting oppression by those whose gods she went after, her compulsive persistence in this matter is nothing if not bizarre and inexplicable. In this respect, her behaviour is not unlike the similarly bizarre and inexplicable behaviour of the protagonists in the epilogue. Third, like the protagonists in the epilogue, Israel's bizarre and inexplicable behaviour is also mirrored by a prominent Israelite leader. In fact, given that all Samson ever got out of his involvement with Philistine women was also trouble from the very people whose women he went

---

[17] Note also how Israel's dalliance with foreign gods is also described in Judg. 2:17 and 8:33 as a form of prostitution (זנה).

after, it is a wonder that he would persist in pursuing them.[18] Finally, in spite of the fact that the behaviour of both Samson and Israel were bizarre and inexplicable in a similar way, in the end, neither is able to throw any additional light on the other that might help to explain such behaviour. Incidentally, this contentment with simply creating close parallels without using such parallels to provide overt explanations for unusual behaviours is also characteristic of the rhetorical approach used in the epilogue. From these observations, it is not hard to see that almost the exact same rhetorical strategy is used to craft the link between Samson and Israel as that which was used to craft the other links between the epilogue and the central section.

To be sure, differences do exist between the link involving Samson and Israel and the links involving the protagonists in the epilogue and the leaders in the central section. One such difference is that whereas in the latter, the actions of Israel's leaders seem to function within the literary chronology of the book as precedents for the behaviour of the protagonists in the epilogue,[19] in the case involving Samson and the Israel, it is the repeated involvement of Israel with foreign cults that is first presented before one encounters Samson's repeated involvement with foreign women. Strictly speaking, therefore, this would eliminate the possibility of seeing Samson's compulsive involvement with foreign women as a precedent for Israel's compulsive involvement with foreign cults.

---

[18] This is probably what prompted Exum and Whedbee (153) and Josipovici (123) to note that the character of Samson does not change or develop, that he was just the same at the end of his life as he was at the beginning. But if this is true of Samson, the same may also be true of the Israel portrayed in Judges. This would thus constitute one more parallel that strengthens the analogy between Samson and Israel.

[19] It should be noted here that in real historical chronological terms, the events narrated in the epilogue probably occurred well before the exploits of the various Israelite leaders narrated in the central section. After all, Jonathan, Micah's priest, is said to be a grandson of Moses in Judg. 18:30, while the war with Benjamin was apparently fought when Phinehas, grandson of Aaron, was still officiating as priest (Judg. 20:28). This means that the events narrated in the epilogue most likely occurred relatively early in the period shortly after the passing away of Joshua. Be that as it may, in the present arrangement of the text, the author/redactor has chosen to place the hero stories before the events narrated in the epilogue, so that as his readers proceed according to the literary chronological schema he constructs, Israel's leaders in this period would have been seen as having set bizarre precedents for the general population once the various links joining the epilogue and the central section become apparent.

But while this difference can potentially be significant, one can also argue that such a difference may be more out of necessity than by design. After all, Israel's repeated apostasy is the triggering action that sets into motion chains of events leading directly to the rise of the various judges. Therefore, both plot-wise and logic-wise, it would be almost impossible to first present Samson's exploits before the very apostasy that gave rise to his judgeship is presented.

But in the end, perhaps a total correspondence between the link involving Samson and Israel and links involving the protagonists in the epilogue and Israel's leaders in the central section may not be absolutely necessary. In view of the fact that the link involving Samson and Israel is wholly contained within the central section, it is entirely possible that this link is designed to serve a slightly different function from the others that connect the epilogue with the central section. But what is this function? And how does it related to the other links it parallels?

To begin, it should be noted that within the literary chronology of the book, the link involving Samson and Israel is the first to suggest a mirroring of behaviour between leader and people. Compared to other such links that are to follow, it also happens to be the most obvious.[20] Given the abrupt change of focus in the epilogue from the exploits of the judges to those of the general populace, can it be that this parallel in behaviour involving Samson and Israel was in fact designed as a bridge that connects two seemingly unrelated sections? Thus, through this parallel, not only is the mirroring of behaviours between leader and people previewed, that preview would also serve to heighten the reader's awareness of this significant rhetorical thrust of the epilogue. After all, since this parallel in behaviour between Samson and Israel only comes to light at the end of the central section, readers who manage to grasp its significance would essentially begin their reading of the epilogue with the idea of behavioural parallels between leader and people still fresh in their mind. Thus, when they next encounter in the epilogue strategically placed allusions that seem to link the bizarre and inexplicable behaviours of its protagonists to those of the various leaders featured in the central section, memory of behavioural parallels between Samson and

[20] This is evident in that while the parallel between Samson and Israel has been noted by numerous scholars, most of the other links between the protagonists in the epilogue and Israel's leaders in the central section have rarely been noticed.

Israel should lead them to consider the possibility that other similar behavioural parallels may also exist between leader and people. This would therefore help increase the likelihood that this subtle yet significant rhetorical thrust of the epilogue is not missed.

But if this is indeed the main function of the link between Samson and Israel, then all it has to do is to introduce the underlying idea of behaviour parallels between leader and people. Granted, because of the literary chronological arrangement of the text, one may eventually conclude that the leaders are in fact presented as having set precedents for the people. But this is a secondary conclusion that is arrived at only as one tries to make further sense of the pattern emerging from the numerous links between the protagonists in the epilogue and Israel's leaders in the central section. For the link between Samson and Israel, however, the issue of precedent may not be relevant.

In any case, the point is that even though the brief episode of Samson's exploits in Gaza in Judg. 16:1–3 does not seem at first glance to have any direct rhetorical connection with the material in the prologue or the epilogue, yet in an indirect way, it too contributes to the heightening of awareness of the rhetorical purpose of the epilogue. What this means is that if the bulk of the material in the central section was indeed included on the basis of its relevance to the rhetorical purpose of the prologue and the epilogue, then the same may also be true of the brief episode of Samson's exploits in Gaza.

What then about the minor judges? Admittedly, in the context of the central section as well as of the book as a whole, the rhetorical function of the narratives of the minor judges in Judg. 3:31,[21] 10:1–5, and 12:8–15 is still somewhat mystifying. In an attempt to understand why they may have been included, a few issues will have to be considered.

---

[21] Whether Shamgar should be considered a minor judge or not is still subject to debate. On the one hand, the narrative lacks the other features of the minor judge framework such as length of rule, death notice, and place of burial. The description of Shamgar's exploit also seems to be closer to the deliverances brought about by the 'major' judges. On the other hand, the narrative does share the same introductory phrase "after him" with the minor judges. If, as Ishida (517), Martin (75–76), Hauser (1975:200), and Mullen (1982:201) assert, there is no real functional difference between the so called 'major' and 'minor' judges, such that the categorisation is only a matter of length and style of narrative, then on account of its brevity, the narrative should probably be categorised together with the minor judges.

First, do the judges mentioned in the book represent a comprehensive list of all the judges known to the book's author/redactor? If so, then there would be no further need to look for a reason for their inclusion other than the desire of the author/redactor to be comprehensive in his record of the period.

Unfortunately, this is something that no one can know for certain. To be sure, Lilley argues that had other judges been known to the book's author/redactor, it would be curious for the non-Israelite Shamgar to be given a place in preference over them.[22] But then again, given the fact that most of the other judges such as Ehud the left-hander, Jephthah the social outcast, Samson the lover of Philistine women, and so on, are all unexpected choices, perhaps Shamgar was chosen precisely because he fits into this theme of unlikely heroes. Thus, Shamgar's presence among the judges should not be taken to mean that no more traditions about other judges are available.

In fact, against the suggestion that the author/redactor of Judges aimed at being comprehensive in his inclusion of material is the fact that for at least one of the minor judges, other traditions apparent exist that have not been included in the book. For while the description of Jair in Judg. 10:3–5 focuses mainly on his thirty sons who rode thirty donkeys and controlled thirty towns, in Num. 32:40–41, Deut. 3:14, and Josh. 13:30, other traditions about Jair, such as his tribal and clan affiliation, the role he played in the military campaign against Og and the Rephaites, and the etiological origin of the name of his towns, are preserved. That at least some of these traditions are available to the author/redactor of Judges seems clear, since it has already been argued earlier that Judges shows significant literary dependence on Joshua. Furthermore, if there is any validity to the Deuteronomistic History hypothesis, then traditions found in Deuteronomy must obviously also be available to the book's author/redactor.

Of course, that is not to say that the author/redactor of Judges is obliged to include every scrap of material available to him. But what this demonstrates is precisely that the principle of selectivity is at work even in the accounts of the minor judges. And if the book's author/redactor had not seen fit to include all the information he

[22] Lilley, 98.

had about Jair, then there is reason to believe that further details may also have been available about Shamgar and his oxgoad, or the military deliverance of Tola,[23] or the exploits of the other minor judges, that the author/redactor had not seen fit to include within the book. Otherwise, one has to wonder why the traditions about these shadowy figures were preserved at all if all they contained are the mundane details recorded in Judges.[24]

But if the inclusion of not only these minor judges, but also the material about them, is by design, then one is confronted with the questions: Why these judges? And why these mundane details about them rather than their more colourful exploits, if these indeed exist and were available to the author/redactor of Judges?

To be sure, for some of these minor judges, a case can be made that their placement within the book and what is said about them may be contextually significant. The fact that Shamgar ben Anath is also mentioned in Deborah's song may indeed explain why Shamgar's brief exploit is placed right before the Deborah-Barak narrative: to provide background information in anticipation of his abrupt mention in Judg. 5:6. As for the mention of the numerous offspring of Jair, Ibzan, and Abdon, that such notices are found amidst the accounts of Gideon's loss of nearly all his children, Jephthah's sacrifice of his only daughter, and Samson's childless death, is likely also not accidental. Perhaps the contrast is meant to highlight the tragic fate of these surrounding 'major' judges.[25]

But even if these reasons are valid, they still do not completely account for all the minor judges. What about the inclusion of Tola and Elon, about whom hardly any information is given other than their tribal origin, length of rule, and place of burial? Hence, some other reason must be sought that can account for the inclusion of all the current slate of minor judges and not just some of them.

---

[23] Although Boling (1975:187) and Beem (149) argue that the "deliverance" Tola effected was none other than the restoration of peace and stability after the rampage of Abimelech, yet within Judges, הושׁיע is consistently used with human subjects to denote military deliverance. See, for example, 2:16,18; 3:9,15,31; 6:15; 7:2; 8:22; 12:2,3; 13:5.

[24] Indeed, Boling (1975:189) notes that even in antiquity, such information that is concerned with the number of a man's sons, daughters, grandsons, donkeys, and weddings would represent an extremely odd antiquarian or administrative interest.

[25] Claassens (206) thinks the contrast is meant to serve as a subtle criticism of Jephthah.

In this regard, the once popular theory about the author/redactor of the book aiming to include twelve judges to represent all the tribes of Israel may be worth another look.[26] After all, the minor judges do include judges from tribes such as Issachar and Zebulun that would otherwise not be represented by a judge.

Granted, this still does not result in every single tribe being represented by a judge, for judges from Reuben, Simeon, Gad, and Asher are still missing. But as Jair and Jephthah are both said to hail from Gilead (10:3, 11:1) without further specification of tribal affiliation, these two judges may have been intended to jointly represent Reuben, Gad, and the half tribe of Manasseh east of the Jordan.

As for Asher, while it is true that no judge is specifically said to be from that tribe, a case can be made that the author/redactor may have intended Ibzan to function as a surrogate Asherite. After all, Ibzan is said to be a Bethlehemite, and while that could refer to the better-known Bethlehem of Judah, scholars are generally of the opinion that it is referring to a northern city of the same name, located close to the border between Zebulun and Asher.[27] This is partly based on the observation that in Judges, the Judean Bethlehem is almost always referred to as "Bethlehem in Judah (17:7,8,9; 19:1,2,18)", whereas in 12:8, the specification 'in Judah' is not present. Since the Judean city is not mentioned at all in Joshua, but Bethlehem in Zebulun is in Josh. 19:15, given the apparent literary dependence of Judges on Joshua, it is reasonable to argue that the unmarked Bethlehem likely refers to the one previously mentioned in Joshua.

---

[26] As Smend (1963:46) points out, the twelve judges proposal had long existed even before Wellhausen. But it has subsequently been associated frequently with Noth's amphictyony hypothesis (see for example, Hertzberg, 1954:286–90; Schunck, 255–56; 1991:364; Soggin, 1980:245–46). Admittedly, Noth's hypothesis has since been discredited (see Orlinsky, 375–87; Mayes, 1973:151–70; 1977:299–308; Lindars 1979:95–112; Whitelam, 166–67), but the twelve judges proposal is not in itself necessarily tied to Noth's hypothesis. Rather, as the following discussion will show, the current attempt to reconsider the twelve judges proposal is based primarily on literary/rhetorical arguments and does not represent an attempt to revive the amphictyony hypothesis. Note too that the make up of the twelve judges in the current proposal is also somewhat different from those put forth earlier. For comparison, see Hertzberg, 1954:288; Schunck, 255.

[27] Moore, 310; Burney, 334; Boling, 1975:215–16; Lemche, 53; Soggin, 1987:223; Globe, 1990:239; Williams, 80. See also editor's note for Judg. 12:8 in the JPS Hebrew-English Tanakh.

But even if this is true, this northern Bethlehem is still located in Zebulun and not in Asher. On what basis then, can one consider Ibzan to be a surrogate Asherite? For one, the next judge, Elon, is specifically said to be a Zebulunite, and this, unlike Bethlehem, is a tribal rather than geographical designation. Thus, if Ibzan is also meant to represent Zebulun, this would result in two judges representing the same tribe, something unique within the list of judges.[28] But since Bethlehem in Zebulun is located very close to the border with Asher, if no tradition of a judge from Asher is available in the source material, the author/redactor might well have included Ibzan to serve as a surrogate Asherite. By deliberately linking Ibzan to a town rather than specifying his tribal affiliation, he might be banking on the willingness of the reader to accept the ambiguity that someone living in a border town could easily hail from the other side of the border.[29]

That would leave Simeon as the only tribe not represented by any judge. But this again poses no insurmountable problem. After all, at the beginning of the book, Simeon is already shown to be in an alliance with Judah in Judg. 1:3. That the territory of Simeon specified in Josh. 19:2–8 consists of many towns already assigned to Judah in Josh. 15:21–32, and that the tribe's inheritance is explicitly said to be taken from Judah and located within the territory of Judah in Josh. 19:1,9 allow for the possibility that Simeon, the smallest of the tribes according to the census in Numbers 26, may have historically been seen as semi-dependent on Judah.[30] This, and the possibility that no judge from Simeon can be found in the source material, may well have explained why the author/redactor of Judges did not deem it necessary to have a separate judge to represent Simeon as long as Judah is represented. In fact, the void created by the absence of a judge from Simeon may have been why Shamgar,

[28] One can of course point out that both Deborah and Abdon are from Ephraim. But whether Deborah is to be considered one of the judges is actually debatable, as the following discussion will show.

[29] Note that Tola, who is explicitly said to be from Issachar in 10:1, apparently lived in the territory of Ephraim. Samson, who is a Danite, was also active within the neighbouring territory of Judah before the Danite migration.

[30] It is also noteworthy that Simeon is not included in Moses' blessing of the tribes in Deuteronomy 33. Nor is it mentioned in Deborah's song in Judges 5, which incidentally, also did not mention Judah.

the non-Israelite judge,[31] was included, so that there would still be twelve judges without any tribe having more than one judge.

In light of the above discussion, the theory that the author/redactor aimed at presenting twelve judges in order to represent all the tribes of Israel seems indeed to be a viable explanation for the inclusion of the six minor judges. In fact, this hypothesis becomes even more compelling when one considers how the arrangement of the twelve judges seems to reflect the same south-to-north geographic trajectory introduced in the prologue of the book in Judges 1.

As has already been pointed out, that the judges in the central section are arranged along a roughly south-to-north geographic trajectory according to their tribal affiliation has not gone unnoticed by scholars.[32] But while most are content to note the rough approximation of this arrangement to the south-to-north trajectory introduced in Judges 1, few have taken the trouble to explain the few apparent irregularities. But a careful examination of the data seems to indicate that even the irregularities are by design and are therefore readily explicable.

First, consider the sequence of the present arrangement. Assuming that the preceding discussion relating to representation for Reuben, Simeon, Gad, and Asher is accepted, the order of judges then begins with Othniel representing Judah and Simeon in the far south, and moves on to Ehud representing Benjamin immediately to the north of Judah. As Shamgar was likely not an Israelite, he therefore does not represent any Israelite tribe. Next, one finds Deborah and Barak, and this presents somewhat of a problem because each of them was affiliated with a different tribe located geographically at a distant from each other. But of the two, since Deborah is explicitly said in 4:5 to be holding court in the hill countries of Ephraim, it appears on the surface that the south-to-north trajectory is at least maintained as Ephraim was located immediately north of Benjamin.

[31] Although Williams (80) sees Shamgar as plausibly identified with Simeon because of his activities in the southwest, the general consensus seems to be that Shamgar is a non-Israelite name. See, for example, Fensham, 1961:197–98; Danelius, 191; Van Selms, 301; Craigie, 1972:239–40; Shupak, 517–25. As for the origin of this name, there is, however, much less consensus, with Hurrian/Hanean and Syrian/Canaanite being the most common suggestions.

[32] See p. 154.

Then comes Gideon, representing the half tribe of Manasseh located immediately to the north of Ephraim. As his son Abimelech is not presented as a judge in the book, the next judge is therefore Tola, affiliated with Issachar immediately north of Manasseh.

Then a slight detour is taken to include the two and a half tribes east of the Jordan as Tola is followed by Jair and Jephthah, both of whom are said to hail from the region of Gilead. The northward progression then resumes with Ibzan and Elon, both technically associated with Zebulun to the north of Issachar, but with Ibzan possibly intending to also represent Asher to the west and northwest of Zebulun.

At this point, one expects the next judge to be from Naphtali, but instead, one finds Abdon the Ephraimite. Why is this northward progression suddenly disrupted? And why is Abdon found at this particular slot, if indeed he was affiliated with a tribe further south? Interestingly, the key to solving this mystery may actually lie with Deborah and Barak.

Earlier, it has been pointed out that as the sequence of judges progress northwards, the simultaneous involvement of Deborah and Barak in the war against Sisera poses somewhat of a dilemma. But since, according to the geographic progression, one would expect a judge from Ephraim, and since Deborah is explicitly said in 4:5 to be holding court in the hill countries of Ephraim, the natural tendency is to immediately see Deborah as the next judge who represents Ephraim. But such an understanding may be problematic on several counts.

To begin, if one carefully analyses the Deborah-Barak narrative, one cannot help but to suspect that the one called to deliver Israel as a military judge was Barak and not Deborah. For from the verbs associated with the two characters in Judges 4, it seems that Deborah's role has to do primarily with her prophetic function. In 4:6, she is associated with two summoning verbs שׁלח and קרא, and in 4:6,9,14, she is associated three times with the speaking verb אמר. True, three verbs of movement קום, הלך, and עלה are also associated with Deborah in 4:9–10, but these are used once each only to report her accompanying Barak. It is worth noting also that with only one exception, all six verbs used of Deborah are found in the pre-battle narrative of 4:6–10. The only action associated with her in the battle portion of the narrative is basically her repetition in 4:14 of YHWH's promise of victory already given in 4:7 when Barak was first called. Otherwise,

Deborah almost played no role in the battle narrative and indeed was not even mentioned again after her repetition of YHWH's promise in 4:14. In contrast, Barak seems to be portrayed as actively involved in battle as verbs associated with him include זעק in 4:10, ירד in 4:14, רדף in 4:16,22, and בוא in 4:22. And most of these occur within the battle narrative in 4:12–16.

In other words, while Barak is seen as actively involving in the military deliverance of Israel from her enemy, the role of Deborah within the narrative seems to be more in line with one of her role as prophetess (4:4) than as military judge. In fact, within the narrative, Deborah functions more like an agent than a full-fledged character, and her role seems to be restricted mainly to the conveying of YHWH's will and not much else.[33] Considering that it was Barak and not Deborah who was called by YHWH to fight Sisera in 4:6–7, and that it was Barak and not Deborah who was referred to in 1 Sam. 12:11[34] as one of the deliverers sent by YHWH,[35] a case can certainly be made that it was Barak and not Deborah who should be considered the primary military/deliverer judge in the narrative.[36]

As for the explicit mention of Deborah's 'judging' Israel in 4:4, while on the surface, this seems indistinguishable from summary statements found with Othniel (3:10), Tola (10:2), Jair (10:3), Jephthah (12:7), Ibzan (12:8,9), Elon (12:11), Abdon (12:13,14), and Samson (15:20, 16:31),[37] it should be noted that it is only with Deborah that

[33] Can this account for the sparseness of rabbinic account about Deborah as noted by Bronner (79)?

[34] Granted, the MT reads בדן rather than ברק, but given the context and the closeness in orthography between the two names, the LXX is surely right in translating the name Barak instead of positing an hitherto unknown deliverer with an orthographically similar name.

[35] Note too that this understanding of Barak as judge also seems to be reflected in later tradition as Heb. 11:32 in the New Testament also lists Barak along with the other judges among the heroes of faith. To be sure, the absence of Deborah's name both in 1 Samuel 12 and in Hebrews 11 does not necessarily mean that she is not counted as one of the deliverer judges. But prominence given to Barak in both lists seems to suggest that even if Deborah were considered a deliverer judge, she would still be occupying a position subordinate to Barak.

[36] Note the series of questions Block (1994:235; 1999:193–94) raises that seem to cast doubt on whether Deborah was ever meant to be portrayed as a deliverer judge.

[37] As for the absence of this formula in the narratives of Ehud, Shamgar, and Gideon, Ishida (521–22) suggests that its omission in the Ehud narrative is only an accident of transmission since the equivalent is found in the LXX. For Shamgar, he argues that his non-Israelite identity may be why he is not said to have "judged"

the precise nature of her judging is specified. According to 4:4–5, she held court to decide the people's disputes. Thus, of all the human characters that are considered judges within the book, Deborah is the only one whose judgeship is explicitly said to fulfil a judicial function.[38] In this respect, the role of Deborah as 'judge' is actually similar to the role of Moses in Exod. 18:13–16 and to the role of Israel's appointed judges mentioned in Exod. 18:21–26; Deut. 1:16–17; 16:18–20; 17:8–13; 19:16–21; 25:1–3. A case can therefore be made that the kind of judgeship exercised by Deborah is actually fundamentally distinct from and much more narrowly defined than the kind of judgeship exercised by the other military/deliverer judges mentioned in Judges.[39]

But if that is the case, then why did the author/redactor of the book allow for this confusion by using similar language when speaking of two different kinds of judges with apparently distinct functions? Given what has been said about the geographic progression of the judges, one can argue that this confusion may in fact be by design. For if the author/redactor of the book was interested in preserving the impression that the judges are presented according to roughly the same south-to-north geographic trajectory introduced in the prologue, but at the same time, realised that thematically, the progressive deterioration theme is better served with Barak the Naphtalite being placed between Ehud the Benjaminite and Gideon the Manassite, then what better way is there to get around the problem than to create an ambiguity which allows for both schemas to be maintained? The fact that the judge from Naphtali so happened

Israel since the term implies rulership. As for Gideon, Ishida argues that the omission of the formula is to avoid contradicting Gideon's own assertion in 8:23 that neither he nor his sons will rule over Israel.

[38] As Martin (69) points out, there are only two places within the book where a judicial sense of 'judging' is clearly demanded. One is the description of Deborah's judging in 4:5, and the other is the description of YHWH's judging in 11:27. This judicial understanding of Deborah's judgeship is, however, disputed by Block (1994:237–40). But some of Block's objections will be answered in the following discussion.

[39] Although the kind of judgeship exercised by the other military/deliverer judges have not really been clearly defined in Judges, yet scholars have generally accepted on the basis of the cognate šāpitum being used in the Mari texts to refer to a high official that the office in Judges may similarly signify rulership. Of particular relevance is the fact that this šāpitum in the Mari texts is apparently one who not only was in charge of administrative duties, but also exercised military leadership. See Marzal, 189–205; Safren, 1–4; Martin, 69–70; Ishida, 519–21. Rozenburg (77–86) also argues from biblical usage that basic meaning of שפט is to rule or govern.

to be associated with an Ephraimite who served as a judge, albeit a different kind of judge, made it possible for the narrative to be placed exactly where the author/redactor wanted it, as long as it is not immediately apparent that the deliverer judge is actually the one from Naphtali and not the one from Ephraim. So, to create this ambiguity, the author/redactor capitalised on the fact that although the functions of Barak and Deborah within the book are different, they were both "judges" in their own right because the same term can legitimately be used to describe both functions. Thus, by describing Deborah, the judicial judge, in language reminiscent of the description of the other military/deliverer judges, and by giving her a role with some prominence within the narrative, the impression is given that the narrative is placed exactly where it is supposed to, even though in reality, it is out of place with respect to the south-to-north geographic trajectory. In fact, one can even argue that, unlike the other judges such as Othniel (3:9), Ehud (3:15), Shamgar (3:31), Gideon (6:14, 8:22), Tola (10:1) and Samson (13:5), the fact that neither Deborah nor Barak is explicitly said within the narrative to have delivered Israel may well be another way to maintain that ambiguity,[40] so that it is not immediately clear which of the two is supposed to be the military/deliverer judge.[41]

But while this ambiguity is necessary mainly for literary reasons, it seems that, for other reasons, the author/redactor of the book also had no wish to leave the matter in a state of permanent ambiguity. Thus, he had left at least two clues that would enable the discerning reader to figure out what he was doing. The first is the clear description of Deborah's role as judge in 4:5. By specifying her role to be judicial, the author/redactor seems to be making sure that the reader will be aware that she is a different kind of judge from the others described within the book. As for the second clue, this is where Abdon comes in.

The fact that Abdon, the Ephraimite judge, appears in the exact spot where one would expect Barak, the Naphtalite judge, to appear is surely no accident. And because this displacement is so obvious,

---

[40] In this regard, one would have to disagree with Boling (1975:7), who, despite acknowledging the lack of direct evidence, nonetheless asserts that the narrator has "clearly conveyed" that Deborah has "saved" Israel.

[41] Also see Amit (1987:92–94) on the ambiguity regarding whether Deborah or Barak is to be the deliverer.

it almost forces those who are aware of the south-to-north geographic progression to go back and recheck who actually occupies the position where Abdon should have. This, of course, would lead them back to Deborah, and by extension, Barak. The realisation that there may have been a transposition between Barak and Abdon according to the south-to-north geographic progression would thus prompt a discerning reader to re-evaluate his earlier understanding of who the military/deliverer judge really is. This would therefore result in the proper recognition that it is actually Barak and not Deborah who is meant to serve in that role.

In any case, with the placement of Abdon accounted for, the progression of judges then moves on to the final judge, Samson, whose tribe, Dan, eventually ended up being the northernmost tribe after its northward migration.[42]

What seems clear from the above discussion is that, if the arguments presented above are indeed valid, then one cannot help but conclude that the current selection and arrangement of all the judges within the book is a result of careful and thoughtful design. And that includes the selection and arrangement of the minor judges. Thus, while there is no denying that the narratives of the minor judges in their present form may have been rooted in a source different from the narratives of the major judges, that they are clustered together in their current arrangement in Judg. 10:1–12:15 may actually have to do with the fact that these narratives happen to fall together under the geographic schema adopted by the book's author/redactor. In other words, rather than the author/redactor having taken the list of minor judges over directly from his source and incorporating it into Judges without substantial modification as Soggin claims,[43] it is entirely possible that the order of the minor judges is in fact rearranged to conform to the south-to-north geographic trajectory that forms one of the two main trajectories that provide structure for the book. If this is true, then one can say that even the inclusion and arrangement of the minor judges is intimately related with one of the main structural schemas introduced in the prologue.

---

[42] See discussion on p. 187 regarding the placement of Dan as the northernmost tribe even though the exploits of Samson apparently took place before the tribe's northward migration.

[43] Soggin, 1987:198.

As for the extreme brevity of these narratives, one suspects that the omission of any detailed exploits of these judges may well be accounted for by the fact that the available traditions must not have contained any material that would further contribute to the deterioration theme being developed by the book's author/redactor. While admittedly, such a suspicion is somewhat speculative because it is essentially an argument from silence, the advantage of the present hypothesis is that by relating the narratives of the minor judges to the overall rhetorical purpose introduced in the prologue, one can simultaneously explain not only the presence of these narratives within the book, but also their perplexing brevity that seems to always hint at more but ends up providing preciously little about possible further exploits of these judges.

But what is important here is that, based on the above discussions, it appears that even the few narratives in the central section that initially seem wholly unrelated to rhetorical purposes of the prologue and epilogue are shown to constitute an integral part of these purposes. What this means therefore is that every single narrative included in the central section can now be shown to be related in one way or another to the rhetorical purposes of the prologue and epilogue of the book. Thus, inasmuch as it has been argued that the prologue and epilogue of Judges were composed specifically to provide a paradigmatic introduction and an evaluative conclusion to the central section, it can equally be argued that the central section of Judges was in fact redacted specifically to support and illustrate the rhetorical purposes found in the prologue and the epilogue. And while these two positions may seem paradoxical at first glance, it is only so if one insists on a linear model of composition. In reality, however, the compositional/redactional process for the book may have been one where the three sections were shaped out of continuous interaction with each other.

To show how this is so, imagine a situation where an author intends to compose an account of Israel's history between the conquest and the monarchy. As he reads through and digests the source material before him, he decides that, rather than presenting a comprehensive and purely factual account, he would instead present a representative and ideological account of the period, reflecting not only the period's major trends, but also his unique understanding and evaluation of it. As ideas begin to formulate in his mind about why events in this period unfolded as they did and how these events relate to the continued development of Israel's history, the selection of material for his work becomes guided by these ideas, so that only material conducive to his unique understanding and evaluation of the period would be included to illustrate that understanding.

But as he continues to digest and work with his source material, initial ideas will receive modifications and expansions as new insights are gained. This will therefore necessitate re-evaluations of his initial selection of material, so that material initially deemed irrelevant but has now taken on new significance will also be included. And this process will go back and forth, until the author is sufficiently satisfied that all relevant materials from his sources are included and are arranged in the right order. This will thus make up the main body of his work.

But although this selection and arrangement of material in the main body of his work is based on some very specific rhetorical/ideological purposes, the fact that the materials themselves come from pre-existing sources means that even when they have been judiciously selected and arranged, the purposes that underlie their selection and arrangement may not be immediately apparent. Therefore, to ensure that the main purposes of his work are not altogether missed, as well as to give unity to the whole, the author decides to compose an introduction and a conclusion to complement the main body. Furthermore, because this author apparently values subtlety over overt declarations, and may even have a penchant for riddles and puzzles, he has so designed these two sections so that it is only when the rhetorical links he plants between these sections and the main body are noticed and understood that his rhetorical/ideological purposes can be discovered.

But in any case, what should be noted here is that although the actual writing of the introduction and conclusion may have come only after the material in the main body has been selected and arranged, the rhetorical/ideological purposes inherent in the introduction and conclusion were actually present right from the very beginning, guiding the selection and arrangement of the material in the main body all along. Therefore, although in terms of the actual composition, one can say that the introduction and conclusion were composed expressly for the main body of the work, it is also true at the same time that main body was in fact redacted expressly to support and illustrate the purposes inherent in the introduction and conclusion.

But if this hypothetical scenario indeed reflects how Judges may have been composed, then the implication is that the key to understanding the book actually lies in the book's prologue and epilogue instead of in its central section. For despite the fact that the central section contains the bulk of traditional material that records the dominant personalities and events of the period, in the end, this material only functions as illustration for a specific interpretation of the period's history. The full extent of that interpretation, however, can come to light only when the central section is read in conjunction with the prologue and epilogue and not when it is read on its own.

And that, incidentally, may be why the book has confounded so many for so long. For the fact that the book has come to be known historically as Judges may have predisposed scholars wishing to understand the book to focus primarily on the very section where the exploits of the judges are recorded. In fact, since neither the prologue nor the epilogue even mentions the judges after whom the book is titled, and especially since the epilogue does contain extensive narratives but features none of the judges, the most natural assumption is that these sections must represent wholly unrelated compositions artificially appended to the central section at a later date. But such an assumption has resulted in a lack of effort to seek continuity between the prologue-epilogue and the central section of book, and that, in turn, has prevented readers from truly understanding not only the individual sections, but also what the book as a whole is really all about.

Rhetorical Purpose of Judges

So what is Judges all about? If one is to sum up the author's portrayal of this period of Israel's history with a single phrase, it would be 'progressive deterioration'. After all, this is a book that opens with a report of tribal cooperation and success but ends with a picture of Israel almost wiping out one of its own tribes in a civil war. How the nation went from the former to the latter is thus never far from the concern of the book's author.

This theme of progressive deterioration is conveyed both through the book's structure as well as its content. Structurally, the theme is first previewed in the prologue through a succinct progress report of the tribes' attempts at dispossessing their foreign enemies as they tried to take possession of the land. The report follows a progressively deteriorating trend as the accomplishments of the tribes or lacks thereof are traced along a roughly south-to-north geographic trajectory. A similar south-to-north trajectory also happens to order the way in which the judges in the central section are arranged according to their tribal affiliation. As it turns out, the same deteriorating trend can also be discerned in the portrayal of the major judges through common themes that link their narratives to each other. In this regard, the primary structure of the prologue is mirrored almost exactly in the central section, and at the heart of both is the idea of progressive deterioration.

As for content, this progressive deterioration is conveyed in a number of ways. First, although the deterioration portrayed within the book primarily concerns those living during the days of the judges, the stage is first set by portraying the generation of the judges as collectively falling short of the accomplishments of their predecessors. This is seen especially in the prologue and the epilogue, where pervasive references are made to events recorded in Joshua through ironic allusions. Through these allusions, the message that emerges is that despite attempts of the generation of the judges to recapture the successes of their predecessors, they inevitably fall short because they only emulated the outward form of those successes without truly understanding the substance behind them. This subtle but consistent message is in fact corroborated by Judg. 2:7–10, which states that the emerging generation no longer knew YHWH and what He had done for the nation the same way the previous generation did. What this highlights therefore is that for the generation of the judges, deterioration has already set in even at the dawn of their generation.

And unfortunately, this deterioration did not abate as the history of the period continues to unfold. In 2:19 one is told that with the passing away of each judge who ruled during this period, the following generation became even more corrupt than the one before it. This therefore alerts the readers to further signs of deterioration as they approach the narratives that follow.

Even as the book opens, this progressive deterioration at the tribal level is already introduced as the conquest report in Judges 1 shows a decreasing ability of the tribes to dispossess their enemies and take possession of the land. In the following narratives that dominate the central section, this deterioration is further applied to the nation as a whole as well as to the various judges who successively led the nation.

At the national level, this deterioration is conveyed primarily through the introduction of a cyclical framework that eventually breaks down. What is noteworthy here is that of the five elements that make up the cycle, the ones most affected by this breakdown are precisely the ones that seem most closely linked to the prospect of a turn-around for Israel from her troubles. For in cycles that begin with Israel's apostasy, leading to YHWH's giving of Israel into the hands of foreign oppressors, it is Israel's crying out to YHWH that essentially precipitates YHWH's raising up of a deliverer to deliver the nation from her oppressors. But it is precisely here that significant breakdowns occur. For not only is YHWH portrayed as becoming increasing impatient with Israel's repeated transgressions, evidenced first by the intervention of a prophet's rebuke in the Gideon cycle and then by YHWH's direct rebuke in the Jephthah cycle before deliverance is eventually granted, but in response, Israel also stopped crying out to YHWH altogether in the Samson cycle, being content apparently to live under foreign domination (15:11). Therefore quite fittingly, Samson also happens to be the only judge who only began to but did not completely deliver the nation from her foreign oppressors.

And this ties in with another element of the cycle that also breaks down, namely the report of a period of rest after each deliverance. Here, one notices that although in earlier cycles, a period of rest is reported after each deliverance, from the Jephthah cycle on, this report is longer found.

But not only is this progressive deterioration at the national level conveyed through the breakdown of the cyclical framework, it is also conveyed by the portrayal of a nation increasing divided. As the narratives progress, one notices that the involvement of the tribes in support of their judges' military campaigns against foreign enemies gradually decreases. Thus, although Ehud's campaign against Moab is still portrayed as enjoying national participation in 3:27, each successive judge after him seems to receive less participation from fewer tribes than the one before. In fact, by the time one reaches the narrative of Samson, not only is he depicted as not receiving any support from any of the tribes, but Judah even sided with the foreign enemies against him. This decreasing participation, mirrored by an increasing refusal of cities and tribes to cooperate with their judges, also led directly to an escalation of internal conflict.

But if the nation as a whole is portrayed as progressively deteriorating throughout the book, her leaders are also not spared from this trend. In fact, the same progressive deterioration that characterises the nation can also be discerned when it comes to the quality of her leaders. For not only do the actions and words of the judges reflect an increasing lack of faith in YHWH, they also betray an increasing tendency to be motivated by self interest. In light of this, it is perhaps not surprising that the tribes become increasingly unwilling to support and cooperate with their leaders. Unfortunately, this unwillingness to support and cooperate is met by a corresponding increase in harshness on the part of the judges to deal with this internal dissent. Given that Jephthah eventually slaughtered forty-two thousand Ephraimites in what sounds like a somewhat personal dispute with the tribe, is it any wonder then that the book eventually ends with the account of a civil war that sees Israel almost wiping out the entire tribe of Benjamin?

But if this progressive deterioration is indeed something that has affected the nation as a whole as well as her leaders, then the questions that beg answering are, "What is the root of this deterioration? What had caused it in the first place?" Having portrayed this deterioration in the prologue and the central section, the author then attempts to offer a subtle diagnosis of the problem in the concluding section of the book.

Contrary to the understanding of many scholars, the problem that plagued the period, and therefore, its possible solution, is not primarily a political one, but a spiritual one. If the oft-repeated refrain in the epilogue is indeed meant to pinpoint the main problem and thereby hint at a solution, then the problem it pinpoints is not the absence of central political authority, nor is the solution the embracing of a human king. Rather, understood in the context of the book as a whole, what the refrain seems to be pinpointing as the central problem is Israel's refusal to recognise YHWH's ultimate kingly authority. The implied solution, therefore, is that the nation must return to YHWH and begin honouring His kingly authority before the deterioration can be halted and reversed.

That such is the evaluation of the book's author should come as no surprise. After all, the foreign oppression that turns out to be Israel's main source of trouble during this period has more than once been directly linked to Israel's disobedience and rejection of YHWH even in the early parts of the book. In 2:1–3 in the prologue, the fact that the nations would remain as thorns in Israel's side is presented as a direct consequence of Israel's disobedience.

That these nations could oppress Israel is further presented in 2:11–13 as punishment from YHWH for Israel's forsaking Him and seeking instead to serve the Baals. Moreover, the reason for this readiness to forsake YHWH also seems to be hinted at in 2:10 as a lack of knowledge of YHWH and what He has done for the nation. Thus, right from the beginning, Israel's problem is already presented as a spiritual one, the centre of which lies in Israel's relationship with YHWH. In fact, to make sure the reader does not forget this, intermittent reminders of this root problem is provided in the central section through two divine rebukes, the first communicated through a prophet in 6:7–10, and the second directly by YHWH in 10:11–14. And in both, the focus is on Israel's disobedience and rejection of YHWH.

Not only so, but in the epilogue where an evaluative refrain is repeatedly found, this refrain also seems to punctuate narratives that highlight non-YHWH-honouring behaviour on the part of Israel's populace. Such behaviour includes the setting up of a private idolatrous cultic shrine by Micah and his mother, the violation of practically every Levitical regulation by Jonathan, the abandoning of their original tribal allotment by the Danites in favour of an easier target, their slaughtering of the people at Laish in apparent violation of the rules of engagement of Deut. 20:10–15, the embracing of the worst form of Canaanite perversity by the people of Gibeah, the presumption by the Israelites of a course of action against their brother without first seeking YHWH's approval, the willingness to deal with their brother with the kind of harshness that should have been reserved for Israel's foreigner enemies but was never applied to them, and so on. As all these actions seem in some way to reflect a rejection of YHWH's authority, mostly through violations of His explicit commands, these narratives being framed by the refrain seems to confirm the interpretation that the refrain is indeed pinpointing the non-honouring of YHWH's kingly authority as the root cause of the problem in this period.

But if the author sees the root cause of Israel's problem as a spiritual one, he also sees the responsibility for this spiritual problem as lying with Israel's leaders. This seems clear from the way most of the non-YHWH-honouring behaviour associated with the general populace in the epilogue actually echoes similar types of behaviour witnessed among Israel's leaders in the central section. Thus, if Israel's leaders were themselves acting in ways incompatible with their core identity, contributing to idolatrous cult, embracing Canaanised behaviour, treating fellow-Israelites more harshly than their foreign enemies, making rash and inappropriate vows, violating stipulations associated with their special calling, going after what was right in their own eyes, and so on, is it any wonder then, that the general populace was doing the very same things? Thus, if the evaluative refrain in the epilogue explicitly identifies Israel's problem in the period as one relating to the non-honouring of YHWH by His people, then in a more subtle way, the shaping of the narratives in the epilogue to highlight similar behaviours between leader and people hints at the need for godly leaders who can set proper examples so as to lead the nation back to a YHWH-honouring path. And this seems to be the central message towards which Judges as a whole and each of its constituent parts consciously point.

Two Closing Comments

As this study draws to a close, there remain two issues that need to be briefly commented on. The first has to do with the implications of the present study for the Deuteronomistic History hypothesis.

In recent years, questions about the validity of the Deuteronomistic History hypothesis have been raised by various scholars.[44] In particular, relating to Judges, Auld has asked concerning the supposedly incontestable key Deuteronomistic passages within the book that if Judg. 2:6–3:6; 6:7–10; 10:6–16, and possibly 3:7–11 can all be shown to be late additions to the book, then in what sense can the book still be properly called Deuteronomistic?[45]

Coming from a very different perspective, the conclusions reached in the present study also raise important questions about the validity of Noth's Deuteronomistic History hypothesis. For if, as has just been argued, the central section of Judges is in fact redacted expressly to provide support and illustration for the ideological/rhetorical purposes inherent in the prologue and epilogue, then it means this central section cannot possibly be excerpted directly from or form an integral part of a larger Deuteronomistic History. For not only would the merging of the Eli-Samuel narratives with the narratives in the

[44] For a brief survey of these, see Auld, 1999:116–23.
[45] Auld, 1998:123–26.

central section of Judges as suggested by Noth destroy the progressive deterioration theme that is so critical to the understanding of those narratives,[46] the forced detachment of the narratives in the central section from the prologue and epilogue would also render it almost impossible to discern any logic behind the selection and arrangement of material in that section. Instead, the evidence presented in this study seems to lend support to a theory of composition for Judges that differs fundamentally from the scholarly consensus in that Judges in its current form is seen to be an artful creation of a single author who, in spite of making use of diverse source materials, was nonetheless the one primarily responsible for shaping the entire book into its current form to reflect his unique ideological understanding of this period of the nation's history. Thus, the book as it stands displays remarkable unity and progression, with every single part of the composition making a unique contribution towards the realisation of an overall rhetorical goal.

What this implies, then, is that if one insists on viewing Judges as Deuteronomistic, then it is Deuteronomistic in a way significantly different from what was envisioned by Noth. Instead of the central section of the book being originally a part of a larger continuous work that has unfortunately been artificially severed from the rest of this work by the later addition and intrusion of the book's prologue and epilogue, one should perhaps speak of a series of self-contained 'Deuteronomistic' compositions of which the current form of Judges in its entirety is but one in the series. In this respect, we may have

[46] Admittedly, Eli is portrayed somewhat negatively in 1 Samuel 1–4. Thus, one can conceivably argue that the narrative about him is not incompatible with the deterioration pattern found in Judges. But as negatively as Eli is portrayed, he is nevertheless portrayed especially in 1 Samuel 4 as someone who does care about YHWH's glory and His ark. That is a marked improvement from Samson, who only seems to care about his own interests. In addition, the attempt of Eli to dissuade his sons from sinning against YHWH in 1 Sam. 2:23–25, and the resignation he expresses in 1 Sam. 3:18 that YHWH should do "what is good in His eyes" also seem to offer positive contrasts to Samson, who seems to be interested only in going after what is right in his own eyes. As for Samuel, although his inability to control and discipline his wicked sons does mar his record, yet he is otherwise portrayed in a positive light throughout 1 Samuel. In fact, if one is to slot him in among the "deliverer" judges along the deterioration continuum presented in Judges, his position would probably be much closer to Othniel than to Samson. For these reasons, the inclusion of the Eli and Samuel narratives with those found in Judges would effectively destroy the progressive deterioration theme the author of Judges has so painstakingly constructed.

arrived in the end at a position not dissimilar to that of Polzin's, who essentially seeks to equate DH with Deuteronomy plus the Former Prophets.[47]

This leads to a second issue that needs to be addressed. If, indeed, as has been argued, Judges in its current form was essentially the artful creation of a single author, then is it still appropriate to speak of the book as consisting of three distinct sections? After all, the labels "prologue", "central section", and "epilogue" primarily originated with the assumption of diverse authorships for the three sections of the book under the Deuteronomistic History hypothesis.

To answer this question, one should recognise that even though the book in its current form may be the artful creation of a single author, yet subtle differences in style and interest are discernible. For example, while the major cultic centres such as Jerusalem, Bethel, and Shiloh are almost unmentioned in the central section,[48] these cities are mentioned at least sixteen times in the prologue and the epilogue.[49] Also, while common חרם-related war terminologies are repeatedly found in the prologue and epilogue, these are surprisingly absent in the central section in spite of numerous reports of wars against foreign enemies.[50] The most likely explanation for such differences is that the process of composition for the central section is slightly different from that of the prologue and epilogue. Specifically, it seems that after their selection, many of the narratives in the central section were probably incorporated with minimal revision from their sources except for minor changes and the addition of framework material that casts the narratives into cycles. Although the prologue and epilogue may also have made use of sources, such as the

[47] See pp. 12–13 for a brief discussion of Polzin's conception of DH.

[48] The only exception is the mention of Bethel in 4:5 as Deborah's place of ministry.

[49] These include reference to Jerusalem in 1:7,8,21; 19:10; Shiloh in 18:31; 21:12,19,21; and Bethel in 1:22,23; 20:18,26,31; 21:2,19. 2:1 may also be counted if Bokim is identified as Bethel.

[50] Such discernible differences in style is perhaps what holds me back from embracing the far more radical proposal made by Deryn Guest (1998:43–61) that Judges may have been composed entirely without sources. Furthermore, although Deryn Guest (59) makes a very good point about how the interlocking network of motifs in the central section may have been indicative of a single hand behind the narratives, the fact that these themes and motifs are connected more on a conceptual level rather than being readily discernible through concrete and obvious linguistic correspondences (see earlier discussion of deterioration themes in the central section in chapter four) seems to argue against their having been 'composed' by a single author.

use of Joshua in the prologue, yet a greater degree of flexibility and creativity seems to have been at work as different words, phrases, and even structures from elsewhere are incorporated to establish the various rhetorical links. Thus, while the prologue and epilogue can perhaps justifiably be called original compositions by their author, the role of the same author when it comes to the central section is perhaps mainly that of a creative redactor.

But while this difference may indeed justify the continued use of the designations 'prologue', 'central section', and 'epilogue' to describe the three sections of the book, the boundary especially between the prologue and the central section may have to be reconsidered. Under the Deuteronomistic History hypothesis, 2:6–3:11 is often considered part of the central section because the cyclical framework organising the rest of the central section (2:6–3:6) and the paradigmatic figure Othniel (3:7–11) are considered essential parts of the Judges portion of DH.

But if, as has been argued in the present study, both the cyclical framework and the arrangement of the judges fall under the umbrella of the progressive deterioration paradigm introduced in the prologue, then 2:6–3:11 is conceivably as much the original work of the book's author as the prologue and the epilogue. Thus, what was previously considered the contribution of the Deuteronomistic redactor of the Judges portion of DH may in fact turn out to be the contribution of the author of the prologue and epilogue. Consequently, what was previously considered the central section of the book should perhaps be redefined to include only the primarily redacted portion of Judges found in 3:12–16:31.

Conclusion

Thus, we have come to the end of our study, and have arrived at a substantially different understanding of Judges than when we first began. By paying attention to synchronically discerned rhetorical links that subtly connect narratives in the various sections of the book, we have arrived at a new understanding of how the book may have been put together in its current form. And this new understanding has significant diachronic implications. For while the standard critical position is to see the book in its current form as a composite work consisting of three independently composed sections that have been artificially stitched together, such a position essentially grows out of a perception that a significant disconnection exists between the three sections at the structural, theological, and plot level. But as significant albeit heretofore little-noticed rhetorical links connecting all three sections of the book are discovered through a close reading of the text, it has become increasing apparent that sections previously thought unrelated are in fact intricately related in terms of structure, theology, and plot. As such intricate relationships are generally considered a sign of literary unity and common authorship, their discovery therefore necessitates a re-evaluation of the existing standard position that two of the three sections of the book are unrelated fragments only artificially appended to the core text at a much later date. And if the three sections that have been thought of until now as unrelated in fact originated from the same hand, then the synchronic approach that reads the entire book as a unified composition would be amply justified and can no longer be accused of being an 'artificial' reading that does not do justice to the points of view of the supposedly multiple authors of the book.

In the end, I suppose what this study has demonstrated is the validity of an interpretive process not too different from that championed by Polzin in his study of the 'Deuteronomistic' corpus. Admittedly, Polzin has approached his subject matter from an essentially structuralist point of view while I have chosen to employ mainly literary/rhetorical tools. Yet both approaches seem to have in common the belief that in the study of biblical material, procedural priority must be given to synchronic literary analysis over diachronic historical analysis.[51] After all, if diachronic analysis is indeed especially geared towards finding solutions to perceived disconnections and inconsistencies, then it goes to reason that before such disconnections and inconsistencies can be identified, synchronic analysis must take priority in order that all facets of a text is first thoroughly explored. Otherwise, one runs the risk of subjecting a text to a fragmentary bias where in fact, what is called for is an integrative approach to a unified text.

[51] Polzin, 5–7. Note that Polzin does not reject wholesale the validity of the diachronic approach. What he emphasises is merely that literary analysis must have operational priority over historical studies. In fact, Polzin thinks that scholarly understanding of biblical material must "result from a circular movement that begins with literary analysis, then turns to historical problems, whose attempted solution then furnishes further refinements and adaptations of one's literary critical conclusions".

SELECTED BIBLIOGRAPHY

Abba, Raymond. "Priests and Levites in Deuteronomy." *VT* 27 (1977): 257–67.

Abrams, Meyer Howard. *A Glossary of Literary Terms.* Third edition. New York: Holt, Rinehart and Winston, 1971.

Ackerman, Susan. "What If Judges Had Been Written by a Philistine?" *BibInt* 8 (2000): 33–41.

Aharoni, Yohanan, Michael Avi-Yonah, Anson F. Rainey, and Ze'ev Safrai, eds. *The Macmillan Bible Atlas.* Completely revised third edition. New York: Simon & Schuster, 1993.

Alonso-Schökel, Luis. "Erzählkunst im Buche der Richter." *Bib* 42 (1961): 143–72.

Alter, Robert. *The Art of Biblical Narrative.* New York: Basic, 1981.

———. "How Convention Helps Us Read: The Case of the Bible's Annunciation Type-Scene." *Proof* 3 (1983): 115–30.

———. "Samson Without Folklore." In *Text and Tradition: The Hebrew Bible and Folklore*, pp. 47–56. Edited by Susan Niditch. Atlanta: Scholars, 1990.

Amit, Yairah. "Judges 4: It's Content and Form." *JSOT* 39 (1987): 89–111.

———. "The Use of Analogy in the Study of the Book of Judges." In *Wünschet Jerusalem Frieden: Collected Communications to the XIIth Congress of the International Organization for the Study of the Old Testament, Jerusalem 1986*, pp. 387–94. Edited by Matthias Augustin and Klaus-Dietrich Schunck. Frankfurt am Main: Peter Lang, 1988.

———. "The Story of Ehud (Judges 3:12–30): The Form and the Message." In *Signs and Wonders: Biblical Texts in Literary Focus*, pp. 97–123. Edited by J. Cheryl Exum. Decatur: Scholars, 1989.

———. "Hidden Polemics in the Conquest of Dan: Judges 17–18." *VT* 40 (1990): 4–20.

———. *The Book of Judges: The Art of Editing.* Biblical Interpretation Series, 38. Translated by Jonathan Chipman. Leiden: Brill, 1998.

———. "Bochim, Bethel, and the Hidden Polemic (Judg 2,1–5). In *Studies in Historical Geography and Biblical Historiography: Presented to Zecharia Kallai*, pp. 121–31. Edited by Gershon Galil and Moshe Weinfeld. Leiden: Brill, 2000.

Andersen, Francis I. and David Noel Freedman. *Hosea: A New Translation with Introduction and Commentary.* The Anchor Bible. Garden City: Doubleday, 1980.

Andersson, Greger. *The Book and Its Narratives: A Critical Examination of Some Synchronic Studies of the Book of Judges.* Örebro Studies in Literary History and Criticism, 1. Örebro: Universitetsbiblioteket, 2001.

Auld, A. Graeme. "Judges 1 and History: A Reconsideration." *VT* 25 (1975): 261–85.

———. *Joshua, Judges, and Ruth.* The Daily Study Bible Series. Louisville: Westminster John Knox, 1984.

———. "Gideon: Hacking at the Heart of the Old Testament." *VT* 39 (1989): 257–67.

———. "What makes Judges Deuteronomistic?" In *Joshua Retold: Synoptic Perspectives*, pp. 120–26. Edinburgh: T. & T. Clark, 1998.

———. "The Deuteronomists and the Former Prophets, Or What Makes the Former Prophets Deuteronomistic?" In *The Elusive Deuteronomists: The Phenomenon of Pan-Deuteronomism*, pp. 116–26. Edited by Linda S. Schearing and Steven L. McKenzie. Sheffield: Sheffield Academic, 1999.

———. "The Deuteronomists Between History and Theology." In *XVIth IOSOT Congress Volume: Oslo 1998*, pp. 353–67. Edited by A. Lemaire and M. Sæbø. VTSup, 80. Leiden: Brill, 2000.

Bal, Mieke. *Death and Dissymmetry: The Politics of Coherence in the Book of Judges*. Chicago: University of Chicago, 1988.

Bar-Efrat, Shimon. *Narrative Art in the Bible*. JSOTSup, 70. Translated by Dorothea Shefer-Vanson and Shimon Bar-Efrat. Sheffield: Almond, 1989.

Bauer, Uwe F.W. "Judges 18 as an Anti-Spy Story in the Context of an Anti-Conquest Story: The Creative Usage of Literary Genres." *JSOT* 88 (2000): 37–47.

———. "A Metaphorical Etiology in Judges 18:12." *JHS* 3 (2001): article 5.

Becker, Uwe. *Richterzeit und Königtum: Redaktionsgeschichtliche Studien zum Richterbuch*. Beihefte zur Zeitschrift für die alttestamentliche Wissenschaft, 192. Berlin: de Gruyter, 1990.

Beem, Beverly. "The Minor Judges: A Literary Reading of Some Very Short Stories." In *The Biblical Canon in Comparative Perspective*, pp. 147–72. Edited by K. Lawson Younger Jr., William W. Hallo, and Bernard F. Batto. Scripture in Context IV. Lampeter: Edwin Mellen, 1991.

Begg, Christopher T. "The Function of Josh 7,1–8,29 in the Deuteronomistic History." *Bib* 67 (1986): 320–33.

Beyerlin, Walter. "Gattung und Herkunft des Rahens im Richterbuch." In *Tradition und Situation: Studien zur alttestamentliche Prophetie*, pp. 1–29. Edited by E. Würthwein and O. Kaiser. Göttingen: Vandenhoeck & Ruprecht, 1963.

Blenkinsopp, Joseph. "Structure and Style in Judges 13–16." *JBL* 82 (1963): 65–76.

———. *Gibeon and Israel: The Role of Gibeon and the Gibeonites in the Political and Religious History of Early Israel*. London: Cambridge University, 1972.

Block, Daniel I. "The Period of the Judges: Religious Disintegration Under Tribal Rule." In *Israel's Apostasy and Restoration: Essays in Honor of Roland K. Harrison*, pp. 39–57. Edited by A. Gileadi. Grand Rapids: Baker, 1988.

———. "Echo Narrative Technique in Hebrew Literature: A Study in Judges 19." *WTJ* 52 (1990): 325–41.

———. "Deborah among the Judges: The Perspective of the Hebrew Historian." In *Faith, Tradition & History: Old Testament Historiography in Its Near Eastern Context*, pp. 229–53. Edited by A.R. Millard, J.K. Hoffmeier, and D.W. Baker. Winona Lake: Eisenbrauns, 1994.

———. "Will the Real Gideon Please Stand Up? Narrative Style and Intention in Judges 6–9." *JETS* 40 (1997): 353–66.

———. *Judges, Ruth*. The New American Commentary. Nashville: Broadman & Holman, 1999.

Bluedorn, Wolfgang. *Yahweh Versus Baalism: A Theological Reading of the Gideon-Abimelech Narrative*. JSOTSup, 329. Sheffield: Sheffield Academic, 2001.

Bohmbach, Karla G. "Conventions/Contraventions: The Meaning of Public and Private for the Judges 19 Concubine." *JSOT* 83 (1999): 83–98.

Boling, Robert G. "In Those Days There Was No King in Israel." In *A Light Unto My Path: Old Testament Studies in Honor of Jacob M. Meyers*, pp. 33–48. Edited by Howard N. Bream, Ralph D. Heim, and Carey A. Moore. Philadelphia: Temple University, 1974.

———. *Judges: Introduction, Translation, and Commentary*. The Anchor Bible. Garden City: Doubleday, 1975.

———. *Joshua: A New Translation, with Notes and Commentary*. The Anchor Bible. Garden City: Doubleday, 1982.

Boogaart, T.A. "Stone for Stone: Retribution in the Story of Abimelek and Shechem." *JSOT* 32 (1985): 45–56.

Brekelmans, Christian. "חרם." In *Theological Lexicon of the Old Testament, Vol. 2*, pp. 474–77. Edited by Ernst Jenni and Claus Westermann. Translated by Mark Biddle. Peabody: Hendrickson, 1997.

Brettler, Marc Zvi. "The Book of Judges: Literature as Politics." *JBL* 108 (1989): 395–418.

———. "Judges 1:1–2:10: From Appendix to Prologue." *ZAW* 101 (1989): 433–35.
———. *The Book of Judges*. London: Routledge, 2002.
Bronner, Leila Leah. "Valorized or Vilified? The Women of Judges in Midrashic Sources." In *Judges: A Feminist Companion to the Bible*, pp. 72–95. Edited by Athalya Brenner. Sheffield: Sheffield Academic, 1993.
Brueggemann, Walter. "Social Criticism and Social Vision in the Deuteronomic Formula of the Judges." In *Die Botschaft und die Boton: Festschrift für Hans Walter Wolff zum 70. Geburtstag*, pp. 101–14. Edited by Jörg Jeremias and Lothar Perlitt. Neukirchen-Vluyn: Neukirchener Verlag, 1981.
Buber, Martin. *Kingship of God*. Third edition. Translated by Richard Scheimann. New York: Harper & Row, 1967.
Burney, C.F. *The Book of Judges*. First published 1903. Reprinted with *Notes on the Hebrew Text of the Books of Kings*. New York: KTAV, 1970.
Butler, Trent C. *Joshua*. Word Biblical Commentary. Waco: Word, 1983.
Callaway, Joseph A. "The Settlement in Canaan: The Period of the Judges." In *Ancient Israel: A Short History from Abraham to the Roman Destruction of the Temple*, pp. 53–84. Edited by Hershel Shanks. Washington D.C.: Biblical Archaeology Society, 1988.
Campbell, Edward Fay, Jr. *Ruth: A New Translation with Introduction, Notes, and Commentary*. The Anchor Bible. Garden City: Doubleday, 1975.
Cassuto, Umberto. *A Commentary on the Book of Exodus*. Translated by Israel Abrahams. Jerusalem: Magnes, 1967.
Chalcraft, D.J. "Deviance and Legitimate Action in the Book of Judges." In *The Bible in Three Dimensions*, pp. 177–201. Edited by David J.A. Clines et al. JSOTSup, 87. Sheffield: Sheffield Academic, 1990.
Chisholm, Robert B. Jr. *Where Have All the Leaders Gone? A Literary and Theological Commentary on the Book of Judges*. An unpublished class notes. Dallas: photocopied, 1998.
Civil, Miguel. "Enlil and Ninlil: The Meaning of Sud." *JAOS* 103 (1983): 43–66.
Claassens, Julie. "Theme and Function in the Jephthah Narrative." *JNSL* 23 (1997): 203–19.
Cooke, G.A. *The Book of Judges*. Reprint. Cambridge: University Press, 1918.
Craig, Kenneth M. Jr. "Bargaining in Tov (Judges 11,4–11): The Many Directions of So-Called Direct Speech." *Bib* 79 (1998): 76–85.
Craigie, Peter C. "A Reconsideration of Shamgar Ben Anath." *JBL* 91 (1972): 239–40.
———. *The Book of Deuteronomy*. The New International Commentary on the Old Testament. Grand Rapids: Eerdmans, 1976.
Crenshaw, James L. "The Samson Saga: Filial Devotion or Erotic Attachment?" *ZAW* 86 (1974): 470–503.
———. *Samson*. London: SPCK, 1979.
Cross, Frank Moore. "The Themes of the Book of Kings and the Structure of the Deuteronomistic History." In *Canaanite Myth and Hebrew Epic: Essays in the History of the Religion of Israel*, 274–89. Cambridge: Harvard, 1973.
Crüsemann, Frank. *Der Widerstand gegan das Königtum: Die antiköniglichen Texte des Alten Testamentes und der Kampf um den frühen israelitischen Staat*. Neukirchen-Vluyn: Neukirchener, 1978.
Culley, Robert C. "Structural Analysis: Is it Done with Mirrors?" *Int* 28 (1974): 165–81.
———. "Themes and Variations in Three Groups of Narratives." *Semeia* 3 (1975): 3–13.
———. *Studies in the Structure of Hebrew Narrative*. Philadelphia: Fortress, 1976.
Cundall, Arthur E. "Judges." In *Judges & Ruth*, pp. 15–215. By Arthur E. Cundall and Leon Morris. Tyndale Old Testament Commentaries. Downers Grove: InterVarsity, 1968.

———. "Judges—An Apology for the Monarchy?" *ExpTim* 81 (1970): 178–81.
Dan, Joseph. "Teraphim: From Popular Belief to a Folktale." In *Studies in Hebrew Narrative Art Throughout the Ages*, pp. 99–106. Edited by Joseph Heinemann and Shmuel Werses. Scripta Hierosolymitana, 27. Jerusalem: Magnes, 1978.
Danelius, Eva. "Shamgar Ben Anath." *JNES* 22 (1963): 191–93.
Davis, Dale R. "Comic Literature—Tragic Theology: a Study of Judges 17–18." *WTJ* 46 (1984): 156–63.
Davies, G. Henton. "Judges VIII 22–23." *VT* 13 (1963): 151–57.
Deryn Guest, Pauline. "Dangerous Liaisons in the Book of Judges." *SJOT* 11 (1997): 241–269.
———. "Can Judges Survive Without Sources? Challenging the Consensus." *JSOT* 78 (1998): 43–61.
Dexinger, Ferdinand. "Ein Plädoyer fur die Linkshänder im Richterbuch." *ZAW* 89 (1977): 268–69.
Dietrich, Walter. *Prophetie und Geschichte: eine redaktionsgeschichteliche Untersuchtung zum deuteronomistischen Geschichtswerk.* Göttingen: Vandenhoeck & Ruprecht, 1977.
———. "History and Law: Deuteronomistic Historiography and Deuteronomic Law Exemplified in the Passage from the Period of the Judges to the Monarchical Period." In *Israel Constructs its History: Deuteronomistic Historiography in Recent Research*, pp. 315–42. Edited by Albert de Pury, Thomas Römer, and Jean-Daniel Macchi. JSOTSup, 306. Sheffield: Sheffield Academic, 2000.
Dillard, Raymond B. *2 Chronicles.* Word Biblical Commentary. Waco: Word, 1987.
Duke, Rodney K. "The Portion of the Levite: Another Reading of Deuteronomy 18:6–8." *JBL* 106 (1987): 193–201.
Dumbrell, W.J. "'In Those Days There Was No King In Israel; Every Man Did What Was Right In His Own Eyes.' The Purpose of the Book of Judges Reconsidered." *JSOT* 25 (1983): 23–33.
Ebach, Jürgen and U. Rüterswörden, "Pointen in der Jothamfabel." *BN* 31 (1986): 11–18.
Eissfeldt, Otto. *Die Quellen des Richterbuches.* Leipzig: Hinrichs, 1925.
Emerton, John Adney. "Priests and Levites in Deuteronomy." *VT* 12 (1962): 129–38.
Erlandsson, S. "זנה." In *Theological Dictionary of the Old Testament, Vol. IV*, pp. 99–104. Edited by G. Johannes Botterweck and Helmer Ringgren. Translated by David E. Green. Grand Rapids: Eerdmans, 1980.
Exum, J. Cheryl. "Promise and Fulfillment: Narrative Art in Judges 13." *JBL* 99 (1980): 43–59.
———. "Aspects of Symmetry and Balance in the Samson Saga." *JSOT* 19 (1981): 3–29.
———. "The Theological Dimension of the Samson Saga." *VT* 33 (1983): 30–45.
———. "The Tragic Vision and Biblical Narrative: The Case of Jephthath." In *Signs and Wonders: Biblical Texts in Literary Focus*, pp. 59–83. Edited by J. Cheryl Exum. Decatur: Scholars, 1989.
———. "The Centre Cannot Hold: Thematic and Textual Instabilities in Judges." *CBQ* 52 (1990): 410–31.
———. "On Judges 11." In *Judges: A Feminist Companion to the Bible*, pp. 130–44. Edited by Athalya Brenner. Sheffield: Sheffield Academic, 1993.
Exum, J. Cheryl and J. William Whedbee. "Isaac, Samson, and Saul: Reflections on the Comic and Tragic Visions." In *On Humour and the Comic in the Hebrew Bible*, pp. 117–59. Edited by Yehuda T. Radday and Athalya Brenner. JSOTSup, 92. Sheffield: Almond, 1990.
Feldman, Louis H. "Josephus's Portrait of Ehud." In *Pursuing the Text: Studies in Honour of Ben Zion Wacholder on the Occasion of his Seventieth Birthday*, pp. 177–201. Edited by John C. Reeves and John Kampen. JSOTSup, 184. Sheffield: Sheffield Academic, 1994.

Fensham, F. Charles. "Shamgar Ben 'Anath'." *JNES* 20 (1961): 197–98.
———. "The Numeral Seventy in the Old Testament and the family of Jerubbaal, Ahab, Panammuwa and Arthirat." *PEQ* 109 (1977): 113–115.
Fishbane, M. *Biblical Interpretation in Ancient Israel.* Oxford: Clarendon, 1986.
Fokkelman, Jan P. "Structural Remarks on Judges 9 and 19." In *"Sha'arei Talmon:" Studies in the Bible, Qumran, and the Ancient Near East Presented to Shemaryahu Talmon*, pp. 33–45. Edited by Michael Fishbane and Emanuel Tov. Winona Lake: Eisenbrauns, 1992.
———. *Reading Biblical Narrative: An Introductory Guide.* Translated by Ineke Smit. Louisville: Westminster John Knox, 1999.
Freeman, James A. "Samson's Dry Bones: A Structural Reading of Judges 13–16." In *Literary Interpretations of Biblical Narratives, Vol. II*, pp. 145–60. Edited by Kenneth R.R. Gros Louis and James S. Ackerman. Nashville: Abingdon, 1982.
Fritz, Volkmar. "Abimelech und Sichem in Jdc. IX." *VT* 32 (1982): 129–44.
Gage, Warren Austin. "Ruth Upon the Threshing Floor and the Sin of Gibeah: a Biblical Theological Study." *WTJ* 51 (1989): 369–375.
Gerbrandt, Gerald Eddie. *Kingship According to the Deuteronomistic History.* SBLDS, 87. Atlanta: Scholar, 1986.
Globe, Alexander. "The Literary Structure and Unity of the Song of Deborah." *JBL* 93 (1974): 493–512.
———. "The Muster of the Tribes in Judges 5:11e–18." *ZAW* 87 (1975): 169–84.
———. "'Enemies Round About': Disintegrative Structure in the Book of Judges." In *Mappings of the Biblical Terrain: The Bible as Text*, pp. 233–51. Edited by Vincent L. Tollers and John Maier. Lewisburg: Bucknell, 1990.
Good, Edwin M. *Irony in the Old Testament.* Reprint. Sheffield: Almond, 1981.
Gooding, D.W. "The Composition of the Book of Judges." *EI* 16 (1982): 70–79.
Gray, George Buchanan. *Numbers.* The International Critical Commentary. Edinburgh: T. & T. Clark, 1903.
Gray, John. *Joshua, Judges and Ruth.* The Century Bible. New edition. London: Nelson, 1967.
Greene, Mark. "Enigma Variation: Aspects of the Samson Story Judges 13–16." *VE* 21 (1991): 53–79.
Greenfield, Jonas C. "Stylistic Aspects of the Sefire Treaty Inscriptions." *ActO* 29 (1965): 1–18.
Greenspahn, Frederick E. "An Egyptian Parallel to Judges 17:6 and 21:25." *JBL* 101 (1982): 129–130.
———. "The Theology of the Framework of Judges." *VT* 36 (1986): 385–96.
Greenstein, Edward L. "Reviews: Biblical Narratology." *Proof* 1 (1981): 201–08.
———. "The Riddle of Samson." *Proof* 1 (1981): 237–60.
Gros Louis, Kenneth R.R. "The Book of Judges." In *Literary Interpretations of Biblical Narratives*, pp. 141–62. Edited by Kenneth R.R. Gros Louis, J.S. Ackerman, and T.S. Warsaw. Nashville: Abingdon, 1974.
Guillaume, Philippe. *Waiting for Josiah: The Judges.* JSOTSup, 385. London: T&T Clark, 2004.
Gunn, David M. "Joshua and Judges." In *The Literary Guide to the Bible*, pp. 102–21. Edited by Robert Alter and F. Kermode. Cambridge: Harvard University, 1987.
———. "Samson of Sorrows: An Isaianic Gloss on Judges 13–16." In *Reading Between Texts*, pp. 225–53. Edited by Danna Nolan Fewell. Louisville: John Knox, 1992.
Gunn, David M. and Danna Nolan Fewell. *Narrative in the Hebrew Bible.* The Oxford Bible Series. Oxford: Oxford University, 1993.
Halpern, Baruch. *The First Historians: The Hebrew Bible and History.* Paperback edition. University Park: Penn State, 1996.
Hamlin, E. John. "Adoni-Bezek—What's in a Name (Judges 1:4–7)?" *Proc* 4 (1984): 146–52.

Handy, Lowell K. "Uneasy Laughter: Ehud and Eglon as Ethnic Humor." *SJOT* 6 (1992): 233–246.
Hauser, Alan J. "The 'Minor Judges': A Re-evaluation." *JBL* 94 (1975): 190–200.
———. "Two Songs of Victory: A Comparison of Exodus 15 and Judges 5." In *Directions in Biblical Hebrew Poetry*, pp. 265–84. Edited by Elaine R. Follis. JSOTSup, 40. Sheffield: Sheffield Academic, 1987.
Hertzberg, Hans Wilhelm. "Die Kleinen Richter." *TLZ* 79 (1954): 286–90.
———. *I & II Samuel.* Old Testament Library. London: SMC, 1964.
Hess, Richard S. "The Dead Sea Scrolls and Higher Criticism of the Hebrew Bible: The Case of 4QJudg[a]." In *Scrolls and the Scriptures: Qumran Fifty Years After*, pp. 122–28. Edited by Stanley E. Porter and Craig A. Evans. JSPSup, 26. Sheffield: Sheffield Academic, 1997.
Hoffman, Yair. "The Deuteronomistic Concept of the Herem." *ZAW* 111 (1999): 196–210.
Hudson, Don Michael. "Living in a Land of Epithets: Anonymity in Judges 19–21." *JSOT* 62 (1994): 49–66.
Ishida, Tomoo. "The Leaders of the Tribal Leagues 'Israel' in the Pre-Monarchic Period." *RB* 80 (1973): 514–30.
Janzen, J. Gerald. "A Certain Woman in the Rhetoric of Judges 9." *JSOT* 38 (1987): 33–37.
Japhet, Sara. *I & II Chronicles.* The Old Testament Library. Louisville: Westminster John Knox, 1993.
Jobling, David. *The Sense of Biblical Narrative: Structural Analysis of the Hebrew Bible II.* JSOTSup, 39. Sheffield: Sheffield Academic, 1986.
Josipovici, Gabriel. "The Rhythm Falters: The Book of Judges." In *The Book of God: A Response to the Bible*, pp. 108–131. New Haven: Yale, 1988.
Joüon, Paul. *A Grammar of Biblical Hebrew.* Translated and revised by T. Muraoka. Rome: Editrice Pontificio Istituto Biblico, 1991.
Jugel, Erwin, and Heinz-Dieter Neef. "Ehud als Linkshänder: Exegetische und Anmerkungen zu Ri 3,15." *BN* 97 (1999): 45–54.
Jüngling, Hans-Winfried. *Richter 19—Ein Plädoyer für das Königtum.* Analecta Biblica, 84. Rome: Biblical Institute, 1981.
Kaminsky, Joel S. "Joshua 7: A Reassessment of Israelite Conceptions of Corporate Punishment." In *The Pitcher is Broken: Memorial Essays for Gösta W. Ahlström*, pp. 315–46. Edited by Steven W. Holloway and Lowell K. Handy. JSOTSup, 190. Sheffield: Sheffield Academic, 1995.
Klein, Lillian. *The Triumph of Irony in the book of Judges.* JSOTSup, 68. Sheffield: Almond, 1988.
———. "Structure, Irony and Meaning in the Book of Judges." In *Proceedings of the Tenth Congress of Jewish Studies; Division A: The Bible and Its World*, pp. 83–90. Edited by D. Assaf. Jerusalem: World Union of Jewish Studies, 1990.
Kornfeld, Walter. "Onomastica aramaica und das Alte Testament." *ZAW* 88 (1976): 105–12.
Lasine, Stuart. "Guest and Host in Judges 19: Lot's Hospitality in an Inverted World." *JSOT* 29 (1984): 37–59.
Lemche, Niels P. "The Judges—Once More." *BN* 20 (1983): 47–55.
Licht, Jacob. *Storytelling in the Bible.* Jerusalem: Magnes, 1978.
Lilley, J.P.U. "A Literary Appreciation of the Book of Judges." *TynBul* 18 (1967): 94–102.
Lindars, Barnabas. "Gideon and Kingship." *JTS* 16 (1965): 315–26.
———. "The Israelite Tribes in Judges." In *Studies in the Historical Books of the Old Testament*, pp. 95–112. Edited by J.A. Emerton. VTSup, 30. Leiden: Brill, 1979.
———. *Judges 1–5.* Edinburgh: T. & T. Clark, 1995.
Lohfink, Norbert. "Die Bedeutungen von hebr. jrš qal und hif." *BZ* 27 (1983): 14–33.

———. "חרם." In *Theological Dictionary of the Old Testament, Vol. V*, pp. 180–99. Edited by G. Johannes Botterweck and Helmer Ringgren. Translated by David E. Green. Grand Rapids: Eerdmans, 1986.

———. "Der heilige Krieg und der Bann in der Bibel." *Communio* 18 (1989): 104–12.

Malamat, Abraham. "The Danite Migration and the Pan-Israelite Exodus-Conquest: A Biblical Narrative Pattern." *Bib* 51 (1970): 1–16.

———. "Charismatic leadership in the Book of Judges." In *Magnalia Dei, the Mighty Acts of God: Essays on the Bible and Archaeology in Memory of G. Ernest Wright*, pp. 152–68. Edited by Frank Moore Cross, Werner E. Lemke, and Patrick D. Miller, Jr. Garden City: Doubleday, 1976.

———. *Mari and the Early Israelite Experience: The Schweich Lectures, 1984.* Oxford: Oxford University, 1989.

Malul, Meir. "Taboo." In *Dictionary of Deities and Demons in the Bible*, pp. 824–27. Edited by Karel van der Toorn, Bob Becking, and Pieter W. van der Horst. Second revised edition. Leiden: Brill, 1999.

Maly, Eugene. "The Jotham Fable—Anti-monarchical?" *CBQ* 22 (1960): 299–305.

Marais, Jacobus. *Representation in Old Testament Narrative Texts.* Biblical Interpretation Series, 36. Leiden: Brill, 1998.

Marcus, David. *Jephthah and His Vow.* Lubbock: Texas Tech, 1986.

———. "The Bargaining between Jephthah and the Elders." *JANES* 19 (1989): 95–100.

———. "The Legal Dispute Between Jephthah and the Elders." *HAR* 12 (1990): 105–14.

Margalith, Othniel. "Samson's Riddle and Samson's Locks." *VT* 36 (1986): 224–34.

Martin, James D. "The Office of Judge in Pre-Monarchic Israel." *Trans* 26 (1978): 64–79.

Marzal, A. "The Provincial Governor at Mari: His Title and Appointment." *JNES* 30 (1971): 186–217.

Matthews, Victor H. "Freedom and Entrapment in the Samson Narrative: A Literary Analysis." *PRS* 16 (1989): 245–57.

———. "Hospitality and Hostility in Genesis 19 and Judges 19." *BTB* 22 (1992): 3–11.

Mayes, Andrew David Hastings. "The Historical Context of the Battle Against Sisera." *VT* 19 (1969): 353–60.

———. "Israel in the Pre-monarchy Period," *VT* 23 (1973): 151–70.

———. "Period of the Judges and the Rise of the Monarchy." In *Israelite and Judaean History*, pp. 285–331. Edited by John H. Hayes. London: SMC, 1977.

———. *Deuteronomy.* New Century Commentary. Grand Rapids: Eerdmans, 1979.

———. *The Story of Israel between Settlement and Exile: A Redactional Study of the Deuteronomistic History.* London: SMC, 1983.

———. *Judges.* Old Testament Guides. Sheffield: JSOT, 1985.

———. "Deuteronomistic Royal Ideology in Judges 17–21." *BibInt* 9 (2001): 241–58.

McCann, Clinton J. *Judges.* Interpretation. Louisville: John Knox, 2002.

McCarter, P. Kyle Jr. *I Samuel: A New Translation with Introduction, Notes and Commentary.* The Anchor Bible. Garden City: Doubleday, 1980.

McMillion, Phillip. "Worship in Judges 17–18." *In Worship and the Hebrew Bible: Essays in Honour of John T. Willis*, pp. 225–43. Edited by M. Patrick Graham, Rick R. Marrs, and Steven L. McKenzie. JSOTSup, 284. Sheffield: Sheffield Academic, 1999.

Mendenhall, George E. *Law and Covenant in Israel and the Ancient Near East.* Reprinted from *BA* 17 (1954): 26–46, 49–76. Pittsburgh: The Biblical Colloquium, 1955.

———. *The Tenth Generation: The Origins of Biblical Tradition.* London: John Hopkins University, 1973.

Milgrom, Jacob. *Numbers.* The JPS Torah Commentary. Philadelphia: The Jewish Publication Society, 1990.

Miller, Geoffrey P. "Verbal Feud in the Hebrew Bible: Judges 3:12–30 and 19–21." *JNES* 55 (1996): 105–17.

Moore, George F. *A Critical and Exegetical Commentary on Judges*. The International Critical Commentary. New York: Charles Scribner's Sons, 1895.

Mullen, E. Theodore. "The 'Minor Judges': Some Literary and Historical Considerations." *CBQ* 44 (1982): 185–201.

———. "Judges 1.1–36: The Deuteronomistic Reintroduction of the Book of Judges." *HTR* 77 (1984): 33–54.

———. *Narrative History and Ethnic Boundaries*. SBLSS. Atlanta: Scholars, 1993.

Müller, Hans-Peter. "Die Konjugation von Nomina im Althebräishen." *ZAW* 96 (1984): 245–63.

Murray, D.F. "Narrative Structure and Technique in the Deborah-Barak Story (Judges IV 4–22)." In *Studies in the Historical Books of the Old Testament*, pp. 155–89. Edited by J.A. Emerton. VTSup, 30. Leiden: Brill, 1979.

Myers, Jacob. *II Chronicles: Introduction, Translation, and Notes*. The Anchor Bible. Garden City: Doubleday, 1965.

Na'aman, Nadav. "Canaanites and Perizzites." *BN* 45 (1988): 42–47.

Nelson, Richard D. *The Double Redaction of the Deuteronomistic History*. JSOTSup, 18. Sheffield: JSOT, 1981.

———. "The Herem and the Deuteronomic Social Conscience." In *Deuteronomy and Deuteronomic Literature: Festschrift C.H.W. Brekelmans*, pp. 39–54. Edited by M. Vervenne and J. Lust. *BETL*, 133. Louvain: Leuven, 1997.

Nelson, Wayne S. "The Book of Judges: Its Structure and Paradigmatic Figures." Part 2. *JRR* 2 (1992): 49–60.

Niditch, Susan. "The 'Sodomite' Theme in Judges 19–20: Family, Community, and Social Disintegration." *CBQ* 44 (1982): 365–78.

———. "Samson as Culture Hero, Trickster, and Bandit: The Empowerment of the Weak." *CBQ* 52 (1990): 608–24.

———. *War in the Hebrew Bible: A Study in the Ethics of Violence*. New York: Oxford, 1993.

———. "Reading Story in Judges 1." In *The Labour of Reading: Desire, Alienation, and Biblical Interpretation*, pp. 193–208. Edited by Fiona C. Black, Roland Boer, and Erin Runions. SBLSS. Atlanta: SBL, 1999.

Noth, Martin. "The Background of Judges 17–18." In *Israel's Prophetic Heritage: Essays in Honor of James Muilenburg*, pp. 68–85. Edited by B.W. Anderson and W. Harrelson. The Preacher's Library. London: SCM, 1962.

———. *The Deuteronomistic History*. Translated by D. Orton from the 1967 German third edition. JSOTSup, 15. Second edition. Sheffield: Sheffield Academic, 1991.

O'Brien, Mark A. *The Deuteronomistic History Hypothesis: A Reassessment*. Gottingen: Vandenhoeck & Ruprecht, 1989.

O'Connell, Robert H. *The Rhetoric of the Book of Judges*. VTSup, 63. Leiden: Brill, 1996.

O'Doherty, Eamonn. "Literary Problem of Judges 1:1–3:6." *CBQ* 18 (1956): 1–7.

Ogden, Graham S. "The Special Features of a Story: a Study of Judges 3:12–30." *BT* 42 (1991): 408–414.

———. "Jotham's Fable: It's Structure and Function in Judges 9." *BT* 46 (1995): 301–08.

Orlinsky, Harry M. "The Tribal System of Israel and Related Groups in the Period of the Judges." In *Studies and Essays in Honor of Abraham A. Neuman*, pp. 375–87. Edited by Meir Ben-Horin, Bernard D. Weinryb, and Solomon Zeitlin. Leiden: Brill, 1962.

Penchansky, David. "Staying the Night: Intertextuality in Genesis and Judges." In *Reading Between Texts*, pp. 77–88. Edited by Danna Noland Fewell. Louisville, John Knox, 1992.

Pennant, David Falconer. "The Significance of Rootplay: Leading Words and Thematic Links in the Book of Judges." Ph.D. dissertation, University of Bristol, 1988.

Peter C.B. "The Anti-Monarchic Tradition in the Old Testament and the Question of Diakonia." *IJT* 32 (1983): 9–18.

Polzin, Robert. *Moses and the Deuteronomist: A Literary Study Of the Deuteronomic History, Part One: Deuteronomy, Joshua, Judges*. New York: Seabury, 1980.

Propp, William H. *Exodus 1–18: A New Translation with Introduction and Commentary*. The Anchor Bible. Garden City: Doubleday, 1999.

Rad, Gerhard von. Genesis: A Commentary. Revised edition. Old Testament Library. Philadelphia: Westminster, 1972.

Revell, E.J. "The Battle with Benjamin (Judges xx 29–48) and Hebrew Narrative Techniques." *VT* 35 (1985): 417–33.

Richter, Wolfgang. *Traditionsgeschichtliche Untersuchungen zum Richterbuch*. BBB, 18. Bonn: P. Hanstein, 1963.

———. *Die Bearbeitungen des 'Retterbuches' in der deuteronomischen Epoche*. BBB, 21. Bonn: P. Hanstein, 1964.

Ringgren, Helmer. "זנח." In *Theological Dictionary of the Old Testament, Vol. IV*, pp. 104–06. Edited by G. Johannes Botterweck and Helmer Ringgren. Translated by David E. Green. Grand Rapids: Eerdmans, 1980.

Robertson, David A. *Linguistic Evidence in Dating Early Hebrew Poetry*. SBLDS, 3. Missoula: SBL, 1972.

Robinson, Bernard. "The Story of Jephthah and His Daughter: Then and Now." *Bib* 85 (2004): 331–48.

Rofé, Alexander. "The End of the Book of Joshua According to the Septuagint." *HENOCH* 4 (1982): 17–35.

Römer, Thomas C. "Why Would the Deuteronomists Tell about the Sacrifice of Jephthah's Daughter?" *JSOT* 77 (1998): 27–38.

Rösel, Hartmut N. "Zur Ehud-Erzählung." *ZAW* 89 (1977): 270–272.

———. "Die Überleitungen vom Josua- ins Richterbuch." *VT* 30 (1980): 342–50.

———. "Das 'Negative Besitzverzeichnis'—traditionsgeschichtliche und historische Überlegungen." In *Wünschet Jerusalem Frieden: Collected Communications to the XIIth Congress of the International Organization for the Study of the Old Testament, Jerusalem 1986*, pp. 121–35. Edited by Matthias Augustin and Klaus-Dietrich Schunck. Frankfurt am Main: Peter Lang, 1988.

———. *Von Josua bis Jojachin: Untersuchungen zu den deuteronomistischen Geschichtsbüchern des Alten Testaments*. VTSup, 75. Leiden: Brill, 1999.

Rosenberg, Abraham J. Editor. *Judges: A New English Translation*. New York: Judaica, 1979.

Roth, Wolfgang. "Deuteronomistisches Geschichtswerk/Deuteronomistische Schule." In *Theologische Realenzyklopädie, Band VIII*, pp. 543–52. Edited by Horst Robert Balz et al. Berlin: Walter de Gruyter, 1981.

Rozenberg, Martin. "The Sofetim in the Bible." *EI* 12 (1975): 77–86.

Safren, Jonathan D. "New Evidence for the Title of the Provincial Governor at Mari." *HUCA* 50 (1979): 1–15.

Satterthwaite, Philip E. "Narrative Artistry in the Composition of Judges 20:29ff." *VT* 42 (1992): 80–89.

———. "'No King in Israel': Narrative Criticism and Judges 17–21." *TynBul* 44 (1993): 75–88.

Schäfer-Lichtenberger, Christa. "Bedeutung und Funktion von Herem in biblisch-hebräischen Texten." *BZ* 38 (1994): 270–75.

Schneider, Tammi J. *Judges*. Berit Olam: Studies in Hebrew Narrative and Poetry. Collegeville: Liturgical, 2000.

Schöpflin, Karin. "Jotham's Speech and Fable as Prophetic Comment on Abimelech's Story: The Genesis of Judges 9." *SJOT* 18 (2004): 3–22.

Schunck, Klaus-Dietrich. "Die Richter Israels und ihr Amt." In *Congress Volume: Genève, 1965*, pp. 252–62. VTSup, 15. Leiden: Brill, 1966.

Seeligmann, I.L. "A Psalm from Pre-Regal Times." *VT* 14 (1964): 75–92.
Shupak, Nili. "New Light on Shamgar ben 'Anath." *Bib* 70 (1989): 517–25.
Simpson, Cuthbert Aikman. *Composition of the Book of Judges*. Oxford: Basil Blackwell, 1958.
Smelik, Willem S. *The Targum of Judges*. OTS, 36. Leiden: Brill, 1995.
Smend, Rudolf. *Jahwekrieg und Sätmmebund: Erwägungen zur ältesten Geschichte Israels*. Göttingen: Vandenhoeck & Ruprecht, 1963.
———. "Das Gesetz und die Völker: ein Beitrag zur deuteronomistischen Redaktionsgeschichte." In *Probleme biblischer Theologie: Gerhard von Rad zum 70. Geburtstag*, pp. 494–509. Edited by Hans Walter Wolff. München: Chr. Kaiser, 1971.
Soggin, J. Alberto. *Introduction to the Old Testament*. Translated by John Bowden. Old Testament Library. London: SCM, 1976.
———. "Das Amt der 'kleinen Richter' in Israel." *VT* 30 (1980): 245–48.
———. *Judges*. Second edition. Old Testament Library. London: SCM, 1987.
———. "'Ehud und 'Eglon: Bemerkung zu Richter III 11b–31." *VT* 39 (1989): 95–100.
Stager, Lawrence E. "Archaeology, Ecology, and Social History: Background Themes to the Song of Deborah." In *Congress Volume: Jerusalem, 1986*, pp. 221–34. Edited by J.A. Emerton. VTSup, 40. Leiden: Brill, 1988.
Stern, Philip D. *The Biblical Herem: A Window on Israel's Religious Experience*. BJS, 211. Atlanta: Scholars: 1991.
Sternberg, Meier. *Poetics of Biblical Narrative*. Bloomington, Indiana University, 1985.
Sweeney, Marvin A. "Davidic Polemics on the Book of Judges." *VT* 47 (1997): 517–29.
Talmon, Shemaryahu. *King, Cult, and Calendar in Ancient Israel: Collected Studies*. Jerusalem: Magnes, 1986.
Tanner, Paul J. "The Gideon Narrative as the Focal Point of Judges." *BSac* 149 (1992): 146–61.
Tigay, Jeffrey H. *Deuteronomy*. The JPS Torah Commentary. Philadelphia: The Jewish Publication Society, 1996.
Tollington, Janet E. "The Book of Judges: The Result of Post-Exilic Exegesis?" In *Intertexuality in Ugarit & Israel*, pp. 186–96. Edited by Johannes C. de Moor. OTS, 40. Leiden: Brill, 1998.
Tov, Emanuel. *Textual Criticism of the Hebrew Bible*. Minneapolis: Fortress, 1992.
Townsend, Theodore P. "The Kingdom of God as a Reality: Israel in the Time of the Judges." *IJT* 32 (1983): 19–36.
Trebolle Barrera, Julio. "Textual Variants in 4QJudg[a] and the Textual and Editorial History of the Book of Judges." *RevQ* 14 (1989): 229–45.
———. "4QJudg[a]." In *Discoveries in the Judaean Desert XIV: Qumran Cave 4 IX: Deuteronomy, Joshua, Judges, Kings*, pp. 161–64. Edited by Eugene Ulrich, Frank Moore Cross, et al. Oxford: Clarendon, 1995
Trible, Phyllis. "A Meditation on Mourning: The Sacrifice of the Daughter of Jephthah." *USQR* 36 (1981): 59–73.
———. *Texts of Terror: Literary-Feminist Readings of Biblical Narratives*. Philadelphia: Fortress, 1984.
Tsang, Jacob C.S. *Judges*. Hong Kong: Tien Dao, 1998 (In Chinese).
Ulrich, Eugene. "Our Sharper Focus on the Bible and Theology Thanks to the Dead Sea Scrolls". *CBQ* 66 (2004): 1–24.
Van Der Hart, R. "The Camp of Dan and the Camp of Yahweh." *VT* 25 (1975): 720–28.
Van Selms, Adrianus. "Judges Shamgar." *VT* 14 (1964): 294–309.
Van Seters, John. *In Search of History: Historiography in the Ancient World and the Origins of Biblical History*. New Haven: Yale, 1983.
Veijola, Timo. *Das Königtum in der Beurteilung der deuteronomistischen Historiographie: ein redaktionsgeschichtliche Untersuchung*. Helsinki: Suomalainen Tiedeakatemia, 1977.

Vickery, John B. "In Strange Ways: The Story of Samson." In *Images of Man and God: Old Testament Short Stories in Literary Focus*, pp. 58–73. Edited by Burke O. Long. Bible and Literature Series, 1. Sheffield: Almond, 1981.

Vincent, Mark A. "The Song of Deborah: A Structural and Literary Consideration." *JSOT* 91 (2000): 61–82.

Wadsworth, Michael. "Making and Intrepreting Scripture." In *Ways of Reading the Bible*, pp. 7–22. Edited by Michael Wadsworth. Brighton: Havester, 1981.

Waltke, Bruce K. and M. O'Connor. *An Introduction to Biblical Hebrew Syntax*. Winona Lake: Eisenbrauns, 1990.

Webb, Barry. "The Theme of Jephthah Story (Judges 10:6–12:7)." *RTR* 45 (1986): 34–43.

———. *The Book of Judges: An Integrated Reading*. JSOTSup, 46. Sheffield: Sheffield Academic, 1987.

Weinfeld, Moshe. "Period of the Conquest and of the Judges as Seen by the Earlier and the Later Sources." *VT* 17 (1967): 93–113.

———. "Judges 1.1–2.5: The Conquest under the Leadership of the House of Judah." In *Understanding Poets and Prophets: Essays in Honour of George Wishart Anderson*, pp. 388–400. Edited by A. Graeme Auld. JSOTSup, 152. Sheffield: Sheffield Academic, 1993.

———. "The Ban on the Canaanites in the Biblical Codes and Its Historical Development." In *History and Traditions of Early Israel: Studies presented to Eduard Nielson*, pp. 142–160. Edited by André Lemaire and Benedikt Otzen. VTSup, 50. Leiden: Brill, 1993.

Weitzman, Steve. "Reopening the Case of the Suspiciously Suspended Nun in Judges 18:30." *CBQ* 61 (1999): 448–60.

Wenham, Gordon J. *Story as Torah: Reading the Old Testament Ethically*. Edinburgh: T. & T. Clark, 2000.

Wharton, James A. "The Secret of Yahweh: Story and Affirmation in Judges 13–16." *Int* 27 (1973): 48–66.

Whitelam, Keith W. "The Former Prophets." In *Creating the Old Testament*, pp. 151–68. Edited by Stephen Bigger. Oxford: Basil Blackwell, 1989.

Williams, Jay G. "The Structure of Judges 2.6–16.31." *JSOT* 49 (1991): 77–85.

Williamson, H.G.M. *1 & 2 Chronicles*. The New Century Bible Commentary. Grand Rapids: Eerdmans, 1982.

Willis, Thomas M. "The Nature of Jephthah's Authority." *CBQ* 59 (1997): 33–44.

Wilson, Michael. "As You Like It: The Idolatry of Micah and the Danites." *RTR* 54 (1995): 73–85.

Wolff, Hans Walter. *Hosea*. Translated by Gary Stansell. Hermeneia. Philadelphia: Fortress, 1974.

Wong, Gregory T.K. "Is There a Direct Pro-Judah Polemic in Judges?" *SJOT* 19 (2005): 84–110.

———. "Ehud and Joab: Separated at Birth?" *VT* 66 (2006), forthcoming.

———. "Narratives and Their Contexts: A Critique of Greger Andersson with Respect to Narrative Autonomy." *SJOT* 20 (2006): 1–15.

———. "Gideon: A New Moses?" In *Reflection and Refraction: Studies in Biblical Historiography in Honour of A. Graeme Auld*, pp. 529–45. Edited by Robert Rezetko, Timothy Lim and Brian Aucker. VTSup, 113. Leiden: Brill, 2006.

———. "Song of Deborah as Polemic." 2007, forthcoming.

Wright, G. Ernest. "The Literary and Historical Problem of Joshua 10 and Judges 1." *JNES* 5 (1946): 105–14.

———. "The Levites in Deuteronomy." *VT* 4 (1954): 325–30.

Yee, Gale A. "Ideological Criticism: Judges 17–19 and the Dismembered Body." In *Judges and Method: New Approaches in Biblical Studies*, pp. 146–70. Edited by Gale A. Yee. Minneapolis: Fortress, 1995.

Younger, K. Lawson, Jr. "Judges 1 in Its Near Eastern Literary Context." In *Faith, Tradition & History: Old Testament Historiography in Its Near Eastern Context*, pp. 207–27. Edited by A.R. Millard, J.K. Hoffmeier, and D.W. Baker. Winona Lake: Eisenbrauns, 1994.

———. "The Configuration of Judicial Preliminaries: Judges 1:1–2:5 and Its Dependence on the Book of Joshua." *JSOT* 68 (1995): 75–92.

Zenger, Erich. "Tradition und Interpretation in Exodus XV 1–21." In *Congress Volume, Vienna, 1980*. Edited by J.A. Emerton. VTSup, 32. Leiden: Brill, 1981.

INDEX OF AUTHORS

INDEX OF BIBLICAL REFERENCES

SUPPLEMENTS TO VETUS TESTAMENTUM

8. Bernhardt, K.-H. *Das Problem der alt-orientalischen Königsideologie im Alten Testament.* Unter besonderer Berücksichtigung der Geschichte der Psalmenexegese dargestellt und kritisch gewürdigt. 1961. ISBN 90 04 02331 3
9. *Congress Volume, Bonn 1962.* 1963. ISBN 90 04 02332 1
11. Donner, H. *Israel unter den Völkern.* Die Stellung der klassischen Propheten des 8. Jahrhunderts v. Chr. zur Aussenpolitik der Könige von Israel und Juda. 1964. ISBN 90 04 02334 8
12. Reider, J. *An Index to Aquila.* Completed and revised by N. Turner. 1966. ISBN 90 04 02335 6
13. Roth, W.M.W. *Numerical sayings in the Old Testament.* A form-critical study. 1965. ISBN 90 04 02336 4
14. Orlinsky, H.M. *Studies on the second part of the Book of Isaiah.* — The so-called 'Servant of the Lord' and 'Suffering Servant' in Second Isaiah. — Snaith, N.H. Isaiah 40-66. A study of the teaching of the Second Isaiah and its consequences. Repr. with additions and corrections. 1977. ISBN 90 04 05437 5
15. *Volume du Congrès* [International pour l'étude de l'Ancien Testament]. *Genève 1965.* 1966. ISBN 90 04 02337 2
17. *Congress Volume, Rome 1968.* 1969. ISBN 90 04 02339 9
19. Thompson, R.J. *Moses and the Law in a century of criticism since Graf.* 1970. ISBN 90 04 02341 0
20. Redford, D.B. *A Study of the Biblical Story of Joseph.* 1970. ISBN 90 04 02342 9
21. Ahlström, G.W. *Joel and the Temple Cult of Jerusalem.* 1971. ISBN 90 04 02620 7
22. *Congress Volume, Uppsala 1971.* 1972. ISBN 90 04 03521 4
23. *Studies in the Religion of Ancient Israel.* 1972. ISBN 90 04 03525 7
24. Schoors, A. *I am God your Saviour.* A form-critical study of the main genres in Is. xl-lv. 1973. ISBN 90 04 03792 2
25. Allen, L.C. *The Greek Chronicles.* The relation of the Septuagint I and II Chronicles to the Massoretic text. Part 1. The translator's craft. 1974. ISBN 90 04 03913 9
26. *Studies on prophecy.* A collection of twelve papers. 1974. ISBN 90 04 03877 9
27. Allen, L.C. *The Greek Chronicles.* Part 2. Textual criticism. 1974. ISBN 90 04 03933 3
28. *Congress Volume, Edinburgh 1974.* 1975. ISBN 90 04 04321 7
29. *Congress Volume, Göttingen 1977.* 1978. ISBN 90 04 05835 4
30. Emerton, J.A. (ed.). *Studies in the historical books of the Old Testament.* 1979. ISBN 90 04 06017 0
31. Meredino, R.P. *Der Erste und der Letzte.* Eine Untersuchung von Jes 40-48. 1981. ISBN 90 04 06199 1
32. Emerton, J.A. (ed.). *Congress Volume, Vienna 1980.* 1981. ISBN 90 04 06514 8
33. Koenig, J. *L'herméneutique analogique du Judaïsme antique d'après les témoins textuels d'Isaïe.* 1982. ISBN 90 04 06762 0
34. Barstad, H.M. *The religious polemics of Amos.* Studies in the preachings of Amos ii 7B-8, iv 1-13, v 1-27, vi 4-7, viii 14. 1984. ISBN 90 04 07017 6
35. Krašovec, J. *Antithetic structure in Biblical Hebrew poetry.* 1984. ISBN 90 04 07244 6
36. Emerton, J.A. (ed.). *Congress Volume, Salamanca 1983.* 1985. ISBN 90 04 07281 0
37. Lemche, N.P. *Early Israel.* Anthropological and historical studies on the Israelite society before the monarchy. 1985. ISBN 90 04 07853 3
38. Nielsen, K. *Incense in Ancient Israel.* 1986. ISBN 90 04 07702 2

39. Pardee, D. *Ugaritic and Hebrew poetic parallelism.* A trial cut. 1988. ISBN 90 04 08368 5
40. Emerton, J.A. (ed.). *Congress Volume, Jerusalem 1986.* 1988. ISBN 90 04 08499 1
41. Emerton, J.A. (ed.). *Studies in the Pentateuch.* 1990. ISBN 90 04 09195 5
42. McKenzie, S.L. *The trouble with Kings.* The composition of the Book of Kings in the Deuteronomistic History. 1991. ISBN 90 04 09402 4
43. Emerton, J.A. (ed.). *Congress Volume, Leuven 1989.* 1991. ISBN 90 04 09398 2
44. Haak, R.D. *Habakkuk.* 1992. ISBN 90 04 09506 3
45. Beyerlin, W. *Im Licht der Traditionen.* Psalm LXVII und CXV. Ein Entwicklungszusammenhang. 1992. ISBN 90 04 09635 3
46. Meier, S.A. *Speaking of Speaking.* Marking direct discourse in the Hebrew Bible. 1992. ISBN 90 04 09602 7
47. Kessler, R. *Staat und Gesellschaft im vorexilischen Juda.* Vom 8. Jahrhundert bis zum Exil. 1992. ISBN 90 04 09646 9
48. Auffret, P. *Voyez de vos yeux.* Étude structurelle de vingt psaumes, dont le psaume 119. 1993. ISBN 90 04 09707 4
49. García Martínez, F., A. Hilhorst and C.J. Labuschagne (eds.). *The Scriptures and the Scrolls.* Studies in honour of A.S. van der Woude on the occasion of his 65th birthday. 1992. ISBN 90 04 09746 5
50. Lemaire, A. and B. Otzen (eds.). *History and Traditions of Early Israel.* Studies presented to Eduard Nielsen, May 8th, 1993. 1993. ISBN 90 04 09851 8
51. Gordon, R.P. *Studies in the Targum to the Twelve Prophets.* From Nahum to Malachi. 1994. ISBN 90 04 09987 5
52. Hugenberger, G.P. *Marriage as a Covenant.* A Study of Biblical Law and Ethics Governing Marriage Developed from the Perspective of Malachi. 1994. ISBN 90 04 09977 8
53. García Martínez, F., A. Hilhorst, J.T.A.G.M. van Ruiten, A.S. van der Woude. *Studies in Deuteronomy.* In Honour of C.J. Labuschagne on the Occasion of His 65th Birthday. 1994. ISBN 90 04 10052 0
54. Fernández Marcos, N. *Septuagint and Old Latin in the Book of Kings.* 1994. ISBN 90 04 10043 1
55. Smith, M.S. *The Ugaritic Baal Cycle. Volume 1.* Introduction with text, translation and commentary of KTU 1.1-1.2. 1994. ISBN 90 04 09995 6
56. Duguid, I.M. *Ezekiel and the Leaders of Israel.* 1994. ISBN 90 04 10074 1
57. Marx, A. *Les offrandes végétales dans l'Ancien Testament.* Du tribut d'hommage au repas eschatologique. 1994. ISBN 90 04 10136 5
58. Schäfer-Lichtenberger, C. *Josua und Salomo.* Eine Studie zu Autorität und Legitimität des Nachfolgers im Alten Testament. 1995. ISBN 90 04 10064 4
59. Lasserre, G. *Synopse des lois du Pentateuque.* 1994. ISBN 90 04 10202 7
60. Dogniez, C. *Bibliography of the Septuagint – Bibliographie de la Septante (1970-1993).* Avec une préface de Pierre-Maurice Bogaert. 1995. ISBN 90 04 10192 6
61. Emerton, J.A. (ed.). *Congress Volume, Paris 1992.* 1995. ISBN 90 04 10259 0
62. Smith, P.A. *Rhetoric and Redaction in Trito-Isaiah.* The Structure, Growth and Authorship of Isaiah 56-66. 1995. ISBN 90 04 10306 6
63. O'Connell, R.H. *The Rhetoric of the Book of Judges.* 1996. ISBN 90 04 10104 7
64. Harland, P.J. *The Value of Human Life.* A Study of the Story of the Flood (Genesis 6-9). 1996. ISBN 90 04 10534 4
65. Roland Page Jr., H. *The Myth of Cosmic Rebellion.* A Study of its Reflexes in Ugaritic and Biblical Literature. 1996. ISBN 90 04 10563 8
66. Emerton, J.A. (ed.). *Congress Volume, Cambridge 1995.* 1997. ISBN 90 04 106871

67. JOOSTEN, J. *People and Land in the Holiness Code.* An Exegetical Study of the Ideational Framework of the Law in Leviticus 17–26. 1996. ISBN 90 04 10557 3
68. BEENTJES, P.C. *The Book of Ben Sira in Hebrew.* A Text Edition of all Extant Hebrew Manuscripts and a Synopsis of all Parallel Hebrew Ben Sira Texts. 1997. ISBN 90 04 10767 3
69. COOK, J. *The Septuagint of Proverbs – Jewish and/or Hellenistic Proverbs?* Concerning the Hellenistic Colouring of LXX Proverbs. 1997. ISBN 90 04 10879 3
70,1 BROYLES, G. and C. EVANS (eds.). *Writing and Reading the Scroll of Isaiah.* Studies of an Interpretive Tradition, I. 1997. ISBN 90 04 10936 6 (*Vol.* I); ISBN 90 04 11027 5 (*Set*)
70,2 BROYLES, G. and C. EVANS (eds.). *Writing and Reading the Scroll of Isaiah.* Studies of an Interpretive Tradition, II. 1997. ISBN 90 04 11026 7 (*Vol.* II); ISBN 90 04 11027 5 (*Set*)
71. KOOIJ, A. VAN DER. *The Oracle of Tyre.* The Septuagint of Isaiah 23 as Version and Vision. 1998. ISBN 90 04 11152 2
72. TOV, E. *The Greek and Hebrew Bible.* Collected Essays on the Septuagint. 1999. ISBN 90 04 11309 6
73. GARCÍA MARTÍNEZ, F. and NOORT, E. (eds.). *Perspectives in the Study of the Old Testament and Early Judaism.* A Symposium in honour of Adam S. van der Woude on the occasion of his 70th birthday. 1998. ISBN 90 04 11322 3
74. KASSIS, R.A. *The Book of Proverbs and Arabic Proverbial Works.* 1999. ISBN 90 04 11305 3
75. RÖSEL, H.N. *Von Josua bis Jojachin.* Untersuchungen zu den deuteronomistischen Geschichtsbüchern des Alten Testaments. 1999. ISBN 90 04 11355 5
76. RENZ, Th. *The Rhetorical Function of the Book of Ezekiel.* 1999. ISBN 90 04 11362 2
77. HARLAND, P.J. and HAYWARD, C.T.R. (eds.). *New Heaven and New Earth Prophecy and the Millenium.* Essays in Honour of Anthony Gelston. 1999. ISBN 90 04 10841 6
78. KRAŠOVEC, J. *Reward, Punishment, and Forgiveness.* The Thinking and Beliefs of Ancient Israel in the Light of Greek and Modern Views. 1999. ISBN 90 04 11443 2.
79. KOSSMANN, R. *Die Esthernovelle – Vom Erzählten zur Erzählung.* Studien zur Traditions- und Redaktionsgeschichte des Estherbuches. 2000. ISBN 90 04 11556 0.
80. LEMAIRE, A. and M. SÆBØ (eds.). *Congress Volume, Oslo 1998.* 2000. ISBN 90 04 11598 6.
81. GALIL, G. and M. WEINFELD (eds.). *Studies in Historical Geography and Biblical Historiography.* Presented to Zecharia Kallai. 2000. ISBN 90 04 11608 7
82. COLLINS, N.L. *The library in Alexandria and the Bible in Greek.* 2001. ISBN 90 04 11866 7
83,1 COLLINS, J.J. and P.W. FLINT (eds.). *The Book of Daniel.* Composition and Reception, I. 2001. ISBN 90 04 11675 3 (*Vol.* I); ISBN 90 04 12202 8 (*Set*).
83,2 COLLINS, J.J. and P.W. FLINT (eds.). *The Book of Daniel.* Composition and Reception, II. 2001. ISBN 90 04 12200 1 (*Vol.* II); ISBN 90 04 12202 8 (*Set*).
84. COHEN, C.H.R. *Contextual Priority in Biblical Hebrew Philology.* An Application of the Held Method for Comparative Semitic Philology. 2001. ISBN 90 04 11670 2 (In preparation).
85. WAGENAAR, J.A. *Judgement and Salvation.* The Composition and Redaction of Micah 2-5. 2001. ISBN 90 04 11936 1
86. MCLAUGHLIN, J.L. *The* Marzēaḥ *in sthe Prophetic Literature.* References and Allusions in Light of the Extra-Biblical Evidence. 2001. ISBN 90 04 12006 8

87. Wong, K.L. *The Idea of Retribution in the Book of Ezekiel* 2001. ISBN 90 04 12256 7
88. Barrick, W. Boyd. *The King and the Cemeteries.* Toward a New Understanding of Josiah's Reform. 2002. ISBN 90 04 12171 4
89. Frankel, D. *The Murmuring Stories of the Priestly School.* A Retrieval of Ancient Sacerdotal Lore. 2002. ISBN 90 04 12368 7
90. Frydrych, T. *Living under the Sun.* Examination of Proverbs and Qoheleth. 2002. ISBN 90 04 12315 6
91. Kessel, J. *The Book of Haggai.* Prophecy and Society in Early Persian Yehud. 2002. ISBN 90 04 12368 7
92. Lemaire, A. (ed.). *Congress Volume, Basel 2001.* 2002. ISBN 90 04 12680 5
93. Rendtorff, R. and R.A. Kugler (eds.). *The Book of Leviticus.* Composition and Reception. 2003. ISBN 90 04 12634 1
94. Paul, S.M., R.A. Kraft, L.H. Schiffman and W.W. Fields (eds.). *Emanuel.* Studies in Hebrew Bible, Septuagint, and Dead Sea Scrolls in Honor of Emanuel Tov. 2003. ISBN 90 04 13007 1
95. Vos, J.C. de. *Das Los Judas.* Über Entstehung und Ziele der Landbeschreibung in Josua 15. ISBN 90 04 12953 7
96. Lehnart, B. *Prophet und König im Nordreich Israel.* Studien zur sogenannten vorklassischen Prophetie im Nordreich Israel anhand der Samuel-, Elija- und Elischa-Überlieferungen. 2003. ISBN 90 04 13237 6
97. Lo, A. *Job 28 as Rhetoric.* An Analysis of Job 28 in the Context of Job 22-31. 2003. ISBN 90 04 13320 8
98. Trudinger, P.L. *The Psalms of the Tamid Service.* A Liturgical Text from the Second Temple. 2004. ISBN 90 04 12968 5
99. Flint, P.W. and P.D. Miller, Jr. (eds.) with the assistance of A. Brunell. *The Book of Psalms.* Composition and Reception. 2004. ISBN 90 04 13842 8
100. Weinfeld, M. *The Place of the Law in the Religion of Ancient Israel.* 2004. ISBN 90 04 13749 1
101. Flint, P.W., J.C. VanderKam and E. Tov. (eds.) *Studies in the Hebrew Bible, Qumran, and the Septuagint.* Essays Presented to Eugene Ulrich on the Occasion of his Sixty-Fifth Birthday. 2004. ISBN 90 04 13738 6
102. Meer, M.N. van der. *Formation and Reformulation.* The Redaction of the Book of Joshua in the Light of the Oldest Textual Witnesses. 2004. ISBN 90 04 13125 6
103. Berman, J.A. *Narrative Analogy in the Hebrew Bible.* Battle Stories and Their Equivalent Non-battle Narratives. 2004. ISBN 90 04 13119 1
104. Keulen, P.S.F. van. *Two Versions of the Solomon Narrative.* An Inquiry into the Relationship between MT 1 Kgs. 2-11 and LXX 3 Reg. 2-11. 2004. ISBN 90 04 13895 1
105. Marx, A. *Les systèmes sacrificiels de l'Ancien Testament.* Forms et fonctions du culte sacrificiel à Yhwh. 2005. ISBN 90 04 14286 X
106. Assis, E. *Self-Interest or Communal Interest.* An Ideology of Leadership in the Gideon, Abimelech and Jephthah Narritives (Judg 6-12). 2005. ISBN 90 04 14354 8
107. Weiss, A.L. *Figurative Language in Biblical Prose Narrative.* Metaphor in the Book of Samuel. 2006. ISBN 90 04 14837 X
108. Wagner, T. *Gottes Herrschaft.* Eine Analyse der Denkschrift (Jes 6, 1-9,6). 2006. ISBN 90 04 14912 0
109. Lemaire, A. (ed.). *Congress Volume Leiden 2004.* 2006. ISBN 90 04 14913 9
110. Goldman, Y.A.P., A. van der Kooij and R.D. Weis (eds.). *Sôfer Mahîr.* Essays in Honour of Adrian Schenker Offered by Editors of *Biblia Hebraica Quinta.* ISBN 90 04 15016 1
111. Wong, G.T.K. *Compositional Strategy of the Book of Judges.* An Inductive, Rhetorical Study. 2006. ISBN 90 04 15086 2